THE DREAM AT THE
END OF THE WORLD

THE DREAM AT THE END OF THE WORLD

Paul Bowles and

the Literary Renegades

in Tangier

Michelle Green

HarperCollins*Publishers*

FIRST EDITION

Designed by Cassandra J. Pappas

Photo insert researched, edited, and designed by Vincent Virga.

Library of Congress Cataloging-in-Publication Data

Green, Michelle–
    The dream at the end of the world : Paul Bowles and the literary
renegades in Tangier / Michelle Green.—1st ed.
        p.   cm.
    Includes index.
    ISBN 0-06-016571-5
    1. Bowles, Paul, 1910– —Homes and haunts—Morocco—Tangier.
2. Tangier (Morocco)—Intellectual life—20th century.
3. Americans—Morocco—Tangier—History—20th century. 4. Bowles,
Paul, 1910– —Friends and associates.   5. Tangier (Morocco)—
Social life and customs.   6. Authors, American—20th century—
Biography.   I. Title.
PS3552.0874Z65   1991
813'.54—dc20   90-55535
    [B]

---

91 92 93 94 95 CC/HC 10 9 8 7 6 5 4 3 2 1

*This book is for
Bobby and Georgia Green,
and for Jim Lyons*

Acknowledgments

During the four years that this book was aborning, a number of people came to my aid by sharing their memories about Tangier and the expatriates who lived there. My greatest debt is to Paul Bowles, who met with me several times a week in the winter of 1987, when I lived in Tangier, and who helped me to construct portraits of expatriates including his wife Jane. I would like to thank William Burroughs and James Grauerholz, with whom I spent a memorable day in Lawrence, Kansas. Allen Ginsberg was extremely generous with his time, as were David Herbert, Edward Field and Neil Derrick. Louise Bourgeois provided a jolt of inspiration when I visited her in her studio in 1988; Francis Bacon gave me his perspective on characters including Ahmed Yacoubi; and Felicity Mason allowed me to read the manuscript of her memoir, "The Love Quest," which later was published by Peter Owen.

I also would like to extend my thanks to Vincent Virga, Terry Wilson, Ira Cohen, Charles Gallagher, Christopher Wanklyn, Dr. Leslie Croxford, Tamara Dragadze, Isabelle Gerofi, Yvonne Gerofi, John Hopkins, Ruth Fainlight, Lyn Austin, Joseph McPhillips, Edouard Roditi, Jack Dunphy, Marguerite McBey, Gavin Lambert,

Kathy Jelen, Peter Orlovsky, Phillip Ramey, Regina Weinreich, Buffie Johnson, Ruth Hopwood, John Giorno, Bill Willis, Robert Shea, Beatrix Pendar, Noël Mostert, Comtesse Guillaume Lecointre, Ian Selley, Dr. Palma Ruspoli, Paul Danquah, Peter Pollock, Michael Scott, Tessa Codrington Wheeler, Hassan Ouakrim, George Staples, Gordon Browne, Ellen Buckingham, Mercedes Guitta, Trishy Haskins, Ian Moxon, Jeffrey Chester, Nadia Benabe, Hamri, Roddy Curry and Boubker Temli. The staffs at Columbia University's Butler Library and the Humanities Research Center at the University of Texas at Austin were also extremely helpful.

I am indebted to Rick Kot for his perspicacious editing, to Kris Dahl for her unflagging support and to Harriet Rubin for her well-timed encouragement. I'd like to thank Jim Gaines at *Life,* Jim Seymore at *Entertainment Weekly,* and John Saar at *People* for their forebearance. Finally, I would like to express my gratitude to Kim Hubbard, Tom Ward, Brian Green, Larry Ashmead, Mitchell J. Shields, Frazier Moore, Beth Vesel, Joanna Powell, Charla Krupp, Stuart Emmrich, Jean-Bernard Dangien, Seth Rosen, Amy Zimmerman, Robert Hershman, Mellon and John Tytell, and Edith Gould.

It's the end of the world, Tangier. Don't you feel it, Bill?
—*An ex-junkie to William Burroughs in a dockside bar, 1955*

Before coming here you should do three things: be inoculated for typhoid, withdraw your savings from the bank, say goodbye to your friends—heaven knows you may never see them again. . . . Because Tangier is a basin that holds you.
—*Truman Capote, 1950*

Prologue

To the expatriates who landed there after World War II, the International Zone of Tangier was an enigmatic, exotic and deliciously depraved version of Eden. A sun-bleached, sybaritic outpost set against the verdant hills of North Africa, it offered a free money market and a moral climate in which only murder and rape were forbidden. Fleeing an angst-ridden Western culture, European émigrés found a haven where homosexuality was accepted, drugs were readily available and eccentricity was a social asset.

But the decadence of the infidels who drifted to Tangier was offset by a singular thread in the city's complex fabric—the mysticism of its native Muslims. Paul Bowles, the most prominent of the literary exiles who settled in Tangier, was acutely aware of its spiritual undercurrent. "I relish the idea that in the night, all around me in my sleep, sorcery is burrowing its invisible tunnels in every direction, from thousands of senders to thousands of unsuspecting recipients," he wrote. "Spells are being cast, poison is running its course; souls are being dispossessed of parasitic pseudo-consciousnesses that lurk in the unguarded recesses of the mind. There is drumming out there most nights. It never awakens me; I hear the drums and incorporate them into my dream, like the nightly cries of the muezzins. . . ."

Taken with the promise of worldly pleasures in an occult setting, a flock of other Western intellectuals assembled in Tangier after Bowles embarked on his self-imposed exile in 1947. Along with Jane Bowles, the idiosyncratic writer whom he married in 1938, Paul became a magnetic force in a scene enlivened, at various junctures, by Truman Capote, Tennessee Williams, William Burroughs, Brion Gysin, Allen Ginsberg and Jack Kerouac. Over a period of two decades, they saw—and wrote about—the city from a remarkable range of perspectives: For twelve months of his four-year sojourn, the gaunt Burroughs languished in a male brothel, where he "had not taken a bath . . . nor changed my clothes or removed them except to stick a needle every hour in the fibrous gray wooden flesh of terminal addiction." Immersed in a junk-fog, "El Hombre Invisible," as he was called by the street urchins, produced the wild scribblings that became *Naked Lunch.* Jane Bowles, whose short story "Everything Is Nice" is a sharply observed portrait of Moroccan women, spent hours in the clamoring souks, wooing the Berber grain-seller who became her lesbian lover. Capote disported himself at the cafés in the medina and at the parties given by flamboyant socialites like Countess Phyllis della Faille, collecting shards of gossip like a crow diving for glinting tin. In 1950, he wrote a luminous précis on Tangier's most outré citizens—including the sinuous Estelle, a half-Chinese, half-Negro prostitute who "walk[ed] like a rope unwinding."

If the literary set was taken with Tangier, international society was also quick to recognize its charms. The Bowleses' lives—if not the Beats'—often intersected with those of the wealthy Americans and Europeans who descended on the city at the same time. The coterie was dominated by Woolworth heiress Barbara Hutton; after her third divorce, she acquired a stone palace in the Casbah (the walled fortress inside the medina), where she staged theatrical fêtes for her friends. Belly dancers, camel drivers and "blue people"—nomadic tribesmen whose skin was tinted by the indigo dye in their robes—were called in like movie extras to parties where Hutton held forth on a throne, wearing an emerald and diamond tiara that once belonged to Catherine the Great. On those shimmering evenings, Charlie Chaplin and Oona O'Neill, Greta Garbo, Cecil Beaton, Claudette Colbert, Aristotle Onassis and Maria Callas wandered with hundreds of other revelers through gilded rooms where detectives stood by to keep souvenir-seekers from gouging precious stones from the tapestries.

Other monied exiles set themselves up on the Old Mountain. A lush promontory studded with white villas, it was perched above the Straits of Gibraltar, and above the fishermen's shacks that clung to the sandy coastline. For the diplomats, socialites and fraying bluebloods who comprised the "Mountain set," the roiling medina (the quarter favored by the bohemian contingent) was something from which one retreated, cocktail glass in hand. The potentate of Mountain social life was the Honorable David Herbert, the second son of the Earl of Pembroke and a particular friend of Jane Bowles's. Like many of his neighbors, he was said to have an interesting past. That, however, was no disadvantage in Tangier, and Herbert's influence was so pervasive that he controlled the guest list even for Hutton's parties.

The postwar boom also brought a wave of desperados to Tangier. Given a special international status in 1912, when Morocco was divided into protectorates controlled by France and Spain, the city had long been a haven for those who lived on the edge; governed by a commission representing nine nations (including Britain, France, Spain, Italy and the United States), it refused entry to almost no one. After the war, its free port was dominated by smugglers, gun runners and latter-day pirates including "Nylon Sid" Paley, a New Jersey native who masterminded hijackings on the high seas. Fast-and-loose financiers made fortunes in the city's international money market, where dollars could be bought, rubles sold, and zlotys bartered at will. And war criminals flourished in its laissez-faire climate: Otto Skorzeny, the Gestapo agent who kidnapped Mussolini, set up a weapons-supply operation in Tangier with a group of erstwhile Nazi officers.

For most of the intellectuals—particularly Burroughs, with his enduring fascination with the underworld—such blackguards only intensified Tangier's allure. As it happened, many of the émigrés who came to Morocco fit the same profile: Each, in some sense, was a renegade. Refusing to accept the psychic and moral rigidity that had overtaken Western culture, iconoclasts like Bowles and Burroughs turned to an oasis where one could give free rein to the unconscious and explore forbidden impulses without fear of reprisal. It was almost as though Tangier had been devised for the delectation of the outlaw artist: The prevailing definition of sanity was idiosyncratic; madmen were free to walk the streets, and even the Beats (no strangers to prisons and mental hospitals) had little to fear from the authorities. Since foreigners were virtually immune to criminal prosecution, American intellectuals had a sense of invulnerability that was particularly exhilarating during the McCarthy era, when their colleagues were under siege. It was a heady setting, and it provided expatriate artists like Paul with a perspective that would influence the next generation of the avant-garde.

Like any earthly paradise, however, Tangier had its perils: Jane Bowles and other impulsive sorts tumbled into disastrous relationships with lower-class Moroccans whose view of love was decidedly pragmatic. (Even Paul became enmeshed in such amours—the most painful of which was with a young painter who conceived mad passions for wealthy European women.) No matter how fiercely one wanted to penetrate the complex Moslem world, it remained fundamentally incomprehensible to Westerners; those expatriates who did manage to open doors found themselves in a maze. Cast adrift in the midst of the International Zone's polyglot culture, tortured souls like Burroughs fell prey to searing loneliness and a wrenching sense of dislocation. *Kif* and hash and opiates like Eukodyl (which pharmacists supplied without a prescription) were easy anodynes, but they only heightened one's sense of unreality. In Tangier's rarefied climate, insecurity blossomed into paranoia, self-indulgence grew into dissipation and eccentricity ripened into madness. Egomaniacs had the advantage, and the International Zone attracted more than its share; only those with a strong carapace could survive in the midst of its moral chaos.

The emotional dramas were played out against a political backdrop that was rife with tension and intrigue. Morocco, as Bowles observed early on, "is a country that always seems to be hanging by a silken thread; everyone wonders how it's managed to hang on this long and not break." The animosity between the Moroccans and the imperious French had been barely contained since the days of Hubert Lyautey, France's first Resident-General, and in 1952 the nationalist revolt began to catch fire. In Tangier, the medina was rocked by a day-long riot in which police killed at least eighteen Moroccans and wounded more than one hundred others. After Sultan Ben Youssef was sent into exile with his two wives and eight concubines, a guerrilla war broke out; terrorist societies like the Black Crescent took hold in the teeming *bidonvilles* of Casablanca, where women fashioned grenades and men plotted assaults on the *colons.* In 1954, seven hundred colonists throughout Morocco were wounded or killed as the nationalists made their desperate bid for independence. In turn, French colonial police beat ten of thousands of rebels in fierce *ratissages* and tossed thousands of others into jail. Like the British settlers who weathered the Mau-Mau uprising in Kenya, the besieged colonists became desperate; seizing the initiative, they recruited counterterrorists among the ragged Spaniards and Corsicans who inhabited the back alleys of Rabat and Fez and Casablanca. During the revolutionary summer of 1955, vigilantes shot Moroccans in the streets and murdered other Frenchmen suspected of being sympathetic to the Istiqlal.[1] And although fewer bullets were fired in the 144-square-mile International Zone than in embattled Casablanca, Tangier's Europeans came to see that their utopia was doomed.

In works like his 1949 novel *The Sheltering Sky*—written as he traveled through the Sahara—Paul explored the dangers that lay in wait for the disaffected expatriate who entered such a cauldron in search of exotic kicks. The story of an estranged American couple who encounter madness and death in the desert, the novel could have been a collaboration between Albert Camus and Edgar Allan Poe—two of the writers whom he most admired. Shot through with an existential despair and tinged with a sable glamour, the book not only made Paul a favorite with critics but spawned a cult of readers who regarded its author as an oracle. The fact that he had used *majoun* (a potent cannabis jam) while writing the book's gripping death scene only heightened his allure; romantics saw him as a latter-day Coleridge, and sixties-era hipsters believed him to be in sympathy with Burroughs and the Beats.

And while Paul continued to make expeditions to other countries (most notably, Ceylon, where he bought an island that he used

as a retreat in the mid-fifties), he never lost his obsession with
North Africa—or his attraction to its troubling undercurrents. In his
second novel, *Let It Come Down,* he took the International Zone as his
de facto protagonist—presenting it as a soulless place in which pilgrims were condemned to discover the ringing emptiness of their
own lives. In *The Spider's House,* begun in 1954, he documented the
upheaval that attended the final ouster of the hated French. Paul
stayed in Morocco even after Tangier went into its traumatic decline—after the International Zone was subsumed by an independent Morocco; after the diplomatic corps pulled up stakes and the
demimonde and the smugglers and the fast-buck bankers fled. In
the sixties, the Bowleses saw the once-thriving port become the
dog-eared city of the moment for unkempt Westerners primed to
embrace an archaic culture—the same nomads who surfaced later in
Katmandu. It was a time when cheap quarters in the Casbah were
advertised in the *Village Voice* and the medina's crooked streets were
alive with antic characters in top hats and leather vests and other
acid-era regalia. Even Timothy Leary turned up—"on top of the
wave, and riding it," as Paul remembered.

It was a succession of such scenarios that lent a surreal quality
to expatriate life in Tangier. Few modern settings have offered such
an alchemical blend of primitivism and sophistication, and few have
spawned so many provocative tales. And while the spirited, raffish
port has long since deteriorated into a desultory tourist town, Europeans who find themselves there still sit for long hours in its caco-
phonous cafés, talking of Paul and Jane and the tawdry glory that
was Tangier. Most of the visitors never knew the Bowleses, but that
hardly seems to matter; we have all become fellow travelers in a
world ruled by entropy, and it was Paul who mapped the course.

Chapter 1

The city had come back to Paul Bowles in a dream. Rising up through the tranquil sleep of a warm May evening in New York, the reverie left in its wake a delicious sense of peace. In it, he had seen himself walking the labyrinthine streets of an inscrutable medina: Step by step, he followed the narrow alleys and corridors and cul-de-sacs, watching the play of afternoon sunlight as it filtered into the maze. He left the mysterious city only reluctantly, and he tried to reconstruct the scene when he awoke. Tracing his path through the dream terrain, Paul felt a thrill of recognition. His unconscious had taken him to an outpost he had first seen sixteen years before: Tangier, the scapegrace North African seaport that was a portal to the unknown. As the sunstruck images returned in a rush, his heart began to pound. Morocco, it seemed, was offering itself up to him again.

In the spring of 1947, Paul Frederick Bowles was a man who needed an escape route. Not because his life was out of control—a fastidious soul, he seldom was sidetracked by untidy passions or impulsive missteps. Messy obsessions were left to Jane Bowles, the extravagantly neurotic writer to whom he was married. Paul's own daring was in his art, and his ambition seemed limitless: He was an accomplished poet as well as a musician, and as a youth he had found mentors in both Gertrude Stein—who had appropriated him as a kind of mascot when he made a pilgrimage to Paris—and Aaron Copland. By the time he was thirty-four, Paul's surrealist-inspired opera *The Wind Remains* had been performed at the Museum of Modern Art, and he had written scores for plays including *The Glass Menagerie* and *Watch on the Rhine.* A gifted linguist, he had made an impression as a translator of fiction and drama, and his version of Sartre's *Huis Clos* (which he transformed into *No Exit*) had completed a successful run on Broadway. Paul also produced a music column for the *New York Herald Tribune,* and readers recognized him as one of the city's brightest, sharpest critics. Still, he was beginning to feel like a hired hand, and he was weary of focusing his energy on works that were not his own. At thirty-seven, he was eager for new creative terrain.

Spurred by the succès d'estime of his wife's stories and her novella, *Two Serious Ladies* (works that prompted Tennessee Williams to laud her as "the most important writer of prose fiction in modern American letters"), Paul had already resumed his own experiments with short stories. Disturbing, nihilistic, quietly bizarre, his efforts had quickly attracted the attention of the literati. In the fall of 1946, *Partisan Review* had accepted "A Distant Episode"—a story that coolly detailed the torture of a linguistics professor at the hands of a primitive North African tribe—and Paul had been galvanized: It seemed that he had found not only an appreciative audience but a literary calling.

For all of that, the breakthrough had heightened Bowles' growing sense that New York—with its perpetual distractions and demands—was no longer the place for him. The dream that came in May 1947 had a portentousness about it that made his escape seem a fait accompli, and as summer approached, his course took shape with perfect clarity: Struck by the power of his stories, editors at Doubleday offered Paul an advance for a novel. He immediately arranged passage to Morocco. For Paul, writing fiction was bound up with the notion of yielding to his unconscious; he needed an occult setting for himself, as well as for his protagonists, and the dream had shown him the way.

*   *   *

Like many expatriates who landed in Tangier that year, the courtly, meticulous Paul had long been at odds with convention. His marriage to Jane Auer Bowles—the headstrong only daughter of prosperous middle-class Jews—was an exercise in incongruity: "Paul and I are so incompatible," she once said, "that we should be in a *museum.*" Their sexual interest in each other had been fleeting, and both had taken homosexual lovers. Paul's exploits were as understated as Jane's were excessive: Flirtatious, seductive, she staged mad crushes and improbable amours. But while their paths often diverged, their bond was unbreakable. She called him "Bupple," and he treasured her ability to astonish; her mind, he said admiringly, "could have been invented by Kafka." With their curious charisma, they had become favorites among the creative elite. The two were regulars at Kurt and Constance Askew's lively New York salon (whose members included e. e. cummings, Virgil Thomson, and George Balanchine); and everyone from Peggy Guggenheim to W. H. Auden admired the charmingly eccentric Bowleses. As Paul's friend Gore Vidal observed, the two may have been unknowns to the rest of the world, but they were "famous among the famous."

By all appearances, however, being accepted had always been a matter of complete indifference to Paul. His sense of isolation had developed early on: The only son of an affluent Long Island couple whose roots were in New England, he never spoke to another child until he was five. Although both Claude Bowles and his wife, Rena, believed that the world was a dangerous place, and discipline the only defense, they had disagreed on the proper means of turning their son into a civilized human being. The benevolent Rena had tried to employ patient moral guidance, while Claude—a bitter man whose parents had forced him to abandon the violin in order to study dentistry—used excoriating verbal abuse to curb him at every turn. In time, Paul had learned to affect compliance without losing his sense of outrage. His only refuge was his imagination: at four, he began writing stories, and at nine, he composed an opera about an opium trafficker who had two wives. Later, he produced his own clandestine daily newspaper, devised secret codes and devoured the works of Poe and Hawthorne. Inspired by his parents' atlas, he invented his own planet—a place where continents had names like

Araplania and where no adults could follow. "Even as a small child," he once said, "I was always trying to get away."

After his years of being closeted on Long Island, the world outside had an irresistible allure for the young Paul. At seventeen, he left for the University of Virginia, and in the middle of his freshman year he fled to Paris, giving his parents no hint where he had gone. Convinced he would never see his family again, Paul found his freedom to be at least as restorative as Paris itself. After four unfettered months he returned to the States—and a surprisingly subdued Claude and Rena. But he was off again in March of 1931, when he contrived an urgent mission: He would sail to Europe to rendezvous with Aaron Copland, the composer who had become his tutor.

Possessed of a diffident charm and a rapidly expanding set of connections, the angular blond prodigy traveled to Paris and met Stein, Jean Cocteau, André Gide and Ezra Pound before Copland even arrived. Stein soon decided that Paul—whom she addressed as "Freddie"—was "delightful and sensible in summer but neither delightful nor sensible in the winter." Morocco, a country where winter's blasts were seldom felt, would be the perfect place for such a spirit, she decreed. Months later, when Paul was casting about for a summer retreat, she directed him to Tangier—a city of which he knew little, save that it seemed thrillingly remote.

When Bowles and Copland arrived in Tangier in August, 1931, they found an enclave that was vital and clamorous. Tangier was a city of strident contrasts: The ancient native quarter, or medina, was a teeming warren where life burst through at the seams; its steep streets were alive with donkeys and water sellers and leathery Berbers bound for the Grand Socco, an outdoor marketplace with the antic bustle of a medieval fair. Arab women were veiled shadows swathed in yards of white cotton; men were wonderfully excessive characters wearing frogged jackets and billowing trousers in hothouse hues. Muezzins summoned the masses to prayer five times each day, and the hard African wind carried the scents of eucalyptus, mint, mutton grease and dung. But the city of sixty thousand was controlled by an international cast of diplomats and administrators and exiled bluebloods who had brought with them the accoutrements of European civilization. Their world was one of elegant hotels and palmy estates; their lives were centered around costume balls, pig-sticking expeditions and martinis at Madame Porte's buzzing tearoom. The infidels had imposed a sense of order on Tangier, and under their influence the Arab city had become a monument to cleanliness and efficiency.

Together, Bowles and Copland took a house on the Mountain—a lush, villa-studded European stronghold perched above Tangier Bay. "The heat here is like that of a Turkish bath," he reported to Daniel Burns, a friend in America. ". . . Steady, hot, dry weather, with a sun that burns a white hole in the ultramarine sky, with a moon that is like the sun when it is full." Copland—who had declared Morocco "a madhouse"—soon grew impatient with their situation; the piano in their isolated house was wildly out of tune, and composing proved difficult. "Up here on the mountain there are drums that beat a lot," Paul wrote to Stein. "That worries Aaron, as he cannot get it out of his head that the Arabs are grieved about something, and are all set to go on the warpath."

In the fall, the two traveled south to Fez, a walled city that seemed to have been preserved intact from the Middle Ages. Deformed beggars and gibbering madmen prowled its narrow streets, and djellabaed[1] shepherds herded clattering sheep past market stalls bedecked with bloody entrails. Wedding processions, circumcision ceremonies, trance dancing—all of it was part of the pageantry. Paul had found "everything [in Fez to be] ten times stranger and bigger and brighter," he wrote later. "I felt that at last I had left the world behind, and the resulting excitement was well-nigh unbearable."

After Copland left for Berlin, Paul stayed on in Morocco to explore. With his close friend Harry Dunham, he roamed through the native quarter in Marrakech and made a bone-jarring trip by truck over the Atlas mountains to Ouarzazate, a desert outpost where the French Foreign Legion was encamped. Paris and its brilliant circle of expatriates reclaimed him by the end of the year, but the images of North Africa lingered. In the spring of 1932, Paul returned to eat opium in Tangier and watch the frenzied rites of religious brotherhoods in Fez; the next winter, he came back to steep himself in the austere beauty of the Sahara, where the sky had a life of its own. The experience was a "baptism of solitude," as he described it: "Once [a man] has been under the spell of the vast, luminous, silent country, no other place is quite strong enough for him, no other surroundings can provide the supremely satisfying sensation of existing in the midst of something that is absolute," he wrote. "He will go back, whatever the cost in comfort and money, for the absolute has no price."

Living on a small sum bequeathed him by an aunt, Paul moved about constantly during the winter of 1933—taking crowded buses at dawn and enduring the outlandish discomforts of camel treks. He found North Africa to be populated by the most extraordinary people he had ever known: Mystical undercurrents ran deep among the nomadic Berbers and their Arab countrymen, and one might witness a man transforming himself into a goat in the midst of a busy souk. Drugs such as *kif* (cannabis mixed with tobacco), hashish and *majoun* underscored the supple nature of reality. It was like being on the other side of the looking glass, and he found the sheer alienness intoxicating. In March 1933 Paul wrote to the poet Charles Henri Ford, "There is one drawback to Arabs, and that is their insupportable jealousy. . . . But once I shall be away from them I shall immediately regret it, and am sure I shall return and spend all my life somewhere among them."

Over the next decade, Paul pursued the exotic with a quiet vehemence. Stein declared him to be self-indulgent, but it seemed to him that "each day lived through on this side of the Atlantic was one more day spent outside prison," as he wrote from Tangier. Work was his only constant; drawing upon the rigid self-discipline imposed upon him by his father, he kept up his creative momentum as he transported himself from one country to another. After a short interlude in New York—where he set texts by Stein and Cocteau to music and published them himself—he left for another tour of Morocco; from there, he made an expedition to Central America. Back in New York in 1937, he met Jane Auer, an untamed twenty-year-old with a shock of hennaed hair. The two soon began to "spin fantasies about how amusing it would be to get married and horrify everyone," as Paul put it; and in February 1938 they did just that. Together, they explored Panama, Costa Rica, Guatemala and Mexico and spent long months in Europe. But North Africa was always Paul's polestar; nowhere else had he encountered people who were guided by the liberating belief that nothing—save the infinite—is real.

As Paul prepared to sail for Casablanca in June of 1947, the memories came crowding in: cold, moonlit dunes; remote palmeries[2] surrounded by rock-strewn wasteland; the harsh expanse of a desert sky. It was a landscape forceful enough to destroy the traveler who came unprepared—a brutal terrain that could serve not as a mere backdrop but as a protagonist in his novel. What would happen to naifs who fled to such a place? The professor in "A Distant Episode" had been annihilated—the tribesmen whom he had hoped to study had kidnapped him, hacked off his tongue and turned him into a macabre jester. As Paul sat on a Fifth Avenue bus one day, surrounded by dowagers wearing white gloves and office workers scanning the *Times,* the plan for his novel crystallized: He would create three American travelers and send them into the Sahara. Like Tangier's flesh-and-blood expatriates, his characters would be restless souls who wanted to explore life outside the boundaries—the boundaries of Western civilization, of social convention, of traditional morality. But living in extremis would send them into a tailspin—stripped of identity, bereft of purpose and spirit, the three would be lured into destruction by the Sahara itself.

Paul left New York on July 1, buoyed by the sense of freedom that settled on him whenever he left America. With him was Gordon Sager, a novelist whom the Bowleses had met during an early-forties sojourn in Taxco, the expatriate haven in Mexico. Jane stayed behind, and their parting was attended by the kind of domestic farce that she orchestrated so often. After lunch, Paul had gone to retrieve the passport he had left on a bookshelf earlier in the day. It had disappeared, and the car that was to take him to the docks in Brooklyn would be at the door in half an hour. A frantic search through a mountain of valises yielded nothing; the passport had simply vanished. "Just before the car came, I unearthed it, buried beneath a neat pile of Jane's underwear in the back of a bureau drawer," Paul remembered. "It was a mystery; Jane earnestly claimed to know nothing about it. Yet no one else had come into the apartment. We looked at her accusingly. She laughed. 'You *know* I don't want you to go,' she said. 'So I must have [hidden it].' "

Jane—who was struggling with a novel—moved for a time to Treetops, the Connecticut estate that belonged to the singer Libby Holman, a close friend of both the Bowleses. Although she had always been the writer in the marriage, Jane had a sense that their roles were about to become blurred. In August, she wrote to Paul, "As for packing your passport away—I thought it was mine—I looked to see whose picture was in it—and I dimly remember my own face and not yours. As Libby said when I told her, 'How psychosomatic can you get.'"

Chapter 2

In 1947, Tangier was not a place that suggested permanence; its quiet colonial air had been shattered, and a flamboyant boomtown spirit had set in. Since Bowles' last visit, the International Zone had become a realm where—for the infidel, at least—all things seemed possible. The gulf between Tangerinos (as European residents were called) and native Tanjawis had widened significantly; much of the native population was struggling merely to survive, while a fresh crop of expatriates were seizing quick profits and inventing new lives for themselves.

With much of the Western world shackled by exchange restrictions, high taxes, trade controls and other economic curbs, the 225-square-mile International Zone was an island of financial opportunity: Corporations and holding companies could be formed overnight and used to shelter tainted money or evade foreign taxes; banking laws were nonexistent, and import duties were kept low. None of the newly minted wealth was taxed, and profits were channeled into consumption of the most conspicuous sort. Smugglers, counterfeiters, sleight-of-hand bankers, real-estate speculators and even honest entrepreneurs found Tangier to be a postwar promised land rivaled only by Beirut. In the city of about 130,000 inhabitants, European and American expatriates numbered 25,000, and more émigrés arrived on every boat.

The amphitheater of sandy hills that surrounded Tangier Bay was dotted with blazing-white buildings in various stages of construction. In the Ville Nouvelle (or European quarter), Spanish and Moroccan laborers worked night shifts to complete private villas and spacious apartment buildings to shelter the nouveaux riches. From the Place de France—a crossroads dominated by the fashionable Café de Paris and the stately chancellery of the French legation—the city was sprawling east and south, claiming the low green hills where goats and sheep had lately grazed. Ablaze with electric lights, the once-modest Boulevard Pasteur had become a thriving shopping street where arrivistes could acquire the requisite Swiss watches, French perfumes and Italian leather goods. Barely in evidence ten years earlier, American-made automobiles were now ubiquitous; the wealthiest expatriates cruised around in Packard clippers and Cadillac convertibles, sharing the roadways with moth-eaten donkeys struggling under teetering loads. A string of new hotels rose above the crescent-shaped bay, and the harbor was crowded with the PT boats and subchasers used by smugglers to dart across the Straits of Gibraltar.

While it seemed at times that every European in Tangier was caught up in its capitalist fervor, some felt that lucre was the least the city had to offer. A pockmarked past was no liability, and an impressive number of misfits, eccentrics, libertines, black sheep and second sons were able to burrow their way into society. Since few questions were asked of new arrivals, any fugitive could shed his sullied persona and take on the coloration of a solid citizen; spies, war criminals, Nazis, remittance men, disbarred lawyers, unlicensed doctors and defrocked priests had all been reborn in Tangier. Poseurs could alter themselves with abandon: In Tangier's rarefied climate, social climbers metamorphosed into bluebloods, bank clerks became barons, and shopgirls, grandes dames. Rakes with real titles came to the Mountain to sit out minor scandals and immerse themselves in a milieu abrim with sensual delights. Even the nastiest spot of bother seemed insignificant when one was lolling in a jasmine-scented garden on a cliffside, lulled by the splashing of water in a fountain and the call of the muezzins from their distant minarets.

The appeal to sybarites was obvious, and after the war thousands made languid pilgrimages to the city where almost any pleasure could be had for a price. Although homosexuality was still a criminal offense in England, it was eminently acceptable among Moroccans, whose male population was largely bisexual. Youngsters of eight or ten prowled the streets, propositioning visitors in French or English or German. A Spanish-run boy-brothel offered partners who would oblige the most esoteric request; patrons made their choices from a photo album, and the youths were dispatched within minutes. Heterosexuals found their own louche amusements: After nights of Dom Perignon and dancing, bejeweled women and their tuxedoed escorts went slumming in the alleys where one could watch tatty sex shows and survey the female prostitutes who draped themselves outside the Chat Noir. Not content with such commonplace pursuits, one wealthy Englishman created his own harem. A tiny man with a taste for tall, dark-skinned maidens, he stocked his Mountain retreat with innocents from the Rif and kept them in line with the help of a fierce black matron.

In the cafés that surrounded the Petit Socco, a thriving plaza deep in the medina, voluptuaries gathered to spend long afternoons sipping sherry or smoking *kif.* Employment was optional for many wellborn exiles, since even a modest inheritance could be stretched to accommodate any number of luxuries. Moroccan servants were paid only fifty cents a day; capacious flats with dramatic views of the bay could be had for one hundred dollars a month, and three-course meals in superior European restaurants were two dollars or less. A room at the self-consciously elegant Minzah Hotel—a bastion of French-inspired hauteur that incorporated a townhouse built by Ion Perdicaris[1]—cost as little as ten dollars a night, and a single day's pension at a less elaborate establishment went for two dollars and fifty cents. A custom-tailored suit cost fifty dollars; a one-way plane ticket to London, nineteen pounds. Even without a decent allowance, a solvent idler with simple tastes could drift along indefinitely; quarters in the medina were absurdly cheap, and market stalls charged pennies for Moroccan staples like *harira* and couscous.

Along with creature comforts, Tangier offered the expatriate a
bracing jolt of cultural diversity. Perched at the northwestern tip of
the continent (where Hercules was said to have separated Africa
from Europe and created the Straits of Gibraltar), it had always been
a lure for foreign invaders. As a Phoenician trading post, it had been
taken over by the Romans before falling into the hands of the
Vandals and then, the Arabs. Occupied by the Spanish, and later by
the Portuguese, it was given to the British Crown in 1662 as part
of the dowry of Catherine of Braganza. Returned to Morocco in
1684, it had remained under the control of successive sultans until
the sovereign state was divided up by Western imperialists on the
eve of World War I. Coveted by rival powers, Tangier eventually
had been incorporated into an International Zone where Britain,
France, Holland, Italy, Belgium, Portugal, Spain and the United
States all asserted their authority. By 1947, the city was well established as the diplomatic capital of Morocco; each of the governing
countries was a palpable presence in the city, and each maintained
a legation staffed with consuls, vice-consuls, attachés and aides.

Tangier's government was a Byzantine collective effort. A Leg-
islative Assembly that included four Frenchmen, one Dutchman,
two Moroccan Jews, three Moroccan Moslems, two Americans, one
Belgian, three Englishmen, one Portuguese and four Spaniards met
monthly to vote on laws that were then ratified by a similarly
heterogeneous Committee of Control. Judicial matters were handled
by a mixed court whose judges were French, Spanish, British, Italian
and Belgian. Executive power rested with a chief administrator, who
served a six-year term. An international staff of subordinates
managed public services: A Spaniard ran the Department of Public
Works, and a Belgian commandant supervised a police force whose
members were primarily Spaniards and Moroccans. Sultan Sidi Mohammed ben Youssef—himself closely controlled by the overseers
of the French Protectorate, which ruled its portion of the country
from the imperial city of Rabat—was represented by His Excellency
Si el Hadj Mohammed ben si el Hadj Abdeldrim Tazi, whose palace
crowned a hill outside the medina. Although he wielded little political power, the Mendoub, as he was called, held religious and judicial
authority over the native population and presided over Assembly
meetings. His most visible role was as part of a weekly ceremony

that marked the Muslim holy day; each Friday morning, a chauffeured Cadillac ferried him to the mosque in the Casbah to pray
with the faithful. His arrival was heralded by a stirring procession
through the town: Led by spirited Tanjawi musicians, members of
his Black Guard—turbaned horsemen in uniforms of blue, white,
red and green—paraded their mounts down the Boulevard Pasteur,
past the Minzah, into the Grand Socco and finally up to the Casbah,
where they stood at attention as the white-robed Mendoub made
his way into the mosque.

Tangier's international character was reflected on every street
corner, where boxes for three different postal systems—Spanish,
British and Moroccan—competed for business. Royal-blue signs
with white lettering designated street names in French, Spanish and
Arabic. Vendors sold the English *Tangier Gazette* (founded in 1883 as
"the first newspaper to be published in the Moorish Empire") along
with two Spanish and three French papers. Every citizen seemed
fluent in at least three languages, and the fleet of money changers
who conducted business on orange crates in the Petit Socco could
rattle off exchange rates in a dozen tongues.

Social life was dominated by the diplomatic corps, whose
members generally had little to do aside from monitoring the low
rumble of the independence movement fomenting in the Spanish
and French Protectorates. After the unending round of official teas,
receptions, cocktail parties and soirées, they revived themselves
with polo or golf or tennis at the Country Club Diplomatique.
Younger couples arranged scavenger hunts and picnic excursions to
the Diplomatic Forest, where one could recline under the umbrella
pines and watch graceful white ibis fluttering over Tangier Bay.

Together with their countrymen, each group formed a nucleus
whose boundaries were seldom breached; polarized by the war, they
clung doggedly to tribal prejudices. The loftiest positions in expatriate society belonged to the members of the British colony. They
worshiped together at St. Andrew's Church (a sedate structure with
its own mossy graveyard), gathered for rugby at the British Sports
Club, traded gossip at the British Library and drank at Dean's Bar,
where one could scan the latest issue of the *Illustrated London News.*
Daphne Fielding (the erstwhile Marchioness of Bath), an author
who had a house in the Casbah, wrote that the "dainty little tea

parties, croquet on the lawn, and more or less harmless and harmful gossip contributed to the creation of a Cranford in Africa tinged with the cantonment heartiness of an Indian Hill station in the palmy days of the Raj." Equally clannish, the French maintained their own library, church and lycée, while the rival Italians supported another church, a hospital, and a school established by Mussolini in the palace once owned by the brigand sheikh Ahmad ibn Muhammad Raisuli. The eighteen-thousand-member Spanish colony (which far outnumbered the other expatriate communities) erected two churches, a hospital, a library and a school as monuments to its own culture. At the bottom of the social order were the Americans, whose only outpost—an august legation in the three-story palace given to the United States in 1821 by Sultan Slimane—was tucked away in the southeastern corner of the medina.

With its wildly disparate elements, the International Zone was marked by an air of unreality. Newcomers saw Tangier as an existentialist Utopia—a place where everyone could seize a part of the same bizarre dream. Charged with a euphoric energy, it was the city of the moment for fantasts who had the means to shop for new settings the way one might try on a string of pearls.

In September of 1946, the peripatetic Woolworth heiress Barbara Hutton had bought a phantasmagoric house near the Casbah. The home of retired American diplomatic agent Maxwell Blake, Sidi Hosni was a mazelike fifteen-room folly that had been created by joining no fewer than five Moroccan houses. Among its lavish chambers were two dining rooms, three bedrooms, a guest cottage and a series of salons that led to a throne room. Surrounded by crenellated stone walls, the pure-white palace was full of rare tiles, graceful Moorish archways, carved panels and flowering courtyards. An imposing fig tree dominated its central patio, and a vast rooftop terrace offered a splendid view of Spain's southern coast and the point where the deep-green Atlantic merged into the azure Mediterranean.

Hutton had been taken to the house by Blake's daughter, Ruth Hopwood, whom she had met at a cocktail party just hours before. Awash in moonlight, Sidi Hosni (which took its name from the saint who was enshrined just outside its gates) seemed magical, and the impulsive Barbara decided on the spot that she wanted it as a pied-à-terre. She knew it was on the market, and she immediately offered Blake seventy-five thousand dollars—outbidding Spain's Generalissimo Franco, who had sent a detachment of experts to evaluate the property. The next morning, while Blake was still considering the offer, Barbara called Ruth Hopwood to demand that she hurry her father to the bank to close the deal.

Sidi Hosni had proved the perfect backdrop for Barbara's poetic fantasies. Enchanted by all things Oriental, she decided that Tangier was a kind of Xanadu. After it was announced that she would be setting up housekeeping in the Casbah, she told the press, "I inherit six servants. I think it's all too sweet for words. . . . I've always wanted to live like an Arab." Divorced from her third husband, Cary Grant, in 1945, she was free to plunge into impetuous affairs, and Sidi Hosni—an opulent pleasure dome in the least judgmental of all cities—was an idyllic trysting spot. "Tangier," as she told Ruth (who stayed on at Sidi Hosni as a lady-in-waiting), "is a place to bring a lover, not a husband." Unpopular in America, where she was seen as self-indulgent and—worse—unpatriotic, Barbara found an unprecedented degree of sympathy in Tangier. Her Arab neighbors applauded her and called out "Bar-bar-a, Bar-bar-a!" whenever her motorcade appeared, and the arched gateways of the medina were widened to accommodate her fleet of Rolls-Royces. Since Moroccans seldom intruded on her privacy, she could allow herself the luxury of exploring the medina in slacks and a simple blouse, with only Ruth for company.

Even in Tangier, however, the provocative Barbara remained in the spotlight. Her presence marked the International Zone as a Mecca for café society, and butterflies began arriving in Tangier to collect at her soirées. The paparazzi recorded her comings and goings, and the gossip mavens who followed the "Huttontot's" every move began echoing—and amplifying—Barbara's own gauzy notions about living among the Moors. When Barbara acquired Sidi Hosni, gossip columnist Elsa Maxwell reported excitedly that Barbara's bathroom looked squarely into the minaret of the mosque in the Casbah and that she could hear the muezzin clear his throat as he sang "Allah Akbar. . . ."

For all of Hutton's rapturous illusions, she noticed something that many émigrés were determined to ignore: While Tangier had its share of wealthy native merchants, dynastic families and old Moroccan money, the native population had been disenfranchised by a top-heavy international administration determined to extract maximum profits from its demesne. The lives of most Arabs stood out in bold relief against those of their European neighbors; just outside the guardhouse at Sidi Hosni, thousands of natives were crowded into a quarter where life was primitive. The least fortunate slept in alleyways and settled into dank cubbyholes that contained little but a charcoal brazier, a pail and a mat to sleep on. On the outskirts of town, entire families lived in wooden packing crates that had contained the Nashes and Packards shipped across the Straits. And in the fertile hills to the southeast, the proud Berbers who had fled the famine-plagued Rif mountains were encamped in a sprawling *bidonville.* A rural slum whose shelters were constructed from cardboard, cast-off sheets of rusty metal and flattened soldiers' canteens (*bidons* in French), it was a wretched testament to the desperation of many natives. Hutton recorded the disturbing sights in her journals (families in quarters "without plumbing or cooking facilities, the ceiling so perilously low they have to crawl to get from room to room") and she took steps to alleviate the suffering. She funded a soup kitchen that fed as many as a thousand refugees a day, and she sent hundreds of thousands of dollars to the charities ministering to Tangier's poor.

Such empathy, however, was in short supply among arrivals who saw Moroccans only as quaint extras in the drama that was Tangier. Moneyed parvenus seldom troubled to study Maghrebi, the Arabic dialect spoken in Morocco, and many used the airy colonial term "Moors" when discussing the natives. Female servants usually were addressed by the generic name of "Fatima," and more than one imperialist referred to Tanjawis as "apes." Virtually invisible to the arriviste, powerful Moroccan families like the Menebhis—whose late patriarch had been the Sultan's ambassador to Great Britain—lived in shuttered splendor in palaces that they had owned for generations. The Moroccans whom most expatriates encountered were servants and shopkeepers, and few Europeans concerned themselves with what such creatures might be thinking.

Citizens had no votes, and Tanjawis of modest means were

reminded at every turn that their city belonged to the interlopers. Since Europeans held the reins, a disgruntled foreigner could slap a native policeman and simply walk away. Once open to the masses, the city beach was about to be marked off-limits to those who didn't belong to one of the European beach clubs lining Tangier Bay. And although visitors from Tunisia and Algeria were allowed to buy liquor, Moroccan Muslims were forbidden by law to drink. (Instead of forswearing alcohol, Tanjawis bought it through sympathetic Europeans or made pilgrimages to the graveyard where Jewish boot-leggers sold wine under cover of darkness.)

For the 105,000 Moroccans who lived in "El Kelba" ("the bitch," as Tangier was known to the rest of the country), the seaport symbolized a foreign domination that was increasingly oppressive. In the late 1940s, nationalism began gaining ground in the Spanish and French Protectorates, and it became obvious that the European stronghold could hardly remain unscathed. Already Tanjawis had staged an enormous—if bloodless—demonstration to protest the painful inequalities. Two months before Paul Bowles sailed for Morocco, Sultan ben Youssef made his first visit to Tangier in almost two decades, sending his subjects into a joyous frenzy. In a defiant address that enraged French Resident General Erik Labonne (who expected him to propagandize on behalf of the European overlords), he called for a strengthening of bonds with the Arab League and hinted that the French usurpers might be packing for Paris sooner than they had imagined.

Tanjawis—and a minority of vigilant Europeans—took the Sultan's daring speech as a sign that a revolution was inevitable, and that the International Zone would not be spared. For all of its polyglot charm, the enclave was structurally unsound; apart from its cavalier treatment of Tanjawis, the administration was as corrupt and rapacious as any other in possession of absolute power, and the zone was riddled with evidence of its quick-profit ethos. The city beach often resembled a midden heap; electrical failures and water shortages were all too frequent, and facades on new buildings were already peeling. A public servant was required to answer only to his own conscience; customs officers were easily bribed, and justice was meted out by a court that reflected the administration's petty jealousies. No one seemed shocked by the fact that some members of the consular corps itself engaged in smuggling—why should diplomats be denied the freedom enjoyed by Tangier's other contrabandiers?

But while pragmatists may have been able to spot the fatal flaws, most expatriates were too busy living for the moment to consider the prospect of a messy rebellion. Having reached an oasis where one could follow any impulse without fear of reprisal, they refused to admit that the International Zone was an illusion of sorts, and that—like all dreams—it was destined to come to an end.

Chapter 3

In spite of his fascination for Tangier, Paul Bowles refused to settle anywhere during his first heady months abroad. After the S.S. *Ferncape* docked in Casablanca, he and Gordon Sager went east to Fez, where he found himself in a state of "perpetual excitement," as he described it. The city's medieval aspect was unchanged, and he took pleasure in the timelessness of it all: the bird market where djellabaed men sold sparrows in little bamboo cages; the carriages that plied the route between the Jewish quarter and Bab Bou Jeloud (an elaborate garden planted by the French); the caravansaries that sheltered shepherds and their bleating charges and the vast tanneries where half-naked workmen heaved dripping skins into stone vats abrim with brilliant dyes. Fez smelled of incense and freshly cut cedar, and it was alive with an ancient clamor—horse bells, beggars' cries, the hammerings of metal workers in the *foudouk*s and the shouts of *"Balek!"* from donkey men squeezing their animals through the streets. Along with its pleasingly sinister elements—the wild-eyed hunchbacks who extorted money from Europeans at sidewalk cafés, the spell shops where one could buy the chameleon's legs and lion's claws necessary to ward off djins—Fez had its fanciful qualities. To Charles Henri Ford, Paul reported, "The lake in Bou Jeloud is covered with little boats full of Arab ladies in pink and lavender *haik*s. It all looks rather as though Versailles had been invaded and remodeled [and] the Europeans kicked out."

After a few days, Sager went to Marrakech, but Paul stayed on in Fez. During the Atlantic crossing, he had written "Pages from Cold Point," a disquieting story about an incestuous relationship between a manipulative sixteen-year-old and his widowed father. Now, in the Hotel Belvedere, he began working on the novel that had brought him to Morocco.

Superficially, at least, *The Sheltering Sky* echoed his life with Jane: Port Moresby (a name appropriated from a town in New Guinea) and his wife, Kit—well-bred expatriates emotionally estranged from each other—have landed in North Africa with a traveling companion named Tunner. A compulsive traveler outraged by the fact that even the most primitive cultures are becoming despoiled, Port is put off by the grayness of the coastal town in which they have docked. Studying his maps, he insists that the three move on into the Sahara, "where there [is] only the sky." Kit consents, if only to please him; although her fastidious husband has abandoned her sexually, their perverse bond has remained intact. For all of the psychological distance between them, the dispassionate Port and the vulnerable Kit are warring aspects of the same psyche.

In the opening chapters of the book, it becomes clear that the couple's weaknesses will be pitilessly exposed during their expedition. Each betrays the other sexually—Port with a beautiful Moroccan prostitute, and Kit with the predatory Tunner. Torn by guilt, obsessed with omens, Kit begins to recognize her own helplessness; as much as she wants to "become whatever [Port] wanted her to become," she is crippled by a sense of dread. Her husband's fascination with the desert is incomprehensible: "It was as if always he held the fresh hope that she, too, would be touched in the same way as he by solitude and the proximity to infinite things, but the very silences and emptinesses that touched his soul terrified her."

Port recognizes Kit's terrors and, although part of him hopes for a rapprochement, he uses them to keep her at bay. On a bicycle trip into the mountains near Boussif, the two hike up a rocky ridge to contemplate the endless plains:

"You know," said Port, and his voice sounded unreal, as voices are likely to do after a long pause in an utterly silent spot, "the sky here's very strange. I often have the sensation when I look at it that it's a solid thing up there, protecting us from what's behind."

Kit shuddered slightly as she said: "From what's behind?"

"Yes."

"But what *is* behind?" Her voice was very small.

"Nothing, I suppose. Just darkness. Absolute night."

"Please don't talk about it now." There was agony in her entreaty. "Everything you say frightens me, up here. It's getting dark, and the wind is blowing, and I can't stand it."

Still writing, Paul left Fez late in the summer of 1947. After a brief stop in Tangier to survey the changes in the city, he crossed the Straits into Spain, where he wandered from Algeciras to Ronda to Córdoba. Content to move about spontaneously and work in hotels, he took with him vast amounts of luggage—most of which contained a wardrobe more suitable for a sojourn in London than an excursion in rural Spain and North Africa. Tweed jackets, silk ties and dressing gowns, oxford-cloth shirts, cashmere vests and pullovers—with the exception of the djellaba he occasionally affected, the decorous Paul declared himself to be at a distinct remove from his surroundings. He traveled as he had before the war, avoiding anything that wasn't cheap and seeking inventive forms of discomfort. He loathed airplanes; far better to wedge oneself (and one's imperious mountain of luggage) into a train compartment spilling over with unorthodox humans, ragged bundles and trussed-up chickens.

Perhaps because of his fascination with the bizarre, Paul displayed an uncanny ability to attract marginal characters. "If a crazy person came into a bar or a railway car he or she came straight at me," he said later. "I don't know why—I must look as though I would play their game with them. I was on a train when an old, lined peasant woman came straight at me and sat right down. She said in Spanish, 'I'm so glad to see you again. I haven't seen you in years.' I said 'No,' and she said, 'Well, you are my son, after all.' I said (laughing), 'No, I'm not.' And she said, 'Come on, don't pretend, I'm your mother.' She had a turkey and she put it in my lap. I couldn't get rid of her; there was nowhere to go, and she knew I was her son.''

In Fez, Paul had been singled out late one night by a madman who haunted Moulay Abdullah, a walled quarter whose lone portal was guarded by Senegalese soldiers. Years later, he spoke of the episode with the same detachment he would use to describe an event that was purely fictional: "I'd just gone inside when this maniac came up and grabbed me," Paul said. "In one hand he had a knife; he was very strong. He began to run, forcing me to run. He was like somebody with hydrophobia—he was saying, 'I'll kill him, I'll kill him.' It wasn't directed at me—he had to have hold of me in order to kill whomever he thought was chasing him. We ran all through this labyrinth, and he never let go of me. Finally, we were crouching under a table in a deserted café; he was panting and repeating, 'I'll kill him.' Of course, nobody ever came. There was never an explanation—he kept looking and waiting and since no one came he let go of me. I thought, 'Well, I'm not going to start running—he'll run after me.' So I just walked off alone. Jane would have said something like, 'Oh, well, what do you expect when you go wandering out at night alone?' Normal people didn't go walking in Fez in the darkness.''

Now, as Paul traveled through Spain and Morocco, he was trailed by a nomadic English couple, a mother and son named Powell,[1] who somehow appeared at every stop on his ad hoc itinerary. Garrulous and abusive, Mrs. Powell complained obsessively about her hapless grown son and about every aspect of their perpetual journey. At breakfast on the roof of a hotel in Fez, she had taken the opportunity to lecture Paul about how impossible the boy was; he had, she announced, caught some terrible disease from a "filthy Arab woman." As Paul observed the two, it became apparent that the pale young Powell was a victim of his mother's malign fantasies. "He didn't do anything for fear she would disapprove," Paul said. "He had to be right next to her all the time—she wanted him to sleep either in the room with her or in a room with a connecting door, so she'd know when he came in and out. She was always saying to him things like, 'You *are* a proper idiot—I could box your ears, you're so stupid.' " The Powells, whom he found simultaneously revolting and amusing, were quickly appropriated as characters in *The Sheltering Sky*. When the unhappy son asked sardonically, 'Isn't married life wonderful?' it seemed to Paul that—in fiction, if not in fact—such a lament implied a torturous sexual relationship. Accordingly, he turned the Lyles, as his characters were named, into a ludicrous pair whose sparring cloaked a repellent secret.

Paul finally parted ways with the Powells in the fall of 1947, when he encamped again in Tangier. Along with Babarhio, an Amazon parrot he had acquired as a traveling companion, he installed himself in a secluded pension opposite the villa where he had lived with Aaron Copland sixteen years before. Although his friends would later shudder at the memory of El Farhar ("rhymes with horror," Tennessee Williams complained to Donald Windham), he was inclined to ignore its dampness and disagreeable odors; for seventy-five pesetas, or under two dollars a day, he was given three meals, a cypress-shaded cottage on a cliff and the privacy that he craved.

The city was a different place from the one that Paul had known as a restless prodigy. In an October letter to Charles Henri Ford (who had become the editor of the surrealist magazine *View*), he described Tangier as "the Boom Town of the Eastern Hemisphere." The International Zone was "so civilized," Paul reported, "that the latest number of *Horizon* hangs from each newsstand, Sartre, Beauvoir, Camus and Lorca decorate the bookshop windows, and the American Legation hangs a copy of the *Random House Selected Writings of Gertrude Stein* in a glass case outside the entrance so the mules can brush against it as they pass."

While the milieu was pleasant enough, Paul kept himself aloof from anything remotely social. "You ask about Tangier's sex-life," he wrote Ford in November. "I have a feeling it is completely changed. I never knew it very well, even when I was young. My feeling now is that the American cinema has taken over, and everyone wants to go dancing swing at the Emsallah Gardens. There are several dance joints with hot jazz. I haven't been to any, and know nothing about it. Of course the people I knew when I was here before are middle-aged and fathers of families, and I'm inclined to avoid them. I haven't met any new friends in the few months I've been here. The reason is that I have a hovering feeling of not being really in Tangier at all. It is terribly changed, and I can't bear to imagine what it used to be like." His mood, however, was hardly elegiac: "As you know perfectly well," he reminded Ford, "I've never yet felt a part of any place I've been, and I never expect to."

Alone on the Mountain, Paul devoted his attention to *The Sheltering Sky*, which moved toward a nightmarish crescendo: On a long bus ride to El Ga'a, a settlement in the wasteland of the Algerian Sahara, Port falls ill with typhoid. Turned away from a mangy hotel whose proprietor shouts at them about an epidemic, Kit rides with the ashen Port in a truck to another outpost called Sbâ, where she finds shelter in a mud-walled one-room hut that serves as a military infirmary. Now, in the depths of the desert, Port is dying. Consciousness has become a fever dream; the only thing that lies ahead is the void. Unhinged by the shock, unable to attend to Port as he makes his final descent, Kit flees into the night.

Port, Paul decided, would die alone, and he wanted to describe precisely his hallucinatory last moments. In other works of fiction, he had avoided writing subjectively about dying, reasoning that it was impossible to capture something so occult. With the death scene before him, however, he conducted an experiment with *majoun*—the cannabis confection that was said to induce fantastic visions. In the medina, he bought a large chunk for ten pesetas. "It was the cheapest kind," he remembered, "and therefore tasted like very old and dusty fudge from which all flavor had long since departed." The drug took hold after Paul had hiked from his cottage to the wooded heights of the Mountain, where he lay in the sun on a great slab of rock. "The effect came upon me suddenly, and I lay absolutely still, feeling myself being lifted, rising to meet the sun," he wrote. ". . . Then I felt that I had risen so far above the rock that I was afraid to open [my eyes]. In another hour my mind was behaving in a fashion I should never have imagined possible."

As the *majoun*'s spell intensified, Paul made his way back down the mountainside to the safety of the Farhar, where he lit a fire against the twilight chill, fixed his gaze on the flames, and, "without any relation to *The Sheltering Sky*, I simply lay there on the bed having a vision," he said later. "I was climbing up a kind of *calle de la playa;*

this car was coming down the hill, out of control, and so it wouldn't get me I rushed to the left of the street, to the entrance of a bakery. I remember being very aware of the pastries in the bakery window. The car did come and hit me anyway. I did feel the blow because the car hit me and cut me into pieces. It was very painful. I wasn't aware of Port or anybody else; I was dying—and I was dead."

Later that night Paul recorded his apocalyptic vision. In the morning, he incorporated it into the dying dreams of Port, the character with whom he identified so closely: During his slow-motion final moments, Port sees himself being mangled by a massive automobile that has careened out of control on a hill. Impaled by shards of glass and metal, he lies bleeding in the doorway of a pastry shop until he rises to flee from an assailant who is coming to step into his torn entrails. The fever-crazed Port watches himself run through endless alleys until a boulder is sent tumbling down upon him, "striking him with the weight of the entire world." On the brink of death, Paul wrote, Port

opened his eyes, shut his eyes, saw only the thin sky stretched across to protect him. Slowly the split would occur, the sky draw back, and he would see what he never had doubted lay behind advance upon him with the speed of a million winds. . . .

His cry went on through the final image: the spots of raw bright blood on the earth. Blood on excrement. The supreme moment, high above the desert, when the two elements, blood and excrement, long kept apart, merge. A black star appears. . . . Point of darkness and gateway to repose. Reach out, pierce the fine fabric of the sheltering sky, take repose.

To Jane, Paul reported that his "little novel" was going well enough, and that he expected to see her in Tangier at any moment. He also wrote her of a visit he had made to a soothsayer who had spoken of a journey that would be attended by illness or death. Like the character Kit, Jane saw omens at every turn, and most of them terrified her. "She had more angst than anyone I've ever seen," Paul said later. In December 1947, she informed him that his letter "threw [her] into a state." Denying at length that she had ever implied that her departure was imminent, she wrote, "Naturally all during the summer there were moments when I thought of simply rushing off and other moments when my deep despond about my own work and your reports about the slow but steady progress in yours somehow combined to make me feel, 'que ce n'était pas le moment encore.' . . . [but] I want to get there and feel I would if it weren't for the Fortune Teller. You never should have written me that, of course." And while her tone was—as always—self-mocking, she declared, "I shall never forgive him or you, really."

Angst or no, Jane clearly missed Paul, and he was eager to have her in Tangier. He had found an aerie that he knew would amuse her: During his solitary walks about the Casbah, he had spotted an odd little house near the Place Amrah, just two doors from Hutton's Sidi Hosni. Three stories high, with a series of infinitesimal rooms and a magnificent view from its flat roof, it was miraculously cheap and "cozy as a raspberry tart," as Truman Capote would observe. Paul persuaded the set designer Oliver Smith, a distant cousin who was part of the Bowleses' New York household, to invest in it with him to use as a communal headquarters. With an anchor thus established, he promptly left Tangier again, this time on an open-ended excursion to Fez and points south. Paul had told Jane of his plans before her December missive, and in it she implored, *"Please* take care of yourself and don't for God's sake get sick down there. . . . Is there any mail delivery in the desert?"

It was in Fez, at the home of a wealthy Moroccan named Abdessalem Ktiri, that Paul met a handsome teenager called Ahmed Ben Driss el-Yacoubi. Paul had had other Arab friends, but none to rival Ahmed—a handsome, sensual, expansive character who was impossible to ignore. Like Jane, he was powerful enough to walk into a room and charm everyone in it without the slightest effort. While natives of Fez had earned a reputation among their countrymen as a dour, devious lot, Ahmed "wasn't a typical Fassi," Paul said. "He had a great sense of humor, and he made everyone laugh. He didn't speak any language except Moghrebi but he could put ideas across easily—he was very expressive."

Born to parents who were both Cherifs, or direct descendants of Mohammed, Ahmed had been trained in a mystical healing art known as *f'qih*. Like his father and paternal grandfather, he had learned to cast out illness by manipulating fire, preparing herbal remedies, writing sacred formulas and practicing the laying on of hands. He had committed to memory parts of the Koran, as well as traditional songs, dances, legends and bits of alchemists' lore. But Ahmed's destiny lay outside the profession of *f'qih*. Since childhood, he had made sculptures and drawings, and his head was filled with images that he wanted to call into existence. None of his friends had ever expressed such a heretical desire, and his pious father had told him that Allah was displeased by those who created idols. Determined to follow his secret calling, Ahmed used goat dung thinned with water to make exuberant sketches that he showed to no one.

Paul was fascinated with Ahmed, but with the cool, wet winter setting in, he left Fez for the Sahara. Bringing with him seven valises and the intrepid Babarhio (who traveled in a brass cage covered with a child's djellaba), he took a train east across the Middle Atlas mountains to Oujda, a trading center on the Algerian border. "I'm in slow route to Colomb-Béchar and thence southward," he reported to Charles Henri Ford on December 13. "With my parrot, who still refuses to talk. I've beat him with a rubber hose, burned his wings with cigarette butts and given him the works time and again, but it's no use. He used at least to cluck, but now he remains obstinately silent. . . ."

Late in December, the pair arrived in Taghit. A spare settlement with a commanding view of stony desert and gilded hillocks of sand, it was occupied by a contingent of French military officers, Pères Blancs (Christian missionaries dedicated to the task of providing a moral example for their Arab brethren) and the dark-skinned descendants of Sudanese slaves imported centuries before by the Arabs. From Taghit south to Timimoun and Adrar, the landscape was one of vertiginous extremes—of temperature, of beauty, of discomfort. In the daytime, a ruthless sun presided over a glaring inferno where every rock was thrown into high relief; after dark, when the sky deepened to midnight blue, a riot of stars assembled and a blazing cold razored through the thickest red-mud walls. Lunar stretches of rocky wasteland, arid river valleys, rhythmic dunes and vestigial mountain ranges were punctuated by fertile oases. The groves had been created through miracles of reclamation;

drawn from deep wells and cleverly constructed reservoirs, precious water was channeled through elaborate networks of canals to neat rows of almond, fig, orange and pomegranate trees. Flute sounds and *kif* scents wafted from fanciful summerhouses where landowners' families gathered for mint tea, and vegetables and grain grew in orderly patches tended by turbaned laborers. Inside the low mud walls, it was easy to forget that one was surrounded by the hushed austerity of the Sahara. Venturing into the desert was arduous, in any case; most travelers moved about by heavy truck or camel caravan, and even without a breakdown a trip of a hundred miles might require several days. Food often was execrable, and sleeping arrangements, uncertain. As Paul wrote later, "There are probably few accessible places on the face of the globe where one can get less comfort for his money than the Sahara." But that, of course, was part of its allure. He confessed to Ford that for him, travel was "a question of finding uncomfortable situations and putting up with them as long as possible before escaping; the desire to escape can then be called perfectly natural. . . ."

Staying, when he could, in the tiny, isolated hotels that had been built by the French, Paul worked on his novel in the cool of the mornings, sitting in bed and writing in longhand. With Port gone, Paul sent the shattered Kit on a hallucinatory trek across the desert. Eluding Tunner (who catches up with her in Sbâ on the eve of Port's death), she strikes out into the dunes, wearing a proper overcoat and carrying talismans from her former life in a small valise. Taken up by wealthy Bedouins traveling by caravan, she is ravished and turned into a sexual chattel; sun-browned, dressed as an Arab boy, she loses all trace of Kit Moresby as they make their slow progress across the Sahara. And while Tunner eventually tracks her down in the Sudan, he is too late; robbed of all identity, Kit has become a catatonic witness to "the horror that lies above."

Paul worked well as he traveled through the Sahara. The desert was everything he required: No one disturbed his psychic peace, and while the French commandants garrisoned in its sprawling, lonely forts could be counted upon for the occasional evening of respectable food and bracing conversation, he never lost the pleasant sense of being an observer. Arabs regarded him as a curiosity; in a setting where songbirds (considered saboteurs in the vulnerable oases) were fair game for hunters using slingshots, here was an inscrutable American who kept a voracious parrot as a pet. In Timimoun, Paul left Babarhio's cage in the window of his hotel and a committee of natives came to suggest that his companion would be safer out of sight. "Nobody likes birds here," they told him gravely. The stories about the *étranger incroyable* seemed to travel faster than he did; by the time he reached Algiers, a journalist who had caught wind of his journey had written "a ridiculous, libelous article" about him for the *Echo d'Alger,* as Paul reported it to Ford. The piece, he wrote, "describ[ed] me as distant, chilly, and eccentric, and, even worse, describ[ed] my parrot as skinny and featherless, which is certainly not the case. So that the staff of the Hotel Saint Georges seemed frightened to let me loose in the lobby, because as soon as I signed my fiche they all knew I was the crazy American from the desert." For all of that, he asserted that nothing could have pleased him more: "Of course I was really delighted. No one can ever heap enough insults upon me to suit my taste. I think we all really thrive on hostility, because it's the most intense kind of massage the ego can undergo."

As Paul was setting off the alarms in Algiers, Jane—who had sailed from New York in mid-January, 1948—cabled to report that she would reach Gibraltar on the thirty-first. Paul and the much-maligned Babarhio set out immediately for the International Zone, a journey that required nine days. Back in Oujda, a customs inspector demanded that Paul present a health certificate for his parrot, and a long, empty Sunday was spent in search of a veterinarian. None materialized, and on the advice of the same functionary he abandoned the quest and, with his companion, took the next train west to Fez: "A horror of slowness, has no diner, sells nothing to eat, and gets me into Fez at some outlandish hour," he reported with satisfaction. An exhausted forty-eight hours in Fez, where he secured the visa needed to travel through the Spanish Zone, and he was on his way back to Tangier—and to a world that, as he saw it, was becoming fatally tainted by Western civilization.

Chapter 4

To a writer imbued with a finely developed appreciation for the absurd, Tangier was paradise. Installed in the Hotel Rembrandt with the dowdy, hard-drinking tea-shop proprietor who was her improbable new lover, Jane Bowles instantly embraced the mongrel city. She was struck by the theatricality of its natives: In a story detailing a visitor's bemused fascination with the cloistered world of Moslem women, she observed, "All the people in the town spoke and gesticulated as though they had studied at the Comédie Française." Like Jane, Tanjawis were clever linguists, acute observers, inventive storytellers and wicked mimics. They shared not only her playfulness but her penchant for performance art; few would hesitate to create a scene to secure a strategic advantage. Moroccans often embraced a paranoid illogicality that reflected Jane's own; years later, in his novel *The Spider's House*, Paul appropriated an aphorism that neatly expressed their common posture: "You tell me you are going to Fez. Now if you say you are going to Fez, that means you are not going. But I happen to know that you are going to Fez. Why have you lied to me, you who are my friend?"

Even among the iconoclasts who had migrated to Tangier, Jane soon became known as an original. With her small-boned frame and close-cropped hair, she looked decidedly gamine, but her wit was sharp enough to wound. Complex, mercurial, she was "constantly giving off different lights and glints, like a prism," in the words of her friend Charles Gallagher, an author who became a Tangier neighbor. At thirty-one, she could be wildly pretty at one moment, painfully plain the next; a fall from a horse had prompted a series of operations that left her with a stiff knee, and her pronounced limp was a Chaplinesque counterpoint to her aura of sophistication. (In mordant moments, Jane called herself "Crippie the Kike Dyke," lampooning her bad leg, her Jewishness and her lesbianism.) Spoiled by a widowed mother, she retained a childish quality that was alternately maddening and endearing. At parties, she nestled into friends' laps and cuddled like a little girl. Moods set in swiftly and then evaporated; given to sulks and tantrums and fits of pique, she created an upheaval whenever she went to a restaurant—terrorizing waiters and summarily rejecting dishes that didn't suit her. Phobic about elevators, trains and snakes, among other things, she had been given the name "Complications Janie" by her friend John LaTouche. "No one would say that Jane was an easy person," said the theater producer Lyn Austin, who became a loyal friend in New York. "That wasn't her gift. Her gift was the wildness and the uniqueness and the fun and the brilliance."

Jokes were Jane's dodge; hounded by anxiety and depression, terrified of her own talent, she used humor to deflect her hard-working demons. But the amusing pronouncements and brilliant non sequiturs only underscored her fragility; beneath it all, her close friends saw a "strained watchfulness," as the poet Ruth Fainlight put it. Even a casual observer could sense the not-so-quiet desperation. "She lived on tiptoe. She really was just like a little kitten running around trying to please everyone," said Jack Dunphy, the writer who would come to Tangier with Truman Capote in 1949.

In literary circles Jane had become known as "a writer's writer's writer," as the poet John Ashbery observed in *The New York Times*. With its elliptical plot and elusive characters, her novella *Two Serious Ladies* had proven too abstruse for most readers, but those who did get the joke often became fanatically devoted to Jane. Alcohol and angst had slowed her creative momentum, and her output was slim.

Since 1943, when *Two Serious Ladies* appeared, she had published just three short stories—"A Guatemalan Idyll," "A Day in the Open," and "Plain Pleasures"—and the first act of her play, *In the Summer House.* Unlike Paul, she found writing to be torturous: "The way I write I never know what's going to happen, which is probably what gives my work its quality of surprise, as if the reader and I were finding out together," she told the writer Jane Howard, who came to Tangier for *Life* in 1967. "That implies it's easy, but it's hell. I hate writing and always have. Anyone, anything can interrupt me from writing. But much as I hate it, I have no interest in anything else, except for the people I love."

By the time Jane reached Tangier, the connection between the Bowleses had withstood not only long separations and involvements with other people but an undercurrent of rivalry that strengthened as *The Sheltering Sky* neared completion. On one level, the two were immensely supportive of each other; in her reply to the letter in which Paul had referred to his "little novel," Jane had taken him to task for underplaying his accomplishment: "I don't care how much better or worse you write than me as long as you don't insist that I'm the writer and not you. We can both be, after all, and it's silly of you to go on this way just because you are afraid to discourage me." But her bravado had faltered as "Camp Cataract," a long story on which she had toiled for months, refused to move ahead. In October 1947, she wrote to Paul, "I hope maybe to have done enough writing by [February] so as not to be completely ashamed and jealous when confronted with your novel. At the moment I can't even think of it without feeling hot all over. And yet if you had *not* been able to do it I would have wrung my hands in grief. . . . However little I have done I am pleased with but shall probably throw it in the rubbish heap when I see yours."

Jane had brought the "Camp Cataract" manuscript with her to Morocco, and she would stay with the story until it was finished. She had been in Tangier for two days by the time Paul made his way back from the desert, and they had little time to commune. After a quick tour of the house in the Casbah, they went on an expedition to Fez with Cory, as her new lover was called, and the poet Edwin Denby, a friend from New York who had come to visit Paul in exile.

Aside from a fondness for cocktails, Cory seemed to have little in common with the vibrant Jane. Paul found her tiresome; an uninspiring conversationalist who warmed only to the subjects of business and sports, she pronounced Morocco to be depressing. Hobbled by a recent injury, she wore a splint on one leg and could barely negotiate the steep streets in Fez. "The idea of bringing someone from New York with a broken hip or whatever seemed absolutely crazy to me," Paul said. "She was the last sort of person you'd want as a traveling companion."

At the Palais Jamai, a nineteenth-century vizier's palace that had been transformed into a hotel, Paul introduced the little group to *majoun*. Since his first encounter with the drug, he had experimented with it again and blissfully concluded that, like Lewis Carroll's Alice, he had "come upon a fantastic secret: to change worlds, I had only to spread a bit of jam on a biscuit and eat it." He also had discovered that the experience had its own psychological protocol: "[I found that it] was imperative to be unmitigatedly content with all the facets of existence beforehand," he wrote later. "The most minimal preoccupation, the merest speck of a cloud on the emotional horizon, had a way of italicizing itself during the alteration of consciousness and assuming gigantic proportions, thus completely ruining the inner journey."

The concoction was supplied by Ahmed Yacoubi, the boy who had caught Bowles' attention at the Ktiri house. After dinner one evening, Ahmed brought a batch to the hotel and—following Paul's instructions—Jane, Cory and Edwin each swallowed a small portion. As Paul had predicted, the drug took hold slowly; after more than an hour, its effects were still imperceptible. "Jane said, 'Ah, this stuff is nothing.' I begged her to not to take any more, but she took a big hunk," Paul said later. "I told her, 'Now you've done it,' but, naturally, she didn't know. She wouldn't believe me." The group soon retired, and the next morning an agitated Jane reported that "her night had been ten nights long and totally horrible." When the generous dose of *majoun* did take effect, it had set off an explosion of paranoia; quivering in her room, she had been convinced alternately that Paul was in mortal danger and that he was about to break in and kill her. The sinister potential that Paul found exhilarating was, to Jane, a source of agony.

As the sojourn in Fez continued, it became apparent that clouds *were* gathering on the emotional horizon. While Paul was fascinated with the city, Jane didn't share his enthusiasm. Lying in a bowl-shaped valley between the Middle Atlas mountains and the peak of Jebel Zalagh, Fez seemed to be a brooding island in the midst of an endless *bled.* "Jane always imagined that there would be trouble and that you could get a ship out from Tangier, but that you would be stranded in the south," Paul said later. Nearly impossible to navigate without a guide, the medina (fifteen kilometers in circumference and the largest in Morocco) was a tangle of streets that, like T. S. Eliot's, "follow[ed] like a tedious argument of insidious intent." Exploring the place with Cory became a chore. In a letter to Tennessee Williams, Paul complained that Jane and Edwin were "not venturesome" and stayed in their rooms.

When Jane and Cory did strike out alone, they fell into adventures that—in retrospect, at least—seemed farcical. Pressing on to Marrakech, 250 miles to the southwest, the two checked into the ornate, elaborately landscaped Hotel Mamounia and prepared to investigate the dusty-pink city outside. On an excursion to a *moussem*—a yearly celebration held at a saint's tomb—they received a jolting introduction to the ecstatic cults that flourished in Morocco. Hearing that the festival of Moulay Brahim was to be held in the nearby mountains, they hired a driver, assembled a picnic and set out in search of the pilgrims. The scene could have been extracted from *The Sheltering Sky:* They had hiked for half an hour through the scrub forest when a contingent of screaming, blood-soaked celebrants came tearing down the mountain at close range. After dancing themselves into a frenzy, it seemed, members of the Aissaoua brotherhood had torn open a bull and devoured the creature alive. "Cory and Jane thought they were going to be covered with blood, too, but the men ran right past them," Paul recalled. "Cory said 'Oh, my Gawd,' and sat down on a rock when they saw them rushing toward them. Jane was sure they were in a state of insanity—probably cannibals. I don't think she thought it was amusing that day or that week, but afterwards she could tell people about it and laugh."

As the two moved about the country, Jane attempted to placate her stolid lover. Working their way north, they found themselves once again in Fez and—searching for an innocuous diversion—Jane tried to interest Cory in the home life of the Moroccan Jews. "She told her, 'They're very calm and peaceful—you'll like them,' " Paul said. "So one day she took her to the Mellah [the Jewish quarter]. Jane said afterwards, 'It was the last place I should have taken her—there was some sort of festival, and outside every house on every street there were decapitated chickens. There was blood everywhere.' Cory said, 'I thought you said they were peaceful.' I think that's when she decided she should go back to Europe."

After seeing Cory off in March, Jane settled briefly into El Farhar with Paul. Although she was working on "Camp Cataract," she also dawdled in the watering holes where Europeans collected. (A nondrinker who was put off by intoxication, Paul seldom set foot in bars.) Ellen Buckingham, El Farhar's proprietor, found her in a lugubrious mood one afternoon. "We had a very sweet little bar— the local children would come in and ask for lemonade or something like that—people didn't get drunk. I went in one day and Jane was sitting there looking very teary and I said, 'But Janie, what's the matter?' She said, 'I've just had absinthe, and it makes me feel very depressed.' She was weeping like anything and I said, 'Then don't have it, why do you have it?' She said, 'Because I *like* to weep.' "

Passionate, emotionally accessible, Jane had never shared Paul's sense of detachment. Perhaps because writing was so agonizing for her, she always had turned outward—becoming embroiled in the dramatic minutiae of daily life rather than focusing her energy on fiction. Even when she was working, Jane was never the sort to sit quietly with her notebooks. She and Paul wrote in adjoining rooms at El Farhar and at the Hotel Belvedere, where they stayed during a May trip to Fez, and she called out questions as she worked: "What genus is the canary?" or "Exactly how do you build a cantilever bridge?"

"I was very busy with Kit somewhere down in the Sahara and I didn't want to talk about cantilevers," Paul recalled. He answered her as best he could; but the bridge, in particular, became an obsession. Jane kept pressing him for details, and "after three or four mornings I became aware that something was wrong. She was still at the bridge. I got up and went into her room. We talked for a while about the problem, and I confessed my mystification. 'Why do you have to *construct* the damned thing?' I demanded. 'Why can't you just say it was there and let it go at that?' She shook her head. 'If I don't know how it was built, I can't see it.' This struck me as incredible. It never had occurred to me that such considerations could enter into the act of writing. Perhaps for the first time I had an inkling of what Jane meant when she remarked, as she often did, that writing was 'so *hard.*' "

While they were still in Fez, Jane managed to finish "Camp Cataract" and Paul completed *The Sheltering Sky*, which he had written in a scant nine months. In a May 10 letter to Libby Holman, Jane reported archly, "Paul finished his novel as he wrote you, I imagine, and will turn out six stories tomorrow." She found Paul's book unsettling; the parallels between the Bowleses and the doomed Moresbys were clear, and the stark tale neatly triggered her terrors of the unknown. To a woman preoccupied with omens, killing off one's fictional counterpart seemed a reckless act. She confessed to Paul that she had felt fiercely protective when Port died: "Seeing you dead in the novel brought out the spitfire in me. . . . Perhaps harpy would be a more suitable word."

Jane's anxiety crested in the weeks after their works were completed. Oliver Smith, a close friend of both the Bowleses and Jane's staunch literary supporter, arrived in Fez late in May and quickly fell ill; while he was still in bed with a raging fever, Jane herself was stricken. The physician she consulted informed her that "there was something organically wrong" with her heart, and Jane became convinced that death was imminent. Paul (whom she had dubbed "Gloompot") fed her fears with a comment about picturing her "in a wheelchair or dead." That provocation, in addition to Jane's frustration at "my failure to like in [Africa] what you do and to like what you do at all anywhere," put the two at odds. "Sometimes I find nice explanations . . . for your attitude and sometimes I feel that you saw the whole thing, I mean the state of my health, as nothing but a threat to your trip, which mattered to you more than anything," she wrote to Paul in July.

It was a conflict that had arisen before. To Jane, Paul's desire to immerse himself in a primitive culture seemed doctrinaire and perverse; his talk about "escap[ing] from Western civilization" made her feel as though the distance between them was unbridgeable. In *Two Serious Ladies*, she had created a couple whose struggles

lampooned their own: On a trip to Panama, Mr. Copperfield—a
dispassionate man with a taste for the exotic—tries to persuade his
skittish, alcoholic wife to visit the jungle. As their bus reaches its
steamy outskirts, she deserts him; while he plunges about in the
jungle's untrammeled depths, she returns guiltily to Panama City
and the beautiful, broken whore for whom she has developed a
fascination.

After Jane had lived in Morocco for a number of months, she
explored the theme more soberly in a story fragment called "The
Iron Table." In it, an unhappy American woman sits on the terrace
of her hotel in an Arab country listening to her husband's "ceaseless
complaining about the West's contamination of Moslem culture."
Knowing his wife "believed it was not possible to continue trying
to escape from the Industrial Revolution," he skillfully draws her
into an argument about going into the desert—looking at her, as he
spoke, "without any light in his blue eyes." She replies irritably:

> "Why do you ask me if I wouldn't love to go into the
> desert, when you know as well as I do I wouldn't. We've
> talked about it over and over. Every few days we talk about
> it." Although the sun was beating down on her chest, mak-
> ing it feel on fire, deep inside she could still feel the cold
> current that seemed to run near her heart.
> "Well," he said. "You change. Sometimes you say you
> would like to go."
> It was true. She did change. Sometimes she would run
> to him with bright eyes. "Let's go," she would say. "Let's go
> into the desert." But she never did this if she was sober.
> There was something wistful in his voice, and she had
> to remind herself that she wanted to feel cranky rather than
> heartbroken. . . .

Later, her husband argues that it would be foolish for her to
go merely to please him:

> "You'd go to an oasis because you wanted to escape
> from Western civilization."
> "My friends and I don't feel there's any way of escap-

ing it. It's not interesting to sit around talking about indus-
trialization."

"What friends?" He liked to make her feel isolated.

"Our friends." Most of them she had not seen in many
years. She turned to him with a certain violence. "I think
you come to these countries so you can complain. I'm tired
of hearing the word *civilization*. . . ."

The moment when they might have felt tenderness had
passed, and secretly they both rejoiced. . . .

Feeling herself on the brink of "a crack-up," as she put it, Jane
was relieved when she, Paul and Oliver returned to Tangier from
Fez to meet Libby Holman, who had come for a visit with her
sixteen-year-old son, Christopher. Still frightened by the doctor's
pronouncement, Jane was in no mood to accompany the group on
their trip around Morocco and over the rugged High Atlas—even if
they were traveling by chauffeured Mercedes, rather than in a sti-
fling bus. Staying alone at Tangier's palmy Hotel Villa de France
(Gertrude Stein's favorite retreat), she threw herself into the life of
the city that her husband found so alluring.

On the road with Oliver, Libby and Topper, as Christopher was
called, Paul had an odd time of it. Libby was an exaggerated character who had become famous first as a torch singer and later as the
cynosure of one of the thirties' biggest scandals. Married in 1931 to
twenty-year-old tobacco heir Smith Reynolds, she had been widowed six months later when Smith died of a gunshot wound after
a bacchanalian barbecue at their estate in Winston-Salem. Two
months pregnant, the twenty-eight-year-old Libby had been in-
dicted for murder along with Smith's best friend, but the powerful
Reynolds family had seen to it that the embarrassing case never
came to trial. The circumstances surrounding Smith's death remained a mystery, and Libby had never shaken the taint: Branded
by the tabloids as a she-devil who seduced and destroyed anything
in her path, she had underscored that image by flaunting an imagi-
native series of male and female lovers—including Montgomery
Clift, Du Pont heiress Louisa Carpenter and a truck driver broken
in by her rival, Tallulah Bankhead. When her second husband, Rafe

Holmes, succumbed to a barbiturate overdose after he separated from Libby in 1947, the death only confirmed what America already knew—that Holman was a femme fatale.

Now, at forty-four, Libby was still a woman of extremes. She smoked constantly, drank until she passed out and embarked on stringent diets to preserve her remarkable figure. She was not a classic beauty, but she had a daring sense of style and an exuberance that touched everyone around her. On stage, she played the enchantress: "Her voice," said Tennessee Williams, "was the voice of a siren in heat." With a portion of the $7 million inherited from Smith, she had built Treetops, an opulent neo-Georgian house where she kept a mutable entourage, a convertible Rolls and a closetful of furs. All the props were in place, but the mercurial Libby was seldom happy; jealous, controlling, she flitted from liaison to liaison, discarding each new lover when the giddiness was gone. What stability she had came from platonic friends; during the years they had known each other, she had forged a close bond with Jane, who shared her sense of humor and applauded her daring.

In Morocco, where the small party spent much of the six-week trip exploring remote outposts like Taroudant and Tiznit, Libby exhibited her typical flamboyance. Instead of the modest, long-sleeved outfits that most European women chose for such expeditions, she had brought along an assortment of revealing dresses that exposed her tanned stomach, and she loaded her arms with gold bracelets. The crowds of Berbers who collected around Libby fixed her with shocked stares, and she loved it. On a visit to the magnificent waterfalls at Ouzoud, she discarded her clothing altogether, running into the icy water and shouting to her son, "Come on in, Topper—this is better than sex!"

To Libby, North Africa seemed like an exotic stage upon which it was possible to enact one's wildest fantasies. In Rabat, disguised as a Berber peasant, she disappeared into the night without giving Paul and Oliver a clue where she had gone. Hours later, she reappeared, but she refused to reveal what had happened to her, except to say that someone had taken her purse. Only later did she announce triumphantly that she had spent the missing hours in the company of a young Moroccan.

The oddest moment of the sojourn came in Ksabi, where the

party stayed for a time in a leopard hunter's lodge. One moon-washed evening, as the two reclined on an outcropping of rocks, Libby proposed to Paul. She had already taken up the subject with his wife, she said, and Jane had told her that she would make no objection if he really wanted to remarry. Startled, Paul said nothing; as much as he admired Libby, marriage was clearly out of the question. His companion broke the silence by laughing. "I don't think Jane likes the idea really," she said. "I think she really wants to be Mrs. Bowles herself." Paul simply stared at the moon, and Libby let the subject drop.

As they traveled about, Libby tried to persuade Paul to compose a score for *Yerma,* which she hoped to mount in New York. She had just read the Federico García Lorca play, and she had conceived a passion for the title role—that of a Spanish peasant who kills her husband because he cannot give her a child. Paul finally agreed to take on the project, but it would be months before he wrote the first song. In mid-July, he was called back to New York by a telegram from Tennessee Williams, who wanted him to write the score for *Summer and Smoke.*

Jane remained in Tangier. She was writing, after a fashion, and she had found a replacement for the absent Cory. While Paul was away, she would focus on the one diversion that always made her feel alive—pursuing a romance that, from the beginning, seemed impossible.

Chapter 5

Sumptuous, riotously stimulating, Tangier's souks were places where the city's cosmopolitan air gave way to a rich confusion that was wholly Moroccan. In the Grand Socco and the smaller markets arrayed near the whitewashed walls of the medina, there was a rural quality that had nothing to do with the new cinema on rue Samuel Pepys or the poodle parlor in the Ville Nouvelle. In the souks, Berber women in striped blankets and straw hats adorned with black pompons squatted in the dust behind modest piles of eggs or bunches of fresh-picked mint; Arab butchers in stark white cubicles lit by a single bulb hacked at sheeps' heads and lambs' livers; shrill, ragged children sold emerald leaf-cones filled with tiny strawberries. The sheer bounty was astonishing; wild artichokes, fennel, avocados, eggplant, tomatoes and peppers were arranged in artful heaps; great shining pyramids of oil-cured olives were piled next to plump preserved lemons; palettes of spices—dusty-green cumin, yellow-orange cayenne, scarlet paprika—were mounded in white enameled bowls. Fragrant bread stands sold long French loaves and sheets of unleavened *therfist* and wholewheat discs called *kisra;* fruit vendors offered mountains of figs, almonds, melons, pomegranates, raisins, prunes and dates. Flower stalls abloom with lilies, roses, daffodils, narcissi and African daisies stood in lyrical contrast to the odoriferous fish market, where armies of flies descended on the sole and *espadon* and *langoustes.*

The manicured Fez Market (where Tanjawi shopkeepers set steep prices for exotica like Marmite and Camembert) was favored by Europeans, but Jane preferred the crowded souks. Her fascination for curious specimens was akin to Paul's, and nowhere in Tangier were so many forms of humanity on display: Hidden behind lithams[1] and djellabas and rhinestoned sunglasses, sharp-voiced Arab women with hennaed hands haggled over chickens for the evening's *tagine;* thin men in cast-off GI uniforms pounced on discarded cigarette butts; swarms of rough-looking little boys argued over who would carry heavy shopping baskets. Children with missing limbs, peasants stricken with river blindness and elderly men wasted by tuberculosis all were familiar sights. Beggars sat with their pants rolled up to reveal twisted legs, and sad-eyed women pinched their infants to make them wail whenever a sympathetic-looking European appeared. Free to walk the streets, madmen twitched their way through throngs of Tanjawis who simply ignored them. But the scene always had its visual jokes—a pair of chickens riding atop a man's turbaned head, or a Berber tribesman pushing an injured sheep in a battered baby carriage.

It was in the busy grain market that Jane began her courtship of a country girl who called herself Cherifa. Paul had met her in the autumn of 1947: "I was taken to see her by Boussif, an Algerian who kept talking about her—he said she was a real primitive, a wild girl, and that he was trying to civilize her. I suppose that means he was trying to get her into bed," he said later. "She was thin and she had long black tresses, and it seemed she was always drunk—Boussif was always giving her liquor. Cherifa knew a lot of people; she had a whole group of Moroccan women who used to come to her *hanootz*[2] and meet rather like a club, and there grew up a whole group of French and English people, sort of pre-beatniks, who used to sit outside and eat with her. And of course they brought her wine."

In the beginning, Paul considered the grain seller to be unremarkable. "She was a zero to me, a bore," he said. But he introduced Jane to her, and she quickly became one of Cherifa's admirers. After

Paul left for New York she began making daily pilgrimages to the booth above the Grand Socco where the "wild girl" sat amid sacks of wheat and oats and barley. Although Cherifa spoke only Moghrebi and Jane had acquired only twenty or thirty words of the difficult dialect, the subtext of the relationship was clear: Jane desperately wanted to sleep with Cherifa, who wanted only money and gifts from her. Before the feast of Aïd el-Kebir, Jane wrote to Paul that Cherifa "is trying to get [a sheep] out of me. . . . She makes a horn out of her hand and says 'Baaa' and then 'Thank you.' "

Even for a woman who habitually formed crushes on droll characters, Jane's choice seemed extreme. At nineteen or so, Cherifa was a formidable figure, one who had little in common with other Tanjawi maidens. Underneath her red-and-white-striped Berber blanket, she wore jeans and brown golfing shoes. Possessed of several gold teeth and a downy mustache, she had a "what-rough-beast-slouching-towards-Bethlehem air about her," in the words of Jane's friend Ruth Fainlight. Cherifa (whose name was the feminine form of "Cherif") claimed to be descended from Bou Arrakia, the patron saint of Tangier. "She would tell people, 'I'm a saint,' " Paul said. "She was so crazy; she carried a switchblade, and she loved to draw it quickly to show what she'd do to men—ripping them from bottom to top. If anyone ridiculed her she'd say, 'Come with me.' She would take them to the police station and say, 'I can prove I'm a virgin'—and she could. She had a piece of paper [that said so]." While some men responded to Cherifa's elemental sexuality and—like Paul's friend Boussif—became members of her claque, she was in fact a lesbian.

In many ways Jane's courtship of Cherifa was less an *affaire du coeur* than an elaborate farce. Jane's role was that of the ardent suitor thwarted by cultural obstacles and a language barrier; Cherifa played the elusory innocent who tortures her patient swain. For months, they enacted absurd little scenes that only whetted Jane's interest in her prey.

As usual, she documented her romantic exploits in letters to Paul in New York:

I am off to Cherifa's *hanootz.* Our relationship is completely static: just as I think that at least it is going backwards (on the days when she sneaks behind a stall) I find that it is right back where it was the next day. Nothing seems to move. I have finally, by wasting hours and hours just hanging about mentioning the [feast of] Aid Es Seghir about every five seconds, managed to get myself invited for tonight. So I shall go soon to the grain market from where we will leave for M'sallah together. I don't know whether I shall walk behind her or in front of her or parallel to her or on the other side of the street. I made my invitation secure by suggesting a chicken. I made wings of my arms and flapped them— "djdedda" . . .

Even when Cherifa agreed to meet her, events often took an ironic turn. When she presented herself at Cherifa's house on the appointed day, bearing a freshly killed chicken, Jane found that the feast—held each year in accordance with a precise phase of the moon—had been conducted earlier than she had calculated. "I therefore went to Cherifa's the very night after the carousing was over," she reported to Paul. "It is all so ridiculous. . . . Then I worried about the chicken rotting." Months later, the courtship was still becalmed: "The great day came when Cherifa consented to go on a picnic . . . but only if she could bring along her friend Kinzah," remembered David Herbert, who became Jane's fast friend.

They arranged to meet in a public garden near the cattle market. Jane prepared the food and took a taxi to the appointed place. She dismissed the taxi and sat waiting patiently for an hour and a half. Finally there appeared the large cream-coloured mule on which were perched the Cherifa and Kinzah. Cherifa was in front and Kinzah behind with a silver tray and teapot between them. They stopped and endless Arab politenesses ensued. Eventually Cherifa asked Janie to hand up the picnic basket: No sooner was it in her hands than she whipped up the mule, which galloped off in a cloud of dust, leaving Janie disconsolate on the side of the road.

Jane's disappointments, however, were offset by an exhilarating sense of being on the threshold "of something that I will one

THE DREAM AT THE END OF THE WORLD   45

day enter," as she wrote to Paul. "This I don't think I could feel if
I didn't know Cherifa and [her friends] the "Mountain Dyke" and
that yellow ugly one (!?). . . . Perhaps I shall be perpetually on the
edge of this civilization of theirs. When I am in Cherifa's house I
am still on the edge of it, and when I come out I can't believe I was
really in it—seeing her afterwards, neither more nor less friendly,
like those tunes that go on and on or seem to, is enough to make
me convinced that I was never there. . . ."

As Jane was discovering, the world to which Moroccan women
belonged was tightly knit and all but impenetrable to the outsider.
Segregated from men in private as well as in public, Tanjawi women
were bound by feudal traditions that kept them insulated from
decadent Europeans. No proper Moslem woman would sit in a café
or walk the streets without a companion or appear in public—as
Cherifa did—without a litham. (Upper-class women seldom ventured outside their homes at all; when Paul arrived in Tangier with
Aaron Copland, there were still female members of the Menebhi
family who had lived their entire lives inside the palace.) Only those
females who were members of wealthy or progressive families received an education. European indulgences like wearing makeup,
smoking or drinking liquor were unthinkable. A girl's virginity was
guarded carefully until the day of her wedding, and heterosexual
liaisons outside marriage were strictly forbidden. (Discreet dalliances with other women, however, were permissible.) Polygamy,
while rare, was still legal, and arranged marriages were the rule. A
woman never disputed her husband's word; no matter how tyranni-
cal her mate, she was required to submit herself and her children to
his will.

Since socializing between Tanjawis and Nazarenes (as the infidels were called) was minimal, few expatriates saw the intimate,
domestic side of Moroccan life—the realm in which women were
comparatively unfettered. While their husbands drank mint tea in
cafés, Moslem wives spent hours tending children, doing needle-
work and trading news on their flat rooftops, where geraniums
bloomed and laundry flapped noisily in the wind. In cramped kitch-
ens, they worked with relatives to orchestrate diffas (feasts)—laboring over bisteeya, tagines, mechoui, [3] salads and sweets and then serving
male family members and their guests. (Leftovers were eaten by the
women behind the scenes after the men had had their fill.) In the

communal baths called *hammams*, they performed their weekly ablutions together in tiled rooms that echoed with laughter and children's voices. The world outside—the world of literacy and politics and social change—had little meaning; their lives were as cloistered as their grandmothers' had been, and that, they believed, was as Allah willed.

Jane was grateful for every glimpse allowed her. "I find myself in a constant state of inferiority vis-à-vis these women," she wrote to Paul. "Of course they live in wonderful long high rooms (the kind I used to hate and now love). Their beds are massive and covered with printed spreads (very Matisse) and white couches line the blue walls. They have hundreds of white frilly cushions too and they put very beautiful seashells into the water pitchers. The room we sit in when I visit Tetum[4] is always the color of early evening because of the blue walls. I know only that room actually but I imagine it rightly as many rooms—there must be hundreds like it."

Even as she tried to enter the world that Cherifa and Tetum knew, Jane found herself drawn to a realm that was wholly European. She had recently discovered Dean's Bar, which was on a little street just below the Minzah, and the Parade Bar on the rue de Fez—outposts that attracted the most prominent British and American exiles as well as a coterie of wealthy visitors. Sorely in need of an audience—and of a fresh cast of characters—Jane entered the drinking scene, where she could assuage her loneliness and laugh about her hopeless crush on Cherifa. With time, she came to know a domain that Paul never explored—a determinedly frivolous society with its own caste system and gin-soaked mythology.

An intimate pub where expatriates collected around a burnished wooden bar, Dean's was as urbane as its engaging proprietor. Short, dark-skinned Joseph Dean had been the barman at the Minzah before setting up his own business. He was surrounded by a tantalizing aura of mystery: No one was certain where he was born or how he had arrived in Tangier. Some Tangerinos insisted that he was Jamaican; others, that he was the son of a Frenchwoman and her wellborn Egyptian consort. He was thought to have been educated in England, where his mother lived, and to have worked variously in New York, Paris, Monte Carlo, Cairo and Berlin. The novelist Robin Maugham maintained that Dean had supported himself as a gigolo. Other patrons whispered that he had served as an informer during the war—that he was a real-life version of Rick in the film *Casablanca*. "He would listen in on deals, ships would later be blown up in the harbor: Who knew how these things came about?" one regular said years later. Many of Tangier's barflies were convinced that the charming Dean was addicted to opium and had served time for drug trafficking.

Whatever else Dean may have been, he was a tart-tongued raconteur with a genius for attracting the haut monde. Errol Flynn, Ava Gardner, Ian Fleming, Francis Bacon and even Barbara Hutton were drawn to Dean's, where it was impossible to miss his spirited monologues. Rupert Crofte-Cooke, a dauntingly prolific British writer who had arrived in Tangier after completing a prison sentence for pederasty, reported that "one of [his] stock stories . . . was of how [Tangier socialite and zoophile] Phyllis della Faille wanted a certain rare tropical fish only found in the remotest part of China. Dean told, miming it up and down behind his bar, how coolies with buckets balanced on long poles ran twenty miles a day to bring the creatures alive to Hong Kong from which port they were shipped to Europe. When they arrived Phyllis was occupied in giving a party and put their bucket in the nearest loo for safety. She was not to know, said Dean rising to his climax, that the water was to fail that day, or that when a lady used the lavatory and found the cistern was dry she would pick up the bucket, supposing it to have been left for the purpose, and pour its precious contents away."

That same Countess della Faille—an alcoholic Anglo-American married to a wealthy Belgian—had bankrolled Americans Jay Haselwood and Bill Chase and a White Russian refugee named Ira Belline, who were Dean's rivals at the Parade Bar. The blond, fortyish Phyllis was a local legend; she collected dogs, cats, horses, birds, monkeys, hedgehogs, desert rats and all manner of other beasts and kept them in a reeking, disheveled rural villa that one visitor pronounced "a concentration camp for animals." Dogs were quartered in the bathrooms or locked into tiny kennels; parrots lived in cages littered with rotting food and two weeks' worth of droppings; foxes were penned up on the patio. Bathrooms were repositories for newts, frogs, snakes and goldfish, and chimpanzees frolicked at the dinner table. At one point, her inventory was said to have included 376 creatures—including 75 dogs, 33 cats, 17 birds and 28 horses—but Phyllis herself was never certain just how large it was; few of her unhappy charges were even given names, and few lasted long in her care. "She would say, 'Oh, where's little doggy so-and-so, we haven't seen him for days,' then he was discovered in a bathroom somewhere, dead since a week," said her friend Kathy Jelen, a Hungarian who came to Tangier as the young wife of the American naval attaché. "It was terrible, terrible."

Unflaggingly melodramatic, the Countess posed for *Life* magazine in a gold caftan, reclining among sea-foam velvet pillows with favorites from her menagerie. Some Tangerinos found her fascinating: "I [fell] straight away under her spell," remembered Daphne Fielding. "The large, round, tortoiseshell-rimmed spectacles perched on her small, beak-like nose made her look like a perky little owl. Her fine-boned wrists were hung with various amulets, including a tiger's claw, charms to ward off the evil eye, articulated fishes of gold and silver, and doll's eyes set in diamonds. The heels of her shoes were studded with gold and silver nails. I . . . delighted in the fantasies and superstitions which she expressed in an incongruously deep voice and with an authority which lent verisimilitude to the most extravagant statements." But even those who didn't like the strident Countess couldn't accuse her of being a bore. If nothing else, there was always the interesting possibility that she would simply pass out in midsentence; she consumed vast quantities of tranquilizers and gin fizzes, and a crisply uniformed Spanish maid was always ready to tuck her in when she lost control.

On holiday from Marseilles, where they had worked as volunteers for the Red Cross, Haselwood, Chase and Belline had run into their benefactress in a Rabat café. "They were sitting there and some extraordinary woman with about twenty dogs and two parrots on her shoulder sat down at the bar," said David Herbert (who became an intimate of Belline's). "She went over to them and she said, 'You're the most interesting people I've seen for years in this country; I'll pick you up tonight and you come and have drinks at my [hotel].' Bill and Jay and Ira just sat there, stunned. They all went to the hotel where she was staying, never thinking she'd turn up; but she [appeared] with more dogs and more parrots, and she fell in love with Jay then—obviously, in a sort of platonic way. And then she said, 'I'll set you up in business,' and she bought the Parade for them and redecorated it."

The Parade's proprietors were an oddly assorted group. Chase was an urbane New Yorker; Haselwood, a rangy southerner. The tall, high-cheekboned Belline—a sweeping figure who described herself as "Igor Stravinsky's favorite niece"—had fled Russia during the revolution and become a success as a costume designer in the Paris theater. With her parents and disabled brother, she had spent the war years hiding from the Germans near Marseilles, where a sympathetic noblewoman quartered the four refugees in her château.

Chase, Haselwood and Belline transformed the Parade into one of the town's smartest bistros. The decor was simple—a jet-black bar set off against a white floor, with framed line drawings displayed against the white walls. Enshrined behind the bar, where Haselwood presided, was a black silk slipper encrusted with rhinestones—a donation from the tempestuous Eugenia Bankhead, Tallulah's sister. An owl attached to a lightweight chain flew about and perched on patrons' shoulders, and outside the French windows was a little garden where supper was served. "It was like a private club," said Ian Selley, a Tangerino whose father was the *London Times* correspondent in Tangier. "People would drink all evening, and you never booked a table for dinner; you ended up in a group ordering food."[5]

Nicknamed "Radio Tangier," the glib Haselwood established an eclectic following that rivaled Joseph Dean's. Within a few years, the Parade's circle would include William Burroughs and the artist Brion Gysin as well as a cast of diplomats, scandal-hungry journalists, nymphomaniacal heiresses, semireformed gangsters and caftaned drag queens. Truman Capote gravitated to the Parade in the summer of 1949, and more than two decades later he appropriated Haselwood as a character in his story "Unspoiled Monsters." Truman's Jay was "a kind and gangling Georgia guy who had made a moderate fortune from dispensing proper martinis and jumbo hamburgers to homesick Americans [in Tangier]; he also, for the favored of his foreign clientele, served up the asses of Arab lads and lassies—without charge of course, just as a courtesy of the house. . . . 'Hard work? I *know,*' [declared Jay's fictional counterpart]. 'I've damn near fucked cobras. That's how I got the pesetas to open this bar.' "

Aside from the Countess who drafted Haselwood as an escort, Jay's greatest admirer was the venerable Jessie Green, who held court every evening, wearing lavender silk and clutching her cane. Like Phyllis, Jessie was a figure whose exploits were much discussed. The niece of Sir William Kirby Green, a British minister assigned to Tangier in the Victorian era, Jessie had been brought to Morocco as a girl to serve as a companion for his daughter, Feridah. Born with an indelible sense of noblesse oblige, she lived on a weedy estate on the side of the Mountain, where she presided over the microcosm of British expatriate society. Jessie spoke freely and did precisely as she pleased. When she wanted to fend off visitors, she unplugged her telephone and had her maid post handwritten notices on her front door: "Miss Jessie, she sick," read one. "Last night she made one baby. Is now lying in. Please not to disturb." And she loved nothing more than laughing at her own acerbic japes; it was said that, at a luncheon party given by proud new parents, she complimented her hosts on the roast pork by saying, "Do you know, it is so tender that I thought for a moment you had roast your new baby." Somehow, Haselwood brought out a more vulnerable side of the contrary Miss Green. Almost two decades later, Jane described the attachment in a letter to Libby: "She is eighty-seven years old and . . . has been in love with [Jay] for many years."

Jane herself came to look upon Jay as a trusted confidant. Still living at the Villa de France, she was supervising the renovation of the Casbah house that Paul and Oliver had bought, and Haselwood helped see her through the inevitable Sturm und Drang. In the meantime, she had spotted another charming Moroccan house in Emsallah (a quiet neighborhood near the European part of town) and she examined the owner's offer in compulsive detail; with four rooms, two terraces, a large bath and space for a garden, it was on the market for two thousand dollars. "Jay says it's the cheapest buy he's ever heard of," she reported to Paul. "But I would certainly make sure that there was no hitch. . . ."

In the end, however, real estate was far less interesting than romance. Haselwood also listened to Jane's daily reports about

Cherifa and Tetum, the other grain seller who had caught her eye. Like Cherifa, Tetum was a tease; she tortured Jane with on-again, off-again invitations and sly promises that were never fulfilled. In a letter to Paul, Jane lamented, "She's a big liar, and each day she says just the opposite of what she said the day before. Do any of the men do that? . . . Whenever I suggest anything to her at all— even a glass of tea—she cuts her throat with an imaginary knife and says something about her family—at least she uses the imaginary knife one day, and on the next is prepared to do anything (verbally only). I am puzzled, vexed and fascinated, but deep inside I have an awful feeling I shall never find out any more than I know now. . . ." Weeks later, she added: "I am always so terribly gloomy when Tetum ties up the grain sacks and says goodbye. Often she and Cherifa leave the market together and we part in front of the hotel. I watch them disappearing up the road in the beautiful soft night and I just can't go yet to my room. The Parade is a warm spot to go to thank God, otherwise I would be too lonely I think—I *know.*"

By December, Tetum and Cherifa were no longer content to share the Nazarene who wooed them with shoes and scarves and djellabas. Cherifa began upping the ante—asking for a taxi as a gift and demanding that Jane pay for twice-weekly visits to a physician who was treating her for a skin disease. "The minute Tetum saw that I was taking Cherifa to the doctor's she wanted to go too" she told Holman. "I asked her what was wrong, and as far as I could gather she merely wanted a thorough checkup. Last month they were burning crocodile dung and pig's bristles and now they all want X-rays. Cherifa was wild and said I couldn't take Tetum to the doctor." And while she recognized the absurdity of it all, Jane didn't argue; not only did she stem the flow of bribes to Cherifa's rival, but she began to avoid Tetum altogether. To Libby, she confessed, "I have never understood why, but I am terrified of going against [Cherifa's] orders."

Chapter 6

It was an unsettled Tennessee Williams who accompanied Paul to Tangier in December of 1948. The critics had not been kind when *Summer and Smoke* finally made it to Broadway's Music Box Theater that October; and although his pain was assuaged by a new and passionate involvement with Frank Merlo, a handsome ex-sailor, Tennessee couldn't shake the storm clouds. During the otherwise pleasant voyage, he began to fret about his "inordinate" lust for Frank, who (like Tennessee) was new to monogamy. "Every evening I would cross his bunk in the stateroom," he remembered. "Aware of my sexual intemperance and what its consequences could be, I began to entertain a suspicion that something was going on between Frankie and Paul Bowles. Nothing was, of course, except friendship—and perhaps . . . an interest in some derivative of cannabis."

Practiced at the art of appearing to ignore such paranoid undercurrents, Paul spent much of his time working in his stateroom. In the fall, editors at Doubleday had turned down *The Sheltering Sky,* demanding that he return the advance. "They told me, 'We asked for a novel,' " he said. "They didn't consider it [fiction]." But the manuscript had not gone begging: John Lehmann would publish the book in England in September 1949, and New Directions would bring out the American edition the following month. Despite Doubleday's rejection, the early word on the novel was extremely favorable, and Paul had been urged by Lehmann, among others, to assemble a collection of short stories.

Alone in his quarters, now, he was crafting "The Delicate Prey," a tale that shocked even his admirers. Paul had taken the plot from an anecdote offered by a French officer in Timimoun: It seemed that a troupe of Filali leather merchants traveling in the desert had been killed for their goods by a Moungari predator who joined their caravan and lured each into a fatal hunting expedition. When the murderer surfaced in an isolated village with the distinctive Filali leather, the elders deduced that he had stolen it from the missing merchants. After hearing the case in private, the local French commandant gave the townsmen leave to punish the Moungari as they wished.

Paul doctored the story by injecting it with sensational elements laid out in exquisite detail. He contrived a hideous death for his character Driss, the youngest Filali: Binding his victim's wrists and ankles, the Moungari used an old barber's razor to hack off the excess rope, then "surveyed the young body lying on the stones. He ran his finger along the razor's blade; a pleasant excitement took possession of him. He stepped over, looked down, and saw the sex that sprouted from the base of the belly. Not entirely conscious of what he was doing, he took it in one hand and brought his other arm down with the motion of a reaper wielding a sickle. . . . A round, dark hole was left, flush with the skin. . . ." After making an incision in Driss's belly and "studiously stuffing the loose organ in until it disappeared," the Moungari "inflicted an ultimate indignity upon the young Filali," allowing himself to be "vociferous and leisurely in his enjoyment." But the murderer himself was punished in a suitably brutal manner: Burying him to the neck in the arid wilderness beyond the town gate, the elders left him to the elements. By the second night, he was delirious, and "the wind blew dust along the ground into his mouth as he sang."

When the story was finished, Paul took it to Tennessee's cabin. The playwright found it both beautiful and scandalous. "He said,

'Oh, I think it's wonderful, Paul, but you mustn't publish that story—people will think you're a monster,' " Paul remembered. "I was very flattered."

Jane was in Gibraltar to meet Bowles, Williams and Merlo when the ship arrived. (Since Tangier's harbor was unable to accommodate ocean liners, passengers disembarked across the Straits and completed the journey by ferry.) Tennessee had met her in Acapulco in the summer of 1940, and to him she seemed a kindred spirit—brave, vulnerable and incandescent enough to have been one of his own characters. She was, he wrote, "a charming girl, so full of humor and affection and curious, touching little attacks of panic—which I thought at first were bits of theater but which I soon found were quite genuine." And if Tennessee was troubled by Paul's apocalyptic vision, he was captivated by the "acute admixture of humor and pathos" that he saw in Jane's work. Her writing, he said, reflected "a unique sensibility . . . that I found even more appealing than that of Carson McCullers."

After a night at the Rock Hotel, the four drove to Málaga in Tennessee's maroon Buick. Convinced that he suffered from a heart defect, Tennessee vetoed Paul's suggestion that they make a detour into the mountains of southern Spain; going to Tangier, he decided, would be far more salubrious than subjecting himself to high altitudes. But a violent rainy season was setting in, and Morocco proved to be a trial for Tennessee. After a chilly ferry crossing, they drove up the muddy Mountain and "for reasons of economy (the Bowles') put up at a perfectly ghastly hotel called the El Far-Har," Tennessee reported to his friend Donald Windham. "Spectacular view: every possible discomfort! The meals were about 25¢ each but were not worth it. I got ill there. A dreadful cold, still coughing from it, and I developed a peculiar affliction—vibrations whenever I lowered my head, running up and down my whole body like an electric vibrator! . . . I thought surely I was about to have a stroke."

The solicitous Jane tried to amuse Tennessee by steering him toward oases like Madame Porte's. A stylish tearoom run by a severe Frenchwoman said to have been a Nazi sympathizer, it offered oversized martinis, delicate pastries and a glimpse of the more respectable characters who populated the International Zone. Although he did take to Porte's, the rest of the city failed to capture his imagination. "Tennessee never had a great response to the country or to the Moroccans; he wasn't mad about them," said the writer Gavin Lambert, whom Tennessee visited in Tangier years later. "They didn't appeal to him the way the Italians or the Mexicans did."

Some of Tennessee's worst impressions were formed during an abortive trip to Fez. Just before Christmas—on a night when, he observed, it was "raining skinned cats and alligators and blowing cross-eyed hyenas"—he and Paul and Frank were detained by border guards at Aqbaa el Khamra, where the Spanish Zone began. The two Spanish soldiers at the customs shed "insist[ed] on everything being hauled out of the car, all *fifteen* of *Paul's* suitcases and our four or five pieces," Tennessee wrote.

> Everything was thoroughly searched, about half the stuff confiscated. Wild arguments, hysteria! In the middle of this, a scream from outside. The Buick had slipped its moorings and had started sliding backwards downhill. Frank rushes out, races it neck and neck down the hill, finally executes a flying leap into it just in time to prevent a serious crash.— We have finally cleared customs and are permitted to go when it is discovered that the car keys are lost. We're sure the Spaniards have stolen them so we turn around and drive back to Tangier to complain to our consulate. In the morning we found the keys had fallen into the window socket of the car. Next day we have to go through the whole procedure again. It was that next day that my vibrations started![1]

The three made a second attempt on a rain-lashed Christmas Eve, and after a long delay at the border of the French Zone and an exasperating search for scarce gasoline coupons, they finally arrived at the Palais Jamai. And although Tennessee was pleased with the majestic hotel, his brief stay was adumbrated by a cablegram reporting that *Summer and Smoke* would soon close in New York. Restless, depressed, he left Paul with Ahmed Yacoubi and drove with Frank to Casablanca, where they immediately booked passage for Marseilles. From the safety of Rome, Tennessee admitted to Donald Windham that Morocco was "wildly beautiful," and that "one night in the Casbah of Tangier was really worth all the difficulties, when we were climbing up a steep, narrow street of mysterious white walls and arches and heard someone chanting the Koran—I believe Paul was quite cross with us for leaving."

If Tennessee's precipitous exit had caused a disturbance, he soon made up for it. By March 1949 he had arranged through the Authors League to give a one-thousand-dollar fellowship to both Paul and Jane, as well as to three other writers whose work he admired. To friends in New York, Jane wrote, "He liked my play. I love him."

For the moment, Jane was working well: since completing "Camp Cataract" (which *Harper's Bazaar* would publish that September), she had resumed work on *Out in the World,* the novel that had been aborning for several years. And she soon would go back to *In the Summer House;* by August, she would be concentrating on a new third act for the play she had begun in 1943. Now, with Paul, she made a month-long trip into the Algerian desert, and there she was able to finish "A Stick of Green Candy," a short story in which she explored the fantasy life of a lonely child.

Since Jane had a fear of unfamiliar landscapes, Paul had expected her to hate the Sahara. To his surprise, however, she pronounced it "the least sinister place on earth." From an oasis near Taghit, where they stayed in the isolated hotel that Paul had discovered the year before, she wrote to friends, "The dunes are extremely high, and I shall not attempt to climb them again—well maybe I will—because it is so beautiful up there. Nothing but mountains and valleys of sand as far as the eye can see. And to know it stretches for literally hundreds of miles is a very strange feeling. . . . It is very quiet, no electricity, no cars. Just *Paul* and *me.* And many empty rooms. The great sand desert begins just outside my window. I might almost stroke the first dune with my hand." After a non sequitur about Cherifa's rivalry with Tetum, she added, "Forgive this disjointed letter, please . . . in the middle of it the Arab who runs the hotel asked me to write a letter for him (naturally he can't write) to a man living in a place called 'Oil Pump Number Five.' It's a famous hell hole south of here. I hope we don't go there to live."

Instead, Paul soon ventured to Paris, where that spring the

pianists Arthur Gold and Robert Fizdale performed the concerto he had written for them in 1947. Alone at the Farhar, Jane resumed her dance with Cherifa and did battle with her novel. She also became caught up with the indelible David Herbert, who, with Cecil Beaton, had just made his entrance upon the scene.

The second son of the fifteenth Earl of Pembroke, David was "a most delightful, gay, alive and witty personality and companion," in the words of his great friend Cecil. Like Beaton, David was a man to whom style was everything; raised at Wilton, a distinguished stately home whose rooms were hung with Rembrandts, he was passionate about interior design. He saw gardening as a form of artistic expression, and he loved to sketch ethereal creatures, including Lady Diana Cooper, the socialite and actress who was a distant relative. Stage-struck since he was at Eton (where he once hired a Daimler to spirit him into the city for a matinee), he had made a stab at a film career in London, sung in cabarets in prewar Berlin and worshiped at the feet of Alfred Lunt and Lynn Fontanne during the Prohibition years in New York. Elinor Glyn, Mrs. Patrick Campbell and Tallulah Bankhead all had sponsored the young aesthete; and although he wisely had abandoned acting as a career, he unfurled his talents as a female impersonator in Tangier's charity musicales.

At forty, David seemed to be linked in some fashion to every significant mortal in the Western world. He counted Augustus John, Noël Coward, Cyril Connolly, the Mitford sisters and Prince Paul of Yugoslavia among his friends and Mrs. Cornelius Vanderbilt among his relatives. It seemed that his lovers were similarly distinguished: In a parlor game called International Daisy Chain (whose players were asked to construct a string of names connected to one another by sexual liaisons), talebearer Truman Capote coupled him with Harold Nicholson. He had met Greta Garbo in the south of France, befriended Barbara Hutton when she was a chubby debutante and spent country weekends with the clever Sitwells. His family had long been part of royal circles; his grandfather had been Lord Steward of the household to Queen Victoria, and his sister Patricia became lady-in-waiting to the Queen Mother. David himself had a cache of amusing stories about dinners with the Duke of Windsor, Queen Marie of Romania, and King George II of Greece, but he was not a classic snob. After he and Jane had known Herbert for two decades, Paul noted that David "wants to know every kind of person there is, and in his house one is likely to meet just about that. All he asks is that each one be himself, and that no one attempt to appear something else. If even the thinnest smoke-screen of pretence is spread, he will be sure to detect it, and then . . . you will hear the expression that denotes the ultimate in David's lexicon of disapproval: *second-rate.*"

As the expatriate community quickly learned, David's greatest talent was as a drawing-room agent provocateur. Practiced in the arts of gossip and intrigue, he moved quickly, gestured extravagantly and punctuated his speech with italics. His looks were not a particular asset; the journalist Ted Morgan (whose thinly veiled portrait of his Tangier neighbor appeared in *Rowing Toward Eden*), observed that he was "tall and thick chested, but his face showed signs of overbreeding with its tiny features and close-set eyes, like a julienne of mixed vegetables in the center of a salad." Loyalists, however, admired his wit and energy and self-possession; to the journalist Noël Mostert, who became a neighbor, he seemed like nothing so much as "an authentic Renaissance man. . . . One can imagine him in the diplomatic service of the Popes with some real Machiavellian bit of diplomacy to effect and doing it with great style and grace."

Other Tangerinos quickly pegged David as a petty opportunist. A master of the veiled barb as well as the effusive compliment, he "could be all sugar and honey one moment, and then be quite happy to stick a little dagger in your back when you turned it," said a titled friend whose stepfather belonged to Tangier's diplomatic corps. He liked having the upper hand, and the expatriate colony was small (and impressionable) enough so that his connections took on a new importance. In Wiltshire, David was merely the unconventional younger brother of the heir to Wilton—an "Hon." who was entitled only to a comparatively modest house on the grounds of the great estate. In a less regimented setting, however, he could use his social skills and his limited allowance to transform himself into "the Queen Mother of Tangier," as his guest Ian Fleming would describe him.

While tale bearers would always say that he had left England because of his sexual preference, David contended that it was his long-standing infatuation with Morocco that prompted him to settle in Tangier. He had made his first foray in 1936, as part of a group that included his cousin Michael Duff; Reine Pittman, a niece of John Singer Sargent; and Poppet John, the eldest daughter of his friend Augustus. As they traveled about the country, the party had been received by Moroccan dignitaries including the powerful Thami el-Glaoui, pasha of Marrakech and a close ally of the French. "He had one eye higher than the other and, in his Moorish clothes, looked like Edith Evans playing him on film," David reported. "He entertained us lavishly. At luncheons and dinners at his various palaces, there were orchestras playing and mountain dancers, beautiful gardens or courtyards with fountains playing, white peacocks strutting to and fro, and gazelles with gold collars and chains eating out of our hands."

In Tangier, David, Diana Cooper, Poppet and the writer A.E.W. Mason had dined with His Excellency Mehedi ben Arbi el-Menebhi at his palace. In a letter to her husband, Diana described the banquet: With Jessie Green and British Consul General Ernest Frederick Gye, the four had been

ushered into an immense white Moorish hall . . . and greeted by our host, a man of rare charm, with a twinkling dark European face. . . . He led us to our seats—low corner banquettes, him in the middle and the others quite comfortable on individual . . . divans. Menebhi did the piling up of cushions round our bums and elbows and took one comfortable little fall in doing it. We were each handed a large towel for our lap and on a six-inch-high table were laid in rapid succession the most delicious foods ever I tasted. The first a boiling dish of pastry, so light you could not get it to your mouth, in which were hidden quails. Between every three people was a shallow plate of clear honey and another plate with a block of butter on it, also each person had a large hunk of bread. . . . The dishes were so large that although we ate liberally of each, one made no impression on them. They were all rather the same, and there seemed little reason why the meal should ever stop or why it should come to the abrupt conclusion it did. Then there was a good deal of washing at a stand-up centre brass ablution arrangement—a slave pouring hot water from a smart kettle. . . .

Conversation never lagged, and of course there is no greater fun than talking to each other about the house and the host in his presence. Miss Green was very good at interpretation—an unchangeable drone of a voice that in the same tone passed you an oriental compliment or said "Of course the old man finds it frightfully difficult to get his daughters off."

At a dinner in Fez given for the group by a cherif who was "a remarkably common descendant of the Prophet but good-looking" in Diana's estimation, the postprandial festivities had included "very smart stomach-dancers and men dancers and delicious mint tea. . . . They sprinkle you with rose water and also bring along a silver brazier of incense and cedar, and put it under the ladies' skirts. You are then invited to put your nose under your dress between your breasts and inhale. You can imagine how some of the old English girls dealt with the situation and what an extraordinarily indecent effect the operation gave," she wrote.

In the spring of 1939, David had returned to Tangier with Cecil and the two had rented a Casbah house which "overlooks the Governor's Palace and is between the prison and the madhouse," as Beaton described it. Owned by the painter Jim Wylie, a venerable Englishman who dressed like a Victorian-era dandy, the house was sheltered by a great fig tree under which Samuel Pepys was said to have composed his Tangier diary. Cecil had fallen in love with the look of the city—its "faded pinks" and "blue-washed walls"—and David had been enchanted by its Byzantine social structure. "After three weeks David has become a complete Tangerine," Cecil wrote in his journal. "Knows all the local gossip of this oriental Cheltenham and knows every square inch of the town. From our roof garden he describes the scenes taking place on the square outside."

When the two returned to Tangier in 1949, they installed themselves in the Villa Mektoub, Loel Guinness' retreat on the Marshan, a scenic hill west of the medina. "His father . . . a millionaire banker, had recently died and left Loel a vast fortune, and houses all over the world," David explained later. "Loel had no idea these existed until after his father's death. Since he could not live in all of them he lent them to his friends while he decided what to do."

As soon as David and Cecil met Jane, they joined the ranks of her admirers. Cecil—who decided that she looked like Gloria Swanson—declared that she became "more wonderful and alluring and brilliant and surprising" as the summer progressed. The three often met at parties: At a wine-soaked soirée at the Villa Mektoub, Jane narrowly escaped serious injury. Late in the evening, she was dancing with an exhilarated Beaton when he scooped her up and swung her around, missing a block of marble by inches. "He could have killed her," said her friend Oliver Smith.

That summer, Tangier was infused with an energy that was almost palpable. The building boom was still on, and the look of the city seemed to change from day to day. The Coca-Cola Company had invaded the International Zone in 1948, opening a bottling plant and introducing its decadent Western beverage to welcoming Tanjawis, and the walls of every dwelling in the Casbah were adorned with posters depicting a dark-haired siren embracing a Coke bottle. Smugglers and speculators continued to thrive, and ostentation was becoming au courant. A wealthy settler who needed a centerpiece for his new house had a massive staircase shipped from England, and "Nylon Sid" Paley, an American who was Tangier's most notorious contrabandier, drove through the streets in a cream-colored Cadillac. At the Minzah, financiers' wives gathered to watch fashion shows staged by Lucian Lelong and Christian Dior, who sent their mannequins and fifty-thousand-franc frocks by plane from Paris.

To Truman Capote, it was a setting that promised high glamour. In Ischia that spring with his lover Jack Dunphy, a cynical writer who was his most recent conquest, he had met Phyllis della Faille, who was traveling in the company of Jay Haselwood, two Chihuahuas, a pair of dachshunds, an Afghan, a Great Dane and a humble mutt. The ebullient Phyllis had made the International Zone sound like a chichi Shangri-la, and Truman (who knew that Beaton and the Bowleses would be there to entertain him) had decided that he and Jack should investigate North Africa. "He was very excited," Jack said. "Although I don't know what the attraction was—maybe he fell in love with Jay Haselwood."

At twenty-four, Truman was a sensation: published in 1948, his first novel, *Other Voices, Other Rooms*, had created an unprecedented stir among readers as well as critics. With its dazzling style, sure voice and skillful treatment of homosexual themes, it was a small masterpiece that instantly marked Capote as a literary contender, and the jacket photo of an indolent-looking Truman draped across a Victorian sofa had contributed to his gilded-youth mystique. Although many found the book troubling ("a deep, murky well of Freudian symbols," shuddered *Newsweek*), few were able to ignore it or its flamboyant author. Wrote *The New York Times*'s Orville Prescott: "It is impossible not to succumb to the potent magic of his writing. . . . Many a first novel is sounder, better balanced, more reasonable than *Other Voices, Other Rooms*. But few are more artistically exciting, more positive proof of the arrival of a new writer of substantial talent."

The newly minted star had constructed his own mythos with the same skill that he brought to writing fiction. Affecting sweeping capes, he offered up purple tales of his childhood in Monroeville, Alabama, and jousted with his literary rivals. Already he had struck up a feud with Gore Vidal, a contemporary whose novel *Williwaw* had created a lesser tempest in 1946. At a party at Tennessee Williams's apartment in New York, "Gore told Truman he got all his plots out of Carson McCullers and Eudora Welty," Tennessee recalled. "Truman said, 'Well, maybe you get all yours from the *Daily News*.'"

After four months in Ischia—where, Tennessee reported, he "was wrapped around [Jack] like a boa practically every minute except when he was making invisible little pencil scratches in a notebook that was supposed to be his next novel"—Truman held court for a time in Paris. Paul was still there, as was Gore, who heard that Truman was about to join the Bowleses in Tangier. Before Capote arrived on July 2, his self-appointed nemesis slipped into Morocco to surprise him. He invited Jane and Paul to witness the scene on the dock: "As the ferry pulled in, Truman leaned out over the railing, grinning widely and waving a very long silk scarf," Paul remembered. "When he saw Gore standing beside me, he did a little comic-strip routine. His face fell like a soufflé placed in the ice compartment, and he disappeared entirely below the level of the railing for several seconds. When he had assumed a standing position again, he was no longer grinning or waving. . . . Gore stayed around Tangier only long enough to make Truman believe he was going to spend the whole summer, and then he quietly left."

At the Farhar with Jane and Paul, Truman quickly became disillusioned. Like Tennessee, he found the pension to be a trial; the tin roof of his cottage magnified the killing summer sun, and his neighbors were a rowdy contingent of hard-drinking British soldiers on leave from Gibraltar. In Jack's estimation, the place was "a dump, depressing beyond words. . . . We dined together with the Bowleses from a table covered with a cracked oilcloth nearly every night and sometimes had drinks in the bar, a small, damp place presided over by a grouchy man with a granite-grey face. When he played his little radio, it sounded exactly like an iron poor box as you drop a penny into it." In a letter to the writer John Malcolm Brinnin, Truman reported, "Janie and Paul Bowles live in this hotel, which means we have company, even too much of it. . . . Cecil Beaton is here . . . wouldn't you know that we two iron-winged butterflies would find ourselves on the same hollyhock? If not for him I'd move on, although I do like these sugar-soft beaches, toward one of which I'm about to repair, to the accompaniment of flutes."

Truman's annoyance was exacerbated by the fact that, aside from Jane, Paul, Phyllis and Cecil (whom he had visited in England), few Tangerinos had heard of him. In America, strangers plied him with impassioned letters; in Europe, he had been toasted by Colette, Dior, Jean Cocteau, Albert Camus, Noël Coward, Somerset Maugham and Natalie Barney. Alice B. Toklas had described him as "the new young Parisian hero." In North Africa, however, "No one knew who he was at all, and that depressed him," Paul said. When he ventured into town for supplies—books from the American library, white chocolate and tins of butter and candies—the strongest response he evoked was simple curiosity; slight, blond and waifish, he looked like a coquettish adolescent on the prowl.

Even in the absence of a proper welcome, however, Truman managed to find amusement. With a reluctant Jack, he entered the social fray with Jane and David and Cecil. In honor of Jack's thirty-fifth birthday, Cecil gave a midnight fête at the seaside Caves of

Hercules, where guests partook of champagne, hashish and toasted marshmallows in a lantern-lined grotto bedecked with flowers. On the beach, an Andalusian orchestra played for revelers who swam in the moonlight or reclined on cushions around a bonfire. Truman, who declared himself to be afraid of scorpions, refused to scramble down the boulders that lead to the beach; instead, he had himself carried down the cliffside by a cadre of Moroccans.

Phyllis herself gave an ambitious soirée that made a distinct impression on Capote. For a costume gala that he attended with the Bowleses, she had the ballroom of her art-filled villa stripped of everything save the Aubussons on the walls and ordered the floors covered in straw for the snake charmers and acrobats she had invited. Despite her efforts, however, the evening proved "a fiasco," in David's words. "Everything went wrong," he reported:

> The refrigerator had broken down and the ice Phyllis had ordered did not arrive. She forgot to send for the food, which had been prepared by a shop in town; by the time she remembered, the shop was closed. The taxi bringing the Moorish musicians and dancers broke down on the way from Tetuan. By this time both the de Lafailles were drunk. The food eventually arrived, and so did the orchestra, but it was too late to save the party. . . . The atmosphere was electric and fights had broken out in every corner. Two guests were severely bitten by the dogs chained under the tables and a young man had the top of a finger removed by an infuriated macaw. . . .

The unfortunate partygoers were an ill-assorted lot. "Many of them had not spoken to each other for years," David remembered.

> A flirtatious Spanish woman noticed a handsome dusky young man in an exquisite uniform; she thought he was a potentate from a Black African state and made flagrant advances to him—to which he naturally responded—only to discover later that he was one of the servants dressed up in the ambassadorial full-dress uniform which had belonged to Charles's Belgian diplomat father. The Spanish woman was

furious at having been made to look foolish and screamed abuse at the young man. She summoned her husband for support, and he threw a glass of champagne at the servant, who ducked. The glass struck a harmless English visitor, Mrs. Malcom, who received a gash in the face and never came to Tangier again. Pandemonium broke loose, sides were taken, someone called the Spanish woman a whore and her husband a crook; the husband retorted that all the men present were pederasts. "What about your own son?" someone shouted. "He's not only a pederast but a cissie [sic] as well!"

For their part, the Moroccan performers ignored the unbalanced Nazarenes. They simply "built a fire in the middle of the room and made themselves completely at home," as Paul remembered it.

Such antics undoubtedly reinforced Truman's notion that Tangier harbored a fine collection of misfits. He described it to Brinnin as "a curious place. . . . There's every kind of activity, most of it raffish, to say the very least, and all manner of humankind—outre, or decadent, elegant or abandoned to hashish or sex, or both of these at once. A little on the scary side, too, and you have to get accustomed to noises the likes of which you've never heard, faces of a character you've never seen, or imagined—and hashish fumes and the smell of the arabe."

To Capote—who even then was a master of observation—Tangier was a collection of bizarre characters, a series of occult tableaux. He sat for hours in the crowded cafés of the Petit Socco—"a display ground for prostitutes, a depot for drug-peddlers, a spy center [and] the place where some simpler folk drink their evening aperitif," in his words. Collecting gossip with the alacrity of a small-town social columnist, he immersed himself in the "swarming drama" around him. In a travel piece written the next year, he polished the stories to a high gloss and embellished them with his own baroque notions:

"The Soko [sic] has its own celebrities, but it is a precarious honor, one is so likely at any second to be cast away, for the Soko audience, having seen just about everything, is excessively fickle," he wrote. The reigning luminaries, as Truman told it, included the flamenco dancer Maumi: "An exotic young man given to cooling his face with a lacy fan," he recently had been stabbed in a bar. His rival was Estelle, "a beautiful girl who walks like a rope unwinding. She is half-Chinese and half-Negro, and she works in a bordello called the Black Cat. Rumor has it that she was once a Paris model, and that she arrived here on a private yacht, planning, of course, to leave by the same means; but it appears that the gentleman to whom the yacht belonged sailed away one fine morning, leaving Estelle stranded. . . ."

Truman claimed that his own favorites were a wealthy woman whom he called Lady Warbanks and the two sycophants who attended her:

Each morning [they] have their breakfast at one of the sidewalk tables: this breakfast is unvarying—a bowl of fried octopus and a bottle of Pernod. Someone who ought really to know says that at one time the now very declasse Lady Warbanks was considered the greatest beauty in London. . . . But her morals are not all they might be, and the same may be said of her companions. About these two: one is a sassy-faced, busy youth whose tongue is like a ladle stirring in a cauldron of scandal—he knows everything; and the other friend is a tough Spanish girl with brief, slippery hair and leather-colored eyes. She is called Sunny, and I am told that financed by Lady Warbanks, she is on her way to becoming the only female in Morocco with an organized gang of smugglers. . . . The precise relation of these three to each other is not altogether printable, suffice to say that between them they combine every known vice. But this does not interest the Soko, for the Soko is concerned by quite another angle: How soon will Lady Warbanks be murdered, and which of the two will do it . . . ?

On the tea-party circuit with David and Cecil, Truman encountered monuments like Jessie Green and her cousin Feridah. Feridah, whose father had become minister to Morocco in the 1880s, had known Tangier in a simpler era—when gentlefolk rode donkeys to dinner parties and packed their children off to public schools. "She has not visited her native England in over fifty years," Truman reported. "Even so, observing the straw skimmer skewered to her hair and the black ribbon trailing from her pince-nez, one knows she goes out in the noonday sun and has never given up tea at five." Although she was past seventy and nearly lame, Feridah possessed a boundless store of energy: "She was the sort who always dashed out in the rain to see how the horses were doing," said Ian Selley, who lived down the lane. The spinster devoted much of her time to helping her Tanjawi neighbors; she ran the Infant Welfare Center, and on Friday mornings she sat in the rambling garden of her house on the Mountain and distributed rations of flour to the poor.

"A hundred or so of these old crones would arrive and Feridah would preside . . . on a high wooden chair at the end of the barn," David remembered. "Feridah knew them all and they loved her; she was completely at home in their language and chatted with each one in turn as they came up to receive their sack of flour. One permanent joke that never failed to amuse [concerned] an old woman who had two hands on one arm, the normal one and an extra one which was slightly smaller, growing at right-angles, just above the wrist. 'Well, Zahara, which hand shall I shake today?' And amid much laughter from the crowd she would reply, 'It's this one's turn. . . .' "

Truman also was taken with Feridah's sister-in-law, the elegant Ada Green. Ada had little in common with her late husband's dowdy sister; a gaunt, heavily rouged beauty, she wore bold jewels and bright turbans and chain-smoked Russian cigarettes through an ivory holder. After long years in sub-Saharan Africa—where her husband had served as a British high commissioner—she had migrated to Tangier, where she lived in a low, verandahed house fashioned after their residence in Nyasaland (which Truman pronounced "Nysieland"). The widow Green received visitors from a chaise-longue in her drawing room, with Coco, her green parrot, perched on her shoulder and Omar, her peacock, lying beside her like a shimmering quilt. Stationed nearby was her ancient African manservant, Putti—a dark-skinned, diminutive figure who wore heavy gold earrings, a white turban and a flowing white linen gown with a dagger at the belt. Equipped with a leather switch, he flicked away flying insects who ventured too close to Madame.

Ada had impressed herself upon Truman at Phyllis della Faille's costume party. As the gathering descended into a sodden brawl, she had moved about the room, coolly inspecting each character through her lorgnette. When she reached Truman, she inquired, "And what are you supposed to represent?"

"The spirit of spring," she was told.

"Well, you don't look it," she snapped. Turning to a snake charmer who was attempting to distract a group of guests, she amazed the assemblage by appropriating the serpent and charming it herself. "You never told me you could do that!" exclaimed Jessie Green.

"You never asked me," Ada retorted.

Truman also came to share David and Cecil's fascination with Jane. To him, she was "a genius imp, a laughing, hilarious, tortured elf." He admired her writing and her potency and her "poignant abilities as a mimic," and he saw a hint of madness in her eyes. "She seemed the eternal urchin, appealing as the most appealing of non-adults, yet . . . some substance cooler than blood invade[d] her veins," he wrote later.

In turn, Jane found him an excellent companion. His wit and energy matched her own, and she recognized him as a fellow truant. "Everything has changed since Truman Capote arrived," she wrote to a friend. "[Before,] all we needed was 'Cecil' on the opposite hill for Africa to pick up its skirts and run. . . ." Each night at dinner, she regaled Truman and Jack and Paul with absurd little stories about her pursuit of Cherifa. After his afternoon swims, she took Capote to Madame Porte's or to Paul's house in the Casbah, where one could climb to the vast third-floor terrace and peer across at Sidi Hosni. Delighted with the Bowleses' retreat, Truman reported that its tiny rooms were "a charming series of postcard-sized Vuillards" with "Moorish cushions spilling over Moorish-patterned carpets . . . [all] illuminated by intricate lanterns and windows that allow the light of sea skies and views that encompass minarets and ships and the blue-washed rooftops. . . ."

Paul's response to Capote was more deliberate than Jane's. He and Truman had little in common, and he sensed that Truman was wary of him. "He was terribly superficial and amusing and not the sort of person you'd pick to be a good friend," said Paul, who perfected an imitation of Capote's nasal drawl. "I don't think he particularly liked me. I don't know what was the matter with him—he kept saying, 'You just finished your novel. I want to read it.' I said, 'I didn't write it for you, Truman—I know you won't like it.' He said, 'You don't know anything of the sort.' " Paul laughed. "I said, 'I don't think you will,' but he insisted.

"So one day I handed it to him; the very next day he came around to my cabin at the Farhar and said, 'Well, here's your novel.' I said, 'Oh, thank you, you mean you read it all?' He said, 'Oh, yes.' And then he looked at me and said, 'There should have been a lot more of you in there.' What does that mean? I don't think he read it. You could never believe what he said, Truman—he was an accomplished liar."

Still, he came to see that Capote's frivolity camouflaged an astonishing resolve. "One day Truman outlined for us his literary plans for the next two decades. It was all in such detail that naturally I discounted it as a fantasy," Paul remembered. "It seemed impossible that anyone could 'know' so far ahead just what he was going to write. However, the works he described in 1949 appeared, one after the other. . . . They were all there in his head, like baby crocodiles, waiting to be hatched."

Despite the heat and the British soldiers, Truman wrote steadily while he was at the Farhar. Each morning was spent working on *Summer Crossing,* the novel he had abandoned in order to write *Other Voices.* The story of a young woman caught up in Manhattan society, it was set in a milieu that began to seem more appealing the longer Truman stayed in Morocco. By late August, he was bored with the boozing and the gossip and the infighting that he encountered. It all seemed suffocatingly provincial, and it left him with an enduring disdain for the "squalid caravan" of hard-core expatriates who shuffled from Taormina to Paris to Tangier. "Among the planet's most pathetic tribes, sadder than a huddle of homeless Eskimos starving through a winter night seven months long, are those Americans who elect . . . to make a career of expatriation," declared the disaffected P. B. Jones, his narrator in "Unspoiled Monsters." "If you're young enough, it's okay for a couple of years—but those who pursue it after age twenty-five, thirty at the limit, learn that what seemed paradise is mere scenery, a curtain that, lifting, reveals pitchforks and fire."

By Jack's account, it was another evening of forced hilarity that prompted their escape to France. Dressed as Topsy and Eva, the boyish Capote and his strapping lover managed to offend *tout* Tangier at a fancy-dress ball: "When we arrived at the party, more than backs turned against us," Jack reported. "Our costumes were simple but perhaps rough. Instead we were given drapes to wear, and the festivities soon came to an end for us."

Retreating to the cold little bar at the Farhar, they found themselves in the company of a lone middle-aged woman who was brooding over a glass of stout. As Truman and Jack shared a ham sandwich lifted from the buffet at the party, she burst into "Galway Bay"—singing the ballad "from beginning to end, looking out of the open door of the bar . . . as if she could see everything she sang about, while beating time with her open-toed, black patent leather shoes on the stone floor," remembered Jack. "Afterwards, except for the sucking sound she made draining her glass of stout, the silence was exceptional."

Clearly, it was time to move on. Traveling with the London-bound Cecil and two African parrots, Dunphy and Capote sailed to France in late September. The pall that had settled on them in Morocco disappeared the moment they landed: "In Aix-en-Provence, we drank new wine from stands on the street. It was good to be back," Jack reported.

Truman never returned to Tangier, but he acknowledged its hypnotic effect. When he wrote about the International Zone in "Local Color," he advised: "Before coming here you should do three things: be inoculated for typhoid, withdraw your savings from the bank, say goodbye to your friends—heaven knows you may never see them again. . . . Because Tangier is a basin that holds you."

Alone in the rambling Guinness villa, David Herbert invited Paul and Jane—who were waiting for workmen to complete the renovation of the Casbah house—to join him. "He said, 'I'd hate to live in this big house all by myself—we could have all the privacy we needed and share the food and servants and so on.' And then he said, 'You could pay two-thirds and I could pay one-third,' " Paul remembered. Although the frugal Paul was unhappy with the financial arrangement, the Bowleses soon installed themselves in the Villa Mektoub. Within days, Jane contracted measles, and her illness claimed the attention of the entire household. Confined to a dark room to protect her weakened eyes, she became bored and querulous. "She said, 'Oh, David, I have to have Cherifa here to help me,' " said Paul. "He said, 'But, darling, there's no place for her to sleep.' Janie said, 'Oh, yes, she'll sleep under my bed.' And David said, 'Oh, we can't have that—Oh, no.' "

In the end, however, Herbert was unable to refuse her, and he dispatched a servant to find Cherifa in the grain market. Told that her admirer would give her a radio if she came to the Villa Mektoub, Cherifa upped the ante, declaring that she would come only if she received a Mercedes and a chauffeur's uniform. Jane held firm; Cherifa settled for the radio.

During the summer, Jane had continued her visits to Cherifa's *hanootz,* but much of her attention had been claimed by David and Cecil and Truman. Herbert had become her most effusive admirer; he led the laughter when she regaled dinner guests with her rapid-fire monologues, and he cherished her every bon mot. "Before you have had time to laugh at some glorious sally she has turned the joke into something so infinitely sad you are almost in tears," he wrote later.

Together, Jane and David traded wicked gossip and commiserated about their love affairs. As David saw it, her crushes on women were mere feints; he insisted that only because Paul had become involved with Ahmed Yacoubi (whom he saw during frequent trips to Fez) did Jane take up with Cherifa. "She was never *really* a lesbian," David declared. "Janie loved Paul more than anything in the world and Paul loved Janie. Physically they had very different lives, but Janie wasn't jealous because she knew Paul loved her best." Like their other friends, David saw that the Bowleses had constructed a cosmos that was closed to outsiders: At times, their entire relationship seemed to be based on a private joke. Together, they spun elaborate fantasies, invented songs and enacted arch little dramas. At parties, they held hands and whispered to one another like teenagers. When the three were at the Villa Mektoub, David could hear them "talking and laughing in the next room as though they had just met and were being at their most scintillating in order to charm each other."

Although David admired Paul—whom he saw as a finely modeled creature with "the beauty of a fallow deer"—the two would never be close. Always uncomfortable in the presence of intellectuals, David found it impossible to tell what Paul was thinking. With Cecil and Truman, Herbert could chatter about Princess Margaret's wardrobe and the indiscretions of Tangier's parvenus. But while Paul had a writer's appreciation of gossip, he abhorred frank discussions about homosexuality, and one could never enlist him in the sort of bitchy gabfests that David loved. Paul dealt in subtle ironies, deadpan humor and double messages, and his remarks had an elusive subtext that David often missed.

It was Jane who was the cornerstone of the triad—the one who inspired a cool devotion from her enigmatic husband and a fierce loyalty from David. After he had known the Bowleses for years, Herbert offered to marry her if anything happened to Paul. Jane was simultaneously amused and horrified: "She told me, 'Don't die, Bupple,' " said Paul.

That summer, David discovered that Paul was at least as fastidious as the ailing Jane, who kept Cherifa busy cooking special dishes and fetching tea. His digestion was a source of much anxiety; a fussy eater who favored hamburgers and chicken, he avoided unfamiliar food and shuddered over unhygienic peasant fare like the soft cheese that he called "typhoid pie." Obsessed with being correct, he kept track of the most improbable domestic minutiae. When David came down with a headache, he went to Jane for aspirin and she sent him to Paul's medicine cabinet, where he found a large bottle. As David told it, Paul asked Jane the next day whether she had taken any aspirin tablets. Informed that David was the culprit, he said, "Oh, that's all right. I just wondered because the last time I took one there were seventy-three left in the bottle and now there are only seventy-one."

When Jane was well enough to travel, the three decided to drive through France to England. Published in September by John Lehmann, *The Sheltering Sky* was causing a stir among British critics, and Lehmann had invited Paul to claim his laurels in London. Unwilling to spend a damp winter in Tangier, Paul decided to go on to Thailand or Ceylon after the London sojourn. Jane made plans to spend the winter in Paris, where she would rendezvous with the long-neglected Cory.

Before they left Morocco, the Bowleses made a brief trip to Fez, where they saw Ahmed Yacoubi. Impressed with the Klee-like drawings he had brought to their hotel on earlier visits, Jane bought him art supplies and encouraged him to continue his experiments. Both she and Paul were pleased with the results: "He still did not know that there were such people as artists; nor had he ever seen a painting," Paul remembered. "Yet he had made enormous stylistic progress [since the last visit], merely working by himself in his father's house in the Medina."

In November, Paul and Jane and David took the *Koutoubia* across the Mediterranean to Marseilles. Traveling in David's Jaguar, they embarked on a gastronomic tour through the Rhône valley— stopping at every three-star restaurant they could find. David and Jane took pleasure in each decadent mouthful, but Paul found the cuisine "hellishly rich." "It just about killed me," he said. "By the time we got to Lyon I couldn't get out of bed." While Paul was nursing his overburdened liver, David and Jane made pilgrimages to one culinary shrine after another. After each meal, the two convened in Paul's hotel room, and the patient recoiled as they relived each spectacular course. "The lingering descriptions and discussion of the food's texture constituted a kind of torture," he remembered.

Paul rallied when they reached London. With *The Sheltering Sky* on the best-seller lists, Lehmann took pains to introduce him to any literary dignitary whom he cared to meet, and "parties were given for him every second," Jane reported. Although her own writing was going badly again and her anxiety was mounting, she said she was pleased for Paul. "I know it did him a great moral good to be at last a *lion* which he has deserved for many years and had somehow never gotten in music," she told Libby Holman. "He is now a famous literary figure in England (well-known anyway) and probably will soon be in New York if he isn't already."

The *Times Literary Supplement* had offered only admiration for Bowles's novel: "As an exercise in futility, in the remorseless exposure of the despair and indifference which place people at the mercy of fate, unsure of their wishes or wants, their loves or their hates,

The Sheltering Sky is an exciting and remarkable book," said its reviewer. In America, where the book had been published in October, reviewers were responding to it as a daring, if imperfect, work. Noting its skillful evocation of "emotional nausea, intellectual despair and desert primitivism," *Time's* critic pegged the book as "a remarkable job of writing . . . the most interesting first novel to come from a U.S. writer this year." Like others, he observed that Paul was less adept at breathing life into characters than in creating a sense of place; Port and Kit, he complained, were "neurotic intellectual playchildren" who seemed like the "novelist's puppets." But if any of Paul's influential friends agreed that the book was flawed, none complained publicly. Writing in *The New York Times Book Review,* the supportive Tennessee offered only admiration; he hailed *The Sheltering Sky* as a novel that "[brought] the reader into sudden, startling communion with a talent of true maturity and sophistication." On one level, he asserted, the book was a "first-rate story of adventure"; on another, it was "a mirror of what is most terrifying and cryptic within the Sahara of moral nihilism, into which . . . man now seems to be wandering blindly."

On the American best-seller lists by January, 1950, *The Sheltering Sky* soon took its place as a cult novel—one that, in its moral anarchy, presaged the work of William Burroughs and the prodigal Beats. Years later, Norman Mailer wrote, "Paul Bowles opened the world of Hip. He let in the murder, the drugs, the incest, the death of the Square . . . the call of the orgy, the end of civilization." And if critics sometimes took Paul to task for his brutality, no one denied the power of his dark vision: With his pitiless fatalism, he had created a world where hope was moribund and life was lived in extremis.

In Morocco, Paul had found a wellspring for his fiction, and he drew from that source even when he was away. Sailing from Antwerp for Ceylon in December 1949, he felt torn when the Polish freighter entered the Straits of Gibraltar and passed the Caves of Hercules. "We entered the Strait . . . at night, and I stood on deck watching the flashes of the lighthouse at Cape Spartel, the northwestern corner of Africa," he remembered. "As we sailed eastward I could distinguish the lights of certain houses on the Old Mountain. Then when we came nearer to Tangier, a thin fog settled over the water, and only the glow of the city's lights was visible, reflected in the sky. That was when I felt an unreasoning and powerful desire to be in Tangier." Retreating to his hard bunk belowdecks, Paul "started right in writing, bang. . . . I decided to write about the very part of the land that I was going by at that second—the nearest part—and it was the beach, the grotto, the cave." By the time the ship landed in Colombo, he had completed the first chapter of *Let It Come Down*—a novel that, like *The Sheltering Sky,* documented the psychic destruction of an unwary pilgrim who sought new life in North Africa.

Chapter 7

In the spring of 1950, Brion Gysin was casting about for a new incarnation. A man who liked to call himself a "moving target," the British-born artist was a wildly energetic soul who had gone through phases as a surrealist painter in Paris, a *hashishin* in Greece, a welder in a New Jersey shipyard, a Canadian Army recruit and, by one account, a CIA operative trained to spy on the Japanese. With Brion, one was never sure; his stories were as mutable as they were engrossing, and after a while one stopped caring about the truth.

At thirty-four, Brion was ruled by a voracious curiosity as well as a dauntless creative spirit. The son of a Scottish-Irish teacher and a prosperous Swiss who migrated to Edmonton, Alberta, he had studied for two years at rigid Downside College in England and, in 1934, escaped to the Sorbonne. His practical education had taken place in the studios and salons and cafés of prewar Paris: Through Sylvia Beach, he had met Max Ernst, Valentine Hugo, Salvador Dali and Pablo Picasso, and he had made the obligatory pilgrimage to see Gertrude Stein and Alice B. Toklas. The flamboyant young artist was asked to be a part of a 1935 surrealist exhibition that included

Arp, Duchamp, Magritte, Miró, Man Ray and others, but his relationship with the group was short-lived: André Breton (who, Brion claimed, was annoyed by his irreverence and his unabashed homosexuality) ordered his work removed from the Galerie Aux Quatre Chemins on the eve of the opening. Brion retrieved his pictures and showed them on the sidewalk instead.

Gysin had always styled himself as the brilliant nonconformist who was ill treated by those in power: Paranoid, defensive, he was often churlish to the patrons who took an interest in his work. But he could also be madly charming, and he was surrounded by friends and lovers who were willing to overlook his spoiled-child side. Intoxicated by his spirit and intelligence and grace, they clustered around him like bees sipping nectar from a particularly exotic flower. "He had enormous charisma," said his friend Felicity Mason, an elegant British bohemian who called Brion her adopted brother. "He was a great catalyst; he brought people together. And he received them very graciously. Even when he had only a cup of tea to share, it was like going to tea with the king."

William Burroughs, who became his great friend and collaborator, described Brion's bearing as being "regal without a trace of pretension." He was, said Burroughs, "the only man I ever respected. I have admired many others, esteemed and valued others, but respected only him."

Brion's intellectual passions were limitless, and his monologues mesmerizing. (At least to his disciples; cooler heads pegged him as a tedious mythomaniac.) He drew inspiration from the literature of the ancient Greeks and Romans, from the Egyptian Book of the Dead, from Celtic folklore and esoteric Eastern religions, as well as from modern sources like the surrealists. Mystics all, the females in his mother's family had passed along a strong belief in things unseen. Clairvoyance, spirit guides, spells, even "little people"—all of it was incorporated into his manic discussions. New York Times music critic Robert Palmer, who became a close friend, remembered Brion's conversation as "some of the cleverest, most mordant and most provocative . . . one could hope to enjoy. The talk would go on for hours, finding fault with the Freudian assumptions of Surrealism one moment, speculating on the mechanisms of dervish trance drumming the next. . . ."

Spilling over with radical notions about painting and literature, Gysin was a galvanic force for other artists. But his intellectual intemperance was his weakness as well as his strength; lacking the discipline (or perhaps the will) to harness his creative powers, he had never found popular success. He seemed destined to chase motes—and to lead others in the same direction. It was Brion, for example, who would introduce fellow exile Burroughs to the cutup—a literary mosaic created by tricks including quartering a page of prose and reassembling it randomly. Paul, among others, would find their brave new writings unreadable. "Anyone who came under Brion's influence," he said, "fell ten years behind in his career."

Along with a flood of other expatriates, Brion Gysin was adrift in Paris in the winter of 1950. Since leaving the army, he had spent much of his time delving into the subject of slavery. (Black culture had a strong appeal for him; convinced he was a changeling who had been "slipped into the wrong-colored package and delivered to the wrong address," he hated his pale, freckled skin and blond hair, and he often chose dark-skinned men as lovers.) After writing a biography of Josiah Henson, the slave preacher who was the prototype for Harriet Beecher Stowe's Uncle Tom, he had completed a book-length study called *The History of Slavery in Canada,* which he had published with the help of a wealthy admirer. Given a Fulbright fellowship to continue his research, he had spent 1949 traveling in France and Spain, where he sifted through arcana at the University of Bordeaux and the Archivos de India in Seville. But that phase was ending, and his next move was uncertain. Fear was settling in; with typical overstatement he announced to one acquaintance that he had "never been so desperate in [his] life."

It was Paul Bowles who drew Brion to Tangier. In the spring, after his trip to Ceylon, Paul joined Jane at the Hôtel de l'Université, where she and Cory had spent the winter. The Bowleses had known Brion since the late thirties, when the splendidly dissolute Denham Fouts had introduced them in Paris. When they ran into Gysin again, Paul suggested that he try Tangier for the summer. Brion liked the sound of the place; he had been to the Algerian Sahara in 1938, and he was drawn to the vast silent spaces of North Africa. Morocco—with its *majoun* and its mysticism and its slim-hipped, dark-eyed boys—promised to be "a wild west of the spirit," and he could think of nothing that would please him more.

As summer began, Brion joined Paul in Tangier. With Jane still in Paris, he invited Gysin to stay with him in the medina. Since the Bowleses had left in November, their narrow, multistoried house had been renovated to accommodate its occupants' separate lives: Brion took the quarters on the second floor, and Paul lived on the fourth, in a tower that afforded a view of the bay. Dual entrances allowed the two to come and go without disturbing each other. "As a cook," Paul remembered, "we got the butler who had worked for David Herbert the year before. He had been employed by Barbara Hutton earlier and still went to her house occasionally; it was just around the corner. Sometimes as we were finishing lunch, he would come and stand in the doorway to the patio, holding a towel in his hand and tell[ing] us unlikely stories about her."

Although he was working steadily—both on *Let It Come Down* and on the music for *Yerma*—Paul also made a point of introducing Brion to Moroccan exotica. In Sidi Kacem, the two went to a *moussem*. Held at the tombs of local saints, the celebrations offered an exhilarating view of native life: Pitched outside the town would be a tent city that looked like a medieval battlefield. Acrobats and snake charmers and storytellers competed for the attention of the pilgrims, and the air was perfumed with the scents of *tagines* and roasted lamb. As day turned into evening, *fantasias* would be staged on the open ground near the saint's tomb: Teams of riders in robes and turbans would line up their splendidly outfitted mounts at one end of the field and, at a signal, urge them into a thundering gallop. At the end of the course, the horsemen would fire their long rifles into the air at the same instant and rein in their mounts as one.

For Brion, music was the most riveting element of the *moussem*. After dark would begin the mellifluous chorus of wind instruments and the seductive rattle of tambourines. Dressed in long white tunics and crimson fezzes encrusted with cowrie shells, ebony-skinned musicians who belonged to the Gnaoua—a brotherhood of adepts said to have the power to exorcise evil spirits—would dance and play themselves into a hypnotic state. Djeballaed musicians from Beni Aros would offer sinuous *rhaita* music, and querulous vocal solos would rise above the tent city like wood smoke.

Amid the exotic cacophony, Brion found a troupe of Moroccans who created music unlike anything he had ever heard. Wearing rough woolen robes and pointed leather slippers that gave them a gnomish aspect, the Master Musicians, as they were called, played wild flute songs—"strangely riveting music, related to the ecstatic trance music of the Sufi brotherhoods but different, [with] a luminous, hieratic quality all its own," as Palmer later described it. Brion became obsessed: "I said, 'Ah! That's my music . . . I just want to hear that music for the rest of my life,' " he told the British writer Terry Wilson.

With the help of a Moroccan lover, Brion eventually traced the troupe to Jajouka, a remote village in the Jibala hills, about sixty miles south of Tangier. When he finally set eyes on the outpost, he felt a shock of joy; set above a lush valley, Jajouka was a place that could have been lifted straight from antiquity. Electricity was unknown; at nightfall, Brion wrote, one could see the "blue kif smoke drop[ping] in veils" around the village. Its occupants were members of the Ahl Serif tribe—Berbers whose ancestors had inhabited the Rif for centuries. Male and female villagers were lodged in separate quarters, and their lives were so discrete that "even women's language isn't immediately understood by men," he reported. Women spent their days close to the village, and men roamed the hills grazing their flocks. Once a year, they joined together to enact an atavistic epic that Brion believed to be the equivalent of Roman Lupercalia, or the Rites of Pan, "hidd[en] under the ragged cloak of Islam." As Brion discovered, the rites of Jajouka were intended to preserve the balance between the male and female forces in nature, just as the Roman rite had been.

Later, Brion explained the connection in a talk with Terry Wilson: "The Lupercalia," he said,

> was a race run from one part of Rome, a cave under the Capitoline Hill . . . and the point was to go out to the gates of Rome and contact Pan, the God of the Forests, the little Goat God, who was Sexuality itself, and to run back through the streets with the news that Pan was still out there fucking as [the runner] flailed the women in the crowds.

Brion believed that Bou Jeloud, Jajouka's patron saint, served as Pan's stand-in in the drama: "Inside the village," he reported,

the thatched houses crouch low in their gardens to hide in the deep cactus-lined lanes. You come through their maze in the broad village green where the pipers are piping; fifty raitas banked against a crumbling wall blow sheet lightning to shatter the sky. Fifty wild flutes blow up a storm in front of them, while a platoon of small boys in long belted white robes and brown wool turbans drum like young thunder. All the villagers, dressed in best white, swirl in great circles and coils around one wildman in skins. Bou Jeloud leaps high in the air on the music, races after the women again and again, lashing at them fiercely with his flails. Scattering like white marabout birds all aflutter, the women throw back their heads to the moon and scream with throats open to the gullet, lolling their tongues around in their heads like the clapper of a bell.

Witnessing the rite in the Jibala hills changed Brion's life forever. Later, he would remember it as a kind of seduction—one that seemed at once heady and perilous. "You know your music when you hear it, one day. You fall into line and dance," he wrote, "until you pay the piper."

In the summer of 1950, Paul Bowles rendezvoused in southern Spain with Libby Holman, who was still obsessed with the idea of staging *Yerma*. It had been two years since Paul had agreed to the collaboration, and the task of composing the score had been neglected in favor of writing fiction. Still, he had finished several songs, and the two decided to work on them while they steeped themselves in Andalusian music. With Paul wedged into the back seat of a black MG driven by Luke Readdy, the Rhodes scholar who was Libby's most recent conquest, they meandered through Seville, Córdoba, Granada, Ronda, and finally Algeciras, where they boarded the ferry to Tangier.

After his visitors were gone, Paul wrote a letter to Charles Henri Ford, complaining that the International Zone had been further despoiled by arrivistes. Still, he was amused by the absurdity of it all: "Libby Holman has left and I am alone with Brion Gysin here in the lighthouse," he reported.

Didn't you and Djuna [Barnes] have the Wiley house one spring? (1933?) A California couple now live in it; she says "Aloha" instead of "good-bye." She also has a $10,000 car which she designed. Everything is changed; the place is very European. Barbara Hutton arrived this week, but she is staying indoors because she is ill. The town is full of American marines who sit and drink in a chichiteux bar decorated with fake zebra-skins, to look like the La El Morocco. They all get rolled by the same two or three Arab bathing-boys, who are making a fortune this season. Everyone is high on hashish ALL THE TIME, including . . . two little . . . princesses, who carry it around with them in silver boxes. . . . You can see what our old town has become. It looks like pictures of Tel Aviv.

Paul's own favorite specimens included a British expatriate known as the Vampire of Tangier: In his sitting room the man kept a large refrigerator filled with glasses of fresh blood sold to him by boys in the medina. Each glass was labeled with the donor's name, and at teatime guests were offered the blood as a tonic.

Sir Cyril Hampson was another Tangerino whom Bowles found amusing. A tiny Englishman who commuted between Morocco and Zanzibar, he relished towering, dark-skinned maidens and stocked his Mountain retreat with Berber innocents whom he lured to the city with the promise of expensive caftans. Surrounded by a sheep pasture and set off by a hillside garden lush with banana plants, papaws and tropical oddities like the flowering Flamboyant Tree, Hampson's villa was an island of madness on the Mountain.

Invited to dine at Sir Cyril's with a company of other Europeans, Paul found himself in a scene from a British farce: A man whose most distinguishing feature was his blinding hostility, the host welcomed Paul's party with a drunken tirade about lazy-sot Moors who hardly knew the meaning of a day's work. The soliloquy—which went on to encompass the filthy French and incompetent Spanish—continued after his guests were seated on hassocks around *taifors*[1] and Hampson's Zanzibarian butler had served the meal.

At length, the raving stopped long enough for Sir Cyril to introduce his unhappy harem and dash into the next room. Dressed in filmy white gowns that resembled negligees, five astonishingly pretty Moroccan girls were ushered from behind a curtain by a muscular black *maîtresse*. Taking their places behind drums covered in zebra hide, the impassive young performers serenaded Sir Cyril's guests with a loud and lunatic tattoo. When the diminutive host burst back into the room, he was wearing high boots and brandishing a circus whip. Cracking it expertly, he urged the girls into fits of feigned terror that soon accelerated into real hysteria. Shrieking and spitting, his handmaidens turned on one another—pulling hair and ripping bodices as they ducked the flying whip. After their keeper broke up the melee and hustled the weeping girls behind the curtain, Sir Cyril returned to his guests. Holding up a key, he announced that anyone who wanted to see the girls privately could simply excuse himself and adjourn to their quarters.

"Of course everyone was completely frozen," Paul remembered. "When we finally began leaving, everyone said, 'Good night, so delicious, thank you' to Sir Cyril, who was at the door. He was mellifluously polite: To each person, he replied, 'Good night, fuck you,' 'Good night, fuck you.' "

In the summer of 1950, social life in Tangier was no less frenetic than it had been when Jane Bowles had been on hand. Aside from the gregarious sybarites who collected at Dean's and the Parade, the scene was enlivened by the diplomatic corps, for whom parties were ceremonial events. Evenings invariably began with cocktail parties and continued with dinners, balls and receptions that were "ridiculously pompous and grand," in David Herbert's words. Being seen at the right functions—and seated next to dinner partners of the proper rank—was a matter of vital concern. Private parties became social battlefields; when Herbert assigned her to the "wrong" place at his table, one Frenchwoman married to an American diplomat turned her plate upside down and declined to talk to her neighbors. Whenever Hutton entertained, climbers unsheathed their daggers; being omitted from one of her balls was a grave blow,

and counterfeiters whose first calling was turning out *faux* green-
backs made handsome profits by selling bogus invitations to Sidi
Hosni.

Tangerines kept late hours, and the mink-coat crowd often
ended the evening at a sleek boîte de nuit or in a boisterous dive.
"We loved to go slumming after dinner parties," said Ruth Hopwood, who accompanied Hutton on her nocturnal rounds. "You
could walk around the Casbah in the moonlight wearing your evening clothes and your jewels and be completely undisturbed." Hopwood and her friends often wandered into spots like the French
brothel whose floor show featured a series of *tableaux amoureux:*
"They showed a woman and a woman, a man with a man, a woman
with a donkey. My husband Binx once asked the madam, 'Why
don't you show a man with a woman?' She drew herself up and said,
'Monsieur, this is a respectable house!' " The indefatigable David
explored all of Tangier's night haunts, and the friends who came to
see him in exile were taken to all his favorites—including "the
smart, expensive Emsallah Gardens, where you danced in the open
air to the smell of orange blossom from the surrounding trees; hot
dark bars where a piano tinkled drearily away till dawn [and] cabarets of every description; some showing belly-dancers . . . some
female impersonators," in David's recollection. Other expatriates
were partial to Freddy's Embassy Club or the Lido Kursaal, with its
South American orchestra and Spanish dancers; or to the Alhambra,
which imported Parisian acts like the Mayol Pin-up Girls, featuring
"the exciting colored dancer Jane d'Ivoire."

"Tangier was so glamorous; it was like a little Paris," remembered Kathy Jelen, who came to Tangier as the wife of the American
naval attaché. Raised among artists and writers in Hungary, where
her father was a novelist, she was just twenty-one when her husband was transferred from Casablanca to the International Zone.
She was thrilled with her new home: "Not only was it very beautiful, but it was full of activity, and everyone I met seemed like a
super-human to me," she said.

Among the expatriates who left an indelible impression on
Kathy were Phyllis and Charles della Faille. That year, the Countess
invited her on a car trip across North Africa to Egypt. To the venturesome Kathy—who was longing for an escape after months at

home with her first baby—the plan sounded irresistible.

On the appointed day, Phyllis and Charles called for her in a huge station wagon that contained four chihuahuas and a big Afghan greyhound—favorites from their unhappy private zoo. The dogs were just the beginning; Phyllis considered herself to be on a mission, and her object was to collect as many animals as she could crowd into the car. "No sooner had we reached Rabat," said Cathy,

than Phyllis exclaimed, "My goodness, I forgot the rat!" During the war, she said, she had got two Egyptian desert rats from some English soldiers as a memento of their battalion. The rats were unhappy in their prison in Tangier, and one of them died. The other one, widow or widower, remained, and she wanted to take it back to Egypt and release it at the foot of the Pyramids. So we stayed in Rabat a couple of days while the rat was packed and sent by plane.

Finally we were underway. We went to Oujda, then Tlemcen, then Algiers. We spent several days in Algiers, because everywhere we went we ordered animals to pick up on the way back, but we needed to get special permission. After Algiers we stopped in Constantine. We arrived at 8 o'clock at night, and every restaurant was closed. We walked all over the town, and finally we said to one of the cashier ladies in a beer hall, "Please, don't you have any bread from yesterday?" She told a waiter to take us to the Black Cat, which was what you think it was. We had a delicious dinner there and a floor show to start with. Phyllis was very merry and had a lot of gin fizzes.

Every day of the journey we had breakfast in our respective rooms and then we gathered to depart. Before we started off, gin fizzes for Phyllis and Charles. Then they'd send them back several times because there wasn't enough gin and too much fizz. Then we started off and there were several gin fizz stops along the road, if possible. When we stopped at a restaurant for a meal, every member of our group was obliged to order spaghetti with meatballs. That was then taken to the car and while the dogs were feasting you could order whatever you liked.

After Tunis the roads were not very good; very often they were covered with sand and the desert was still mined in places so that from time to time you heard the detonation when an animal of the desert or an unfortunate camel stepped on a mine there. One morning we started off on the left foot—whether it was the hardships of the road, I don't know, but Phyllis was very nervous and Charles was also nervous. They started a terrible fight. Charles was driving, Phyllis was sitting next to him and the shouting between them became louder and louder and stronger and stronger.

Suddenly Phyllis was grabbing our passports from the glove compartment and Charles was trying to stop her and the car was moving back and forth. Phyllis became frenetic and she began throwing out things from the picnic basket onto the road—cups and plates and tins. She wanted to throw our passports out also. Charles was screaming at the top of his voice. I meekly tried to calm them down, not that they took any notice of me. Finally Charles stopped the car, opened the door and kicked Phyllis out. Then off we went on this road that was covered with sand sometimes, at about 110 miles an hour, I trembling in the back.

Not until Charles had driven for miles could Kathy persuade him to turn back. "But we didn't know where this dreadful thing had happened," she said. "It's so sandy you don't know where you are. Our landmarks were the thrown-out cups and saucers, but Phyllis was nowhere. So we got more and more frenetic, and finally in a little town where the caravans stop and let their camels relax we found her in a cafe, very self-possessed and cool." Refusing to rejoin the party, Phyllis informed the pair that she had made arrangements to return to Tunis. Only after Kathy pleaded with her did she consent to continue the trip, but she declined to speak to Charles except through Kathy.

When the three finally reached Egypt, Phyllis obtained permission from King Farouk to buy kangaroo rats and a mongoose from the Cairo zoo. "We kept the mongoose and the chihuahuas in the bathroom at the Mena House and we thought they would be the best of friends, but not at all—the mongoose bit all of the chihuahuas and made a terrible row," Kathy remembered. "We thought to release the mongoose in the desert on the way back and it was the worst thing to do—often they're infected with rabies, so we never knew whether he had given it to the chihuahuas. In Cairo we also bought another desert rat; unfortunately I had to open my big mouth and say that if you leave this rat in freedom after how many years in captivity, it will die. Phyllis said 'You're right,' so instead of keeping her alone in a cage we bought her a mate. In a matter of minutes we had babies, and the kangaroo rats had babies also." On the way back to Tangier, Phyllis bought two crows, three desert foxes and a giant lizard, and Kathy herself acquired a hedgehog.

Although one of the desert foxes bit the Countess on the nose, the return trip went well enough until the group stopped for a picnic in the desert. "We tied the Afghan greyhound to the rear bumper of the car, we had lunch, then we packed everything up and started again," Kathy said. "When we passed the next village, all the people were waving; we said, 'What are they waving about?' We had forgotten the dog tied to the bumper, and it was lucky he was a greyhound because he could keep up the pace." Miraculously, the animal was unharmed except for his paws, which were raw and bleeding.

Despite their unconventional cargo (which included Egyptian artworks, as well as the expanding population of animals) the della Failles made it through the Tunisian and Algerian frontiers without incident. "The border guards said, 'Menagerie, menagerie, are you going to perform?' and we said 'Yes, yes' and we sailed through absolutely unscathed," Kathy said. "You can imagine the smell that we had in the car by the time we got back to Tangier."

Through the rain-soaked autumn of 1950, Paul labored on *Let It Come Down*—using the International Zone as the novel's setting and creating characters who echoed the city's mad esprit. His story centered on Nelson Dyar, a blank-slate New York bank teller who flees to Tangier in hopes of shaking his chronic numbness. As soon as he checks into the Hotel de la Playa, he falls in with a flock of predators who could have been lifted straight from the Parade. (Bowles later admitted that with the exception of Dyar, each European had been modeled on a fellow expatriate; he even created a self-parody in the character of the priggish Richard Holland.) Jack Wilcox, a fast-talking American who has made a modest killing in the black market, recruits Dyar as a confederate in his currency deals. Mme Jouvenon, a blue-haired spy, tries to enlist him as a Soviet informant. The calculating Eunice Goode—an overweight, alcoholic lesbian who is "supremely conscious of being a comic character"—becomes Dyar's rival for the affections of Hadija, an artful young prostitute whose English is limited to phrases like "Hello, Jack." Dyar himself is pursued by Daisy de Valverde, a manipulative marquesa who manages to seduce him after plying him with *majoun.* Of Tangier, Daisy says, "It's a madhouse. . . . A complete, utter madhouse. I only hope to God it remains one."

Discovering the truth in Daisy's words, Dyar comes to see the International Zone is a psychotic's dream made manifest. Early on, he pauses to survey a drizzly street-scene outside the American Legation: "A little Moroccan boy, his face ravaged by a virulent skin disease, stood near him, studying him silently. . . . A man wearing a tattered outmoded woman's coat, high-waisted, with peaked shoulders and puffed sleeves, walked up and stopped near the boy, also to stare. In one hand he carried a live hen by its wings; the hen was protesting noisily. . . . The street looked insane with its cheap bazaar architecture, its Coca-Cola signs in Arabic script, its anarchic assortment of people in damp garments struggling up and down." Feeling himself to be "supremely anonymous," Dyar realizes that "he was no one, and he was standing here in the middle of no country. The place was counterfeit, a waiting room between connections, a transition from one way of being to another, which for the moment was neither way, no way."

Destined to be a pawn for Tangier's "moral derelicts," as Paul described them, Dyar becomes enmeshed not only in a sleight-of-hand currency scheme but in a plot devised by Eunice to expose him as a Russian spy. Imagining that the authorities are closing in, he makes a desperate attempt to seize control of his fate—slipping out of the International Zone with nine thousand pounds that belongs to one of Wilcox's clients. But Dyar's ballast is gone; heightened by *kif* and *majoun,* his sense of unreality takes possession of him. In an isolated mountain cottage in the neighboring Spanish Protectorate, he turns on Thami, the Moroccan who has engineered his escape from Tangier. As his companion lies deep in a *majoun* dream, Dyar (who himself is *m'hashish*) inserts a long nail into the man's ear and hammers it into his brain. After the murder, Paul wrote, Dyar still sensed that "he was not real, but he knew he was alive."

As he sent his protagonist hurtling towards psychic destruction, Paul himself kept moving. With Brion Gysin, he made a long visit to Fez, where he saw Ahmed, and another to Marrakech, where the late-fall sun was still strong. When he and Brion returned to Tangier at the end of 1950, Paul left his visitor in the medina house (which again needed repairs) and retreated to the Villa Mimosa. A newly constructed pension with a bracing view of the bay, it was run by a jocular Englishwoman who had been part of Kenya's Happy Valley set. The pension's airy name belied its discomforts; during the winter rains, water cascaded down the walls in Paul's room, flowed into the halls and dripped down the stairs into the entranceway. The only dry spot was his bed, and he spent much of his time stretched out there, writing in his notebooks.

Even in his damp little cocoon, however, it was difficult for Bowles to keep the world at bay. Published in America by Random House, *The Delicate Prey and Other Stories* was drawing heated reactions from some reviewers. "Horrific, unpleasant, sadistic, these stories just avoid the deep end, but are unqualifyingly talented," said *Kirkus Reviews.* The *New York Herald Tribune* critic pronounced Paul to be "preoccupied with violence and death" and added that his characters were "if not mad, severely neurotic, hugging to themselves some quietly terrible frustration, some taint, some malevolent perverseness that finally can no longer be controlled and explodes with twisted fury. . . ." In a letter to his editor, David McDowell, Paul noted that the reviewers were "shocked, scandalized and disapproving. And all wrong. . . ." But as the critics grew more strident, McDowell urged Paul to come to America and take advantage of his succès de scandale. "Whether you know it or not," McDowell wrote, "you are the subject of a great deal of interest here in this country: a musician, a writer, an 'ex-patriate' and a very exotic man who wanders around deep in the sands of the Sahara. All that makes good copy and makes lady columnists' and bored reviewers' tongues hang out."

Aside from the fact that he was little disposed to offer himself up as a curiosity, Paul was convinced that if he did return to New York, the State Department would seize his passport. In 1939, he and Jane had joined the Communist Party—an organization that not only helped the penurious young composer get on the welfare rolls but reinforced his sense of being an outsider. (Later, he admitted that his infatuation was inspired by the organization's "disruptive potential," as he put it; the party, he wrote, "was well organized and could cause a lot of trouble; this seemed sufficient reason to support it.") Like most iconoclasts, Paul and Jane had made sorry comrades, and they had regretted the move almost immediately. Terrified of authority in any form, they had gone into a panic in 1942, when an FBI agent grilled Jane about a telegram that Paul sent her from Mexico. Now, with the specter of Joe McCarthy looming large, Paul's paranoia was in high gear. To McDowell, he wrote, "I have nothing against being [in the States] except the fear of being detained there. And I don't know DOS policy on reformed political criminals. . . ."

The political atmosphere in Morocco was hardly benign, of course, and Paul saw that the horizon was darkening. In an effort to undermine the growing spirit of nationalism, the French colonial government was squaring off against Sultan Mohammed ben Youssef, who had infuriated Paris by making an appeal for Arab unity and showing sympathy for the Istiqlal. Early in 1951, Resident General Alphonse Juin, an imperious hard-liner who had been dispatched from France to subdue the palace, forced the Sultan to replace his "subversive" personal cabinet with a fleet of pro-French ministers and to denounce the methods of the increasingly strident nationalist party. His supporters were outraged by the Sultan's public defeat; members of the Arab League rose up in protest, and anti-French demonstrations erupted in Egypt, Lebanon and Pakistan. Rumors exploded like fireworks: In Cairo, press reports detailed an alleged French plot against the throne, and it was said that the French planned to bombard Fez and make martyrs of its troublesome intellectuals.

A consummate strategist, Juin exploited the long-standing enmity between the urban Arabs, who supported the Sultan and his cause, and the nomadic Berbers, who retained strong tribal loyalties and whose feudal chiefs were allied with the Protectorate. Juin's most powerful Moroccan ally was His excellency Hadj Thami el-Glaoui; a Berber born in the High Atlas around 1900, the feral Glaoui had begun his career as a bandit and had risen to become the Pasha of Marrakech. Along the way, he had become one of the world's richest, most ruthless men; worth an estimated $50 million, he was rumored to receive a tithe from the six thousand prostitutes who worked in Marrakech and to ride about Morocco with a machine gun in his lap.

At Juin's urging, the Glaoui rounded up tribesmen from the Middle Atlas—provincials who had little sense of the issues at stake—and sent them to demonstrate against the Sultan in Fez and Rabat that December. Under heavy pressure, ben Youssef finally agreed to sign a decree prepared for him by Juin's administration that substantially reduced his power. By spring, Paris was openly debating the notion of removing him from the throne, and the sound of rattling sabers was heard throughout the Maghreb.[2]

With its liberal climate, the International Zone became a command post for the nationalist movement. In a city where smugglers had no fear, political dissidents could fade into the background with relative ease. Still, open rebellion did not go unpunished: Early in 1951, the city was the scene of a trial in which Ahmed Ghomara, chief of the Darkawa brotherhood, was brought before the Tribunal on charges of smuggling weapons into the Zone in preparation for an attack against the neighboring Spanish Protectorate. Declaring that Moroccans were treated like animals by the Spanish and that he would extract justice no matter what the cost, the insurrectionist received a three-year prison sentence and an enormous fine. Istiqlal founder Allal al-Fassi then chose Tangier as a forum in which to claim that nationalists were being censored by the French; charged with using the Cairo press to make false allegations against the Protectorate, he, too, was made to face the Tribunal. Al-Fassi was freed, but his trial sparked a confrontation between armed police and the Tanjawis who gathered outside the courthouse; when the crowd grew unruly, the gendarmes drove them from the building with fire hoses.

Paul took a perverse satisfaction in such upheavals, which

seemed to confirm his own notion that Morocco was "hanging by a silken thread." As an evangelical pessimist, he felt vindicated when external events took on an ominous cast. "Paul and Jane loved disasters," said David Herbert. "When things went well, they couldn't believe it."

Chapter 8

As it happened, Paul Bowles had a talent for creating interesting conflicts in his own life. Skilled at setting himself up as a victim for the mavericks who attached themselves to him, he had already squared off with Brion Gysin over Hamri, a fifteen-year-old whom he had met in a train station and brought to his house in Place Amrah.

A voluble bantam, Hamri had left his mountain village at a tender age and embarked on a career as a smuggler. Riding the crowded trains that traveled across the frontiers, he worked alone—running live hens and other contraband from the International Zone into the French and Spanish Protectorates. Like many of Tangier's knaves, Hamri took pride in his craft. "He always said he was the king of the *trapelistas*," remembered Paul. "As far as I could tell, he spent his entire time trying to get hold of money illicitly."

Delighted with Paul's find, Brion appropriated the boy and invited him to share his narrow room. In a matter of weeks, Hamri had become Brion's protégé; convinced that he was meant to be a painter rather than a petty criminal, Brion bought him art supplies and set him to work.

Hamri's avarice, however, seemed to be even stronger than his desire to please his generous Nazarene, and he soon began backsliding. Saying that he had to attend an important wedding, he asked Paul to lend him a proper outfit for the occasion. "He wanted a white shirt, good tie, socks, shoes, everything, so I fitted him out in all of this, and I gave him the suit I wore when Jane and I got married," Paul said. "He said, 'I'll be home very late because weddings take forever,' but he never came. I went to Brion downstairs and said, 'Where is he?' Brion said, 'How should I know?' I said, 'He's got all my clothes.' Brion said, 'That's your own fault, what did you give them to him for?' He wasn't at all sympathetic.

"Hamri didn't come back that day or any other day. Then one day Brion came to me and said, 'If you want your clothing go fast to the *jotea;* you'll find everything on sale there.' Hamri had taken everything and sold it. I was very angry; I said, 'I will not spend a penny on my own clothing.' Brion said, 'All right, you won't have it, that's all.' I never saw the suit again."

Although Bowles was as angry with Brion as with Hamri (who eventually swaggered back into their lives), he continued to see him. He had found few kindred spirits in Tangier, and Brion shared his fascination for the more baroque forms of humanity. "Brion knew the strangest people—they smelled him out," Paul said. "That was a reason to admire him. When he was around crazy people he was slightly crazier himself; he seemed to be raving part of the time."

At Brion's suggestion, Paul bought a Jaguar convertible in the winter of 1951 and broke it in by making a long trip through the south and into the Sahara. He did not go alone; with him were Brion and Mohammed Temsamany, a well-built young Riffian whom Paul hired as a driver. Outfitted in high boots and a military-style uniform, Temsamany was an imposing figure who exuded disdain for the folk whom they encountered in desert outposts like Taza, where their Jaguar seemed like an apparition.

Their journey ended in Fez, where Paul again spent time with Ahmed Yacoubi. When Jane cabled from Paris, saying she was ready to return to Tangier, Paul promised to rendezvous with her at the French border, and he asked Ahmed to come along. Leaving Brion in Tangier, Bowles, Temsamany and Yacoubi made the long drive up through Madrid, where Paul took the two to see the Bosches in the Prado.

In her long months away from Africa—and from her husband—Jane had grown homesick for them both. Early in 1951, she wrote to Libby Holman, "Deep inside my heart is a tiny picture of Tangier in color. . . . Some days I am in misery because I seem to feel two equally strong destinies and one of them is to be with Paul. I miss him of course terribly."

While Paul had been exploring the tea plantations of Ceylon and the temples of southern India, Jane had been living with the burdensome Cory in Paris, drinking and agonizing over *Out in the World.* Heartened by the news that her play, *In the Summer House,* was to be staged in Westport, Connecticut, she had booked passage to America in the summer of 1950. That production had fallen through, but Jane had lingered in the States until the following winter. In part, she had stayed on to comfort the shattered Libby, whose son Christopher had been killed in a mountain-climbing accident just as she and Luke were leaving Morocco. Jane's other mission was a headier one; with Cory out of the way, she had embarked on an affair with a younger woman who, in her words, was "sweet and trusting and gay and brave." To Libby, Jane reported that her new quarry "looks not only beautiful but distinguished and as if she could not even possibly have met me."

When Jane did return to Paris in the frigid winter of 1951, she had settled back into the shabby comfort of the Hôtel de l'Université, where Truman Capote was her next-door neighbor. Together, he remembered, the two spent "many a cold evening . . . in Jane's snug room (fat with books and papers and foodstuffs and a snappy Pekingese puppy bought from a Spanish sailor) . . . listening to a phonograph and drinking warm applejack while Jane built sloppy, marvelous stews atop an electric burner. . . ." Working sporadically on the third act of the play as well as on the novel, Jane had been unhappy with virtually every line that she produced. Since Paul had become known as the author of *The Sheltering Sky,* her sense of doom had gained momentum; terrified that she had lost her own creative powers, she was flirting with the notion of abandoning her notebooks. In a letter written in January, she spun a fantasy about becoming "the wife of a writer," and added, "I don't think you'd like that, and could I do it well? I think I'd nag and be mean, and then I would be ashamed. Oh, what a black future it would be!"

Reunited with Paul in Tangier that summer, Jane took up the life that she had missed so badly. Spending long hours with Cherifa and her circle, she made rapid progress in Maghrebi. (Kouche Said, her tutor, reported that she was one of the brightest students he had ever had, and that her grasp of gutter language was truly amazing.) Although the city itself still pleased her, her mood was precarious; Paul's orderly stack of notebooks was a painful counterpoint to her own fitful efforts, and it was increasingly difficult to dispel the morbid wife-of-a-writer fantasy.

Eager to complete *Let It Come Down,* Paul decided in July to go into seclusion until the novel was finished. As a retreat, he chose Xauen, which was known as the most beguiling town in Morocco. Deep in the Rif mountains about sixty miles southeast of Tangier, it was perched over the rim of an arresting valley. With fewer than seventeen thousand inhabitants, it had the air of an Andalusian village painted by Gauguin; the Spanish-style buildings were tiled in shocking blue, bright coral, amber and umber, and flowering trees and exuberant gardens added more jolts of color. Long inaccessible to "Christian dogs" (as a local described *London Times* correspondent Walter Harris, who penetrated the town in disguise), it was considered sacred ground by the Jilala tribe. Buried nearby was Moulay Abdessalem ben Mchich, their patron saint, and his *zaouia* was a gathering place for pilgrims and the holy men called marabouts.

In a letter to his mother, Rena, Paul reported that it was easier to focus in a setting that was splendidly isolated. "With a novel," he wrote, "the work is a good deal more than just consecrating so many hours of the day to sitting at a desk writing words;—it is living in the midst of an artificial world one is creating, and letting no detail of everyday life enter sufficiently into one's mind to become more real than or take precedence over what one is inventing. That is, living in the atmosphere of the novel has to become and stay more real than living in one's own life. Which is why it is almost impossible to work in a city, or with people around. At least, for me." He reported that his retreat was "amazingly pure in aspect, and the customs have remained more or less what they were centuries ago. The people grind their own flour, spin their own wool from their own sheep, make their own clothing as well as very fine blankets and thick rugs, and live largely on their own produce, each family having an orchard at the edge of town. I am astonished at the beauty of the town, and can't understand why it isn't full of tourists and vacationists. I suppose that will come soon enough, and when it does, *I* shan't come any longer, but will have to seek out some more isolated spot."

As the novel moved more swiftly, Paul agreed to receive an occasional visitor. Jane came for several weekends, and twenty-one-year-old Irving Thalberg, Jr., (who had been given a letter of introduction by a writer whom he had met in Paris) stayed with him for three days at the end of the summer.

During Thalberg's visit, the two went to hear Jilala music in a crowded café. As they stood in a dim, smoke-filled room that pulsed with the sound of drums, a member of the Jilala brotherhood rose and began to perform a trance dance. Shaken by spasms that "forced his body this way and that, in perfect rhythm with the increasing hysteria of the drums and the low cracked voice of the flute," as Paul described it, the dancer drew his audience into the frenzy; leaping and moaning, he was answered with a rhythmic chorus that mingled with the drumbeats. Pulling out a long knife, the man cut long gashes into his forearms and licked the blood that streamed from the wounds. After slashing the backs of his legs, he sank into unconsciousness, a beatific look on his blood-slick face. Looking around him, Paul saw the same expression on every countenance in the crowd.

The scene was so forceful that he was compelled to incorporate it into his novel. Before murdering Thami, the Moroccan ally who has hidden him in the mountains, Dyar steals into a nearby village and joins the throng in a noisy café. Transported by the drums and the *kif* and the wild, bloody dance, the fugitive feels himself becoming a participant rather than an observer: "With each gesture the man made [Dyar] felt a sympathetic desire to cry out. . . . The mutilation was being done for him, to him; it was his own blood that spattered onto the drums and made the floor slippery. In a world which had not yet been muddied by the discovery of thought, there was this certainty, as solid as a boulder, as real as the beating of his heart, that the man was dancing to purify all who watched."

By autumn, when Paul was ready to leave Xauen, *Let It Come Down* was nearly completed. After a few weeks with Jane in Tangier, he persuaded her to accompany him to Fez. When she left, he stayed on with Ahmed Yacoubi.

Despite their long separations, Bowles was becoming increasingly caught up with the young Fassi. Not only did Ahmed have a powerful creative vision, but he was as animated and beguiling as Jane herself. He charmed Paul by playing the flute to his just-finished paintings—"to bring them to life," he explained—and by impersonating the Europeans whom he knew. A quick study, Ahmed had no trouble fitting in among his friends, even though his English was poor. Said Paul, "He laughed with everybody as if he were one of the crowd." Nothing pleased him more than discovering characters who had the ability to astonish; and in Ahmed, he found both a companion and a source of wonder.

For Bowles, the attachment to Ahmed marked a new phase. "Until he settled in Morocco I think his relationships with boys were never very complex," said Edouard Roditi, a critic and translator who had known him since the thirties. In the past, he had given the exquisitely insecure Jane little reason to be jealous; confident that she was the most important person in his life, his wife had paid far less attention to his sporadic entanglements than to her own romantic exploits. In any case, even those who knew him best were seldom privy to his intimate secrets; although he took pleasure in serving up sodomy and incest in his fiction, Paul was fiercely reticent about his own affairs. Said a writer who knew him in Tangier, "His whole sexual life [was] a very strange one and a very closed one."

Now, while he continued to behave as though nothing had changed, Paul was making a point of incorporating his protégé into his life. When he returned to Tangier early in December, Ahmed came to live with him. To Jane, the threat was clear, but the Bowleses' conflict played itself out in a typically oblique fashion. Said Roditi, "Paul and Jane resolved the situation in a very odd way. As time went on, there was no overt jealousy, but a total disapproval of each other's choices. Paul couldn't stand Cherifa, and Jane couldn't stand [Ahmed]. They were both busy denying what they really felt."

"Of course Janie was jealous," asserted Christopher Wanklyn, the Canadian journalist who became a close friend of both the Bowleses. "She didn't really like Yacoubi but at the same time she realized that Paul needed a friend, a lover. She was given to jealousies which were irrational, and she recognized them as irrational. [But] I think she had a fairly good reason not to like Yacoubi. He was definitely difficult; he was manipulative, in a sense. He was always trying to get money and other things out of [Paul]."

Of course, trying to extract favors from a European lover was hardly an original ploy; to a lower-class Moroccan who became involved with a Nazarene, love and commerce were often inextricable. In an era when at least 90 percent of all natives were illiterate and the best that many youths could hope for was a job as a sweeper, impoverished Moslems saw nothing shameful about playing consort to a discreet foreigner. The prevailing view was that Christians had been put on earth in order to be exploited, and most Moroccans believed that overcharging a Nazarene for a glass of tea and entering his household as a paid companion were equally acceptable. As the local proverb expressed it, *"Nada es mala que gana la plata"*—"Nothing is bad that makes money."

Aside from its material benefits, a lasting liaison could provide a wealth of other advantages for young men like Ahmed. "Boys could learn a great deal [from their lovers], and they were often taken to places that they'd never have a chance to see otherwise," said Gavin Lambert. "The relationship became a special and intriguing adventure for them." Often, patrons provided for their friends after the sexual relationship had ended; one prominent Tangerino (who himself had been rescued from poverty by a homosexual Hungarian prelate) set up his companion as an antiques dealer, and other expatriates employed ex-lovers as majordomos or chauffeurs.

Years later, Paul explored the darker aspect of such arrangements in a story called "Here to Learn." Malika, a striking girl who lives in a dusty little town on the coast, is taken up by a European who has a beautiful apartment in Tangier. Eager to become a part of his world, she learns to wear smart clothing and to charm the "eunuchs" who collect at his cocktail parties. When her lover leaves for a few days, one of his friends spirits her away to Paris, where she continues her education. One rich sponsor takes her to Balenciaga; another sends her to Berlitz. But while the ambitious Malika moves among Christians, she never comprehends them. Two years after leaving her mother's house, the beautiful expatriate (now an exceedingly wealthy widow) goes on a cruise that takes her back to Morocco. When she visits her native village, Malika discovers that her past has been razed: Her mother is dead, her sister has disappeared; even the family home has been torn down to make way for a new road. Weeping, the displaced Malika realizes that "there [is] no longer any reason to do anything," and she watches as a cloud moves across the moon.

If Paul chose to portray the Moroccan as a victim in his story, that was seldom the case in real relationships. Outside of fiction, Europeans were often the ones who fell in love and who found themselves at the mercy of calculating partners. Like Jane Bowles, they found themselves bartering for favors and trying to plumb a psyche that was impenetrable. To a masochist—or a hopeless romantic—it was a satisfying equation indeed: The pursuit was fraught with tension, and the prey was unobtainable.

"Moroccans invariably have the upper hand," asserted Noël Mostert, the South African writer who settled into a house on the Mountain. "They always have their own best interests in mind, and they'll take everything they can, yet they don't grab. . . . They're very witty, very charming; they have a sense of irony about it."

Infinitely more subtle than Cherifa, Ahmed Yacoubi knew that it was enough to place himself in the hands of a powerful foreigner who admired his work. As soon as he moved to Tangier, Paul began to promote him: In November, he went to Yvonne and Isabelle Gerofi, the genteel Belgians who were proprietors of the Librairie des Colonnes, to suggest that they mount an exhibit of Ahmed's paintings. The Gerofis agreed, and the show was a great success; crowds collected on the sidewalk along the Boulevard Pasteur to look into the window of the bookstore, and twenty-eight paintings were sold. Amazed by the response, the artist (who took pride in being pious) expressed his thanks not to Paul but to Allah.

Ahmed's success was not lost on Jane, who later encouraged Cherifa to make her own drawings. The results were childish and crude, and the project was soon abandoned—but not before she prevailed upon several friends to buy the works. (The loyal David, who was among her victims, pronounced Cherifa's style "extraordinary.")

Brion, too, was inspired by the response to Yacoubi's work. During the show, he brought Hamri to inspect Ahmed's paintings and told him that Nazarenes were willing to pay handsome sums for such efforts. "Hamri said something to the effect that, 'Well, I could do that with one hand behind me,' " Paul remembered. "Brion said, 'Go ahead and do it.' So what Hamri did was to copy to the last detail Yacoubi's pictures. He didn't realize you're not supposed to copy someone else's work. Brion was horrified; he said, 'No, no, no, that's not the way to do it, you have to invent your own.' So Hamri did; he was perfectly able to invent his own subject."

Hamri had real talent as an artist, but he had lived by his wits for too long to make the transition so abruptly. When Paul discovered that an expensive new radio had been taken from his house, he immediately suspected Hamri, who, with Brion, had stayed there during his absence. "Both Temsamany and Yacoubi said, 'We know Hamri stole it,' " remembered Paul. "I wasn't there, but they confronted him and they said he turned white."

The incident caused a rift between Paul and Brion, who insisted that Paul should have known better than to leave valuables in the house when he was away. "As far as I was concerned Brion was responsible; he knew perfectly well Hamri had taken the radio," said Paul. With Temsamany and Yacoubi, he paid a call to Brion, who had moved into a cottage on the Marshan. "My two henchmen threatened him in no uncertain terms," he remembered. "They said, 'We're going to get the police and have you and Hamri in jail by tonight.' Brion was very angry to be threatened that way, and I was trying to placate. He left that very day, and I didn't speak to him for months."

Hamri himself would later claim that the blowup had been prompted by sexual jealousy between Paul and Brion—a charge that Paul found preposterous. "He obviously thinks that everybody was very taken with him, that he was very attractive. I don't know, but there wasn't anything like that," said Bowles, adding, "I wasn't angry about Hamri. I really get angry not over people, but over objects."

When the show at the Librairie des Colonnes was over, Paul continued his protégé's ad hoc education—taking him along on his travels and introducing him to his friends. In December, the two left Tangier for a month in Tetuán, a handsome town that was the capital of the Spanish Zone. For company, they had the artist Robert Rauschenberg, who happened to be staying down the street from their hotel on the rue General Franco.

One night, Paul and Ahmed repeated the *majoun* experiment that they had performed on Jane in 1948—this time, without warning their subject that he was consuming a powerful drug. After eating a substantial portion of the confection, Rauschenberg left Paul's hotel in "a very strange state," as Paul described it. Later, the two went to check on his progress. Standing outside Rauschenberg's hotel room, they heard a series of groans and chose not to disturb him. "We decided that since he was already embarked on an unhappy journey, our arrival could only make it worse," Paul reported.

The pair found the stunt so amusing that they repeated it whenever they could. "Paul and Ahmed were notorious for giving people *majoun* and scaring the hell out of them," said William Burroughs. Whenever their subjects had a bad time of it, "Paul would say things like, 'Oh, my God, you know sometimes people get in these states and they never come out. . . . Really, I'm sorry I gave you that *majoun.* I can see you're having a *terrible* reaction to it.' Oh, he was a real ministering angel when you were having the horrors."

Ready to make another expedition in order to escape the Tangier winter, Paul decided after the Tetuán trip to take Ahmed to India. Jane, who had no inclination to accompany the two, found a mission in New York. *In the Summer House* had been staged in August at the Hedgerow Theater in Pennsylvania, and Oliver Smith hoped to bring the play to Broadway. For Jane, New York held a kind of promise that Tangier no longer offered; she needed an audience, and her best critic had turned his attention elsewhere.

By the spring of 1952, Bowles and Yacoubi had reached the island of Cochin off the Malabar coast. There, Paul received news that the

International Zone had been rocked by one of the worst riots in its history. The scene, as he discovered, had been a bloody one: On March 30, Tanjawis had massed to demand that the infidels loose their grip on Morocco. Storming through the medina and up the steep rue Siaghins, they had surged into the Socco Grande, where police tried to contain them by blocking off the surrounding streets. Since most of their commandants were away, the gendarmes had no one to stop them from firing into the crowd, and at least a hundred demonstrators had been wounded by the time the Moroccans retreated. Shaken, the police had locked themselves into their headquarters, leaving Tangier's Europeans to the mercy of the mob. As they made their way through the city—looting hundreds of shops and burning scores of cars—the enraged Tanjawis had beaten a Dutchman to death and severely injured two British residents. Not until reinforcements were sent in from the French and Spanish Zones had the melee been quelled.

At least eighteen Moroccans had died and forty policemen had been injured in the day-long riot, which was believed to have been set off by the Spanish: Eager to wrest control of Tangier away from their European rivals, officers in Tetuán allegedly had floated a rumor that the Treaty of Fez would expire on March 30 but that the administration was refusing to grant Tanjawis their independence. The conspirators seemed not only to have bribed tribesmen from their protectorate to slip into Tangier and lead the fracas but to have arranged a picnic that lured the commandants into the countryside.

Although they were furious with the Spanish, most Tangerinos decided that the unpleasantness (which coincided with a wave of riots in Tunis) was a routine display of Arab nationalism. Serious investors were more alarmed—clearly, the issue of Moroccan independence was not going to disappear, and no one was eager to construct an office building that would be torched by a horde of rioters. Few fled immediately, but building projects were slowing and the prudent had begun to transfer their gold to safer havens.

Along with the news from Morocco, Paul had received reports from America that *Let It Come Down*, published that February by Random House, had drawn strong reactions from critics. *The New York Times Book Review* had offered high praise, lauding the novel for its "nightmare clarity and hallucinative exoticism"; but a number of reviewers had been put off by Paul's nihilism and the depravity of his fictional Tangier. "The fruit of which Paul Bowles has eaten is, unfortunately, that which confers knowledge only of evil, not of good," lamented Richard Hayes in *Commonweal.* The *Spectator*'s critic was particularly acerbic: "I can imagine Mr. Graham Greene turning over some of this material and deciding, with a wry smile, not to use it," he wrote. "As a morality about the mess people can get into who believe neither in this life nor in any other, *Let It Come Down* has lots to say, but I do not see that much is gained by assembling a crowd of rootless creatures in a swamp and watching them rot."

Paul, of course, professed to be pleased by such pronouncements; chronically at odds with American culture, he delighted in shocking its literary mullahs. In India, however, his pleasure in the news about his book and about the ominous events in Tangier was eclipsed by his excitement over being held for two days in a Ceylonese "screening" camp and visiting cobra-infested islands inhabited by Buddhist monks. Caught up in the drama of daily life there and content to be with Ahmed, he was savoring his companion's reactions to the world outside Morocco: Cocky, thoroughly certain of the superiority of his own culture, the young Fassi never hesitated to say what he was thinking or to flout local customs. "He . . . has an intuitive gift for the immediate understanding of a situation and at the same time is completely lacking in reticence or inhibitions," Paul wrote of him:

He can lie so well that he convinces himself straightaway, and he is a master at bargaining; it is a black day for him when he has to pay the asking price for anything. He never knows what is printed on a sign because he is totally illiterate; besides, even if he did know he would pay no attention, for he is wholly deficient in respect for law. If you mention that this or that thing is forbidden, he is contemptuous: "Agh! a decree for the wind!" Obviously, he is far better equipped than I to squeeze the last drop of adventure out of any occasion.

After leaving India, Paul and Ahmed continued to Ceylon. There, Paul fell in love with Taprobane, a minute island that had captured his imagination when he saw it in a photo in one of David Herbert's scrapbooks. Only when the monsoons threatened did they leave for Europe, taking a Norwegian freighter that docked in Genoa. Much of the summer was spent in Italy; the two ran into the peripatetic Brion at Lago di Orta, where he was painting, and they stayed with Peggy Guggenheim at her Venice palazzo, where Ahmed was shocked by the sight of the heiress sunning in the nude. When they moved on to Madrid, Paul arranged for a show of Yacoubi's works at the Galería Clan, and the response was as enthusiastic as it had been in Tangier: Others, it seemed, had no trouble understanding what he saw in his gifted protégé.

It was Jane who drew Paul and Ahmed to America. For months she had been laboring over the recalcitrant third act of *In the Summer House,* and Oliver Smith hoped to bring the play to Broadway by the end of 1953. The production would soon be ready for out-of-town tryouts, and a score was needed. Overcoming his fear of being greeted at the docks by the State Department, Paul agreed to come to New York to compose the music. Ahmed had a mission as well: Jane—who was supportive of his work, if not his role in her husband's life—had brought a collection of his paintings to New York with her, and she had shown them to gallery owner Betty Parsons. Parsons already had mounted a successful show of Ahmed's dreamlike paintings, and Jane had persuaded the owner of the Weyhe Gallery to stage another.

Libby Holman invited Paul and Ahmed to Treetops, and by the late winter of 1953 the two were comfortably installed at the sumptuous estate near Greenwich. For Ahmed, America was a dizzying place; already, he had decided that New York City was a vast illusion created by evil djins. At Libby's, he was bedazzled by the sheer opulence that he encountered: Her three-story house had fifty-six rooms, including sixteen bedchambers, a formal dining room, an immense living room, a wood-paneled library and a playroom that occupied an entire floor. Among the most spectacular enclaves was Libby's own bath, where she received guests from an ornate chaise longue; with its white fur rugs, fireplace, copper sink, gold-domed ceiling and mirrored tub with brass fittings in the shape of dolphins, it was as showy as Holman herself. Perfumed by the roses and fuchsias that came from Libby's lavish gardens, the rest of the house was awash in seductive little luxuries—Persian carpets, English silver, monogrammed satin sheets and lap robes of sable and vicuña. To Ahmed, Treetops seemed a magnificent mirage, and he was happy enough to be left there with Libby when Paul was called to Washington, D.C., where Jane's play was in rehearsal.

In some ways, the affair that blossomed in Paul's absence seemed preordained. As a man who savored disasters, who excelled in the role of victim, he seemed to be setting himself up by allowing the sexually ambitious Libby (who had no lover on hand) to be alone with Ahmed. It took only weeks for her to seduce the twenty-four-year-old painter, but the pursuit was an invigorating one. Beneath the coy smiles and the fragmented English, the well-built Yacoubi was a formidable character who was assertive enough to provide the kind of challenge that Libby adored. The chase, she told Jane, was well rewarded; Ahmed, she said, was the best lover she had ever had—wholly uncivilized and brutally sublime.

Always generous to her beaux, Libby proceeded to do everything in her power for Ahmed. Charmed by his paintings, she adopted the project of arranging exhibitions of his work, and she asked her lawyer to help extend his six-month visa. Although she loved his handsome djellabas, she also bought him a closetful of suits and shirts and shoes. No indulgence was overlooked; when the two went on an excursion and Ahmed saw something he wanted, he simply pointed it out to Libby, whose secretary made sure that the item was sent to Treetops the next day. True to his Fassi roots, he was relentlessly practical about the treasures around him; since he considered Libby's possessions to be his own, he felt no compunction about stripping the precious metal from a set of her silver brushes and combs and hammering it into cubes—the better to barter with, when the time came.

When Paul and Jane returned to Connecticut, Libby's house was in an interesting state of disarray. The avant-garde filmmaker Hans Richter, with whom Paul had worked in 1947, was producing an experimental film called *8 × 8*—a "surrealist commentary on chess," as he described it—and had asked Libby to allow him to stage a segment at Treetops that spring. As his set, Richter used the oval swimming pool; after it was drained, he brought in an organ and an assortment of playroom furniture. Paul and Ahmed were appropriated as actors in the piece, which was titled "The Fatal Move." Bowles played a composer who is lured into the woods by a flute-playing Pan figure—Ahmed—who leaves in Libby's Jaguar after abandoning his prey. Holman herself appeared only in passing, but the swimming-pool set was dominated by a large poster depicting her as a femme fatale.

Even as Richter's surrealist scenario came to life, Paul began to see that another drama was playing itself out around them: Libby, it seemed, had risen to the challenge of seducing Ahmed. He was not surprised when she confessed to him that she had fallen in love. "I feel so guilty," she said. "But I couldn't help myself."

Paul took the blow without flinching. Saying that he wanted to work on the half-finished *Yerma,* he immediately removed himself from the scene. When he left for Tangier early in May, Ahmed did not come with him.

Later, when Bowles talked about Ahmed's defection, he said very little about his own pain. Christopher Wanklyn observed that even close friends were forced to read between the lines; Paul, he said, "was capable of discussing these things without giving any hint of how he felt." In fact, Bowles often camouflaged the story by reporting how Yacoubi's mother had reacted when he and Temsamany went to Fez to give her the news: Told that Ahmed was staying in America with a woman, she immediately asked whether his new friend was rich. Informed that she was very wealthy indeed, she overlooked the fact that she might never see her son again. "Hamdoul'lah," she cried—"Praise Allah!"

As it happened, however, Ahmed was not destined to become the master of Treetops. Never easy to live with, Libby put her young lover to the test—trying to evoke the sort of jealous display that stimulates a jaded palate. Late one night, after a drunken dinner at Treetops with Ted Benedict, a young Harvard graduate who had been one of her amours, she staged a scene straight from a B-movie. Fetching two loaded pistols from a closet, she handed one of the guns to Ahmed, telling him that they should make a suicide pact. "You shoot yourself and then I'll shoot myself," she said. The inebriated Ahmed managed to take Libby's gun away, but the theatrics weren't over.

Soon afterward, she made a distraught phone call to Jane

Bowles, who had gone to stay in Libby's Upper East Side townhouse after her play finished its run in Ann Arbor. Ahmed, she said, had just tried to drown her seven-year-old son, Timmy, in the pool, and she was about to call the police. Jane (who shared Paul's phobia about the authorities) persuaded her to avoid turning the incident into a public scandal; promising that she would keep Ahmed at Holman's pied-à-terre until he could be put on a ship for Morocco, she convinced her to dispatch him to New York in her Jaguar. Claiming that the contretemps was a misunderstanding, Ahmed did not leave Treetops without a fight: As a sign of his contempt, he cut up every piece of clothing that Libby had given him and tossed the expensive scraps into her mirrored bathtub. When Libby told him he was crazy, he slapped her and called her "a camel."

Generous to the end, Holman arranged for Yacoubi to travel first-class on the U.S.S. *Constitution*. Locked into her townhouse for three days before the ship sailed, he went into a frenzy of grief, moaning and keening and calling her name. The voyage calmed him only slightly; still distraught when he arrived in Morocco, he retreated to Fez after a brief reunion with Bowles.

In July, Paul received a compassionate letter from Tennessee Williams, who was in Rome. "Has Ahmed come back?" he wrote. "I hope so, for I sense your loneliness without him. . . . I think what happened was a very temporary thing, a sort of *'coup de feu'* or derangement that came from the sudden collision of two very different cultures at a critical time. It is nothing that could not be understood by a man of your philosophical latitude. . . . Somehow I feel it is very sad for Libby . . . not for you."

Ahmed and Paul continued their lives together after a few weeks, but the strain was unmistakable—at least to the sympathetic Tennessee. Summoned to Rome to write the English dialogue for Luchino Visconti's film *Senso*, Paul took Ahmed and Temsamany along. There, Tennessee saw just what the break had done. On July 28, he wrote to Donald Windham:

[Paul Bowles] has two Arabs with him, his lover [-] (stolen but now relinquished by Libby Holman) and a chauffeur and we all live on the same floor of this apartment building, a top floor which has only a trickle of water for us to divide among us. The Arabs smoke kif and eat "majum" . . . and Paul sweats and fumes over constant anxieties and discomforts which I find rather endearing as I do the same thing. He has some liver trouble and is down to 115 pounds. . . . [-] is torturing Paul by not sleeping with him. It seems that Libby [said] that such relations were very evil and the opinions of a lady with thirty million dollars cannot be taken lightly by a young Arab whose family live in one room. Paul looks haggard and is almost too disturbed to do a good job on the film. "They call it love-hatred and it hails from the pit" is one of the best lines Strindberg ever wrote.

Chapter 9

In the sweltering summer of 1953, every Moslem in Morocco was looking ahead to the solemn festival of Aïd el-Kebir, which was to be celebrated on August 21. Despite the growing sense of political unease, even the poorest families were preparing to buy a sheep to be slain in the ritual that commemorated Abraham's sacrifice of his son, Isaac. For those who knew few luxuries, the Aïd presented a rare opportunity to glory in the fat of the land; the feasting went on for several days, and mutton could be seen drying on clotheslines for weeks afterwards. In some Berber villages, men extended the celebration by blackening their faces, covering themselves in sheepskins and chasing their neighbors, flailing them with hides. But the festival was no mere exercise in hedonism; if performed properly, the ritual slaughter and feasting were taken to be good omens for the following year. According to tradition, the Sultan, as commander of the faithful, was required to slaughter the first sheep with his own hands.

During this abortive Aïd, however, it was Mohammed ben Youssef who became the victim. Still infuriated with the headstrong Sultan, Resident General Augustin Guillaume—helped by his

Machiavellian friend the Glaoui—had spent the summer preparing to depose him. A petition demanding that ben Youssef be forced to abdicate had been signed by 356 Berber chieftains and sent to Paris, and the Glaoui had announced that if the French failed to act, he himself would remove the Sultan from his throne. As the festival approached, the crisis came to a head. On August 14, pashas loyal to the Glaoui gathered in Marrakech and proclaimed that ben Youssef was no longer their spiritual leader; that position, they declared, belonged to the Glaoui's aged uncle, Sidi Mohammed ben Moulay Arafa—a timorous, illiterate man who could easily be transformed into a French puppet. Although the French-backed proclamation allowed ben Youssef to remain as temporal ruler, the message was clear. The Sultan's nationalist supporters were outraged; riots broke out in Marrakech, and thirty-six people were killed in Arab-Berber fighting across the country.

On August 17, the embattled Sultan appealed to the rest of the world to support him against the French, but Guillaume and the Glaoui were preparing the final blow. Three days after ben Youssef made his plea, Berber horsemen converged upon Rabat, as they had in 1951, and French tanks took up their positions around the palace. It was on August 20 that ben Youssef was arrested "for his own protection," as his captors explained it, and the doddering ben Arafa was placed on the throne. The French trundled the deposed Sultan out of the palace without giving him time to put on his shoes. Within hours, he was flown to Corsica, where he was joined by his two wives, eight concubines and four of his children. In the midst of the drama, the Aïd was all but forgotten.

Nothing could have harmed the French position as severely as the banishment of ben Youssef. Moroccans who had been indifferent to the cause of nationalism were outraged by the insult to their imam, and the people rallied behind the Sultan as never before. Forbidden to speak his name in public, his subjects regarded him as a national martyr; peasants claimed that they could see his face in the full moon. In the following months, the Istiqlal and its rival parties launched a campaign of terrorism that included an attempt to kill the detested ben Arafa, and few of their countrymen took issue with their methods.

*   *   *

In Rome with Ahmed Yacoubi, Paul decided that it was an excellent time to return to Tangier. "I was in a hurry to see what Morocco would be like now that the terrorists had started their campaign against the French," he remembered. "Behind my curiosity lurked the fear that the country would cease to be inhabitable for foreigners under the new circumstances." With Tennessee, Ahmed and Temsamany, Bowles drove from Italy back to Tangier, where he sensed a new and pleasing aura of menace. "My fears seemed well grounded," he wrote later. "There was now an element of distinct unfriendliness abroad in the streets of Tangier. I had the impression that everyone was waiting for a signal to be given, and that when it came, all hell would break loose."

If Paul was savoring the prospect of disaster, other Tangerinos were happy to ignore the heightened tension. Content to live from one untroubled day to the next, they simply clung to their old lives, floating from Porte's to Dean's to the Parade with hardly a glance at the "Moors." In spite of the occasional uprising, there was little enough to remind Tangier's expatriates that the country was on the edge of a revolt; the struggle against the French was a far more immediate issue in cities like Casablanca, where *colons* brought loaded revolvers to dinner parties. In the International Zone, anyone who didn't make his living as a diplomat was free to concentrate on matters that were truly vital—topics like who was sleeping with whom and who was staging the liveliest soirées.

One of the Tangerinos whom people were discussing that season was the spirited Louise de Meuron, who gave extravagant parties at her sumptuous house on the Mountain. A German-Swiss who had married a French nobleman, the Countess was a quick, birdlike woman with an astringent wit. She liked to sunbathe nude on Tangier's lonelier beaches, where she startled passing fishermen, and she said absolutely anything that came to mind: In the words of one neighbor, she "often, and not entirely innocently, would refer to uncomfortable truths [other ladies] would rather have left discreetly unmentioned." A beauty who managed to look at least twenty years younger than she was, she buried her face in a bowl of cracked ice for thirty minutes every morning. Long separated from the Count, she had her choice of beaux, but she shocked even

Tangier by taking up with a Moroccan schoolteacher and insisting that her friends invite him to their parties.

Already, Tangerinos had amassed an entire stock of tales about the Countess; one of the most notable concerned the evening that she and a group of friends were stopped by gendarmes on their way to a fancy-dress party: "Louise, who was driving, was dressed as a snake, and the others were in equally weird costumes," remembered a neighbor. "When the gendarme leaned into where Louise was sitting and said, *'Et vous, madame?'* she grabbed his arm and bit him. I think they ended up at the Commissariat, because they always took very seriously people making a scandal."

Paul Bowles was among those who admired the Countess's audacity. "She wasn't afraid of anything," he said. "She came by one day in her station wagon to take us to Tetuán; when we got to the frontier at the Spanish Zone, the soldiers tried to stop her, but she made a funny noise and drove past the roadblock at about eighty miles an hour. It was unheard of. We came back another way and she got out to talk with the guards. I think she settled it with money, which you can do very easily here. She got back in the car and said, *'Voilà.'*

"Her husband came to visit occasionally, and she brought him and one of her daughters on another trip that we made together to Tetuán. On the way there, her husband said, 'I want to go to a brothel.' The daughter wanted to go, too. Louise and I went to a café and listened to music—she loved Moroccan music, and so did I—and the father and the girl went to a whorehouse together. All the girl said later was, 'It was very interesting.'"

As it happened, one of de Meuron's suitors was Bowles's chauffeur, who had an eye for European matrons. The ambitious Temsamany was also trying to seduce Beatrix Pendar, a beautiful socialite who lived on the Mountain, and Louise was furious when she heard about the flirtation. "Louise used to follow him to Beatrix's house," said Paul. "She would crawl under the house, which was on a steep incline, so she could hear everything that was said in the living room. Beatrix, she said, gave Temsamany long lectures about how awful it was to have sex, and he'd pat her and say, 'I understand, I understand,' then he'd begin again and say, 'Just this once.' She'd say, 'No, no—come to the window and look at the stars,' and she'd begin reciting poetry.''

After eavesdropping on one such rendezvous, the Countess decided to extract revenge. "When she finally heard that Temsamany was about to go home, she went out and got in my Jaguar, which he was driving, and crouched in the back where she wouldn't be seen," Paul said. "As they were on the way down the steep mountainside she suddenly stood up and put her arms around him from behind, and he went 'Ay!' He didn't know what it was—a devil who wanted to kill him? And then she began—'C'est comme ça que tu te fais tes amis. Oui, oui, je comprends, j'ai entendu tout que tu as dit ce soir.' He came to me the next day and said, 'You know that woman is crazy!' But I thought it was one of the funniest things of the year. It was typical Tangier behavior."

Aside from the Countess de Meuron, the favorite subjects of 1953 included public scandals like the grave-robbing epidemic that had hit the city. According to Ruth Maxwell, the *Tangier Gazette*'s social columnist, one widowed expatriate had been shocked to see a stranger strolling about town in her late husband's favorite suit. The escapades of New Jersey–born pirate "Nylon Sid" Paley were another diversion for *Gazette* readers: An ex-GI who had invested in a small nylon manufacturing plant, Paley had been charged with plotting the hijacking of a Dutch ship that had been boarded on the high seas by masked gunmen who made away with thousands of cases of cigarettes. Like all American citizens, Paley could be tried only in the American Consular Court, where he made a lasting impression by peeling off ten thousand dollars in bail money from an enormous roll of banknotes. Convicted and given a ten-thousand-dollar fine and a three-year jail sentence, he served only a few months in jail before his appeal suddenly was granted. To celebrate his freedom, Paley dug out his tuxedo and made a surprise appearance at the Rif Hotel on the night of the annual Press Club Ball, sending a thrill of fear through celebrants who had written unkind stories about him.

At the Parade Bar, Jay Haselwood's customers were busily dissecting the lives of their neighbors, including David Herbert and his friend Jamie Caffrey, who was the *Gazette*'s gardening columnist. A witty southerner who was the nephew of the American ambassador to France, Caffrey had worked as a researcher for *Fortune* before meeting Herbert in England. In 1950, when David finally moved from his family's estate in Wiltshire into a house that he rented from Jessie Green, Jamie had come with him. Now, the two were converting Jessie's rambling Moorish villa into an exquisite aerie. Set into the side of a hill near the village of Djamaa el-Mokra, the pale-ocher hideaway—originally a prayer house for a local saint— was surrounded by a brilliant garden planted with *copa di ora* and arum lilies and Chinese fuchsia. Lovebirds sang in ironwork cages, and goldfish darted about in a pond near the terrace. Inside, rooms of apricot and parrot-green had been done in a lush, breezy style that was charmingly unconventional; Regency-period painted furniture, chinoiserie, and the occasional Van Dyck were intermingled with portraits of David's favorites (including Lady Diana Cooper) and bibelots given to him by friends like Tallulah Bankhead. With the help of a staff that included a cook, a major-domo and two housemaids, David had begun to stage spirited dinners and lively luncheons where one was apt to encounter at least one obscure royal. But if many of his neighbors were eager to be invited to Herbert's house, Tangier's true snobs were still eyeing him from afar. David, as they saw it, made too much of his family connections. "They didn't invite him to parties," remembered a countess whose stepfather was a Belgian diplomat. "He invited very smart people to stay, but he was a bit hard up otherwise."

Those who kept track of such things were pleased to note that Herbert already had earned an interesting rival. A tradesman's son who had worked his way from a gray Midland town to a palace in the Casbah, David Edge was a man who was entirely self-invented. Unlike Herbert, whose tales about the Duchess of Kent and Prince Paul of Yugoslavia were true, if a trifle exaggerated, Edge lied with abandon about his ties to European nobility. Tall and fair and hawk-nosed, he exuded "glamour and evil," in the words of Tessa Codrington Wheeler, who often came to Tangier to visit grandfather Jack Sinclair (Zanzibar's governor emeritus). "I first met David when I was seventeen and I thought he was the most amazing person," said Codrington. "He was really wicked—I remember someone saying to me, 'I've never felt such an aura of evil about

anybody.' He screwed anything he wanted and he completely corrupted people."

In residence at Edge's house in the Casbah was a young boy
whom he had picked up on the street in Spain. "Adolfo was just
kind of scurrying around learning how to use a knife and fork and
shine shoes and do anything else David wanted him to do," said
Codrington. "He was completely in awe of his surroundings." Unlike Herbert, the extravagant Edge had exercised absolutely no restraint in adorning his lair. "The house was so exotic it was unbelievable," she said. "It was an old harem—square, with the alcoves
all round it. In the middle there was a huge fountain with banana
plants, and everything was in black and gold. The beds were these
mad-looking four-posters covered in black or purple velvet. David
would give terribly grand parties, and he'd walk around in this
purple caftan with a gold cross that he said had been stolen from
a church. On his bed there would be a crucifix, just thrown on the
velvet spread—it was wonderfully macabre." And if some Tangerinos were put off by such overstatement, others were wild to see
the place for themselves: "He had such a reputation as one of the
frights of Tangier that they would sort of fight to get in," Codrington said.

Like many of his neighbors, Edge seldom told his life story the
same way twice. According to one version, he had been spirited
away to Europe as a young boy by a lecherous bishop who visited
his parish, spotted him in the choir and offered to pay for his
education. In Austria, he said, he had attracted the attention of a
Hungarian cardinal who took him on as a companion. After acquir-
ing a certain patina and learning just enough about art, Edge had
found his way to Tangier, where he transformed himself into
a decorator and antiques dealer—"passing off these things that
he knew had been made yesterday in the souk," as one observer
put it.

For the inventive Edge, every *objet* told a story—usually, a tale
that was completely untrue. "When I first came here I brought with
me a couple of big Japanese lacquered chests with the Shogun crest
on them," reported a well-born British émigré. "David Edge saw
them and asked if he could buy them, and I sold them to him. Some
time later, I went to his house and there they were on two elaborate

stands. I heard him telling people how this was the Shogun crest and how they had been presented to the Empress of Japan, who had presented them to his grandmother. Afterwards I said to David, 'You know it's absolutely untrue, all that nonsense you were telling; how dare you say that, you know perfectly well you got them from me.' And he said, 'It made their afternoon, didn't it?' "

Paul Bowles regarded Edge as "a poor man's David Herbert"—a figure who "was so absurd that he was amusing." Said Paul, "The interior of his house was like something from Beverly Hills. He would say, 'But you haven't seen my bathroom—the doorknobs are real gold and they cost eight thousand pounds.' There would be bits of fakery that you wouldn't see until you looked closely: a magnificent indoor garden with orchids that were artificial but you wouldn't notice because they'd be twenty feet above your head."

When Edge went on errands, he traveled in a Rolls-Royce which he drove himself—wearing elegant leather driving gloves that buttoned up the side. "He told me, 'You and I have the only presentable automobiles in Tangier: Mine is the father and yours is the son,' " Paul said. Seldom did he fail to make an impression; he was the master of the grand gesture, the sweeping entrance. At parties, he sometimes received guests "while reclining on a canopied bed which had reputedly belonged to Catherine the Great," remembered Patrick Higgins, who came to visit Edge in Tangier with his friend Helena Rubinstein. "On these occasions he wore a jeweled caftan and looked not unlike an Anglican bishop dressed by Dior." Paul's favorite vision of Edge was at a costume party given by Louise de Meuron: "He appeared at just the right moment, completely naked and painted silver, borne by a team of Moroccans who were also painted silver. He looked like the Caterpillar from 'Alice in Wonderland.' "

Edge knew that some of his neighbors were scandalized by such gestures, but "he didn't give a damn what anybody thought," said Codrington. The one person whose opinion did seem to matter to him was David Herbert, who found him "beneath contempt," as Edouard Roditi remembered it. Although he was delighted to appear in drag for charity musicales, Herbert had no use for Edge's affectations, and he would never have considered taking in a Spanish urchin like Adolfo. The wild lies and grand airs that amused others only irritated Herbert, who reserved his deepest backstabs for climbers. And although Herbert behaved as though the rivalry were a great joke, some of his friends believed that he was more than half-serious about "the War of the Two Davids," as it was known. "He told me, 'Anyone who sees the other David can't see me,'" remembered one friend. "I said, 'My dear, I'm independent.' I saw both, but he wasn't happy about it."

"It was very, very polarized," said Codrington, whose family knew Herbert well. "David Edge went so much farther than David Herbert would have dreamt, and I think in a way that was a slight niggle. He disapproved profoundly of anyone like me being friends with David Edge, and I didn't let David know I saw very much of him. But of course it was all a question of the pot calling the kettle black."

In the winter of 1952, Brion Gysin made a long retreat into the Sahara. After the madness of Tangier, the desert seemed a sort of minimalist paradise; he loved its severity, its hush, its piercing contrasts. Days were filled with heat and light; nights, with a deep black cold that brought out the brilliance of the stars. Insistent, uncompromising, it was a heady setting for a man who adored visual drama. To Brion, the desert was a place of blasted beauty—a feast of "shattered mountains, rotted valleys and shifting bare plains in an infinite variety of desolations."

If Paul was taken with the desert sky, Brion was dazzled by its light. In notes and sketches ("postcards," he called them) he recorded the silvered images that found their way into later works like *The Process*—a novel that begins with a *kif*-stoked journey across the Algerian desert. Sunset was "a blue tide of darkness rac[ing] across the Sahara, bowling over the giant purple shadows of the amethyst mountains like ninepins." Camels "more like yachts under sail than four-footed beasts" carried travelers through "volcanic moon-surface landscape[s] which fled past like painted stage sets or . . . a nightmare series of absurdly old-fashioned surrealist lantern-slide pictures projected on the curtains of air, almost solid with wind-borne sand." After days in a land of "running shadows but no shade," every scene became a trompe l'oeil: One "march[es] in the eye of the mirage with the dancing and swooning horizon a full wavering circle closing [in]," he wrote. "Heat billows up out of the ground like the breath of a glass factory rolling out the mirage. . . . The watering eye of the mirage is the great Show of The World. On its dazzling round screen you assist at the creation and destruction of the world in flames."

Brion noted that the Sahara played tricks on the psyche as well as on the eye. As one pressed on into the desert, he observed, the mind began "playing about like a mind [confronting] the parallel mirrors of a barbershop"—struggling against the illusion of infinity. Cast adrift in time and space, a stranger could invent a thousand versions of reality, each one based on a different image. Like his alter-ego protagonist in *The Process,* a black academic who studies the history of slavery, Brion liked to say that "all truth is a tale I am telling myself." He found proof of that notion in the Sahara.

Gysin's journey ended in Marrakech, but he continued to mine for magic. With his sketchbook, he sat in the Djemaa el-Fna ("the assembly of the dead," as it was often translated), the ancient square that anchored the medina. The traditional gathering place of Berber tribesmen from the Atlas, Blue People from the Sahara and black Africans from Timbuktu, Senegal and the Sudan, it was the liveliest theater on the continent. By day, it was a crowded, dusty market where tradesmen sold limes and oranges and cactus fruit. At night, with hissing lanterns throwing shadows into the crowd, it became a confusion of fortune-tellers, contortionists, fire eaters, water sellers, scribes, street barbers and musicians. Self-trained dentists squatted amid displays of brown teeth and secondhand dentures; healers formulated potions to banish tumors or mend broken bones. Lithe Berber boys dressed as maidens performed seductive *cheluh* dances, and animal trainers worked their sullen little troupes of Barbary apes. In the midst of it all, storytellers spun out the tales told in the square by their great-grandfathers—"grandiose stories about the Sultan and his daughter and the rich Jew who tries to get her . . . very full of plot . . . with lots of magic and transportation," as Paul Bowles described them.

It was in that setting that Gysin encountered an unlikely fellow traveler. The British-born beauty Felicity Mason was making a solo trip through Morocco "to get over being too much in love with my husband," as she explained it. Cultivated, well-spoken, Mason had been raised in a setting where every character seemed touched by the spark of fame or genius; in the south of France, where her mother lived when Felicity was young, she had known everyone from the Gerald Murphys to the Scott Fitzgeralds to the Dolly sisters. Twice married—most recently to Richard Mason, the Englishman who would write *The World of Suzie Wong*—Felicity was an intrepid sexual adventurer. Morocco, where unaccompanied European women attracted sibilant catcalls and penetrating stares, suited her perfectly. Later, she remembered Marrakech as "the most sensual city in the world. . . . There was a sex souk for all sexes known as 'Le Quartier Reservé,' with girls imported from Marseilles and elsewhere. There were also plenty of Cheluh dancers for gay gentlemen, who were still known as queers. . . . I could never see anything queer about men liking men. I liked men myself, so I understood what it was they saw in each other—good, hard cocks."

When Felicity got off the bus from Tangier one warm spring day, she headed across the Djemaa el-Fna, trailed by three boys who balanced her red suitcases on their heads. When they reached the Café de France, the little procession walked past a cluster of Arab men who were lingering over mint tea. "A dozen pairs of dark Arab eyes watched my arrival. Sitting amongst them in a Harris tweed jacket but nevertheless looking as much a part of them as if he had been wearing a djellaba, was a handsome European man with strange, light green eyes," she remembered. "He looked as if he had been sitting there for centuries. I felt as if I already knew him, but I passed him by without a greeting. I did not yet know that he was my soul brother."

From the balcony of the noisy room that she rented from the patron of the café, Felicity watched the European stroll across the square to an Arab restaurant. Minutes later, she was standing at Brion's table, asking whether she could join him. After he ordered in Arabic for them both, she discovered that "he was a painter, a poet, and the most interesting man I had ever met. . . . He was singular, unique, extraordinary, monstrous and wonderful. He was both negative and positive at the same time. I loved him, admired him, respected him, hated him, all by turns in the space of one short lunch."

As she fell under Brion's spell, Felicity realized that she "felt a profound understanding of him which could not logically be explained . . . [and] he felt the same about me. We had been in all the same places, done all the same things. We even looked alike." Brion, she said, declared that they were "irrevocably linked" after he discovered that she had been born in Walton-on-Thames in 1917—almost two years after he was born in a village just down the towpath. She asked him whether he thought their parents knew one another, and he suggested that perhaps they "visited each other by punt—pushing that long pole into the dark Thames water, lying side by side under the weeping willows."

"Do you think they swapped wives as well as punts? Are we really brother and sister?" Felicity asked.

"Why not?" Brion said. "Do you have a brother?"

"He was killed in the war," she told him. "Do you have a sister?"

"I did. She's dead."

Felicity recalled that Brion "turned his mysterious other-world eyes on me . . . [and] we looked at one another in silent recognition." At that moment, the British writer Peter Mayne (who was writing a vivid, somber memoir called *The Alleys of Marrakesh*) walked into the café and Brian introduced the two. "This is my sister," he told Mayne. "She's just arrived."

Brion and Felicity spent much of the next two months together. When he wasn't painting, he would take her on his little Italian motorcycle to the Agdal Gardens, where one could walk in the shade of olive trees and gaze into mirrorlike pools. At sunset, the two would rendezvous on the terrace of the Café de France with a clique of gay expatriates whom Brion had befriended. Felicity found them agreeable, and she was happy to listen to their war stories. Before long, she had snared a pair of young Arab lovers— "the heavenly twins," she called them—and could offer her own perspective on Moroccan men.

Moroccans, she discovered, considered European women to be a major challenge, but their lovemaking was marked by more energy than finesse. Not for them the subtle machinations of the French or the poetic murmurings of the Italians. "Moroccan men are extremely quick to pick it up when you're available—it's said that because of the veil they learn to read a woman's eyes," she said. "They're very passionate, but there's no real courtship period and very little foreplay. Women are very much sex objects for them—as far as they're concerned, they're there to be fucked and that's it. One's real life is spent among men."

By Felicity's account, Brion and his friends approved of the fact that she "lived as a gay man"—taking lover after lover without becoming emotionally entangled. To Brion, such behavior seemed *évolué,* since he believed that women were poised to devour any male whom they could entrap. As she was learning, her new friend harbored a voluptuous contempt for her kind, and it was the rare female who earned his admiration. Inspired by his mother, a zealous Catholic who raised her children alone after her husband died, Gysin's aversion to the opposite sex had blossomed into a gynephobia that he never troubled to conceal: Women were either harpies or Amazons, and the world would have been better off without them. William Burroughs—whose own misogyny paled beside Brion's—allowed that Gysin's thinking "[left] no room for compromise. . . . The whole concept of woman [was] a biological mistake."

Not that Brion avoided the creatures altogether. He confided to Felicity that he had had a brush with heterosexuality during his early twenties, when he was living in Greece, but that the affair had ended badly. Mad about the well-built blond artist, his Greek girlfriend had given him no rest. "He considered that he suffered a great deal at her hands," said Mason. "She very much chased him and he found that rather obsessive, and I think that terrified him. They were more or less engaged until Brion ran away from that situation." Later, he admitted that he could have been the father of her child—a boy who killed himself in early adulthood.

Gysin never repeated that sexual experiment, but he found it expedient to collect female admirers. Always short of money, he learned to use his mystique—and his "mysterious, other-world eyes"—to bedazzle anyone who would buy his paintings or bankroll his *folies.* "Although he said extremely rude things about women in general, there were many who did a great deal for him," Mason remembered.

Of course, not everyone was willing to look past his all-women-are-whores routine—or to succumb to Brion's legerdemain. Jane

Bowles—who had much in common with the melodramatic, manipulative Gysin—lost her taste for him early on. To her, he was just another Tangier con man besotted with mirages: "She thought he was a fake," said Paul.

By the beginning of 1954, Brion was back in Tangier, where he was transforming himself into an entrepreneur. Still obsessed with the Master Musicians of Jajouka, he had decided to open a restaurant that would serve as a forum for their music. "I said, 'I would like to hear [you play] every day,'" Brion remembered. "And they said, 'Well, why don't you just stick around in the village?' I [told them], 'No, that isn't possible. I have to go back and earn my living.' . . . They said, 'Well, then, why don't you open a little café . . . and we'll come down and make the music.'"

With the help of a few high-rollers and the prodigal Hamri, who was an inspired cook, Brion created a restaurant that he christened the 1001 Nights. Located in a narrow wing of the Menebhi palace on the Marshan, it was a stylish ode to Moroccan culture. Low tables were inlaid with brilliant tiles, banquettes were upholstered with fine native wools and elaborate lanterns with colored-glass panels threw a tremulous light on the sketches that Brion had done in the desert. The menu was burned into wooden schoolboy's tablets—*tagines, mechoui,* "black" couscous and *bisteeya,* the cinnamon-spiked pigeon pie, along with wines from North Africa's best vineyards. Every detail was authentic; even the sugary tea was brewed in the traditional silver pots and poured, burning hot, into glasses brimming with fresh mint.

The musicians from Jajouka held forth in the restaurant's main salon. Aside from playing its own songs, the five-man troupe pounded out accompaniment for the acrobats and fire eaters whom Hamri and Brion recruited as part of the spectacle. The final act was often a particularly agile dancing boy: As the musicians broke into a frenzied rhythm, the young performer would tear into the room, balancing on his head a large tray upon which were perched full tea-glasses and a lighted candle. Without touching the tray or spilling a drop, he would fly from one corner to the next, then stop and wriggle to the floor, where he managed to stretch out his body and make one full turn before coming to his feet again and bounding back into the wings, his burden miraculously intact.

In a hedonistic city where first-class restaurants prospered, Brion's Arabian Nights fantasy was a strong draw: Soon, he was able to boast that the coatroom was "stacked with minks" every evening. A born host and self-promoter, he knew precisely how to cultivate the parvenus to whom profligacy was an art; greeting them with a regal courtesy, he treated them as though they were guests in his own palazzo. Wealthy Tanjawis flocked to him, too, and the restaurant became one of the few spots where the Mountain set mingled with the Moroccan upper class. As skillfully as Brion played his role, however, he couldn't court the rich without striking the occasional note of perversity; he was capable of informing credulous expatriates that an uprising was expected later in the evening, and that anyone caught on the streets was likely to be torn to bits by a ravening mob.

Intrigue, of course, was an important part of Brion's life, and if his restaurant was a success, it was in spite of the sorcery and sabotage that went on behind the scenes. Later, he wrote that the 1001 Nights had been well named, "for some unforeseen, complex, cataclysmic catastrophe occurred every night." The domineering Hamri terrorized the staff and went to any lengths to get his hands on an extra dirham. Moroccan cooks and waiters went into jealous tirades about the musicians, who were Brion's houseguests. And Gysin himself was busy cutting his own throat: Fascinated with the magic practiced by his "Pan people," he had begun to keep covert notes for a book of spells—never suspecting that his treachery would be revealed and the magic used against him.

Chapter 10

Early in the winter of 1954, Brion Gysin found time to mount an exhibit of his work in the gallery of the Rembrandt Hotel. The haut-bourgeois establishment was right on the Boulevard Pasteur, and all manner of Tangerinos wandered in to have a look at his sketches of the Sahara. Just before closing time one afternoon, he found himself listening to a monologue delivered by the pallid junkie who had lately taken up residence in the medina—a man who, in his shiny business suit and greasy fedora, had the air of an FBI agent who had been drummed from the corps. Few expatriates knew his name, but to the wild boys who prowled his seedy neighborhood he was "El Hombre Invisible."

Brion had a horror of narcotics, and he was put off by the cryptic visitor. Later, he remembered that the man had "wheeled in . . . arms and legs flailing, looking very Occidental. He trailed long vines of Bannisteria Caapi from the Upper Amazon after him and old Mexican bullfight posters fluttered out from under his long trench coat instead of a shirt. An odd blue light often flashed under the brim of his hat. . . ." Pegging the man as a bottom feeder who had come to the International Zone for all the wrong reasons,

"Hamri and I decided, rather smugly, that we could not afford to know him," he wrote.

In fact, the newcomer was a well-bred midwesterner who had graduated from Harvard before embarking on his life as a renegade. At forty, William Seward Burroughs II was a laconic adventurer with a mordant wit and an attraction to all things forbidden. An eclectic scholar, he had immersed himself in anthropology, pharmacology and linguistics; studied medicine for a time in Vienna; and devoured the works of Kafka, Céline, Baudelaire, Gide, Rimbaud and Blake. He had just made a pilgrimage to South America in search of a hallucinogen called *yage,* and he had written a sprawling, painfully explicit book that chronicled his expeditions into the netherworld of drugs and depravity. Titled *Queer,* the second part of the two-volume book remained unpublished; but the first had been issued as a paperback called *Junky: Confessions of an Unredeemed Drug Addict.* Impelled by an indestructible urge to create, William had continued to rip out disjointed, farcical "routines," as he called them, but he wasn't convinced that he was a real writer. "I was," he said later, "a nobody."

Burroughs had always been haunted by the sense of being an outsider. The grandson of a clerk who had made his fortune by perfecting the adding machine, he was raised in comfort in St. Louis, where his family lived in a substantial brick townhouse and an English nanny tended to William and his older brother, Mortimer. Disdainful of new money, St. Louis society pegged the family as interlopers, and the furtive, remote William was regarded as a particular threat. Declared one neighbor, "I don't want that boy in the house again—he looks like a sheep-killing dog." Beset by nightmares and hallucinations, young William developed an unorthodox sensibility that was heavily influenced by his mother, a beautiful and cultivated neurasthenic who was fascinated with magic and extrasensory perception. A charming but melancholy woman, Laura Lee fostered William's belief in the unseen and passed along her own brooding sense of despair. Like any minister's child, she also tried to instill in William an abhorrence of bodily functions—an approach that only fueled his obsession with scatology. From his father, a remote but benevolent businessman, he acquired little save a sense of humor that often turned perverse.

Feeling himself to be an alien in the austere Midwest, William decided when he was eight that he wanted to become a writer. "Writers," he later explained, "were rich and famous. They lounged around Singapore and Rangoon smoking opium in yellow pongee silk suits. They sniffed cocaine in Mayfair and they penetrated forbidden swamps with a faithful native boy and lived in the native quarter of Tangier smoking hashish and languidly caressing a pet gazelle."

Outlaws and gangsters were the protagonists of his first short stories, and his infatuation with desperados never waned. In the aimless decade after he left Harvard, William turned himself into a maverick; drifting to Chicago, he worked as a bartender, an exterminator and, later, a private detective, and he surrounded himself with specimens who were straight from the pulps. He landed in New York in 1943 and fell in with Herbert Huncke, a Times Square hustler and drug addict who became his guide to the underworld. William paid for a fifteen-dollar-a-month tenement that Huncke turned into a den for petty thieves, and in return the drifter taught him to use morphine—an initiation that would lead straight into the inferno of addiction.

For all of his slumming and debauchery, the patrician Burroughs was no less an alien in the gutter than he had been in the Bible Belt. He needed to connect with other artistic spirits, to discuss Yeats and Auden and Spengler and Cocteau. With his black humor and rogue intelligence, he had no trouble making an impression on a coterie of creative apostates whom he encountered in 1943. Through David Kammerer, a wealthy fellow exile and childhood friend from St. Louis, William, then twenty-nine, met Allen Ginsberg and Jack Kerouac. At seventeen, the New Jersey–born Ginsberg was an inspired poet and rebellious jester; at twenty-one, Kerouac was a cerebral jock who already had spilled forth his first million words of fiction. Kerouac and Ginsberg became Burroughs's acolytes; but it was Joan Vollmer Adams—a strong-willed and alluring Columbia journalism student who was part of their circle—with whom he cast his fate.

Acute, irreverent, original, Joan shared William's interest in mind control and the Mayan codices as well as his attraction to drugs; her own favorite was speed, and she popped massive doses of Benzedrine. Early in 1946, the sexually adventurous twenty-two-year-old (then pregnant and separated from her husband) began living with the inscrutable William, whose contempt for rank-and-file females didn't prevent him from "experimenting with hetero-sexual amity," as Ginsberg described it. That summer, he left New York after being arrested for forging a prescription, and Joan and her infant daughter joined him when he headed for the hinterlands. Together, the two tried farming in east Texas—where William's primary crop was marijuana—and in Algiers, Louisiana, where Burroughs was arrested in 1949 for drug possession. Skipping bail, he took Joan (by then the mother of William S. Burroughs III) to Mexico City, where they eventually settled into an apartment on Orizaba Street. There, William shot morphine, the faded Joan steeped herself in drink, and the last threads of their fragile alliance began to unravel.

An expert marksman who spent hours at target practice, William brought along his revolver on the evening of September 6, 1951, when the unhappy pair went to a small party at the home of another American expatriate. Late in the gin-suffused evening, William announced that he was ready to do his "William Tell act" with his wife. The reckless Joan obligingly balanced her highball glass on her head, but the drunken stunt went hideously awry. Firing at close range, Burroughs somehow sent the bullet smashing into her brain, and she died without regaining consciousness.

To William, the tragedy had a demonic cast: "I thought myself to be controlled by this ugly spirit," he said of the shooting. "My whole life has been resistance to the ugly spirit." Charged with criminal "imprudence," he jumped bail and headed for Panama before moving on to New York to visit Allen. Desperate to lose himself in a romance, Burroughs pressed his protégé into sleeping with him, but the arrangement proved unsatisfactory for both: William required total devotion, and Allen—who was physically unin-spired by the bony, needle-scarred Burroughs—felt suffocated. Wounded by Allen's sexual rejection, William took flight once again. Somewhere along the way, he read both *The Sheltering Sky* and *Let It Come Down* (whose *majoun*-fueled murder scene had captured his imagination), and he decided that Tangier was a place where one could live precisely as he pleased. After a brief trip to Rome, then, he made his first trip to North Africa.

Arriving in time for the 1954 rainy season, with its chill gray skies and cheerless streets, Burroughs immediately installed himself in the most dispiriting lodgings he could find—a small, mildew-ridden brothel near the Socco Chico, where he paid fifty cents a day for a single room. The place was run by Anthony Reitshorst, a portly Dutch-born pimp who wore makeup and walked his five poodles *ensemble.* Everyone knew that Dutch Tony could arrange any sort of liaison one required, and that the house was the scene of many a sixty-minute dalliance. But William paid little mind to the endless parade of urchins and their pasty-white clients; still hounded by the narcotics habit that he had been trying to kick for years, he spent much of his time buying drugs at the *farmacia* or lying in his room, "sticking needle[s] . . . into the fibrous grey wooden flesh of terminal addiction," as he described it.

When the loneliness set in, Burroughs ventured into the tattier bars and cafés near the Socco Chico. Like a rogue anthropologist, he took pleasure in examining the city's human flotsam. Soon after his arrival, he wrote to Allen Ginsberg:

> Meeting the local expatriates. Junkies, queers, drunks, about like Mexico. Most of them came from someplace else for obvious reasons.
>
> Sample Tanger [*sic*] nocturne: Arrive in the Mar Chica, all-night bar where everybody goes after midnight. With me an Irish boy who left England after a spot of trouble, and a Portuguese who can't go home again. Both queer. Both ex-junkies. Both chippying with dollies[1] . . . Two Lesbians who work on a smuggling ship drunk at a table. Spanish work-men, queers, British sailors. [A drinking companion] seizes me and drags me to the bar, throwing an arm around my shoulder, and tightening his grip whenever I try to edge away. He gazes into my face, putting down a sincere routine. "Life is rotten, here, Bill. Rotten. It's the end of the world, Tanger. Don't you feel it, Bill?"

Burroughs quickly befriended David Woolman, an American journalist who also lived at Dutch Tony's and had a passing acquaintance with Paul Bowles. Eager to commune with other writers, he persuaded Woolman to take him around to see Paul. Stricken with paratyphoid that spring, Bowles was convalescing in a drafty room at the Massilia, a Spanish-run hotel where he was attended by Yacoubi, Temsamany, Jane (who had just returned from the States) and a pair of maids. The meeting lasted less than fifteen minutes; still bedridden, Paul received the two in his dressing gown, "evinc[ing] no cordiality," as Burroughs reported to Jack Kerouac.

For his part, Paul was unimpressed with the drug addict who came to see him on the pretext of asking advice. He had spotted him once or twice before, "passing along a back street in the rain," and noted that Burroughs "didn't look very fit." He wasn't particularly enthusiastic when "Woolman appeared with this gaunt undertaker," as he remembered it. "Burroughs had come because he wanted me to look at a contract for *Junky,*" Paul said. "He wanted to know what I thought, and I thought it was terrible. He'd already signed it, so there was no real point in asking me about it. There was a small advance, about five hundred dollars, and that was it."

After he recovered, Paul made no effort to get to know Burroughs. Nor did Brion, whom William saw on the rare occasions when he ventured out for dinner at the 1001 Nights. To Burroughs, Gysin seemed manipulative and remote; like Paul, he had an aura of impenetrability that William found both annoying and absurd. In one of his *kif*-inspired "routines," Burroughs described Brion (whom he called "Algren") as a "tall, broad-shouldered, handsome [man] with a cold, imperious manner. . . . As a fashionable restaurateur, Algren is superb, just the correct frequency of glacial geniality. . . . [He] doesn't have dime one, but he's a character who will get rich by acting like he is rich already. And Algren is crazy in a way that will help. He has a paranoid conceit. He is a man who never has one good word to say for anybody, and that's the way a man should be to run a fashionable night spot. Everyone will want to be the exception, the one person he really likes."

Burroughs was similarly caustic about Bowles. In an early letter to Allen, he portrayed Paul as a willing victim for the controlling Ahmed: "Paul Bowles is . . . kept in seclusion by an Arab boy who is insanely jealous and given to the practice of black magic," he reported. Later, in communiqués to Jack, he lampooned him as "Andrew Keif," a cold-blooded fake married to an eccentric named Miggles and attended by a chauffeur called Arachnid. In one letter, he wrote, "Miggles looked up at her husband. She sniffed sharply: 'Have you been rolling in carrion again?' she demanded. . . . 'Yes,' he said. . . . 'I have. *But,* believe it or not, I've been rolling in a dead *woman!* That's a good sign don't you think?' Like many homosexuals, Keif decided periodically that he wanted to be 'cured'. . . ."

In another letter to Kerouac, William offered up a Bowles-inspired riff that he claimed to have composed in an attempt to appeal to the mass market:

The only person in Interzone who is neither queer nor available is Andrew Keif's chauffeur, which is . . . a useful pretext to break off relations with anyone [Keif] doesn't want to see. "You made a pass at Arachnid last night. I can't have you to the house again." . . . Arachnid is the worst driver in the Zone. On one occasion he ran down a pregnant woman . . . with a load of charcoal on her back, and she miscarried . . . on the street, and Keif got out and sat on the curb stirring the blood with a stick while the police questioned Arachnid and finally arrested the woman.

Added Burroughs: "I can just see that serialized in *Cosmopolitan* or *Good Housekeeping.* I mean it's hopeless, Jack. I can't write in a popular vein."

Burroughs returned to the subject of Paul's rejection like a child worrying a scab: In the summer, he wrote to Allen, "It has occurred to me that Bowles perhaps wishes to avoid contact with me because of my narcotic associations, fearing possible hassles with . . . authorities in general if he is known to be on familiar terms with me." To Jack, he wrote: "[Paul] invites the dreariest queens in Tangier to tea, but has never invited me, which, seeing how small the town is, seems like a deliberate affront. . . . It may well be that he is himself engaged in some sort of illegal currency operations—like many solid citizens of Tangier—and does not want anybody tracking heat into his trap."

*   *   *

If Burroughs had harbored any romantic notions about Tangier, they evaporated in the face of his loneliness. He branded Arabs as bores who "[sat] around smoking cut weed and playing some silly card game." To Allen, he wrote, "Don't ever fall for this inscrutable oriental shit like Bowles puts down. They are just a gabby, gossipy, simple minded, lazy crew of citizens. . . ." As for the Mountain set, he observed that it fairly throbbed with hypocrisy and hauteur. On a visit to Dean's Bar with Kells Elvins, a dashing boyhood friend who lived in Rome, the wraithlike Burroughs "encountered a barrage of hostility" from the barkeep—who, of course, was rumored to be an opium addict himself. "Dean wanted not to serve me," he wrote, ". . . but there was Kells, a good customer. . . . So I sat there, loaded on tea, savoring [his] disapproval, rolling it on my tongue with [a] glass of good dry sherry." Later, he reported to Allen that "Tanger is a marrowbone conventional town. . . . No snotty uptown fags can compare with these for utter, pretentious, insincere, inhuman snobishness [sic]." Wrote Burroughs, "Jane Bowles asks people, 'Who are you?'. . . . Surrounded by these monsters, I feel understandably alone and frightened."

William's sense of isolation was exacerbated by his longing for Allen. Time and distance had not diminished his desire for the young poet, who—despite the "disturbance of erotic rapport," as Ginsberg put it—was still the most important figure in his life. For Burroughs, the flight to Tangier had been, in part, an attempt to demonstrate to Allen that he was an invincible adventurer who could live—and flourish—in a sphere where the sensitive Ginsberg might have foundered. Allen, however, not only refused to be chastised but made his own four-month pilgrimage to Mexico before landing in San Francisco, where he would "shack up with a fellow worker girl in the market research and advertising world of Nob Hill"—an exercise in heterosexual respectability that, as Allen admitted, "appeared as a terrible affront to Bill's hope of marriage of heart and soul with me." When weeks went by without a letter, the desperate William sent out a plea to Jack Kerouac, asking him to petition Allen to "write me a fix." Wrote Burroughs, "Tell Allen I plead guilty to vampirism and other crimes against life, but I love him, and nothing cancels love."

Although the renegade found much to complain about in "Interzone," as he called it, he also found reasons not to move on. The Spanish-influenced city was pleasantly familiar to a traveler who knew Mexico and South America, and the police were far less troublesome than the *federales*. Burroughs was pleased with Tangier's hilly medina, where one caught sight of something new on every outing, and he liked the windy bay, where he sometimes went rowing. Living on a two-hundred-dollar-a-month allowance from Mortimer and Laura Lee, he could easily pay for drugs, street boys, Spartan quarters and four-course meals in good French restaurants—"snails to Camembert for $1," as he wrote to Allen. (Later, Paul noted: "[Burroughs] spends more money on food than most of us other Tangerines. Perhaps he has more to spend—I don't know—but the fact remains that he insists on eating well, which is part of his insistence upon living just as he likes at all times.")

Opiates, of course, came straight from the *farmacia,* and William's life was infinitely simpler than it had been in the days when he had been forced to stalk the alleys of Mexico City looking for his next fix. "There was none of that nonsense about going to a pusher," he said. "You couldn't get morphine or heroin, but you could buy the equivalent over the counter. I found injectable methadone, which is almost as strong as heroin, and a preparation known as Eukodyl, which was a dehydrated [form of] codeine. It was one of many variations on the morphine formula which were rejected in other countries because it was too euphoric, too enjoyable. Well, they had a lot of this stuff in a warehouse somewhere, and I slowly bought out the batch." William also stocked up on dollies, which he used when he was trying to cut down on opiates, and sampled the local cannabis. Unlike Eukodyl, which dulled his wit, *majoun* inspired wild flights of creativity, and he learned to take it before facing a blank page.

But if buying drugs was easy enough, controlling his habit was another matter. Burroughs had been addicted to narcotics for eight years, and he had subjected himself to every cure he could devise. Nothing worked for long, and by May 1954 he was shooting Eukodyl every two hours. Crippled by depression and paranoia, desperate to kick, he paid an impecunious Englishman named Eric Gifford to hide his clothes, bring in food and ration out dollies until he had weaned himself from Eukodyl. On the second day, however, Burroughs managed to steal clothes from David Woolman and dash off to the *farmacia,* where he bought enough Eukodyl for a fine binge. When Gifford found out, he forced Burroughs to turn over both his stash and his money and warned Woolman to start locking his door. "By God," he told William, "I'm being paid to do it and I'm going to do it right."

William made it through the ten-day cure, but by summertime he was back on Eukodyl. Rheumatic fever set in, and he was bedridden for a time when a secondary infection invaded his ankle. In his illness, he was attended by a sweet-tempered Spanish boy called Kiki, who had become his lover. Although Burroughs had kept him on the line with money and gifts, the loyal Kiki continued to attend his feverish patron when a check from home was lost and he was forced to exist on bread and tea. In dispatches to the distant Allen, Burroughs rhapsodized about their relationship: "Kiki and I spent one of our delightful afternoons today, lying on the bed naked, dozing and making desultory love, smoking a little *kif* and eating great, sweet grapes. What a tranquil, healthy young male he is. There doesn't seem to be a conflict in him. . . . As you say, he is a dream for which I will have nostalgia."

As self-absorbed as he was, William also was aware that political tensions were mounting as the summer wore on. It pleased him to think that the medina might erupt at any moment: As the anniversary of the Sultan's kidnapping approached, he reported to Allen that he had invented two weapons—one, a lead pipe on a short length of cord, and the other, a flit gun full of ammonia—to use "in case a mob tries to force [its] way into the house." He lamented, "And me caught without a pistol the one time in my life I really need one! If only I had my curare at least I could buy game darts and smear them with [the poison]. . . . As it is, I bought a meat-cleaver and a razor sharp knife." Added Burroughs, "They have a hundred troops in readiness, and the police are armed with submachine guns. They would likely be as much a menace to us as to the Arabs, when they start spraying bullets around these narrow streets that all lead around in a circle. You could fire a bullet in one side of the Kasbah and it would ricochet around corners and come out the other end." Even if Tangier failed to give Burroughs a sense of belonging, then, it offered him the promise of macabre thrills.

Chapter 11

Paul Bowles was extracting the most from the foreboding situation. After he recovered from typhoid, he had hurried with Yacoubi and Temsamany to Fez, where, in the wake of two assassination attempts on ben Arafa, the French secret police were conducting a vendetta against the outlawed Istiqlal. Aside from waging war against the French and the Glaoui's Berber tribesmen, terrorist societies like the Black Hand were assassinating countrymen who were suspected of colluding with their enemies. No one, it seemed, was safe.

Expecting to see a city in upheaval, Bowles had not been disappointed: Even before they arrived, Temsamany had been forced to pull the Jaguar to the side of the road to allow French tanks and armored cars to rumble by. In Fez, they had seen more tanks stationed outside the ancient walls at Bab Feteuch. Later, Paul wrote: "A startling change had come over the city. Each day the newspapers published lists of the previous day's atrocities. No one knew where the next dead body would be found or whose body it would prove to be. The faces of passersby in the streets showed only fear, suspicion and hostility."

In letters to friends overseas, Bowles played the scenario for all it was worth. From Tangier, he wrote to John Lehmann, his British publisher: "Political disagreements here have now reached the point where every two nights or so a policeman is murdered in the streets. . . . No one minds so much. Except perhaps the French, who don't want a word about the situation (save what they themselves send out) to reach the outside world. But they are being extremely difficult these days; they all have the jitters and one can't talk calmly with them. Their famous logic has grown astigmatic. . . ."

Even personal news was punctuated with deliciously ominous asides; in another letter to Lehmann, Paul reported casually, "Ahmed is on his way to market to buy food for a dinner he is going to prepare this evening in the Casbah for David Herbert and Oliver Messel and some others. . . . Did I tell you that Peter Mayne was wounded by a hand grenade while he was sitting at the Cafe de France in Marrakech? . . . Jane missed it by a stroke of luck; then she went on to Fez where a bomb went off in the post office the day she arrived. . . . The place is a mess."

Paul used the continuing drama as a springboard when, in the summer of 1954, he began to write another novel—this one to be called *The Spider's House*. [1] From the beginning, he had intended to set the story in Fez, the city where tradition had held sway for so long. Like the rest of Morocco, however, the ancient capital already had been shaken to its roots, and Paul soon realized that even the nationalists were cold to the notion of preserving the place. Instead of restoring the country to its precolonial state of innocence, it seemed, they were interested only in making it more "progressive" after expelling the hated French. Aware that he was witnessing the end of an epoch, he saw that he would have to write "not about the traditional pattern of life in Fez, but about its dissolution."

Taking a house on the edge of a cliff at Sidi Bouknadel, Paul woke each day at dawn and wrote until noon. The complex story that he was crafting centered on three disparate characters caught up in the struggle for independence. In the beginning of the book, he focused on a fifteen-year-old Moroccan who seemed to have been modeled, in part, on Yacoubi. Through Amar, a cherif with a gift for healing, Bowles explored a world that was about to be destroyed—a place in which Allah reigns supreme, and where one accepts fate as it is written. Warned against both the infidels and the nationalists by his father (a holy man who beats him to drive home his lessons) and strong-armed by boys who have joined the Istiqlal, Amar is a stoic who struggles to preserve his integrity. Pious, intelligent, intuitive, he realizes that he is surrounded by corruption, and that he must walk a fine line to avoid being tainted.

Amar loses his footing, however, when he is taken up by a pair of Nazarenes—John Stenham, a successful novelist, and Lee Burroughs Veyron,[2] a glamorous American who settled in Paris after divorcing her French husband. A New Englander who has lived in Fez for five years, Stenham is fascinated with the great medieval city, and he knows that it is doomed. The relentlessly unsentimental Lee, a new arrival who becomes his lover, argues that Moroccan culture is obsolete and that the country should be roused from its slumber. Unlike Stenham, who has mastered Moghrebi, she has scarcely spoken to a native who is not a servant.

Sitting together in a café one afternoon, Lee and John strike up a conversation with the wary Amar. Suddenly, the three are interrupted by the growing roar of an approaching Arab mob, which is storming through the quarter. In a bloody instant, the French police have turned their machine guns on the demonstrators and Berber soldiers have fanned out through the streets, searching for anyone who looks like a dissident. Offering to shelter Amar in their hotel until the melee is over, the Americans slip him past the soldiers. Driven from that refuge the next day, when police conduct a *ratissage*[3] and the hotel is closed, they retreat into the countryside, and Amar comes along.

In the hills, the three share a journey in which they are forced to confront a series of unpleasant truths about the troubled country. For Amar—who loses his sense of superiority and forms an attachment to the Nazarenes he once loathed—their three-day trip is an odyssey. For Stenham and Veyron, however, the journey is merely an adventure. When it ends, they move on to Casablanca, and they refuse to take along their young comrade. No longer certain of his place in the world, Amar must return to his besieged home and struggle with a sense of hopelessness. In the end, wrote Paul, the boy felt "supremely deserted, exquisitely conscious of his own weakness and insignificance. His gift meant nothing; he was not even sure that he had any gift, or ever had had one. The world was something different from what he had thought it. . . ."

Bowles wrote quickly—perhaps because in his words, his subject was "decomposing before my eyes, hour by hour, and there was no alternative to recording the process of violent transformation." In his correspondence, he spoke about the sense of unease that reached even to Tangier. On August 24, he wrote to his friend Oliver Evans:

Everybody was expecting difficulties between the Aïd el-Kebir and the Anniversary of the Sultan's deposition. Personally I think you were fortunate not to have come at this time. Everyone is in a foul temper, people are throwing stones at my house and screaming, Nazarene! (No one answers but the parrot, who gives wolf calls, laughs like a hysterical old maid, and then caws like a flock of crows.) It isn't even amusing for the Arabs, who want nothing more than to see great bloodshed, and spend their time moping around the house engaging in hunger strikes and ripping pictures of Mendès-France[4] out of the papers, after which they either spit on them or, which is more likely, put them into their mouths and chew them up, grinding the saliva-soaked paper between their teeth until it's nothing but paste. It's not amusing because it's not going anywhere and can never [accomplish] anything.

The country escaped an outbreak of violence on the anniversary itself, but the month of August was a tumultuous one. In Fez, nineteen people died in demonstrations set off by rumors that the deposed ben Youssef was on his way back from Madagascar; days later, twenty-five hundred French legionnaires occupied the medina and arrested 135 suspected terrorists. In Port Lyautey, eleven people were killed and more than thirty were injured in riots that erupted when Moroccan police attempted to force owners to reopen shops closed in compliance with an Istiqlal strike order; afterwards, three thousand Arabs were detained for questioning. Twenty people were injured in a bomb explosion near Casablanca, where an Istiqlal member was assassinated and terrorists murdered at least five people, including a pro-French Moroccan and a French bureaucrat.

The drama was heightened by the rising tension between the French and their Spanish rivals. Outraged by the removal of the Sultan, General Franco had announced that Spain would not recognize the authority of ben Arafa; the Spanish Zone, he declared, would retain the leadership of Caliph Hassan el-Mehdi, who was loyal to ben Youssef. Officials in the Spanish Protectorate asked Madrid to separate Spanish territory from the rest of Morocco, and they began to make it difficult for travelers to move from their zone into the French Protectorate. In Tetuán (where ben Youssef's picture was still displayed in shops) anti-French propaganda was broadcast daily, and demonstrators massed to demand the Sultan's return.

While the French were standing firm on the issue of bringing ben Youssef back from exile, there were signs that they would be forced to make concessions to their critics. Aside from Franco's wrath, they faced strong opposition from the Arab League, which was backing the struggle for independence in Algeria and Tunisia. In mid-August, then, Paris ordered a search for a new Sultan, one who would be acceptable to both French and Moroccan leaders. Later that month, the French National Assembly approved a plan for eventual self-rule for Morocco. It was a step forward, but much of the bloodshed was yet to come.

For Jane Bowles, the summer of 1954 was an unproductive one. She had left America feeling dispirited; *In the Summer House* had closed in February after less than two months on Broadway, and although the play had garnered high praise from supporters (including Tennessee and Truman), many reviewers had found it vague. A moody, morbid comedy that focused on a pair of painfully neurotic mothers and their odd-duck daughters, it explored their claustrophobic relationships in a way that made one character seem more off-putting than the next. Even the *Times*'s Brooks Atkinson, who admired Jane's work, had tempered his praise with criticism. "Scene by scene her play is original, exotic and adventuresome, but very little of it survives the final curtain," he wrote. "From the literary point of view it is distinguished. . . . But when [it] is finished it leaves [one] . . . with a feeling of flatness about the whole play, as if the total achievement were unequal to the labor and talent involved." In a postmortem interview with *Vogue,* Jane had said that she took little comfort in the fact that *In the Summer House* had been wildly popular among a small group of theatergoers. "There's no point in writing a play for your five hundred goony friends," she said. "You have to reach more people."

After nursing Paul through his illness, she had settled into the little house in the Casbah and tried to conquer her paralysis. But as he worked steadily on his own novel, she drank and agonized about her inability to move forward. In America, she had written a fragment of a new play, and she was trying desperately to begin another. Instead of bringing a new work to life, however, she was filling her leather-bound notebook with musings about her own state. "Is it writing I'm putting off, or was it always something else—a religious sacrifice? The only time I wrote well, when I passed through the inner door, I felt guilt," she wrote. "I must find that [door] again. If I can't, maybe I shall find a way to give it up. I cannot go on this way."

Ironically, Jane did manage to write long dispatches to friends, and in them she made herself sound like the heroine of a comic novel. To Katharine Hamill and Natasha von Hoershelman, New Yorkers who had just visited her, she reported that she had

> kept out of the David [Herbert] life very successfully except on occasion. . . . The ex-Marchioness of Bath [Daphne Fielding] is here for the moment (married her lover, Mister Fielding, a charming man). I went to a dinner party for her in slacks—a thing that I did not do on purpose. . . . [Later I met] a pitch black boy called George Broadfield who called himself "The New American Negro," and attached himself to me and Paul. I liked him but almost went mad because he was determined to stay in Tangier and thought nothing of talking for seven or eight hours in a row. I told him he should go and live where there were other artists because there were so few of them here. (He himself is a young writer, or is going to be??) He said that Paul and I were enough for him and I was horrified. . . .

In the same letter, Jane offered a rambling account of a picnic with Tetum, Temsamany and a company of "laundry bundles" at a saint's tomb outside the city. When tea was ready, she reported, Tetum and her friends

> sat down and lowered their veils so that they hung under their chins like ugly bibs. They had bought an excellent sponge cake. As usual something sweet. I thought: "Romance here is impossible." Tetum's neighbors were ugly. One in particular. "Like a turtle," Temsamany said. She kept looking down into her lap. Tetum, the captain of the group, said to the turtle: "Look at the world, look at the world." "I am looking at the world," the other woman said, but she kept looking down into her lap. They cut up all the sponge cake. I said: "Stop! Leave it. We'll never eat it all." Temsamany said, "I'm going to roller skate." He went off and we could see him through the trees. After a while the conversation stopped. Even Tetum was at a loss. There was a little excitement when they spotted the woman who runs the toilets under the grain market, seated not far off with a group . . . but nothing else happened. I went to look for Temsamany on the highway. He had roller skated out of sight. I felt that all my pursuits here were hopeless. I looked back over my shoulder into the grove. Tetum was swinging upside down from an olive tree her knees hooked over a branch, and she is, after all, forty five and veiled and a miser.

To Katharine and Natasha, Jane made no mention of her anxiety over the growing bond between Paul and Ahmed. She had never forgiven Yacoubi for wounding Paul, and she had felt shut out when the two moved into the cliffside house together. Despite her discomfort, she usually betrayed her feelings only in cryptic pronouncements like "Eccch, Yacoubi—he has no eyes." "She spoke very little of [her relationship] with Paul," remembered Yvonne Gerofi, who, with her sister-in-law Isabelle, was among Jane's closest confidantes. "She spoke of Paul's needs, of the salad and chicken she had to cook for Paul, but that was all."

Instead of turning to her friends for comfort, Jane countered by renewing her efforts to seduce Cherifa. Still holding court in the grain market, the Berber woman was parceling out chaste kisses that only fueled Jane's frustration. The entire game, she reported, was exquisitely complex: "It's so hard to know what is clever maneuvering on her part, what is a lack of passion, and what is fear—just plain fear of losing all her marketable value and that I won't care once I've had her," she wrote to Katharine and Natasha.

> She asked for five thousand pesetas so that she could fill her grain stall to the brim. I have given her, so far, fifteen hundred pesetas. . . . I find her completely beautiful. A little smaller than myself but with strong shoulders, strong legs with a great deal of hair on them. At the same time soft soft skin—and twenty-eight years old. Last night we went up on the topmost terrace and looked at all of Tangier. The boats and the stars and the long curved line of lights along the beach. There was a cold wind blowing and Cherifa was shivering. I kissed her just a little. Later downstairs she said the roof was very beautiful, and she wondered whether or not God had seen us. . . .

Added Jane: "I wish to Christ you were here. I can talk to Paul and he is interested but not that interested because we are all women."

In the summer of 1954, Jane prevailed upon Cherifa to begin staying overnight with her, but the struggle wasn't over. Cherifa was a controlling presence, and she continued to press her benefactor for money—even though Jane (whose finances were separate from Paul's) had little to spare. At the same time, Jane played host to a cadre of her friends whom Paul, at least, thoroughly disliked: One was the proprietor of a whorehouse; another, the wife of a well-known mobster. "Cherifa knew a lot of people," said Bowles. "She had a whole group of Moroccan women, and they used to meet, rather like a club. Temsamany told me some of them were retired prostitutes. Whether that's true, I don't know." In any case, the cabal consumed Jane's liquor and, of course, created an atmosphere that made writing all but impossible. Angst-ridden and unhappy, she began lecturing Cherifa about her own drinking—treating her not as a lover but as a child.

Jane's friend Christopher Wanklyn occasionally witnessed their standoffs. "Jane and Cherifa and I traveled together after I bought my first used car," he said. "Once, we were starting off for Rabat and Jane said, 'Ask Cherifa if she's been to the bathroom. I'm not speaking to her.' I said I'd do no such thing," said Wanklyn, who was amused by the display. "I don't know what they fought about—one or the other would get drunk, I suppose, if they didn't get drunk together. They'd fight about that; they fought about food and I suppose they fought about money."

Most of Jane's friends were horrified by Cherifa. "I hated her," said Yvonne Gerofi. "She was like a beast. So rough, like a rock. She never smiled. Always very severe, always looking like she hates us." But the Gerofis never saw the spats: "In front of Cherifa, Jane was very respectful," said Yvonne. "Alone with us, when she came to our house, she [would] telephone a lot to Cherifa at home; she would get up just to say, 'I'm here and I'm thinking of you.' "

To those who knew her well, Jane's continuing fascination with Cherifa seemed perverse but entirely in character. Again and again, she had professed to be in love with creatures whom her friends found unbearable. "I think she unconsciously thought of them all as material, although she would have said, 'Certainly not,' " said Paul. "She had to have the normal [friends] to describe the freaks to; otherwise, they wouldn't have been of any interest. She would tell them [about her crushes] and they would say, 'Jane! you're out of your mind. You don't mean it. You're not serious.' " Added David Herbert, "Janie always pretended to fall in love with someone she was quite incapable of getting—that was half the joke."

For all of their shock value, Jane's dalliances almost never involved fulfilling sexual experiences. Not that she didn't care about lovemaking: "When she was with us, she wanted to talk always of food and sex," remembered Isabelle Gerofi. But her affairs always seemed to be conceptual, rather than emotional, and physical passion was seldom part of the scenario. In the mid-sixties, Jane confessed to Isabelle and her sister-in-law that she had found satisfaction with only one partner—a wellborn (and unorthodox) British novelist with whom she had been involved a few years earlier.

Given Jane's peculiar set of requirements, then, Cherifa "couldn't have been better for her," as Paul observed. The brusque, hard-drinking peasant woman was nothing if not original, and Jane delighted in repeating tales about her and her family. "There was a constant discussion of Cherifa's friends and relations," said Wanklyn. "One of Jane's favorites was a cousin who was a house-breaker and highwayman who rode around on a motorcycle, disguised in women's clothes." Said Lyn Austin, who became close to Jane when *In the Summer House* was in production, "When she spoke about Cherifa, it was in comic terms as a domineering Moroccan ordering her about. Her affairs were all like that, and that's why they never seemed very interesting or very important—they were just little sideshows."

Still, Jane's ability to put Cherifa in perspective went only so far. A schemer who knew how to trigger Jane's acute sense of guilt, Cherifa was able to control her to an astonishing degree. "Later, Jane said, 'I consider her my daughter.' She said she felt a great responsibility for *poor* Cherifa," remembered Paul. "She was afraid Cherifa would become a freak because she'd been taken out of the grain market. She had tried for years to get her out, then she finally did and felt guilty. But Jane felt guilty about everything."

It was just after Cherifa began staying with Jane that she sparked a rift between the Bowleses. Although Paul tolerated her in the beginning, she and Ahmed disliked one another on sight. "When Ahmed met Cherifa he was terrified of her. And Cherifa was contemptuous of him because he lived with me," said Paul. Fiercely possessive, she became jealous whenever Jane had a polite conversation with Yacoubi (or, for that matter, when she spoke to another Moroccan on the street). She also was envious because Ahmed had earned money selling his paintings, and she knew that Jane had helped him.

The turning point came when Jane found bundles of *tseuheur* beneath her pillow and her mattress. Used in the practice of black magic, the little packets contained excreta including dried menstrual blood, fingernail clippings and pubic hair. Such amulets were believed to be extraordinarily powerful, and even the most sophisticated Moroccans found them unsettling. When Ahmed heard about Jane's discovery, it confirmed his belief that Cherifa was a witch who intended to poison Jane. From that point on, he refused to go to her house, and he tried to persuade Bowles to stay away as well. "He wouldn't go near her," said Paul. "He thought she wanted to kill us all."

While Jane herself had confided to Truman Capote that Cherifa "tries very seriously to poison me at least every six months," she scoffed at Ahmed's warning. Saying that Cherifa couldn't possibly be plotting to harm her, she told friends that Yacoubi was trying to wrest Paul away by claiming to be afraid of her lover. "She didn't care whether Yacoubi came to her house, but she minded very much that he thought I shouldn't go there," said Paul. "I did stay away—not because I was afraid of Cherifa but because I was trying to humor Ahmed."

During the summer, at least, the Bowleses continued to see each other at Paul's house, and Jane and Yacoubi managed to be civil in spite of the tension. "Jane behaved perfectly naturally, and so did Ahmed," said Bowles. "He still liked her well enough, but he thought she was under Cherifa's power—that she was like a zombie. That was partly true," he said. "She was [mesmerized]."

By the fall, however, the détente was crumbling. "Janie didn't say much to us, but we knew she was anguished about Yacoubi," said Isabelle Gerofi. "She [worshiped] Paul, and she was very jealous." Afraid that she had finally lost her husband to Yacoubi, she began arguing that Paul should be more discreet about their relationship. There was no need, she said, to stroll with him in the Ville Nouvelle or to take him along when they went to restaurants.

Tumbling into a depression, Jane began to drink even harder—a perilous move, since she suffered from high blood pressure and took medication that was dangerous in combination with alcohol. She found little solace in her relationship with Cherifa; unable to write, estranged from Paul, she felt herself in danger of losing everything that mattered. Years later, her friend Charles Gallagher observed, "I always thought of Paul and Jane as being like two twisted cypress trees that had become entwined. . . . Her life wouldn't have had any meaning if she hadn't had him. And perhaps his writing wouldn't have had any meaning if he hadn't had her to outshine."

As Tangier's winter storms were setting in, Paul decided to return to Ceylon. After his last expedition, he had arranged to buy Taprobane, the tiny island near Weligama that he had visited with Yacoubi. To his mind, it was a perfect retreat: The weather was brutally hot and humid, and the place itself was wonderfully primitive; at low tide, visitors simply waded in from the mainland. An elaborate octagonal structure positioned on a low rise and surrounded by a snake-infested forest, the island's single house had neither running water nor electricity, and it offered little in the way of privacy; it was dominated by a sprawling sala with carved pillars and a thirty-foot ceiling, and a cluster of curtained alcoves served as bedrooms. After darkness fell, bats with long teeth and three-foot wing spans invaded the garden, and the sala was cloaked in shadow.

Ahmed, of course, was to be his traveling companion, and Paul decided that Jane should make the trip as well. Anxious to please, she agreed—even though she disliked tropical climates, was mortally afraid of snakes and felt displaced by her husband's lover. Just before the party sailed for Colombo, Paul wrote to David McDowell: "[Jane] hates the idea [of the trip], but she's going along anyway, just to have something concrete to object to."

Bowles and his retinue—which included Jane, Ahmed and Temsamany—arrived in Weligama a few days after Christmas, 1954. "When she saw the island of Taprobane there in front of her, a mere tuft of rain forest rising out of the sea, [Jane] groaned," Paul remembered. "We waded across and climbed onto the jetty. A newspaper photographer from the *Times of Ceylon* snapped our pictures as we did so. Then we came to the gate, and she looked up the long series of stairways through the unfamiliar vegetation, toward the invisible house. 'It's a Poe story,' she said, shrugging. 'I can see why you'd like it.' "

To Jane, the place was a horror—an isolated outpost that was simultaneously tedious and threatening. Paul, who was writing the final chapters of *The Spider's House,* fell to work immediately, but she found it impossible to concentrate. With Temsamany, she made an expedition to Colombo in search of liquor; when they returned, she drank heavily to ward off the guilt and the pain and the terror. Peggy Guggenheim came to Taprobane after they had been on the island for about a month, and she found Jane in a pathetic state; her hair had begun to fall out by the handful, and she was depressed and hysterical by turns. Said Guggenheim, "I think she was having a nervous breakdown."

In many ways, it was a replay of the drama that had been enacted in Fez in 1948, when the panicky Jane had become obsessed with the notion that something was wrong with her heart. After that episode, she had written the anguished letter to Paul about her frustration over "my failure to like (in Africa) what you do and to like what you do at all anywhere." Now, in Ceylon, she was going through the same torment, and Paul was reacting precisely as he had earlier—by focusing his attention on his work, and on Yacoubi. Later, she told her friend Charles Gallagher that Paul had been distinctly unsympathetic when she told him that she thought she was losing her mind. By her account, he simply looked up from his manuscript and said, "I think you are, too, but I wish you'd go crazy in a less expensive place."

By February, Jane's fears—of isolation, of being blocked, of being stranded with a seemingly indifferent Paul—had won out over her sense of duty. Late that month, she sailed for Gibraltar with Temsamany, and there was an air of defeat about her departure. When she wrote to Paul from Tangier, the sense of failure was still palpable: She had "hit bottom" after leaving, she said, and the voyage home had been "a nightmare to the end because it was the twin of the other trip I might have made with you."

In her desperate state, Jane was ill equipped to deal with the problems that were waiting for her in Morocco. She had neglected to pay taxes on the money she had received for *In the Summer House,* and a notice from the tax collector had sent her straight to bed, convinced that she was on the brink of penury. The next day, she had tried to conquer the hysteria, but her head had been "pounding with blood-pressure symptoms." Friends, she claimed, had offered little in the way of support; aside from Phyllis della Faille—who had had given her a blue bead "to ward off the evil eye"—no one seemed to realize how fragile she felt. "[They] think I am mad, and that I should write or live on you, or both," she informed Paul. "It is not easy to make friends take my plight seriously. Not easy at all, unless I were to say that I was starving to death, which would be shameful and untrue." Writing, she reported, was no easier in Tangier than it had been in Ceylon. "I am terrified of beginning to work," she told him, " . . . but I must."

To Jane, Tangier itself seemed to be deteriorating, and she interpreted the decline as a pathetic fallacy. In the days after she returned, a sewer line had ruptured and a flood of chemicals had been dumped into the sea, triggering a stench that permeated the entire Casbah. "I thought I alone could smell it, and it was like the madness I had been living in . . . a special punishment for me, for my return," she told Paul, adding, "There is a terrible depression [here]. . . . Hotels empty, the Massilia closing, and ten people waiting for every job. . . . The Socco in the afternoon is mostly filled with old clothes. . . . Brion's restaurant is the only thing that does business in town."

In fact, the escalating political turmoil had taken its toll on Tangier's economy. The city's reputation as a haven for investors had been tarnished by the 1952 riots, when it became clear that the once-secure International Zone was not immune to violence. Tension between Tanjawis and their European neighbors (who now were outnumbered by five to one) had been mounting ever since, and the visa war between France and Spain had made it difficult to move about. Wealthy tourists and ambitious settlers no longer arrived on every ship, and an uneasy silence had descended upon the Ville Nouvelle, where hotels stood empty and half-finished buildings had been abandoned. Although smuggling was still profitable, the port had lost the frenzied quality that it had acquired during the boom years. Even moneychanger's row had been all but obliterated; European currencies were becoming less fickle, and the free money market was no longer a draw.

For his part, William Burroughs felt inspired by the slump. Back at Dutch Tony's after a trip to Palm Beach (where Laura Lee and Mortimer were raising his motherless son), he was constructing an anarchic novel based on what he saw around him—a tattered, corrupt city where all the rules had been suspended. "Interzone" was an unholy hybrid—a debauched crossroads populated by rapacious natives, pathetic poseurs, failed dreamers and migratory predators, each one desperate to start a new life. Dazzled by the mirage, Burroughs's fugitives would fail to see that the place was moribund, and that, like the city itself, they would fall victim to entropy. In an early essay called "International Zone," he noted, "Tanger [*sic*] is running down like the dying universe, where no movement is possible because all energy is equally distributed."

Complaining to Ginsberg about his "deplorable" financial state, Burroughs sent along odd bits like "International Zone," which he hoped could be sold to a magazine. ("Perhaps *New Yorker:* 'Letter from Tangier,' " he suggested.) In that piece, as well as in essays like "In the Cafe Central," he proved that his long years in a junk fog had not diminished his powers of observation. A passage that centered on a social climber named Morton—a living cliché who provided endless entertainment for the vultures who watched him from their café tables—would have sounded credible to anyone who had ever spent an evening in the Parade: "[Morton] twisted in hideous convulsions of ingratiation, desperate as he saw every pitiful attempt fail flatly, often shitting in his pants with fear and excitement," wrote Burroughs.

> Morton's attempts to please socially prominent residents and visiting celebrities, ending usually in flat failure, or a snub in the Cafe Central, attracted a special sort of scavenger who feeds on the humiliation and disintegration of others. These decayed queens never tired of retailing the endless saga of Morton's social failures.
>
> So he sat right down with Tennessee Williams on the beach, and Tennessee said to him: "I'm not feeling well this morning, *Michael.* I'd rather not talk to anybody." *Michael!* Doesn't even know his name! And he says, "Oh, yes, Tennessee is a good friend of mine!" And they would laugh, and throw themselves around and flip their wrists, their eyes glowing with loathsome lust.

Characters like Morton, of course, were not alone in their pathos, and Burroughs found dozens of variations on the theme simply by looking around him. There was Chris, the public-school man; a penniless British expatriate who had "lost all his savings in a bee-raising venture in the West Indies"; he was "carefully shunned by the Jaguar-driving set, who fear[ed] contagion. . . ."

There was Robbins, a whining mooch who claimed that a "perfidious Australian" had stolen both his money and his wife; with his
cruelly deformed hands and a face like that of "a Cockney informer," he "look[ed] like some unsuccessful species of Homo non
sapiens, blackmailing the human race with his existence." And of
course there was Burroughs—a wellborn pariah who skewered
snobs in the privacy of his dank room. In an early routine, William
re-created his own expedition to a fashionable bar—a place much
like Dean's, where one could sense the "miasma of suspicion and
snobbery" that pervaded the European quarter, and where junkies
were distinctly unwelcome. "I started conversation with a man on
my right," he reported.

> He answered my questions in cautious, short sentences,
> carefully deleting any tinge of warmth or friendliness.
> "Did you come here direct from the States?" I persisted.
> "No. From Brazil."
> *He's warming up,* I thought. I expected it would take two
> sentences to elicit that much information.
> "So? And how did you come?"
> "By yacht, *of course.*"
> I felt that anything would be an anticlimax after that,
> and allowed my shaky option on his notice to lapse.

Despite his progress, Burroughs felt himself to be in an impossible situation. He found little satisfaction in his work; with no one
in Tangier to act as a critic, he became convinced that everything
he had written was absurd. Still hoping to transform his relationship
with Allen into a romance, he was disturbed by letters from Ginsberg in which he rhapsodized about Peter Orlovsky, the angelic-
looking twenty-year-old who had just become his lover. Burroughs
had managed to find intelligent company (including the poet Alan
Ansen, who came from Rome for a month, and Jane's friend Charles
Gallagher, whom he pronounced "charming"), but nothing in the
way of love. Kiki, in the end, was only a bedmate, and he needed
more.

Like many writers, William had a pronounced tendency to
dramatize his own plight, and in the spring of 1955 his letters to

Allen took on a desperate tone. (Years later he scoffed, "I sounded like I was dying.") But for all of his ability to cry wolf, he did face an impressive array of obstacles—including, of course, his addiction. By late April, he was spending most of his allowance on drugs, and Tangier had pegged him as a modern-day De Quincey. To Allen, he reported, "I am famous all over town, and the druggists bring out the best they can sell without RX when I walk in, saying: 'Bueno . . . fuerto.'" As much as he liked *escargots* and Camembert, Burroughs was sometimes forced to subsist on stale crusts, and he fretted about every peseta.

Thoroughly disgusted with junk that spring, William devised a new succession of plans for kicking his habit. First, he turned over his supply of Eukodyl to Kiki, who was charged with doling out small doses on schedule. After that tack failed, he began hoarding Demerol and codeine, on the theory that the drugs would ease the pain of a self-administered cure. Early in May, he decided to submit himself to a fourteen-day sleep treatment at a local clinic. He was given enough barbiturates to knock him out for seventy-eight hours, but he went into a bone-shaking withdrawal when he awoke—sweating and tossing through days of delirium. After he left, the backsliding began; first, he dipped into the codeine, then the more powerful Demerol. By July, he was hooked again, and he could think of little save his need to kick. "I have been buying absolutely the last box of demerol ampules every day for the past 3 weeks," he wrote Allen. "Such a dreary display of weakness. . . . I would gladly go to jail for a month and kick cold."

It was a difficult summer indeed, and the single note of hope came when William received an invitation to tea from Paul Bowles. After returning from Ceylon with Ahmed, Paul had rented a small house on the Mountain, where he had taken up the long-neglected *Yerma*. With *The Spider's House* behind him, he had more energy for seeing visitors, and he decided to take a closer look at the specimen whom gossips called "Morphine Minnie."

To Paul's surprise, the deadpan Burroughs proved to be vital and engaging and funny. An inspired storyteller, he had a buzz-saw drawl that lent irony to every phrase. He could talk for hours about lemurs or *yage* or telepathy, and his sensibility was decidedly bizarre. In the next few months, Paul did an about-face on Burroughs—he appropriated him as one of his admirers, and he asked him to tea with other expatriates, including Brion Gysin.

In the beginning, the imperious Brion was cool to the notion of seeing William: He had made a dismal impression when he appeared at the Hotel Rembrandt, and Gysin saw little reason to cultivate a junkie who preferred Spanish boys to Arabs like Hamri. At tea, however, Brion found that Paul was right—there was more to this character than one might think. Burroughs, he discovered, had a kind of crackpot mystique; fantastically mutable, he was simultaneously vulnerable and threatening, proper and debauched. If one watched him long enough, he assumed another persona: The cowboy became the dreamer, and the predator became the prey.

Still caught up in the 1001 Nights, Brion had little time to pursue the friendship. But Burroughs had captured his imagination, and Gysin began to take notice of the pallid midwesterner who haunted the medina. "I cannot say I saw Burroughs clear during the restaurant days that followed," he remembered. "Caught a glimpse of him glimmering rapidly along through the shadows from one farmacia to the next, hugging a bottle of paregoric. I close my eyes and see him in winter, cold silver blue, rain dripping from the points of his hat and his nose. . . . Willie the Rat scuttles over the purple sheen of wet pavements, sniffing. . . . When you squint up your eyes at him, he turns into Coleridge, De Quincey, Poe, Baudelaire. . . ."

Among the other expatriates whom Bowles saw that season was the painter Francis Bacon, who was spending the summer at the Villa Muniria—a modest but well-kept place run by a Vietnamese woman who was said to have been a madam in Saigon. At forty-five, Bacon had made his name among the cognoscenti, but he still lived like a student; in London, he occupied a single room in a Battersea house that belonged to his friends Peter Pollock and Paul Danquah, who had persuaded him to accompany them to Tangier.

The city itself suited Francis; bars were lively and plentiful, and he quickly became a devotee of Joseph Dean, whom he found "very charming." Work was another matter; Bacon complained about the light in Tangier, saying that it was unsuitable for painting.

Still, he stayed at it, and he even acquired a protégé—the ambitious Yacoubi, who needed help in mastering oils.

That summer, Francis painted for long hours while Ahmed sat behind him, "watching him like a cat," as Paul put it. "Ahmed and I had no common language, but between my limited Spanish and French and his very good Spanish we were able to talk a lot," Bacon remembered. When Yacoubi took him to see Bowles, he said, "Paul was very kind, but I don't feel I was ever able to make much contact with him. He liked marijuana and I liked alcohol, and they create very different worlds." He found Jane to be far more accessible: "I liked her very much," he said. "In between her [episodes of] distress she was extremely amusing."

As Bacon noted, drinkers and *kif* smokers often did find themselves at odds, and Paul Bowles was becoming increasingly caught up in his experiments with cannabis. He had always been drawn to the notion of exploring the unconscious, and through the years he had tried an assortment of potions that promised new perspectives. At the University of Virginia, he had inhaled ether—the drug of choice for daring undergraduates. He had sampled marijuana during a 1934 sojourn in Mexico, and he had discovered the power of *majoun* in Morocco. Only in 1955, however, did he begin to draw smoke into his lungs when he was offered a *sebsi* and to feel the effects of *kif*. (Later, he claimed to have been ignorant about the drug during his first years in Tangier: "If they passed the pipe, I smoked it, but I didn't inhale, because I thought it was just very bad tobacco," he said. "Finally, I realized it was a special plant.") Now, he was discovering that unlike *majoun*, which required absolute surrender, *kif* could be used simply to put a spin on reality—and to stoke the imagination while one was bringing forth a piece of fiction.

Moroccans like Yacoubi, of course, were already familiar with the ways in which *kif* could enhance one's creative powers. A popular proverb asserted that "a pipeful of *kif* before breakfast gives a man the strength of a hundred camels in the courtyard," and it seemed that Ahmed (who, like many natives, had listened for hours to professional tale spinners) could launch into fantastic stories after using cannabis. That summer, Paul began what would become a long series of sessions in which he transcribed and translated tales told by illiterate Moroccans who were under the influence of the drug. Investing in a tape recorder, he went to work with Yacoubi, who invented stories in Maghrebi after the two had smoked several pipes of *kif.* (One of Ahmed's fables was accepted by the *Evergreen Review,* which published it as "The Night Before Thinking.")

Paul's newfound interest in *kif* did nothing to improve his strained relationship with Jane, who had turned against cannabis after her traumatic experience with *majoun.* As it was, the two were living in different quarters and seeing one another infrequently; Paul had moved with Ahmed into the San Francisco, a luxurious apartment building on the city's outskirts, and Jane was still in the Casbah with Cherifa. When she did come to Paul's flat, she often caught the odor of *kif,* and it irritated her. Cannabis only exaggerated Paul's well-developed sense of detachment, and he seemed unreachable when he was under its influence. "She would look at me and say, 'I know you've been smoking,' and she would criticize my conversation at dinner," he said. "Sometimes when I'd smoke I'd start laughing and she didn't like that. She didn't like it when she felt shut out."

Paul, in turn, was losing patience with Jane's continuing inability to conquer either her anxiety or her creative block. It was impossible for him to know whether she was even trying to write; she refused to talk with him about her work, and she threw visitors like Wanklyn off the track by scattering papers about to make it look as though she had been toiling. The only thing that Paul could be sure of was that Jane was still drinking, and that she spent most of her waking hours either obsessing about Cherifa or immersing herself in "the David life," as she called it.

From the beginning of their marriage, Paul had taken a profound interest in Jane's writing; he admired it, promoted it, and—according to friends like Charles Gallagher—was compelled to try to eclipse it with his own. Overtly, at least, he played the role of literary taskmaster, and when she was in a slump, he kept at her until there were signs of progress. As Oliver Smith observed, "Paul has to nag and force and push her to write, which is like teaching a kitten to stand on its head." This time, however, she would not be moved, and Paul gave her an ultimatum. "I don't want to see you," he told her, "unless you're working."

Although Bowles had intended only to spur her into action, Jane was devastated. Leaving Cherifa in the house in the Casbah, she went to stay with Beatrix Pendar, whom she had known for several years. Beatrix was sympathetic, but she could do little to stem Jane's sense of dread. After a week in exile, she returned to the medina, still feeling as though she were under siege.

Apart from her paralysis and her standoff with Paul, Jane had a fresh source of anguish that summer: A new wave of violence was sweeping the country, and every day brought reports of bombings in Fez or riots in Marrakech or shootings in Casablanca. Tangier was tense, and for anyone inclined to paranoia, the Casbah seemed menacing indeed.

Typically, she turned her pain into a sort of joke. Said Wanklyn, "I remember her coming to see me one morning after there had been some tremors of agitation in Tangier. I had a little house in the medina, and the front door was usually open. When I was shaving, I looked up and there behind me, visible in the mirror, was Janie, who was wearing a huge hat. She announced, 'They're on the march again.' Of course, it was very self-conscious, very theatrical—even when Jane was frightened, she could be the actress."

Chapter 12

No one was able to ignore the chaos that had set in that summer. Although newly appointed Resident General Gilbert Grandval had made an urgent attempt to negotiate a settlement with nationalist leaders, France was preparing for a bloody last stand in the Maghreb. Rejecting Grandval's bold reforms, embattled *colons* dug in their heels, and vigilantes gunned down both Moroccans and Europeans suspected of being sympathetic to the Istiqlal. In turn, Moroccan extremists shouted down the moderates who supported Grandval, and they urged the masses to mark the August 20 anniversary of Ben Youssef's dethronement with demonstrations against Ben Arafa. In the weeks before *La Date Fatidique,* as it was designated, Arab terrorists littered the country with tracts urging the faithful to "avenge our dead heroes cut down by Imperialist French bullets."

By the evening of August 19, the tension had reached a crescendo. Wealthy Europeans deserted embattled Casablanca and took shelter in Tangier; legionnaires set up machine guns and searchlights in medinas across the country, and French marines and security police were flown in to back the sixty thousand troops already on alert. Those who expected more violence were not disappointed: Gunshots began ringing out before dawn on August 20, and in the days that followed, ninety-two Frenchmen and at least a thousand Moroccans lost their lives. The bloodiest battles were in the Atlas, where Berber tribesmen who had turned against the Glaoui joined forces with Arab nationalists. Rebels laid siege to the fortified town of Khenifra and fought hand to hand with legionnaires who rushed in to save the settlers. Members of the Smala tribe galloped down from the hills and massacred *colons* in prosperous Oued Zem; nearby, in the mining town of Ait Amar, iron workers dragged their French overseers into the streets, raped women and set fire to anything that would burn. The French struck back with brutal force; supported by planes, tanks and field guns, soldiers spread out across central Morocco and destroyed scores of remote villages. More than four thousand legionnaires moved into the Smala tribal area around Oued Zem and surrounded the Berber stronghold with tanks. After two days of fighting, ten thousand tribesmen and five thousand Arab townspeople surrendered in a formal ceremony held in a wheat field. An ancient *caïd* made a contrite speech, and the rebels piled their guns on the ground. General André Franchi then addressed the masses through a loudspeaker. "You have behaved like stinking jackals," he announced. "If France did not have a heart, all of you would be dead."

When news of the carnage reached Tangier, it stoked the hysteria that had been building for weeks. Later, Bowles wrote: "Tangier was more turbulent than ever. . . . Men [installed] iron bars outside entrance doors all over the city. At the beginning of the trouble it had been strictly forbidden to shout publicly for the return of [Ben Youssef], however, with fifty thousand people demonstrating every day, up and down the city, there was not very much the few policemen here could do other than exercise restraint. . . . When the police did throw tear-gas bombs, these exploded with a roar that was audible all over the city, and the shrapnel wounded dozens."

William Burroughs found the scene invigorating. In August, he wrote to Allen Ginsberg: "Just had a riot here. Details not yet available. I hear 4 casualties, all Arab, of course. All I saw was people running, shop shutters slamming down, women jerking their babies inside. So I went home and loaded my shotgun, but the riot was promptly quelled." William, of course, would have preferred to be in the thick of it: "I figure maybe I will take a trip through the French Zone," he said. "I simply *must* see some of this bloodshed."

With the rest of the country in turmoil, the stabbings committed by a religious fanatic who went amok in the Socco one afternoon seemed especially ominous—particularly to Burroughs, who knew the killer. A gaunt young fundamentalist who made his living selling pastries, Marnissi, as the murderer was called, had always had a sinister quality about him; he had once erupted when Burroughs refused to lend him money, and he had sidled up to one of William's neighbors and whispered, "You go with little boys—Allah doesn't like that." Said Burroughs, "He was a complete paranoid. The day before he went on his rampage he came up to me in front of the drugstore where I bought Eukodyl and he said, 'Why does the American Embassy have wires in my head?' I said, 'Well, Marnissi, I don't want to hear about it. Go get yourself psychoanalyzed.' "

A creature of habit, William was on his way to the *farmacia* at the same time the next afternoon when he ran into a mooch called the Ancient Mariner. Instead of appearing at the drugstore at his usual hour, Burroughs ducked into a café with his compatriot. He was still inside when he heard shouts and screams and slamming shutters: Marnissi, it seemed, had armed himself with a meat cleaver and was slashing his way through the Socco, attacking every Nazarene in his path. After killing a Jewish businessman in the gold district, he had butchered a Spaniard and headed down the rue Amérique to the American consulate, which was locked tight. Running out of the Medina and down the rue de Portugal, he killed a British tourist and stabbed the man's wife before the police stopped him with a bullet in the thigh. When he heard about the spree, Burroughs had a thrilling suspicion that Marnissi had meant to kill him as well. "If I had followed my usual routine, I would have been right where he started [slashing]," he said. "Not to be paranoid, but I felt that in some ways this was aimed at me."

Paul Bowles also took a ghoulish interest in the murderer, who could have been one of his own fictional madmen. As it happened, Marnissi recovered and was sent to Malabata Prison, and Paul obtained a report on his behavior there: "He was so violent that they were afraid he was going to kill other inmates, so they built a special little cell for him, off the court, with one little window," he said later. "He decorated the whole inside with [photos of] ships and guns and modern military equipment . . . airplane carriers, cannons. And then he'd stick his head out and say to the [guards], 'Don't you want to see the pictures? Look in!' And when they did, he'd grab them around the neck."

In the midst of the upheaval, William decided to make another serious attempt to "evict the Chinaman once and for all," as he described it. His habit was again wildly out of hand, and he was creating scenes at Dutch Tony's. To Ginsberg, he reported that a cocktail of dolophine and hyoscine had sent him straight through the roof: "The ex-captain[1] found me sitting stark naked in the hall on the toilet seat (which I had wrenched from its moorings), playing in a bucket of water and singing 'Deep in the Heart of Texas,' at the same time complaining, in clearly enunciated tones, of the high cost of living—'It all goes into razor blades.' And I attempted to go out in the street naked at 2 A.M.—What a horrible nightmare if I had succeeded and came to myself wandering around the Native Quarter naked. . . . Naturally Dave and the Old Dutch Auntie who runs this whorehouse were alarmed, thinking my state was permanent."

At the beginning of September, William arranged to enter Benchimal Hospital, where he was to undergo a six-week dolophine treatment. Eager to turn out something saleable, he brought along his new typewriter and tried to apply himself to "Interzone." As his mood lifted, he began writing urgent routines and finding inspiration at every turn. After reading Jean Genêt's *Journal of a Thief,* he confessed to Allen that he was "seething with ideas to make a $ (some of them not exactly legit)" and went on to praise blackmail— the most "artistically satisfying" of all crimes. When he wasn't training his field glasses on the nubile lads at the nearby Italian School, Burroughs was concocting plans for the future ("may make overland trip to Persia with Charles Gallagher, may visit [Alan] Ansen in Venice, would like to dig Yugoslavia and the queer monasteries of Greece") or composing feverish accounts of his brief excursions outside the hospital. Determined to lure Allen to Tangier, he tried to make the place sound menacing and exotic. On October 23, 1955, he wrote:

I went in an Arab cafe for a glass of mint tea. One room 15 by 15, a few tables and chairs, a raised platform covered with mats stretched across one end of the room where the Arabs sit with their shoes off smoking kif. . . . I draw some dirty looks from a table of Arabs and stare at them til they drop their eyes and fumble with kif pipes. If they insist to make something out of it, I'd as soon die now as anytime. . . . Here on the red tile floor of this cafe, with a knife in my kidney. . . .

When he left Benchimal, Burroughs felt triumphant. Free from his addiction once again, he found new quarters in the medina—this time, a small house owned by the painter Jim Wylie, a British fop who affected flowing cloaks and floppy ties. Within days, his loneliness began to lift; life in Tangier had taken on a kind of jittery intensity, and foxhole friendships were easy to come by. So, too, was *kif,* and one of William's first outings was to an Arab café where he could sample the pleasures of "Miss Green." Under her influence, he reported, the International Zone seemed particularly surreal; to Jack and Allen, he wrote, "Tanger is the prognostic pulse of the world, like a dream extending from past into the future, a frontier between dream and reality. . . ."

While Burroughs was reveling in his comparative sobriety, other Tangerinos were watching as the struggle for independence reached its denouement. Shocked by the August bloodletting (which touched off more tremors in Algeria), the French had realized that the Moroccan revolt could not be contained, and even the Glaoui had begun to urge that Ben Youssef be restored to the throne. As the strikes and bombings and riots raged on, French premier Edgar Faure (who had refused to support Grandval's attempts to forge a compromise with the nationalists) finally met with Moroccan leaders at Aix-le-Bain. In the weeks that followed, the agile Faure moved quickly—mollifying right-wingers by sacrificing Grandval and pushing through a compromise that called for the formation of a new government and the removal of the *faux* Sultan. In October, the timorous Ben Arafa was packed off to Tangier, and Ben Youssef was received in Paris with full honors. On November 6, the long-awaited agreement was announced: Morocco was to become a sovereign state, and Ben Youssef would assume leadership of a constitutional monarchy backed by a democratic government. France would retain certain short-term rights and responsibilities, but the colonial days were now over.[2]

When the Sultan returned to the Imperial Palace on November 16, the country's nine million Moslems erupted into a joyous frenzy. In a letter to John Lehmann, Paul described the scene in Tangier: "It is a crystalline day with a burning sun, for which the Moroccans can give thanks, since today was set aside for rejoicing at the return of the Sultan," he wrote.

> My personal feeling . . . is that they have little cause for such rejoicing, but it is certain that they need a festival, having suppressed all the normal holidays ever since August 1953, when the God-appointed Mohammed ben Yussef was replaced by the Bidault[3]-appointed Arafa. The town is a-flutter with banners, all of them scarlet, and triumphal arches have been erected, flanked with incredible portraits of the Sultan dressed as an angel of mercy extending his arms in a gesture of mercy to the Moroccan masses. The palms of Tangier, infrequent enough, have been stripped of their branches, which now adorn the shop fronts, garlanded with chrysanthemums. The medina is transformed into a series of rustic niches and arcades, red, white and green; at night it is truly unrecognizable, because the lighting accentuates unfamiliar forms, while the landmarks recede into shadows. And how the women can scream for so many hours on end is a small mystery. . . .

Observers like Bowles knew that after facing down the French, Moroccan nationalists were unlikely to ignore the International Zone—a wealthy (if minuscule) enclave that was a monument to Western decadence. In the next few months, expatriates who had arrived during the postwar boom began to feel distinctly unwelcome in Tangier. After Dutch Tony was set upon and beaten by five Tanjawis and Christopher Wanklyn was knifed by a gang near the Socco Chico, few felt secure living in the medina. Even Burroughs retreated to the Ville Nouvelle; with Woolman, he moved into the Villa Muniria, where he set himself up in a fifteen-dollar-a-month room. To Allen, William reported: "The natives are getting uppity. Time for some counter-terrorism, seems to me. The police are quite worthless, the Arab police now quite openly taking sides against Europeans or Americans in any contretemps. A number of queers got notes warning them to leave town and signed 'The Red Hand.' (No note for me.) As usual, puritanism and Nationalism come on together in a most disagreeable melange."

Bowles maintained that a quick survey of the cafés in the Socco Chico proved that the International Zone was on the brink of being reclaimed by Moroccans. In a piece for *The Nation,* he reported: "Instead of the customary assortment of European tourists and residents, elderly Moslems in *djellabas* and native Jews from the nearby streets of the Medina, you are likely to see sitting at the tables no one but young Moslems in European dress—mostly blue jeans. . . . And the Europeans who used to be here every night, where are they? Safe in their houses, or sitting in the fluorescent glare of the French and Italian cafes of the Boulevard Pasteur. They know better than to wander down into the part of town where they are not wanted."

While the dust was settling in Morocco, reviewers began responding to *The Spider's House,* which was published in America that November. Writing in *The New York Times Book Review,* Charles Rollo voiced a complaint echoed by other critics; although he praised Bowles for his skill in limning the conflict between two discordant cultures, he found John Stenham "unimpressive," and the novel itself, unfocused. Anthony West, who reviewed the book for *The New Yorker,* was more enthusiastic; Bowles, he argued, had provided "an unusually successful description of the erosion of private lives by public events. The creation of the awareness of gathering crisis and its movement from background to foreground has rarely been better done," wrote West. "[It is,] moreover, a thoroughly sound piece of political reporting. . . ."

As was his habit, Paul professed to have only a passing interest in what the literary establishment had to say about his fiction; in Tangier, he was at a comfortable remove from critics, and he could dismiss any barb as a primitive weapon wielded by a provincial. To David McDowell, he wrote, "I thought the Mary McCarthy review a milestone along the road to utter destruction of literary reporting. It could easily have been a piece on Audrey Hepburn's newest film, for all it had to do with the business of writing."

Aside from the political disorder, Paul's attention had been claimed by the continuing drama that was Jane. Sensing her neediness, Cherifa had threatened to desert her unless Jane gave her a handsome sum of money. Explaining that she had no cash, Jane offered to give her the house in the Casbah instead. In the fall, she asked Paul to sign the property over to her so that it could be transferred to Cherifa, and he agreed.

As her relationship with Cherifa became more problematic, Jane prepared for another excursion to the States. There she could visit Libby Holman and, for a time, take up her old life. *In the Summer House* would soon be included in a volume called *Best Plays of 1953–54*, and there had been talk of republishing *Two Serious Ladies*. If Paul could exist in a milieu where he had no real presence as a writer, Jane could not, and the trip home promised to restore some of the perspective that she had lost.

Even in Jane's absence, Bowles managed to conjure up intrigue. One rainy night that winter, he received a visit from Christopher Isherwood, whom he had met in Berlin in 1931.[4] Unwilling to miss an opportunity to introduce a novice to *majoun,* Paul and Ahmed offered Isherwood a substantial portion of the drug and watched him "[go] out into the gale in a state of disorientation," as Paul described it. Reported Bowles, "He wrote me later from Italy describing the (largely subjective) difficulties he encountered before managing to reach the Hotel Minzah."

There was also a minor contretemps with his new friend William Burroughs. Unflaggingly generous with books and advice and ideas, Bowles let Burroughs borrow a first edition of a volume of Tennessee Williams's short stories. When William returned the book, its pages were mottled with rust-colored stains. Later, Burroughs remembered, "I was on junk at the time and I dripped blood all over it. Paul," he said, "was furious."

*   *   *

By February 1956, William was "at the end of the junk line," as he put it. Back on dolophine, he had fallen into a kind of paralysis; able to think only of his next shot, he lay in a room littered with discarded ampules and gave himself over to junk dreams. "I did absolutely nothing," he remembered. "I could look at the end of my shoe for eight hours. I was only roused to action when the hourglass of junk ran out. If a friend came to visit . . . I sat there not caring that he had entered my field of vision—a grey screen always blanker and fainter—and not caring when he walked out of it. If he had died on the spot I would have sat there looking at my shoe waiting to go through his pockets."

Desperate to kick, Burroughs decided to take a cure at a clinic in London, where Dr. John Yerbury Dent was treating addicts with an emetic called apomorphine—a morphine derivative that was said to regulate the metabolism. In April, after receiving five hundred dollars from Laura Lee and Mortimer, William cleared up his debts in Tangier and flew to London. The treatment lasted just eight days, and it was only moderately torturous: Twenty-four hours of delirium, followed by prolonged vomiting and sleeplessness. When it was over, he felt more stable than he had in years; he was eating well, and he had no desire to score when he hit the streets.

In no hurry to return to Tangier, the newly energized Burroughs explored London for a time before moving on to Venice, where he rendezvoused with Alan Ansen. Together, the two cruised the local lads, consumed vast quantities of alcohol and scandalized expatriates including Peggy Guggenheim, who gave an elaborate cocktail party at which a dead-drunk William managed to disgrace himself.

When he was ready to return to North Africa, Burroughs headed first to Algeria, where France was trying to quell another uprising. Still eager to see rioting in the streets, he was excited by the scene in Algiers; rebels were lobbing bombs left and right, and an afternoon visit to a tearoom could be transformed into a festival of maimed bodies and broken glass. "I was staying in this big dumpy hotel, and I used to eat every day in this Milk Bar which had big jars of passion fruit, various banana splits, all kinds of juices and little sandwiches; there were pillars made of mirror all around," he remembered. "About a week after I left, a bomb exploded in that

Milk Bar and there was this terrible mess. Brion [Gysin] was there very shortly after the bomb exploded and he later described the scene. People were lying around with their legs cut off, spattered with maraschino cherries, passion fruit, ice cream, brains, pieces of mirror and blood."

As Burroughs would discover, Gysin was having his own adventures in Algiers. Since the tea at Paul's, he had been taken up by an unlikely pair of patrons called John and Mary Cooke—nomads who had wafted into the 1001 Nights looking like Lawrence of Arabia and his overdressed handmaiden. Followers of L. Ron Hubbard, who had just founded the Church of Scientology, the two pseudo-mystics had informed Brion that they had been sent to him by their Ouija board. "They just came floating in giving me the impression that they were really *Magic* People, and that they had all of these things at their *fingertips* . . . most particularly money," Brion told Terry Wilson. "They were the first rich hippies I had ever seen in sandals and saris and sarouels but dripping with real jewels of great price in the best possible taste, paying cash and drinking only champagne." In desperate straits, as always, Brion had happily taken on the role of courtier—making the Cookes feel as though his restaurant were their private salon and being solicitous to the credulous souls who clustered around them. When summer came, the two had taken a magnificent villa on the coast near Algiers, and (as Brion told it) offered him money to close the restaurant and join them. John, it seemed, had been stricken by a mysterious paralysis, and they said that only Brion could restore his spirits.

Gysin had agreed to go to Algeria because of his affection for John—a lovable, spontaneous sort who laughed easily and impressed Moroccans with his skill as a dervish dancer. The scion of a "rich, far-out [family] from the Hawaiian Islands," in Brion's words, he seemed like a blithe version of Gysin himself. "He had big Buddha ears sticking out on both sides of a wide grin full of great big square white teeth and big bugged-out green eyes," said Gysin. "He shaved his head, of course, and went barefoot wearing jewels on his big toes. He could sign a check with his right foot and often did for any amount that was needed. . . ." Cooke's wife— "Scary Mary," as Brion christened her—was another matter. Ever the misogynist, Gysin pegged her as a woman who would overpower any man who allowed her. As Brion reported it, it was she who controlled their money, and who used it to keep their entourage afloat.

After Gysin arrived in Algiers, Brion spent much of his time attending to John—working with him in the indoor pool or carrying him on his back to various shamans. Most French physicians had fled to Paris, and no one could say what had caused John's paralysis. ("Magic practices? Spooky sex?" asked Brion. "Don't know.")

When he wasn't looking after John, Gysin was submitting to the Cookes' ad hoc lectures on Scientology or practicing their party line on visitors. "When guests came they had to stay all night because of the curfew," remembered Brion. "The house was huge and well-known; people came in droves although we didn't know any of them personally. People will go anywhere for free food and drink, especially in wartime. . . . They counted on me to start a big drive on the French captive audience we could get every time we gave a party." Typically, Gysin threw himself into the role of propaganda minister; shaving his head and growing an ascetic-looking beard like John's, he wore simple djellabas that made him look like a holy man who had been wandering in the wilderness.

Even when he wearied of Algiers, Brion found it difficult to extricate himself from the ménage. It seemed that Mary, in particular, was destined to have a hand in his affairs. She had given Brion money to keep the 1001 Nights afloat, and she was not one to forget a debt. When Gysin left Algeria, he knew that her Ouija board was likely to send her back in his direction.

Like other Tangier entrepreneurs who catered to wealthy clients, Brion found himself in a precarious situation when he returned to Morocco in the fall of 1956; business had never been so shaky, and the future was wildly uncertain. Since March 2, when the country had formally been granted its independence and the Treaty of Fez had been abolished, it had been clear that the international regime would be dissolved. In July, Professor Abdullah Genoun had been appointed Tangier's first Moroccan governor, and Tanjawis had been moved into the posts once held by European bureaucrats. Although the savvy Ben Youssef had mapped out a "liberal economic regime" that would temporarily preserve Tangier's free port and money market and absolve residents from income tax, speculators were clearing out. Within three months, much of the gold bullion in Tangier banks (more than $50 million worth, by one estimate) had been loaded onto Caravelle jets and flown to Europe. Bankers and diplomats had accepted new assignments, and their villas on the Mountain were left empty.

Overnight, it seemed, the city had lost its vigor. In the Ville Nouvelle, where real-estate prices had dropped by a third, smart boutiques were giving way to garish souvenir stands; smugglers' boats had disappeared from the harbor, and the waterfront had taken on an eerie calm. Eager to make its mark, the new administration was churning out edicts designed to erase all traces of foreign decadence. Suddenly, street and shop signs were posted in Arabic. Serving liquor within so many meters of a mosque was declared illegal, and bars in the medina were shut down. The proprietor of a French restaurant was required to remove its striped awnings on the grounds that they were "inauthentic," and a camera-shop owner was forced to dismantle a display of street-scene photos on the grounds that they portrayed Tanjawis as "primitives."

With businesses collapsing and the tourist trade evaporating, thousands of Moroccans found themselves unemployed, and the young men who had been part of the resistance began lashing out against Europeans. "Thugs were to be seen all over town, organizing strikes and, in the name of Freedom and Independence, ordering shops and cafes to close," remembered David Herbert's friend Daphne Fielding, who moved from the Casbah to the Mountain. "For good measure, they also closed the brothels and banned the smoking of *kif*. They had no authority to do this, but the local police seemed unwilling or unable to stop them. It was hateful to see the free and easy international regime replaced by the puritanical 'reforms' of the new Moroccan government . . . [but] the sight of thousands of *kif* pipes strung up by their stems on the Kasbah gates, like birds of prey shot by a gamekeeper, was less painful to us than to the Arabs."

Most of the Tangerinos who remained were hedging their bets and mourning the loss of the city's esprit. In a long dispatch headlined "Tangier Turmoil," *The Wall Street Journal* reported that "the wife of one multimillionaire banker is so uncertain of the future that she's suddenly stopped going to the hairdresser. . . . So acute is the sense of crisis that Gilbert Mari, manager of the El Minzah Hotel, a lavish and Moorish edifice, is moved to rebuke his fellow Tangerinos: 'Everyone should go to the bars as usual. A fellow doesn't need to order his customary ten drinks. Two—or even one—will do. But he should present himself. And keep smiling.' "

Among the expatriates who still came to see Jay Haselwood at the Parade, a deep sense of shock prevailed. "No one had seen it coming," said Ian Selley. "People had thought that the International Zone would never change. They thought that they were in a little paradise that would go on forever, untouched by the world. When it did end, everyone panicked."

Jay's benefactor, Phyllis della Faille, was preparing to join the exodus. In Portugal, she found a ruined castle that would accommodate her menagerie, but the move was not an easy one. She and Charles were obliged to charter a cargo ship to ferry most of their dogs, cats, horses, birds and rodents to Lisbon, and she insisted on loading the older dogs into their station wagon and driving them through Spain herself.

The Countess's flight from Tangier was typically eventful: Somewhere in Spain she dozed off, and her car went hurtling into a ravine. Trapped in the driver's seat, the bleeding Phyllis was unable to move or to help the injured animals who were whimpering all around her. Finally, she was rescued and taken to the hospital, where nurses shaved her head in order to dress her scalp wounds. When Daphne Fielding saw her afterwards at their new home in Portuguese hunt country, Phyllis's hair was "just beginning to sprout again, and, to encourage its growth, she daubed her scalp every day with henna paste," Fielding reported. "The result was a fuzzy fiery-red crop which made her look like a Picasso clown. Undaunted as usual, however, she was soon in the saddle again, risking further hazards from her horses which were wilder than ever after days of well-fed inactivity at sea followed by several weeks of an increased ration of vitamins and pep-pills to restore them from the shock of the voyage."

For his part, Paul Bowles was making dark pronouncements about the future and complaining about the chaos that had set in. Not that he was willing to uproot himself; his life in Morocco had a certain momentum, and he had little reason to believe that he would be singled out by the new regime. In any case, he had less to lose than did the members of the mink-coat crowd. Years later, he said: "People left because they believed the government was going to requisition their property. We didn't have any—Jane had given the house to Cherifa, and I was careful not to keep money in the bank in Tangier."[5]

That June, Jane had returned from the States in time to prepare for a visit from Paul's parents—the "Old Bowleses," as they were called. While his relationship with Claude and Rena had thawed in the years since he had lived abroad, Paul was hardly prepared to give them an accurate picture of his relationship with Ahmed—or of Jane's arrangement with her own lover. Seizing the opportunity to stage an *opéra-bouffe,* his wife (who was living with Cherifa next door) had managed to create a domestic scenario that was entertaining, if counterfeit. As far as the Old Bowleses were concerned, Jane and Paul lived together as man and wife in his flat at the San Francisco, and the only Moroccans in their lives were servants. "It was one of Jane's theatrical things—a whole French farce," said Christopher Wanklyn. "She had Cherifa dressed up like a Spanish maid, and Yacoubi was banished from the scene."

"Paul's chauffeur, Temsamany, was very much in evidence during their visit because he was considered rather respectable," remembered Charles Gallagher, who was a neighbor at the San Francisco. "He gave a dinner for the Old Bowleses one night at his family's house, which was marvelous. Afterwards, Jane said, 'Oh, come back and talk to me in my flat.' We were standing on the terrace together when Mr. Old Bowles suddenly walked out onto Paul's terrace. Jane said, 'Duck, duck, quick!'—as if we were having an affair and meeting at midnight. Then we began to imagine that we *were* having an affair and that the Old Bowleses suspected it. Jane loved building that sort of fantasy."

Apparently undaunted by the political tension, Claude and Rena (both in their late seventies) allowed Paul and Jane to take them on drives into the hills and on excursions to towns like Xauen. By Paul's account, they liked the city that their son had chosen as a refuge: "They smoked *kif* when it was offered to them (although naturally they preferred whiskey) and in general made a point of enjoying all the little, specifically Moroccan details of life which visitors either overlook or criticize," he remembered. "There was a place called the American Club, which they immediately joined. When I was not showing them the countryside, they passed their time sitting by the swimming pool. . . ."

After the charade was over, Paul picked up the threads of his working life—returning to *Yerma* and writing travel pieces for *The Nation*. He also looked in on William Burroughs, who was back at the Villa Muniria. Still off junk, William was rowing in Tangier Bay every morning and spending long hours at his desk, ripping out fresh routines.

Years later, Paul described his excursions to Burroughs's sanctum:

> One wall of the room, his shooting gallery, was pockmarked with bullet holes.[6] Another wall was completely covered with snapshots, most of which he had taken on a recent trip to the headwaters of the Amazon. I liked to hear about that voyage, and always got him to talk lengthily about it. He had a little stove in his room over which he cooked his own hashish candy, of which he was very proud, and which he distributed to anyone who was interested. . . . The litter on his desk and under it, on the floor, was chaotic, but it consisted only of pages of *Naked Lunch,* at which he was constantly working. When he read aloud from it, at random (any sheet of paper he happened to grab would do) he laughed a good deal, as well he might, since it is very funny, but from reading he would suddenly (paper still in hand) go into a bitter conversational attack upon whatever aspect of life had prompted the passage he had just read.

For once, Burroughs wasn't worrying about about whether his routines would see print. Instead, "I wrote and I wrote and I wrote," he remembered. "I'd usually take *majoun* every other day and on the off days I would just have a bunch of big joints lined up on my desk and smoke them as I typed. . . . I doubted that [the manuscript] would ever be published, but I was terrifically turned on by what I was writing."

Released from the straitjacket of junk, William found frissons at every turn. To Allen, he reported that he not only was dallying with a succession of boys but had decided that women were "downright piquant." Wrote Burroughs, "What are these strange feelings that come over me when I look at a cunt, little tits sticking out so cute? Could it be that?? No! No! He thrust the thought from him in horror. [Even] physical exercise, the contracting and relaxing of muscles, is for me an exquisite sensual pleasure. . . . So [many] things give me pleasure, walking around town, sitting in a cafe. . . . I think I must be very happy."

His friendship with the Bowleses was another source of satisfaction. Not only was Paul an excellent audience, but he appreciated Burroughs's brand of anarchy. One afternoon, he invited William to tea along with a wealthy American woman who listened, uncomprehending, as Burroughs talked about *yage*, the hallucinogen he had tracked down in the Amazon. "How long does it take to rot you?" she asked. "Lady, you should live so long," Burroughs retorted, and she swept out of the room. William had worried that Paul, too, was mortally offended; but in fact he savored such little episodes. "I have seen him twice since, and dig him like I never dig anyone that quick before," he told Ginsberg. "Our minds similar, telepathy flows like water, I mean there is something portentously familiar about him."

An accomplished gamesman himself, William had no trouble identifying Paul's maneuvers. Later, he said of Bowles: "He's so private. He never says what he thinks. He's never talking about the real thing—always something else." Bowles's primary defensive strategy, he discovered, involved a false naiveté intended to throw off opponents and destroy the notion that he was responsible for whatever circumstance was at hand. "It's a very old trick—'Oh, I don't quite understand.' Well, he understands very goddamn well," Burroughs said. Bowles, it seemed, left the scene-making to others; his own forte was a kind of hypercivil social torture. Remembered William, "He's very precise, very insistent about people arriving on time. I was supposed to go to his house one afternoon to listen to some Gnaoua music he'd recorded, and for some reason or another got hung up and arrived about fifteen minutes late. Paul said, 'Oh!—it's too bad. Well, listen, I was just playing some Gnaoua music. And now I'll have to play something else, won't I?' He was punishing me for being late."

William saw that enigmatic pronouncements were an integral part of Bowles's repertoire, and that he used them as another device for keeping visitors off guard. "He always said that if you had any religion it must be private," he remembered. "Paul was sort of shocked that I believed in the possibility of an afterlife, and when I said 'Why?' he said, 'Because all my friends are atheists.' I said, 'Paul, if I've ever heard a non sequitur, that's it.'"

As Burroughs came to know Bowles, he also began to understand why his wife inspired such devotion. Jane, he found, threw off a kind of energy that touched everyone around her. Later, he said, "She was very, very funny, and she had a sort of chic quality that everyone commented on . . . David Herbert, all of those very high people in Tangier—she had this very admiring set of [followers] whose eyes would get all misty when they said, 'Oh, Janie!'" And while William was hardly given to fawning, he decided that he liked her a great deal. Somehow, he even managed to establish a rapport with her menacing inamorata; Cherifa, he remembered, "thought I was a holy man."

Chapter 13

The sense of exhilaration that William felt that season didn't diminish his desire to see Jack Kerouac and Allen Ginsberg. The two were still his most loyal literary supporters, and after he returned from Algeria he renewed his efforts to lure them to Morocco. Aside from promising Ginsberg not to be jealous of Peter Orlovsky ("Jealousy is one of the emotions of which I am no longer capable," he asserted), he offered reassurance to Kerouac, who was worried that the Arabs would stage a *jihad* as soon as he stepped off the boat. To Allen, he wrote, "Tell Jack that Paul Bowles, who is very much afraid of violence, [has lived] twenty years in Morocco and wouldn't live anywhere else."

In February 1957, Jack Kerouac heeded Burroughs's call and joined him in Tangier—sailing from New York on a Yugoslavian freighter called the S.S. *Slovenia.* In the years since he had seen William in Mexico City, the lonesome traveler had continued his own odyssey; bouncing from the East Coast to the West, hopping freighters to Panama and making a pass through Mexico with Allen and Peter, he had devoured texts on Buddhism and struggled with his sense of despair. Although Jack was impossibly prolific, only one of his twelve novels had been published, and his prophetic *On the Road* had been rejected repeatedly since he completed it in 1951. Perpetually broke, he had taken a succession of blue-collar jobs to keep himself afloat, and he had learned to embrace the anonymity that once had seemed like punishment. By the end of 1956, however, the silence was broken: *On the Road* had been accepted by Viking Press, *The Subterraneans* had been bought by Grove, and the charismatic Jack had attracted the attention of the cognoscenti. To them, he was a handsome, hard-drinking hipster who, with confederates like Ginsberg (already notorious for "Howl"), had dedicated himself to shattering all the rules. Just before he shipped out to Morocco, the thirty-five-year-old Kerouac had been discovered by the press. After a photo of Jack, Allen, Michael McClure and Lawrence Ferlinghetti—antiheroes of the San Francisco poetry renaissance—had appeared in *Mademoiselle,* the fledgling *Village Voice* had sent a scout to collect bons mots from Kerouac, Ginsberg and comrade Gregory Corso. Branded by the *Voice* reporter as a "witless madcap," Jack (who had turned up drunk and offered aphorisms like "Pity dogs and forgive men") had sounded like anything but what he was—a wild, sad creature about to be anointed as a prophet. All at once, he had seen fame coming toward him "like a dirty newspaper blowing down Bleecker Street," and he felt a surge of panic. Burroughs offered an escape route, and he took it.

Jack landed in Morocco on February 27, delighted by the prospect of exploring the "the City of Vice," as he called it. He was met by an unexpectedly tanned, muscular, and vigorous Burroughs, who wasted no time in unveiling the pleasures of *kif* and whores and waterfront dives. After installing him in a rooftop room at the Muniria, William had produced a joint and taken him on a tour of the Casbah. The thoroughly *kif*ed Kerouac had been overcome by a sense of déjà vu; to him, "Maghreb Land" looked precisely like Mexico.

For the next few days, at least, Jack found Tangier to be thrilling. He went for long walks along the beach, where he was taken with "the ancient rhythmic fishermen who hauled nets in singing gangs with some ancient song along the surf, leaving the fish slopping in sea-eye sand. . . ." He liked the strong light and the shepherd boys and the "brown ragged robe priest" who sat near him in a café, "dreaming of Sufi." He was pleased with the "whanging music" that he heard in the Casbah and with the peddlers whose cries echoed through the medina. In a "late afternoon cafe where sat all the decayed aristocrats of America and Europe and a few eager enlightened healthy Arabs," he inquired about women, and that night he found himself at the Muniria with a prostitute in a *haik* and litham. "I watched her flip off the shroud and veil and saw standing there a perfect little Mexican (that is to say Arab) beauty perfect and brown as ye old October grapes," he remembered. "[She] turned to me with her lips parted in curious 'Well what are you doing standing there?' so I lighted a candle on my desk."

Pleased to be reunited with the responsive Jack—who, aside from his other virtues, could bring him news of Allen—William spared no effort in trying to keep him amused. Bowles was on a long trip to Ceylon, but he rounded up everyone else of interest, including David Woolman and Dutch Tony and Paul Lund, an ex-gangster who ran a scruffy bar. He took him to his favorite *farmacias,* where they stocked up on speed and barbiturates, and to the Socco Chico, where they bought raw opium from a Tanjawi in a red fez. Later, the two "made some home made pipes with old olive oil cans and smoked singing 'Willie the Moocher,'" Jack remembered. "The next day [we] mixed hash and kif with honey and spices and made big 'Majoun' cakes and ate them, chewing, with hot tea, and went on long prophetic walks to the fields of little white flowers. . . ."

At the Muniria, Burroughs showed Kerouac the avalanche of stained pages that was his manuscript. Although William was still uncertain how his routines would be received, Jack found them both brilliant and savage. To Kerouac, Burroughs had always seemed a "mad genius," and this outpouring demonstrated just how provocative he could be. "I'm shitting out my educated Middlewest background once and for all," William told him.[1] "It's a matter of catharsis where I say the most horrible thing I can think of—realize that, the most horrible dirty slimy awful niggardliest posture possible." It was Jack who found the right title; William had considered *Word Hoard,* but Kerouac christened the opus *Naked Lunch.*"[2]

Jack volunteered to type up the confusion of pages marked with Burroughs's "strange Etruscan script," and he spent much of the next few weeks elbow-deep in blood and guts and buggery. The *kif* and *majoun* gave it all a terrible resonance, and he began to be haunted by nightmares. Worried about the fate of his own novels, he went into a rage when the proofs of *The Subterraneans* arrived from New York and he saw that the manuscript had been heavily edited. After he ate a generous portion of the opium that he and Burroughs bought in the Socco, Kerouac slid into a depression. The drug hit him full force, like the heroin that they had done together in Mexico; he threw up until there was nothing left, and then he lay motionless for a full day, locked in his chaotic dreams and listening to "the creaks of pederast love" from the room next door. When it was over, he felt worn and wraithlike, and he began complaining about Tangier. The city was alien, unkempt, perverse. Arabs were listless, the expatriate community was dull and the mail was impossibly slow. He hated the Berbers who beat their mules in the streets and the "stiff officious squares" who worked in the American Legation. To New York girlfriend Joyce Glassman, he wrote, "Not too many good vibrations in Tangier . . . mostly fags abound in this sinister international hive of queens."

Aside from his distaste for Morocco, Jack felt burdened by Burroughs's impassioned inquiries about Ginsberg, who planned to join them in March. Although he loved William "just for his big stupid soul," Kerouac was impatient with his romantic obsession; it seemed to him that there was something decadent about William's eagerness to play the flagellant. Of late, Burroughs had begun to struggle with his homosexuality—saying it was a "horrible sickness" and describing "the emergence of my nonqueer persona as a separate personality." Still, he was unable to extinguish his spiritual and sexual attraction to Allen, and it seemed that he was indeed jealous of the half-mad manchild with whom Ginsberg was besotted.

After dinner one evening, the two went out on the broad terrace outside Jack's room, where they watched the silent harbor and talked about Ginsberg's impending visit. As Jack described the scene in *Desolation Angels*, William stared out to sea and asked petulantly, "When will he get here?" Leaning on Jack's shoulder, Burroughs burst into sobs. He pleaded with Jack to describe his rival, and Kerouac did a pencil sketch of Peter's "crazy eyes and face." Lost in his own self-pity, William went downstairs to his opium pipe. Jack (who knew that Ginsberg would never change his mind about sleeping with Burroughs) thought it all seemed absurd; later, he wrote, "What's all this love business between grownup men. . . . Not that [Allen] wasnt [sic] worthy of him but how on earth could they consummate this great romantic love with Vaseline and K.Y.?"

In the days that followed, Jack began spending more time alone—locked into his room with a bottle of cheap Málaga wine or sitting cross-legged on his terrace, reading the Diamond Sutra. In the evenings, he watched the Catholic priests at the nearby church facing the sea to say their prayers. Homesick for "Wheaties by a pine breeze kitchen window," he thought about the other expatriates who had suffered the same pangs: "Wolfe suddenly remembering the lonely milkman's bottle clink at dawn in North Carolina as he lies there tormented in an Oxford room, or Hemingway suddenly seeing the autumn leaves of Ann Arbor in a Berlin brothel. Scott Fitz tears coming into his eyes in Spain to think of his father's old shoes in the farmhouse door. . . ." Painfully out of place, Kerouac no longer saw the street boys or the Socco or the sullen cafés; instead, he was planning his escape.

Along with Peter Orlovsky, Allen Ginsberg arrived in Tangier on March 21, interrupting Jack's reverie and shaking up the lovesick William. At thirty-one, Ginsberg was no longer the guilt-ridden, insecure soul whom Burroughs had left behind. As Michael McClure put it, he had made the "metamorphosis from quiet brilliant burning bohemian scholar, trapped by his flames and repressions, to epic vocal bard." Since making "direct heart exchange" with Peter, he had given up his quest to establish himself as a heterosexual, and his flirtation with middle-class respectability had gone the way of his unhappy girlfriends. Along with his explorations into Buddhist philosophy and dream symbolism and psychoanalysis, Ginsberg had had his own adventures on the road—climbing volcanoes in the Yucatán and sailing to the Arctic Circle as a yeoman on a cargo ship. On October 13, 1955, he had broken through as a poet—giving a stunning reading of "Howl" at the avant-garde Six Gallery in San Francisco. In his urgent, jazz-influenced epic, Allen had put forth the desperation of "angel-headed hipsters" trapped in "I Like Ike" America, and he had taken on the role of laureate for the newly christened Beat Generation. It was a position for which he was well suited; reckless, intense, he was an evangelist dedicated to the cause of liberating the true self. He was eager to take on the literary establishment, and (like Paul Bowles) he understood the importance of having high-profile allies. He had persuaded longtime mentor William Carlos Williams to write the introduction to *Howl and Other Poems,* which was selling out at hip bookstores; he had lunched at the Russian Tea Room with Salvador Dalí, and he had lured Anaïs Nin to a Los Angeles reading in which he removed his clothes—the better to express his "spiritual naked-ness." Now, it seemed, everyone who mattered knew that Ginsberg was the enfant terrible who spoke for the "new barbarians."

William Burroughs was on edge from the moment he and Jack spotted Ginsberg's ship in the harbor. After everyone had re-grouped at the Muniria, he got extravagantly drunk and pulled out his machete, waving it about until Allen told him to stop. As Ker-ouac noted, it was not the "big lovely arrival" that they had antici-pated: "[Bill] had waited so long, and in such torment, and now he realized probably in an opium turningabout of his own that it was all nonsense anyway."

Apart from Ginsberg's heightened sense of emotional indepen-dence, there was the issue of St. Peter, as Jack called him. Even under the best of circumstances, Allen's lover was not the sort of character whom William appreciated. At twenty-three, the wide-eyed Orlovsky had the aspect of a "voluble autistic child," in Bowles's words. "He seemed crazy," said Paul. "He couldn't follow a rational conversational path—he was like a bird flitting from branch to branch on a tree." The spottily educated son of a Russian immigrant, he had earned his keep as a hospital orderly before being drafted into the army. After declaring to a lieutenant that armies were "against love," he had been shipped to San Francisco to work in a military hospital. When Allen met the quixotic Peter, he had pegged him as a "nature boy." Wrote Ginsberg: "He was very moody, very sweet, tender, gentle and open, but every month or two months he'd go into a very dark, Russian, Dostoevskian black mood and lock himself in his room and weep for days; and then he'd come out totally cheerful and friendly. . . ." To Allen (who had spent seven months in a mental hospital and whose own mother had been a schizophrenic), Orlovsky seemed merely erratic. William, however, decided that Peter was a lunatic; he hated it when he made nonsensical pronouncements or spoke in non sequiturs. And, of course, he hated the fact that it was Peter, not he, who was sharing Allen's bed.

After the first evening, the tension escalated: Soon, William was alternately mocking Peter and refusing to speak to him. Ginsberg tried to make peace, but usually succeeded only in irritating the fractious Burroughs. Out of sorts, plagued by asthma, Peter began saying that he wanted to go to Europe to meet girls.

Waiting for the publisher's advance that would pay for his escape home via Marseilles, Kerouac tried to remove himself from the fray. Later, he remembered, "At the time I sincerely believed that the only decent activity . . . was to pray for everyone, in solitude. I had many mystic joys on my roof, even while [Bill and Allen] were waiting for me downstairs." Cannabis, he reported, had helped to set the contemplative mood: "One afternoon high on hasheesh I meditated on my sun roof thinking 'All things that move are God, and all things that dont move are God' and at this utterance of the ancient secret all things that moved and made noise in the Tangier afternoon seemed to suddenly rejoice, and all things that didn't move seemed pleased. . . ."

Determined to quell the psychic disturbance, Allen mapped out plans for afternoons at the beach, hikes in the countryside, even a journey to Fez. Burroughs, however, was reluctant to interrupt the routine he had been following for months—working steadily until 4 P.M., when friends convened in his room to drink cognac—and Kerouac was content to stay in his aerie. "It was a little sad," Jack remembered. "[Burroughs] would be too tired to go out so [Allen] and [Peter] would call up to me from the garden just like little kids calling at your childhood window, 'Jack-Kee!' which would bring tears to my eyes almost and force me to go down and join them. 'Why are you so *withdrawn* all of a sudden!' cried [Peter]. I couldn't explain it without telling them they bored me as well as everything else, a strange thing to have to say to people you've spent years with. . . ."

When the three did go out together, they spent most of their time in the medina, which Allen saw as an explosion of "clear, sharp images." In a letter to his friend Lucien Carr, Ginsberg reported that he had been pleased with his glimpses of Moroccan life—"veiled women, Arabs in long white or black hooded shroudy stranger robes, [adobe] walled tenements, crisscross of crooked alleys, arches, roofs, rembrandt-interior cafes & shops, streetpeddlers selling delicious 2 cent napoleons & French pastries, deformed feet & blind or earsore beggars crouched in doorways, an old palsied Jew in black hood & skullcap in sunlight in middle of sidewalk with palm outstretched & left hand shaking clutching a few brass coins. . . ." Burroughs had warned them never to go into Arab cafés, where Europeans were still unwelcome; but Allen wanted to see everything. With Kerouac, they headed into drowsy enclaves where men smoked *sebsis* and listened to Radio Cairo, and into a "crazy jukebox hangout full of pinball machines," as Jack described it, where "gangs of bluejeaned Arab teenagers play[ed] rock n roll records . . . just like Albuquerque New Mexico or anywhere." To Kerouac, the young Tanjawis seemed oddly familiar—"an absolutely cool bunch of hipsters and urchins probably of a new 'beat' east—'Beat' in the original true sense of mind-your-own-business."

Although Ginsberg had reported to Carr that "the only danger here is predatory leechlike guides & shoeboys & vendors of rubber spiders," Tangier still had its tense moments. Just after Allen arrived, Burroughs led his visitors straight into a riot in the Grand Socco. The local police, it seemed, had gotten into a face-off with a band of Moroccan soldiers, and Tanjawis were taking sides. "All of a sudden a seething yelling mass of cops and soldiers and robed oldsters and blue-jeaned hoodlums came piling up the alley from wall to wall," Jack remembered. Everyone scattered, and Kerouac headed down a cul-de-sac trailing a pair of ten-year-olds who echoed his giddy laughter. Ducking into a wine shop just before the owner pulled down his shutter, he drank a glass of Málaga "as the riot boomed on by." Later, Jack found his companions sitting in an outdoor café, surveying the disorder. Burroughs, he noted, seemed peculiarly satisfied: "Riots every day," he said proudly.

Oddly, Kerouac was less disturbed by that scene than by the one he witnessed in William's room a few days later. Early in April, Ginsberg called to him at midnight from the garden at the Muniria, telling him to come and meet a "big bunch of hipsters and chicks from Paris" who had landed in Tangier. Downstairs, Jack found himself among long-legged girls in slacks and would-be poets with little goatees. Splendidly *kif*ed, the visitors were languidly discussing Charlie Parker and offering obeisance to Ginsberg. Jack had a terrible sense of foreboding; like the poseurs who had sniffed out the Beats in New York and San Francisco, these converts had a calculating sort of coolness that he found completely dreary. Later, he lamented, "To think that I had so much to do with it, too, in fact that at that very moment the manuscript of *Road* was being linotyped . . . and I was already sick of the whole subject." At that moment, Jack confessed, all he could do was "sit on the edge of the bed in despair like Lazarus listening to their awful 'likes' and 'like you know' and 'wow crazy' and 'a wig, man, a real gas' "—knowing that it was only the beginning.

Cutting short his visit by months, Kerouac bought passage on a packet boat bound for France as soon as his advance arrived. In some ways, William was ready to see him go; he had grown weary of Jack's complaints about the contaminated food and the bad hash and the three-dollar whores. Still, Kerouac was one of his acolytes, and he had taken the edge off the loneliness that was always waiting to consume him. On April 5, when Jack walked into William's room to take his leave, he found him still in bed. Later, he wrote, "[Burroughs] actually looked sad when he gripped my hand and said 'Take care of yourself, Jack,' with that upward lilt on my name which tries to ease the seriousness of goodbye."

After seeing off Kerouac, Allen moved with Peter into Jack's old quarters. There, he established a working routine that began at sunrise, when he slipped out of bed to write on the terrace. Later, he headed downstairs to spend the bulk of the day laboring over William's manuscript. A patient editor and inspired literary entrepreneur, he had long served as William's agent; it was Allen who had given shape to *Junky* in 1952 and who had peddled the manuscript to Ace Books. Now, along with their friend Alan Ansen (the part-time Tangerino who had been W. H. Auden's amanuensis), he approached the task of assembling *Naked Lunch*. To Lucien, Ginsberg reported, "Ansen arrived from Venice to help work on Bill's book, we type & edit vast amount of material in relays, and also farm out some typing too, quite a bit done—one whole section of 120 pages finished and another about equal size to be done this week, then the harder job of going thru [his] letters . . . extrapolating and integrating material, autobiography, routines & fragments of narrative. Quite a job—we work 6 hours a day or more, goof, drink, lunch, I cook big suppers, live in Jack's old veranda great room overlooking bay and spain."

Although Allen was still troubled by the hostile undercurrents between William and Peter, he was in an expansive mood. He had long since decided that Burroughs was a genius, and he was happy to see the manuscript of *Naked Lunch* taking shape. Endlessly curious, he was pleased to be in a milieu where he could explore *hammam*s and experiment with *majoun* and commune with other expatriates. Paul Bowles was still overseas, but Allen made himself known to Jane soon after Jack left. As he told it, he simply ran into her on the Boulevard Pasteur: "I don't remember who I was with, but we were introduced," said Ginsberg. "I was talking quite a bit about the change in American poesy: I said my ideal was to be a bop poet, as in be-bop, and I explained about Charlie Parker and others who had transformed the cadences of music, and Kerouac using that [rhythm] in his prose. I was then preoccupied with the notion of the divine vision, and I did ask her whether she believed in God. . . ."

Jane put a more dramatic spin on the story. In a dispatch to Paul, she reported that Ginsberg—a member of the "Zen Buddhist–Bebop–Jesus Christ–Peyote group," as she described him—had taken it upon himself to telephone. "He was given a letter to us through Leo Lerman," she wrote. "I suppose I must see him, but he is much more up your alley than mine. . . . On the telephone he said: 'Do you know Philip Lamantia?' I said: 'No.' He said: 'He's this hep poet, been writing since he was thirteen, and he just had a vision in Mexico on *peyote* . . .' I said: '*Oy weh.*' Then he said, 'Honest, it was a real vision, and now he's a Catholic.' I said, '*Oy weh!*' Then he named twenty-five men, none of whom I'd ever heard of, and I told him I'd been away for a long time, and was too old anyway, and that I wasn't interested in *peyote* or visions. . . . And he said, 'Well, don't you take *majoun* day and night?' and I said: 'I hate all that, and I'm sure you shouldn't see me.' " According to Jane, Ginsberg finally had asked her whether she believed in God, and she had

told him, "I'm certainly not going to discuss it on the telephone."
Later, Bowles observed, "I have a feeling she didn't want to discuss
it on the telephone because she thought God might be listening.
God and the FBI—to her, they were interchangeable."

In the spring of 1957, Jane Bowles was too preoccupied to have
patience with an earnest newcomer who was searching for the exotic. Since returning from New York (where the producer Roger
Stevens had offered her an advance to write a new play), she had
been trying to command a cast of fictional characters who refused
to submit to her will. After producing a series of abortive scenes, she
had been unable to pull the fragments together. Terrified of being
blocked, she had written the same passages over and over, hoping
to find her way out of the labyrinth. To Paul, she complained, "It
is impossible to write a play in the dark without having some idea
of where one is going. . . ." She refused to take comfort in the fact
that *Vogue* had just published "A Stick of Green Candy," her 1949
story about an eccentric child who loses control over her own fantasies. Along with everything else she had written, Jane had dismissed
that long-finished piece on her fortieth birthday. Reaching that
milestone, she told Paul, had been a "bad shock"—one that made
"the full horror of having no serious work behind me at this age . . .
[seem] an official fact." (She had added that he could hardly be
expected to understand her plight, as he had had "quite enough
stacked up behind [him]" at forty.) Jane had decided that she could
redeem herself only by bringing forth a new play, and she went into
a guilty panic when she thought about having to show her husband
how little she had produced. "Failure," she wrote, "follows me into
my dreams."

For all of her talk about being defeated, Jane still was able to
cast herself as the heroine of an antic tragicomedy—at least, in the
letters that she sent to Paul and to Libby Holman. Early in April,
she wrote to Libby about her vigil at the bedside of a friend who
had undergone a difficult abortion. Jane and Christopher Wanklyn
had stayed at her house on the Mountain for a week, and the
experience, she reported, had been "sheer hell." Not only had the
patient insisted on getting out of bed almost immediately—setting
back her recovery "and imprison[ing] us, too," as Jane noted—but

she had scolded her attendants as though they were the hired help. "We had fish and squashed spinach the whole time and once just spinach and potatoes, but when her clandestine lover came (who has no chin and trains horses), she gave him souffle and chicken and gave us the afternoon off. I thought it was very ungracious," wrote Jane. After escaping from her captor ("whom I now HATE") she had returned to her flat at the San Francisco. In her absence, she said, Cherifa had taken to wearing a "truss-like corset with a rubber pump" to correct "a dropped stomach." Jane told Libby that the device seemed to be working, because "she ate a pound of bananas all at once last night like a monkey." She also reported that Cherifa had "taken up playing cards with two women [who] look like Pekingese. I cannot believe they do—not both of them—and think she says this to please me," she wrote. "They are black and their husbands are dead white and work in movie houses. I believe it's really only one woman. How could they be so identical?"

In a letter sent to Paul, she reported that one of their cats had developed a psychosomatic case of eczema and that Paul's parrot had nearly broken the bars of his cage "because I went into the bathroom with a hat on, and he thought I was someone else." She also noted that Ramadan—the month of short tempers and self-denial—had begun and that she had been having vigorous arguments with Cherifa. Both were observing the customary day-long fasts and rising in the early hours for the meal that, by tradition, was taken just before sunrise. Alcohol, of course, was forbidden; all other beverages were prohibited during daylight hours, and sexual relations were taboo. It was a demanding regimen, and nerves often grew frayed as the days wore on. To Paul, she wrote: "Cherifa and I almost came to blows the other night. I insist that she joke at three in the morning if we are to get up then (and we do), but she refuses to treat the meal as a gay occasion. I have threatened to send her home for the month, and she in turn has threatened to stay there. I can't decide which is worse, to be alone or to go through it."

After that dispatch, however, Paul heard nothing more. At the end of the journey that had taken them to Ceylon[3] and Kenya and Zanzibar, he and Ahmed Yacoubi were on a long, slow voyage around Africa—stopping in Cape Town and docking in the Canary Islands before making their way back to Morocco. Despite her reports about her depression and her creative block, Paul had no reason to think that Jane had met the fate that she had long since assigned to herself. It was the middle of May before an urgent message from Tangier reached him in Casablanca; as he and Ahmed stepped off the ship, he was handed a telegram informing him that she had suffered a small stroke. "In my innocence," Paul remembered, "I failed to recognize this message as the first statement of a theme which would become the principal leitmotiv of our lives. I did not know it, but the good years were over."

On April 4, before the end of Ramadan, it seemed that there had been a particularly heated confrontation in Jane's flat—one that involved either Jane and Cherifa or Cherifa and the Moroccan servants. A distraught Jane had left the scene at about 5 P.M. to take refuge with her old friend Gordon Sager, who lived several blocks away. Avoiding the dreaded lift, she had climbed the three flights of stairs to Sager's apartment as quickly as her stiff right knee would allow. Light-headed from hunger, she had fortified herself with several cognacs. After darkness fell, she had ventured back to the San Francisco, where she had climbed eight more flights of stairs to her flat. "Cherifa was always furious if she didn't get back by a certain hour, and as soon as she got back to the apartment she began yelling at her: 'You slut, you . . .'" Bowles remembered.

At some point during that long night, Jane had become violently ill. After vomiting and putting a cold compress on her forehead, she had lost consciousness. By the time Cherifa summoned Christopher Wanklyn (who was staying in Paul's apartment next door), Jane had come around, but she was partially paralyzed on her right side and her vision was impaired. Weak, confused, she could barely speak. Still, she managed to ask Wanklyn what she had taken that evening, and she added what sounded like a riddle. Remembered Wanklyn: "She said, 'What is worse than *baisar?*'"

To Jane's mind, only one thing was worse than the dried-pea soup known as *baisar,* and that was *majoun.* She had loathed the drug since her experiment at the Palais Jamai, but Wanklyn wondered whether she might have tried it again—perhaps with Cherifa, who might have used it during Ramadan as a substitute for alcohol. The frightened Cherifa offered little explanation, and Jane, of course, was too disoriented to give a clear account of what she had done after she had left Gordon.

Even if Jane had consumed *majoun*, however, the drug need only have played a minor role in her seizure: A frail specimen whose father had died from hypertension at forty-five, she had suffered for years from high blood pressure. When she was stricken, she was taking both Sparine—an anti-hypertensive medication that was hazardous when combined with alcohol—and any number of sedatives. Taken on an empty stomach and washed down with five or more glasses of cognac, the prescription drugs could have been responsible for her stroke. Other drugs—including *majoun*—would simply have made the combination more toxic.

When Paul reached Tangier, Jane was in a state that her friends, at least, found alarming. Six weeks after the attack, her vision was still impaired and her right hand refused to function. When she spoke, the words came slowly, and she was plagued by a peculiar aphasia that caused her to confuse pronouns. Paul, however, noted that she didn't look particularly ill, and that her spirits weren't as low as he had feared. He tried to help her recall the day she had been stricken, and eventually, he said, she admitted that she had taken *majoun*.

Already, the stories about Jane's illness were circulating at Dean's and Porte's and the Parade. Some Tangerinos believed that she had actually suffered a stroke, but others were whispering that she had been poisoned by Cherifa and that Cherifa had always wanted to claim what property Jane had. As lurid as it was, the theory was not without logic: Sorcery, of course, was part of everyday life for illiterate Moroccans, who believed in djinns almost as strongly as they believed in the Prophet. Someone in Jane's household had planted the packet of *tseuheur* under her pillow in the summer of 1954, and Yacoubi, at least, was convinced that it had been Cherifa's work. And although Jane had defended Cherifa when he branded her a witch, her friends knew that she distrusted the woman whom she had worked so hard to win. Said Yvonne Gerofi, "She was afraid of her, that's all."

In the months after the stroke, even Paul gave credence to the notion that Cherifa had tried to bring Jane under her control by poisoning her. For any expatriate who savored the idea that, "in the night, all around me in my sleep, sorcery is burrowing its invisible tunnels in every direction," the threat of being struck down by an exotic toxin seemed thrilling. His own short stories were rife with such scenarios, and, as a writer, he appreciated the fact that sabotage was far more interesting than a simple stroke. Years later, he remembered that even her primary physician, Dr. Yvonne Marillier Roux, had believed that Cherifa could have been responsible for Jane's seizure. "She was inclined to think that Cherifa *had* given Jane something," he said. "Not *majoun* and not *kif*, but something else. She said, 'I've practiced medicine in this country for eighteen years and I've known so many such cases. I've seen the results. You'll never know, but I think it was something given to her by a Moroccan, and the only Moroccan who could have done it was *that woman.*' Of course, she hated Cherifa."

But while Paul himself believed Cherifa to be "a monster," neither he nor anyone else could prove that she had tried to harm his wife. Long after Jane fell ill, their friend Edouard Roditi observed, "I wouldn't put it past Cherifa to try [to influence Jane], but she wasn't interested in poisoning her; she was interested in getting Jane to be so attached to her that she wouldn't abandon her." Even if she had plied Jane with some potion meant to transform her into a somnambulist, Roditi said, "I wouldn't trust the efficacy of Cherifa's magic."

Still in shock when Paul returned, Jane herself was reluctant to discuss Cherifa. Paul said nothing to her of his suspicions, but in the weeks that followed, she denied that she had ever said anything about *majoun.* Unable to read or to write, she was forced to give herself over to the business of consulting with an array of physicians. One told her that she had suffered a *"gros accident cérébral"*; another described the problem as a "small bleed," while a third said that the attack could have been triggered by a "microlesion." To Jane, the diagnoses sounded like a babble of disembodied voices in a nightmare; isolated by her terror, she saw omens at every turn, just as the doomed Kit Moresby had done.

In the wake of her seizure, it took little to send her into hysterics. Allen Ginsberg triggered a paroxysm of anxiety when he spoke to her about the episode: "He made all the wrong remarks," said Paul. "He said it had been only two years since William Carlos

Williams had had his stroke, and that *already* he could write a little."
According to Bowles, Allen suggested that Jane learn braille. "That
really upset her," said Bowles. "Right after that she had an epileptiform fit, which had never happened before. Obviously the fits
came as a result of pressure on the cortex because of the stroke—
that was physical. But I [later] noticed that she had them when she
was particularly upset."

Aside from her fear of having sustained irreparable physical
damage, Jane soon seized upon the notion that the stroke had
robbed her of her sanity. "She kept saying, 'Maybe it's made me
crazy,'" said Charles Gallagher. "She was terribly worried about
being sent to the looney bin. And I kept saying, 'No, no, don't be
silly.'"

While friends like Gallagher were quick to offer Jane the reassurance that she needed, Paul's own reaction to the crisis was enigmatic.

On one hand, he could give the appearance of being deeply
concerned about Jane's fate. Tennessee Williams, among others,
believed that he wanted nothing more than for her to regain her
powers. Months later, as Paul made the round of doctors with his
wife and tried to help her regain her equilibrium, he would receive
a letter from Tennessee offering Jane the use of his house in Key
West. "I've always admired you more than anyone else, but never
as much as I have during this ordeal," wrote Tennessee. "It justifies
my own feeling that a hard and clear view of things, which you've
always given them, does not predicate a lack of humanity but makes
a true humanity possible. . . ."

Yet it seemed to some observers that Bowles underplayed her
illness to an astonishing degree—falling back on his mock naiveté
and refusing to acknowledge how damaging the stroke had been.
"It's hard to explain, but [he responded with] a sort of indifference,"
said Gallagher. "That wasn't my feeling alone; Christopher got furious with Paul—he said, 'I'll *kill* him for the way he's treating her.'"

In a letter written to the composer Peggy Glanville-Hicks, Paul
discussed a telling rumor—one that neatly encapsulated the collective perception of his attitude toward Jane. Reporting that she was
"obsessively terrified that her mother will hear of it and drop dead
of the shock," he asked Glanville-Hicks not to spread the news

about her stroke. "Such things have a way of getting around in the most mysterious fashion," he observed. "She had told no one of it at all, and suddenly letters began arriving from unlikely people asking me for details, because they had heard from Themistocles Hoetis[4] who had heard from Gore Vidal who had heard from Truman Capote who had heard from Cecil Beaton who had heard from David Herbert that Jane had had a stroke and that I refused to allow her to have a doctor because I wanted her to die immediately." Instead of pausing to marvel over the story, Paul complained, "Too many gossip vultures hovering overhead."

Chapter 14

It was in the spring of 1957 that Paul Bowles first encountered William Burroughs's mad salon. Eager for an escape from the upheaval at Jane's, he called at the Muniria (known to the Beats as the Villa Delirium) and found a scene that was considerably livelier than the one he had witnessed before he left for Ceylon: Allen Ginsberg and Alan Ansen were laboring over the manuscript of *Naked Lunch,* and David Woolman, Eric Gifford and Paul Lund, the Cockney-blackguard barkeep who had attached himself to William, were on hand to drink cognac and watch the literary festivities. William himself was still turning out routines and giving spontaneous readings of the work as it emerged. "Allen would phone to say, 'Bill's going to read some of *Naked Lunch,'* which Allen was gathering off the floor," said Bowles. "Burroughs would be lying on his bed with a light behind his shoulder, [reading aloud]." Paul, who had heard William's earlier routines, considered the material to be less a novel than a wildly funny collection of drug-induced fantasies. "I took it all as an hallucination under heroin," he said.

At the Muniria, Bowles was struck by the intensity of the debates between Ginsberg and Burroughs, who would "sit around

half the night having endless fights about literature and aesthetics,"
as he remembered it. According to Paul, "It was always Bill who
attacked the intellect from all sides, which I suspect was exactly
what Allen wanted to hear." Launching into a diatribe, "shouting
in his cowboy voice," as Paul described it, William would lurch
about, stirring his drink with two fingers and stopping to drag on
the joints that had been left burning in ashtrays around the room.
After watching the two, Paul decided that although he didn't admire the explicit "Howl," he did approve of Ginsberg. Said Bowles,
"I liked Allen because he was a friend of Burroughs, whom I respected enormously."

In turn, Allen found Paul to be both courtly and distant. After
their first meeting, Ginsberg reported to Lucien Carr that Bowles
was a "short frail blond, closecropped hair, nylon suit, very courte-
ous & lively, also a little mechanical or remote somewhere. . . ."
Allen told of spending a day with Paul and Yacoubi, smoking
Bowles's Tanganyikan grass and listening to his reports about the
unrest in Kenya. In spite of his reserve, Allen reported, Paul was
extremely hospitable; to Lucien, he wrote, "He took me out to
Escargot and talked about Gertrude Stein & we went over to his
house & anson fell asleep on [couch] at 3 A.M. & he played Indian
music on tape & rolled huge bombers & talked medicine with Bill."

Still caught up in his own affair with Peter, Allen was curious
about Bowles's relationship with Yacoubi. "I had considerable
prurient interest in what was going on because I thought Ahmed
was very beautiful," he remembered. "I asked Paul whether he was
still making out with Ahmed, but I think they'd long since ceased."
Noting that Paul said very little about Yacoubi, Ginsberg decided
not that Bowles was hypocritical about his sexuality (as some had
suggested) but that he was merely being politic: "Paul was concerned with his reputation," said Allen. "Given the situation, he had
to be discreet—he didn't want to get Ahmed in trouble [with the
authorities] by making notorious the fact that they were lovers or
that they had been lovers."

During the next few weeks, Yacoubi began making solo visits
to commune with Burroughs's cabal. "We were a younger set,"
remembered Ginsberg, "and he appreciated us as poets, storyteller-
magicians." He was taken with Ahmed's "brain-dazzling" paintings

and his stories about parading down Fifth Avenue in his djellaba, and he liked sitting with him in the Café de Paris, where Ahmed whistled at girls. In a letter to Lucien, Allen reported that Paul's friend was "Klee like in work & quite straightforward & sincere & lively and likeable." For his part, Peter felt an immediate kinship with Ahmed—pronouncing him to be "hip." Added Allen, "He *was* hip, if that's an honorific use of the word, as in innately understanding and all-tolerant."

Francis Bacon, who had come down from London that season, was obliging Paul by continuing to tutor Yacoubi. After meeting Allen and Peter, he sometimes joined the raucous late-night sessions at the Muniria, where all manner of misfits washed up in William's room. Bacon liked William and Allen a great deal, but he was put off when one of their companions made a show of retrieving a tin can from the trash, splashing liquor into it, and offering it to him in place of a glass. (Later, he explained: "I was only afraid of getting typhoid.") When he had a gathering in the bare-bones flat that he had taken nearby, he invited Burroughs and Ginsberg, as well as Yacoubi. "Yacoubi had made a marvelous lot of majoun, and Bill Burroughs was going around with a great spoon and the pot in an old-fashioned jam jar, growling, 'Now have some of this,'" remembered Paul Danquah, the actor-turned-lawyer who was one of Bacon's Battersea landlords. "We learned later that you only needed a thumbnail's worth of *majoun*, so we spent the rest of the night flying around." Later, Danquah and Bacon experimented with the *kif* that Burroughs regarded as a staple. "Francis had no use for it because he had asthma and it made his face blow up like a balloon," reported Danquah. "He never ever did it again."

Allen pegged Bacon as a fellow apostate—a perverse genius who drank hard, gambled recklessly and said he would go back to work as a cook if his muse ever failed him. In a dispatch to Kerouac, he described Francis as a man with the soul of a satyr and the aspect of an English schoolboy: "wears sneakers & tight dungarees and black silk shirts & always looks like going [to] tennis, . . . & paints mad gorillas in grey hotel rooms drest in evening dress with deathly black umbrellas—said he would paint big pornographic picture of me & Peter." Ginsberg—who saw a parallel between Francis's brutally powerful paintings and William's shocking prose—found common ground with him on the subject of art. Saddled with the problem of bringing Burroughs's amorphous novel to a conclusion, Allen asked Francis how he finished a painting. Bacon described the act in a way that made perfect sense to the poet: "He said he did it with a chance brush stroke that locked in the magic—a fortuitous thing that he couldn't predict or orchestrate," Ginsberg remembered.

Late in the spring, Allen and Peter received an invitation from the Bowleses to have dinner at the San Francisco. If Jane was still in a state of crisis, it was not apparent to their visitors; later, Ginsberg recalled an engaging woman who presided over "a gala night with couscous" and who described Peter as "a saint." He was struck by Jane's resemblance to the late Mrs. William Burroughs: Joan had done battle with polio, and she walked with a limp, as Jane did; as Allen remembered it, she had the same "sharp, intelligent eyes" and the same round face. Quick and wry, Jane shared Joan's literary sensibility and, he thought, her "cutting perception of detail." Said Ginsberg, "They were shy, very strong characters, both self-deprecating, with low self-esteem. And both were very fond of their men, although the men's emotions were centered on younger male companions."

As much as he liked the company in Tangier, Ginsberg was ready to leave for Europe by late May. *Naked Lunch* had yet to take its final form, but the finished manuscript had grown to two hundred pages, and he and Ansen had waded through reams of Burroughs's letters. The setting had yielded up much of its exotica; he had read the Koran and made a pilgrimage to Chaouen and, like Jack, discovered that *majoun* was not his drug of choice: "I tried getting high continuously all day every day for two weeks, and it didn't work well—I was hypersensitive, and it caused a lot of anxiety," he said.

That anxiety was stoked by Burroughs, who continued to mock the hapless Peter. Orlovsky retreated to his room and immersed himself in Melville, but the hostilities continued. One evening after they all had taken *majoun*, William zeroed in on Peter once again. Allen snapped: Picking up one of Burroughs's hunting knives, he jumped up and ripped the front of William's khaki shirt—an act he soon regretted. Early in June, Allen and Peter left

for Spain. With him, Ginsberg took a draft of William's manuscript—that, and an enduring sense of unease about the man who
had been his mentor.

In the summer, William Burroughs went to Copenhagen to visit his
friend Kells Elvins, and Paul found few diversions from the task of
attending to Jane. Although she had managed to make a good showing when she saw Ginsberg, she remained in a precarious state: Her
vision was still impaired, and it took hours for her to scribble a
simple sentence. When she suffered a second epileptiform seizure,
she "lost what was left of her morale, and became quasi-hysterical,"
as Paul reported to Virgil Thomson on July 27. She needed expert
care, and it was clear that he would have to take her abroad.

The Bowleses left for London early in August. "I hate to fly and
I had to fly and Jane changed her mind every two minutes," Paul
said later. "That was awful—it was the most depressing trip." At
Oxford, she was admitted to the Radcliffe Infirmary, but she
pleaded for Paul to take her out after twenty-four hours. He quickly
arranged for her to be moved to St. Mary's Hospital in London,
where she underwent a series of X-rays and angiograms and blood
tests. After ten days, her physicians ruled out the possibility of a
brain tumor, but they also told her that her lesion was microscopic
and that surgery could offer no relief. Said one doctor, "My dear
Mrs. Bowles, go back to your pots and pans and try to cope."

Coping, however, seemed to be out of the question. "Jane was
hopelessly depressed," said Bowles. "She didn't believe it if
you gave her good news and the bad news she said she already
knew. . . . She said, 'I *know* I'll never be better.'" To Thomson, he
wrote, "The simple fact of the matter now is that Jane has lost her
nerve and is at the brink of a mental breakdown. When things get
to that point there is no end visible. . . . She is convinced that no
one can diagnose her illness and that suicide is the only solution."

While they were still in London, Paul took Jane to Dr. P. D.
Trevor-Roper, a Harley Street eye specialist. After the examination,
he told Paul that while there could be compensatory effects, the
damage to Jane's vision was irreversible. Afraid that the news would
send her over the edge, Paul kept the news to himself, reporting to

Jane only that her symptoms were believed to be a natural concomi-
tant of the stroke.

By late August, it seemed that nothing more could be done in
England, and the Bowleses sailed for Morocco. From the first moment, their voyage home was an ordeal: Jane began to have palpitations, and then she suffered another seizure. Paul persuaded her to
enter a clinic in Gibraltar, but before the ship reached the Straits she
changed her mind and insisted that they return to Tangier. The
moment they landed in Morocco, she began begging him to take her
back to London.

Unable to face another journey, Paul bought a plane ticket for
Anne Harbach, a wealthy Parade regular who offered her services
as a companion. Before they left, Jane descended into a state that
was unlike anything he had ever seen: Heavily sedated, she seemed
to be sleepwalking through a nightmare. Although she could speak
clearly, she was incapable of making any real contact. She refused
to walk unless someone was at her elbow to guide her, and even
then her steps were tentative. Despite her uncertainty, she was
anything but passive; Paul saw in her "an undercurrent of violence"
that was directed against herself, as well as against anyone who
happened to be within shouting range. He reported to Virgil Thomson that in moments of distress, she would "take hold of heavy
objects with the idea of hurling them across the room." As Paul told
it, she also began talking to herself—repeating the phrase "Complete isolation, complete isolation."

In September, Jane and Anne flew to London via Paris. Convinced that she was about to be tortured, Jane tried to break loose
from her escort at Orly. Said Paul, "Anne turned her back, and Jane
escaped. She had to go running across the airport to get her." When
they reached England, Jane was admitted to the Radcliffe Infirmary
and, soon afterward, to a psychiatric clinic in Northhampton. At the
clinic, her psychiatrists recommended electroshock therapy—a
treatment that she refused to allow.

A few weeks after Jane's arrival, Paul followed her to England.
With him was Ahmed Yacoubi, who, with Bacon's help, had been
given a show at the Hanover Gallery. Paul found his wife slightly
better, although she still seemed "profoundly unhappy and depressed," as he described it. Desperately bored with the other pa-

tients, she was passing the time playing Ping-Pong and weaving.

Along with their friend Sonia Orwell, Paul urged Jane to sign the release that would allow her physicians to administer shock therapy. For days, she resisted; to Thomson, Bowles reported: "She sees its effect on the other patients around her and rejects it, without understanding that the others are manic-depressives, schizophrenics, and alcoholics on whom it is often tried without much hope of being successful." Finally, she relented, and the document was signed.

Paul contracted a severe case of the Asian flu almost immediately, and Jane was forced to endure the treatment without him. Confined to bed in a London hospital, Bowles decided to write a story whose protagonist would fall into a fever-dream that echoed his own. In the midst of his delirium, he completed "Tapiama"—a tale in which he explored the fate of a photographer who travels to Central America and loses himself in a hallucinogen called *cumbiamba*. Although it was productive at first, Paul's convalescence was not an easy one; he was sent home from the hospital after his fever abated, but hours later he was back, suffering from pneumonia, which quickly was followed by pleurisy. It was three weeks before he recovered, and by the time he was reunited with Jane, she had been subjected to seven sessions of electroshock. Later, she would tell him that the treatment had been torture: "She said she'd rather die than go through it again," he remembered.

As difficult as it had been, however, the regime produced a slight improvement in Jane's mood and on November 11 her doctors pronounced her stable enough to leave the hospital. In London, she joined Paul at Sonia Orwell's house on Percy Street, where they were to stay until they sailed on the S.S. *Orion*.

Paul made use of his remaining days in London by trying to find a publisher for a collection of stories that he had written since 1950—among them, "The Frozen Fields," an arresting study of a sensitive child emotionally abused by a father much like Claude Bowles. His well-connected hostess (an editor who was a *Horizon* veteran and the widow of George Orwell) made an appointment for him at the offices of Hamish Hamilton. Somehow, Paul and his manila envelope found their way instead to the headquarters of William Heinemann, and the editor who saw him there immediately offered a contract. ("Sonia," Bowles remembered obliquely, "had to call Hamish Hamilton and explain.")

Heartened by his success and by Jane's gradual improvement, Paul left London late that November with his wife and Ahmed. From the S.S. *Orion,* he wrote a note to John Lehmann to report that he was on his way back to Tangier: "Jane is with me," he said. "She is quite well now, which is the best news of 1957, at least for me."

Bowles's sense of relief was short-lived. As soon as he arrived in Tangier, Paul found himself in the unlikely position of being a player in a public scandal—one that had been created by the impetuous Ahmed Yacoubi. The prelude to the drama had taken place in late June, when the parents of a fourteen-year-old German boy had accused Yacoubi of seducing their son. After they complained to the police, Ahmed had been arrested. Quietly bailed out by Paul, he had been detained a second time and plied with questions about the Bowleses and other infidels. The day after the three returned from England, the authorities zeroed in—arresting Yacoubi on charges of "assault with intent to kill" and taking him to the jail in the Casbah. There, he was allowed to languish while his trial date was postponed repeatedly.

For the Bowleses, the episode was a paranoid fantasy come true. Being thrown out of the country was one of Jane's chief fears; and being branded as a homosexual, of course, was one of Paul's. He was appalled at the prospect of his relationship with Yacoubi being subjected to scrutiny; and as the weeks wore on, his apprehension blossomed into a full-blown panic. Terrified of authority, he convinced himself that it was only a matter of time before the police came for him. "I don't know how much of it was in his own mind and how much was actual, but he felt he'd been accused of espionage," remembered William Burroughs. "He was always afraid that if he left Tangier he wouldn't be allowed to return."

As it happened, the Bowleses' fears of being deported were not unfounded. Aside from the fact that the government was taking a hard line against Nazarene decadence, Moroccan bureaucrats were concerned about the way the country was presented to the rest of the world; eager to establish themselves as progressives, they took exception to novels like *The Spider's House,* which focused on the more exotic aspects of native culture. "They knew about Paul's writing, and they didn't like it at all—they thought it was 'folkloric,' and that it was condescending propaganda about rug merchants," Burroughs said later.

In the beginning, at least, Paul seemed prepared to stand by Yacoubi; he brought food to him in jail, and he hired a cadre of lawyers to lobby for his release. When he heard reports that Ahmed's trial at last had been scheduled and that he would be called to testify, however, he lost his resolve. "He panicked," remembered David Herbert. "Jane said, 'Oh, I'm sure you won't be involved at all.' But Paul wanted to flee."

While some friends placed the blame on Ahmed, others believed that in his own passive manner, Paul himself had orchestrated the crisis. Knowing that Yacoubi could be impulsive and hubristic and indiscreet, he had continued the relationship even after it became clear that expatriates in Tangier were no longer free to behave as they wished. Skilled in the art of "teaching others how to blackmail him," as Wanklyn put it, Bowles had found a perfect companion in the reckless Yacoubi.

Late in January of 1958, after he was called in for questioning and his lawyer warned that Jane would be next, Paul decided to leave Tangier once again. With Jane, he made preparations to escape to Funchal in Madeira. By the middle of February, the Bowleses had closed their flats and flown to Lisbon, where they arranged for passage to Funchal. Ahmed remained in jail, and Cherifa took refuge with relatives in the countryside.

Two dark, rainy months later, Jane flew to New York alone, leaving Paul in Portugal. Both her anxiety and her blood pressure were out of control, and she again needed constant care. From the States, she wrote an anguished, garbled letter that offered a glimpse of what had transpired between them in Madeira. After asking Paul to write a note to her mother, she added, "I don't think you should mention suiside as glibly as you have on occasion—but I don't think you would use that way out really," she wrote. "This may sound like a nonsequator but I am in a hurry and I reffer to a conversation we had in Portugal. You threatened suiside if you had no money or if you were trapped with me and I didn't cheer up or if you were trapped in America. Naturally I have been in a bad state but I have to face it and not die of it. . . . Please for God's sake don't send me any masages saying that Cherifa is waiting for my return or expecting. I will only go back if you go back because the government has changed." Still, her longing for Morocco was palpable: "The episode in Tangier has nearly broken my heart . . ." wrote Jane. "Berred[1] and Cherifa I can't bear to think about, and must tretend there dead as you did Ahmed."

With Yacoubi still in prison, every expatriate who had ever slept with a Moroccan found himself waiting for a knock on the door. Ahmed's arrest, it seemed, had presaged a search-and-destroy operation; unwilling to ignore foreign pederasts and homosexuals, as his predecessors had done, the city's new Algerian police chief was rumored to have composed a blacklist that included some of Tangier's most prominent expatriates. In the months that followed Yacoubi's imprisonment, scores of foreigners were interrogated at the police station in the Grand Socco, and sixteen were kept behind bars. Suddenly, travel agencies were crowded with Europeans trying to arrange passage to Rome or Paris or Lisbon, and patrons at the Parade were eyeing their neighbors with distrust.

William Burroughs, who had returned to the Muniria in September 1957, was busy with his own escape plans. Aside from the fact that he was hardly prepared to offer himself up for questioning, he had grown impatient with the expatriate community. In the Bowleses' absence, the scene seemed spectacularly dull. To Allen, he complained that the town had become an exercise in absurdity; after reporting that he was "sick of [Tangier] and everybody in it," he added, "Brion Gysin has [re]opened the Thousand and One Nights with a troop of sorry dancing boys all with ferret faces and narrow shoulders and bad teeth looking rather like a bowling team from Newark. . . ." The whole Tangier ethos, he added, was repellent: He reported to Ginsberg that one neighbor—a man with a well-documented fondness for little boys—was bringing eight-year-old Arab hustlers back to his room. "It is really disgusting pre-pubescent gooks prowling about the house . . . and he says gaily, 'Oh, its just that I feel INADEQUATE with older people' and LAUGHS. . . . The stupid bastard is in the middle of a particularly undesirable section of Hell and DOESN'T EVEN KNOW IT," wrote William.

Burroughs himself was in the middle of another spiritual upheaval. He had given up drinking, halted work on *Naked Lunch* and embarked on an orgy of introspection. Kiki was gone—stabbed to death in Madrid by a jealous lover who had caught him dallying with a girl. Struggling once again to subdue his homosexual impulses, William spent long hours meditating and thinking about his relationship with Allen. Deciding that he loved Ginsberg only in a platonic sense, he concluded that as much as he liked boys, he was meant to be a heterosexual. Writing *Naked Lunch* had been the turning point—he had purged himself, and the "horrible sickness" was no more. William promptly announced his epiphany to Allen, who was encamped in Paris with Peter. "Changes in my psyche profound and basic," he asserted. "Must have some cunt. I was never supposed to be queer at all."

To Burroughs, Tangier suddenly seemed part of the past—a past in which he had been ruled by the "ugly spirit." In January, then, he took his leave—stripping his minimal room at the Muniria and never looking back. By the middle of the month, he had joined Ginsberg in Paris, where they had an emotional reunion at a scruffy hotel on the rue Gît-le-Coeur.

The gun-shy Orlovsky had headed for New York when Burroughs arrived, but Ginsberg immediately sent him a report on their encounter. Burroughs, he said, had indeed undergone a transformation: The two had faced one another across a kitchen table and talked until 3 A.M. about the difficult interlude in Tangier. "I confessed all my doubt and misery—and in front of my eyes he turned into an Angel!" wrote Allen. William had told him that he had become aware of "a benevolent sentient [feeling] center to the whole Creation," and that he had made the trip to Paris not to conquer him but to consult an analyst who could help banish his remaining blocks. "We talked a long time, got into tremendous rapport, very delicate, I almost trembled," he told Peter. ". . . I woke this morning with great bliss of freedom & joy in my heart. Bill's saved, I'm saved, you're saved, we're all saved. . . ."

*   *   *

While Burroughs had been confronting his demons, Brion Gysin had been wrestling with the sort of intrigue that only he could create. Since his return from Algeria, he had struggled to keep 1001 Nights from going under, but chaos was setting in. After a falling out with the domineering Hamri (who supervised the kitchen and a contingent of relatives who served as helpers), he had arranged to sever their business relationship. Later, Hamri remembered: "Brion says, 'You don't have no relaxation—I want to give you two months' holiday.' I say, 'Good idea.' I go to Madrid and make exhibition there for three months. I got my foot back in Tangier, I feel something black around me. Brion says, 'You can't come back to work. The people who are part of our association don't want you.' He says, 'If you have any problem, then go to the solicitor.'" As Hamri told it, he protested loudly and then sold his share of the business to Brion for ten thousand dollars. "I took my Jajouka [musicians]," he said, "and opened another place."

In the meantime, Brion had brought in other performers and addressed himself to the task of trying to control his staff, which still included a contingent of "Pan people," as he called them. But the battle lines had been drawn, and the real hostilities erupted when it was discovered that Brion had secretly been making notes and drawings for a "recipe book" of Moroccan magic. Furious that an infidel had pried into their secrets, his unwilling informants had extracted revenge. Said Brion, "They poisoned my food twice and then, apparently, resorted to more efficacious means to get rid of me."

During a routine inspection of the kitchen at his restaurant, Gysin had reached into a ventilator and found an evil-looking amulet—an object that drew gasps from his Moroccan workers. "A treasure trove for an ethnographer," in Brion's words, it was not unlike the *tseuheur* that Jane Bowles had found in her bed: "Seven round, speckled pebbles; seven big seeds in their pods; seven shards of mirror surrounded a small square paper packet, barely dusted over with soot," he remembered. "The charm stuck together with goo, probably made of newt's eyes, menstrual blood, pubic hair and chewing gum. Inside was the text, written in rusty ink from right to left across the square of paper, which had then been turned on its side and written again to form a cabalistic grid. The invocation, when I got it hazily made out, called on the Jinn of the Hearth: 'May Massa Brahim leave this house as the smoke leaves this fire, never to return. . . .' "

By Brion's account, it was only days later that Mary Cooke—who by then was his major backer—informed him that she was relieving him of his responsibilities at 1001 Nights. Many a restaurateur had fallen prey to the same fate, of course, and Brion had never been a businessman. ("He don't count the money—he wants to live now," said Hamri. "Tomorrow is incha'Allah."[2]) Despite his own failings, however, Gysin refused to believe that Cooke was acting independently. As he told it, he had been undone by magic, and "Scary Mary" had been summoned up by his enemies.

Under the circumstances, Brion was hardly inclined to remain in Tangier and wait for the next development. In January 1958, he headed for London, where he sold his Sahara paintings before moving on to Paris. In the Place St-Michel, he would run into a "gray-green" William Burroughs. Still uncertain about this cryptic specimen, he would pause, and then think of something that Paul Bowles had said of the Beats: "I really don't know; they're all so taken up with madness and drugs—I don't get it. But you'd like Burroughs if only you'd get to know him."

As it happened, he was right: Over the next few years, Gysin and Burroughs would forge a bond that was eerily intimate—one that would change forever the relationships between William and the compatriots who had come to visit him in Tangier. Despite his air of indifference, it seemed that Paul Bowles took a certain pleasure in throwing together such iconoclasts; one could never predict how they would react, and there was always the interesting possibility that something disastrous would come to pass.

Chapter 15

In 1958, the campaign against undesirables—con men and dead-beats and tax dodgers, as well as those who slept with the wrong companions—was only one of the urgent topics among the foreigners who remained in Tangier. Since the country had wrested its independence from the French, the territory that had once belonged to the infidels had seen dozens of changes, and expatriates found only a few of them to be agreeable. Although the city had been given a charter that allowed it to regain its economic independence, its cosmopolitan aspect was vanishing. The Spanish peseta and the French franc had been replaced by the Moroccan dirham; the press faced government censorship; and French—not the Spanish mastered by most natives—was the second language. The problem of unemployment was growing more severe, and the government had been obliged to spend 200 million francs to help the fifty thousand Tanjawis who were threatened with starvation. For Europeans who depended upon goods that were subject to stiff new import duties, the cost of living had nearly doubled, and the quality of life had dropped dramatically: Not only was it more expensive to buy a new Cadillac, but the Moroccan policemen who had replaced the local gendarmes refused to look the other way when one double-parked it in front of the Minzah.

Under the new regime, beloved landmarks had begun to disappear or to be appropriated by Moroccan entrepreneurs. In the medina, the imposing Spanish post office had been transformed into an undistinguished Tanjawi hotel. The fraying charm of the Café Central—where visitors like Truman Capote had lingered over wine and tapas—was no more. Don Felipe Sacarella, a Spaniard whose family had held the lease for half a century, had been ousted in favor of Tanjawis who had installed fluorescent lights and Formica tables and, of course, replaced the wine with sticky tea. The charming Grand Socco, with its ancient oaks and fragrant flower stalls, had been all but destroyed: After a city bus plowed into a crowd at the plaza, authorities had ordered that the trees be razed and the wooden stalls carted away. Expatriates had mounted a campaign to save the oaks, but the administration had prevailed; now, the trees were gone and the marketplace had all the allure of a parking lot.

Ironically, the Tanjawi administration was eager to attract foreign visitors, and it had spared no effort to make the city seem more sophisticated. Its most ambitious project was the Municipal Casino: An elaborate pleasure palace near the Place de France, it offered roulette, haute cuisine and entertainers like Charles Aznavour. Kept away by reports that the city was a shambles, tourists refused to take the bait. Closed to natives (who could not legally be served alcohol), the casino attracted only a few high-rolling expatriates— Francis Bacon among them. In a city that had lost much of its wealth, the glittering gaming house seemed hopelessly out of place.

Tangier's new regime had been more successful when it turned its attention to the roiling port. In the past, Europeans arriving from Spain and Gibraltar had been besieged by a strident mob of touts, beggars and small-time con men—an experience that was remarkably unpleasant at best. Now the welcoming committee was considerably smaller and infinitely more restrained, and baggage was handled by efficient teams of Tanjawi porters who belonged to the Moroccan Labor Union.

Expatriates were pleased to note that the medina was no longer the unwelcoming place it had been in 1955, and that they could visit the souks without feeling that they were in hostile territory. Still, those attached to the odd pageantry of the native quarter felt that something was missing: Boys now wore blue jeans and girls ventured into the streets without lithams. Prostitutes like those who had loitered outside the Chat Noir had disappeared, and a cold silence fell at night over streets that once had been alive until dawn broke. As Bowles observed in an essay written shortly before his flight to Portugal, the Istiqlal reformers seemed to have crushed Tangier's scapegrace spirit: "The Tangier of the dubious bars, the *maisons closes,* the pimps and panderers, the smugglers and refugees from Scotland Yard and the F.B.I., the old Tangier that tried valiantly if unsuccessfully to live up to its inflated reputation as a 'sin city' is dead and buried," he wrote. ". . . The atmosphere is that of an entr'acte; people are waiting for the spectacle to recommence."

While the Bowleses waited at a safe distance, they received dispatches from friends who told them that the Moroccan police were still hard at work. At the end of March 1958, Christopher Wanklyn posted a letter to Jane from Gibraltar:

> The Tangier situation is not too good, and I think it would be very unwise for you to go there for quite some time. Temsamani has been called in four times for questioning. He was asked about Paul's relations with Ahmed, and yours with Cherifa. He gave the right answers, that Cherifa was your maid, that A and P slept in separate rooms, and that he was only the chauffeur and didn't know anything about your private lives.
>
> Ahmed is still in the Casbah, and his case has not yet come up for trial. Temsamani went to see him regularly, and took him food etc, until he was warned by the warden that he was putting himself in a bad position, so he stopped. Apparently Ahmed caused a lot of trouble in the jail, and talked of his influential European friends who would get him out. I haven't seen Cherifa, I don't know whether she is in town. I didn't think it would be a good idea to go to her house, either for her sake or my own. Everybody is very worried about the whole thing, and anxious not to be drawn into it. Anne [Harbach] is convinced her phone is being tapped. . . . T[emsamany] has been very loyal about the

whole affair, but has finally had enough, and asks me to say please not to write him any more directly. I am also to pass on messages from Charles [Gallagher]—please no more mysterious telegrams to his flat, and from Anne—to write only on open postcards, and that if any definite news comes up she will get a letter out by Gibraltar.

This is all most unpleasant, I know, and there may be an element of hysteria in it, on our parts. But the atmosphere in Tangier is grim. Police are like locusts everywhere, demanding passports and drivers licenses, and throwing people into jail for no reason. . . .

Days later, Francis Bacon mailed a dispatch to Paul, reporting that he had sent two canvases to Yacoubi in jail and would send more when he saw Temsamany. Saying that he had little news of Ahmed, Francis wrote that the authorities were divulging nothing to Nazarenes and added that reporters had asked why he had left Tangier. "I think you should be careful . . . about coming back for your sake as well as Ahmed's. If you write to me please do not put your name on the back of the envelope," said Francis.

On May 14, more than five months after he was imprisoned, Yacoubi was taken to court. Acquitted during a hearing that lasted less than five minutes, he suddenly found himself a free man. Bacon immediately sent a note to Paul, saying that Ahmed was eager to retrieve his possessions from Bowles's flat.

Although Yacoubi was safe, the inquisition continued through the summer. When William Burroughs ventured back to Morocco that August, he sent a gloomy report to Allen Ginsberg: "Tangier is finished. The Arab dogs are upon us. Many a queen has been dragged shrieking from the Parade, the Socco Chico, and lodged in the local box where sixty sons of Sodom now languish. . . . The boy[s], many beaten to a pulp, have spelled a list of hundreds. . . ."

Two months later, Burroughs dispatched a slightly less pessimistic letter from London to Bowles, who had sailed to New York to join Jane: "As to the adviseability [sic] of your return to Tanger it is for the Clouded Crystal Ball Dept," wrote William. "I have it from Paul Lund who allegedly read it in ESPANA that you were officially expelled from the Sherifian Empire no reason given by Rabat. . . . Others deny that such a notice appeared. . . . Gallagher has it straight from Securite that you can return at any time. . . . Brion Gysin, surprisingly thinks you could return without danger. . . . So?"

Yacoubi himself had applied for the visa that he would need to enter the States. In a letter written to Bowles that fall, he declared that he trusted no one in Tangier. He had spent the summer at the Villa Muniria, lying low, but he reported that he was deeply in debt after paying off his lawyers. He also admitted that he had written to Libby Holman to ask her to buy several paintings.

As traumatic as Ahmed's experience may have been, there was little need to flee; even then, authorities were slacking off on the campaign to cast out the city's foreign devils. Perhaps they had grown bored; perhaps they had realized that the crusade was a threat to settlers whom they couldn't afford to lose. In any case, the inquiries stopped as precipitously as they had begun, and the "queens who had been dragged shrieking from the Parade" were set free. Like the half-built high-rises that stood rusting in the Ville Nouvelle, the purge was simply abandoned.

In December 1958, Paul and Jane headed back to Morocco to pick up the threads of their lives. After two and a half months in the psychiatric clinic at New York Hospital–Cornell Medical Center (where she had been treated for high blood pressure and neurological complaints), Jane had seemed strong enough to make the journey to Tangier. From the moment she boarded the ship with Paul, however, she was overcome by anxiety; plagued by headaches, palpitations and a laundry list of other symptoms, she gave him no rest. During the day, she said she couldn't eat; at four in the morning, she would order up sixteen sliced-chicken sandwiches. When they reached Algeciras, she convinced herself that she and Paul would be arrested if they entered Moroccan territory. She insisted that he cable the Tangier police asking whether they could return, but she panicked as soon as the wire had been sent—saying that contacting the authorities was the worst thing they could have done. Only after the American consul had dispatched a reassuring cable did she agree to leave the safety of Spain.

Once they arrived in Tangier, the picture changed dramatically: Jane's panic broke, and she relaxed her grip on the exhausted Paul. Since there had been no uniformed police waiting for them at the port, she saw that one crisis, at least, was over. In a letter sent to Virgil Thomson just after they reached Morocco, Bowles reported: "She began to laugh and take pleasure in food, and become her old normal self, more so than she has been at any time since the stroke. I think all will go well now for a while, perhaps for good, until some external situation changes everything. . . ."

In the weeks after their return, Jane and Paul settled into the Inmueble Itesa, an unpretentious five-story building on the outskirts of the Ville Nouvelle. After he had found a cook and a full-time helper for his wife, Bowles seized his chance to come and go. In mid-February, he went back to New York to attend the opening of Tennessee Williams's *Sweet Bird of Youth,* for which he had written the score. Returning to Tangier late that spring, he began a project that he had wanted to carry out since he heard his first *rhaita.* With grant money and a professional tape recorder given to him by the Rockefeller Foundation, he undertook four separate expeditions in which he was to capture as much tribal music as he could find. The tapes were to be sent to the Library of Congress, and, it was hoped, be released as a record.

Paul's traveling companions were the unflappable Wanklyn, who spoke fluent Maghrebi, and Mohammed Larbi Jilali, a Moroccan who had served as a guide on a year-long British trek through the Sahara. Wedged into Christopher's old Volkswagen along with Paul's endless suitcases (one of which, Wanklyn noted, contained only ties), they set out in July on the first of their five-week journeys—this one to southwestern Morocco. The escape, Paul remembered, was a welcome one: "It was summer; we knew that it would not rain and that there would be many nights with fires and drums under the stars."

There were also enough political entanglements to satisfy even Paul. Before they left Tangier, he had tried to secure the approval of the Moroccan government—which, of course, would have noth-

1. As he traveled through the desert while writing The Sheltering Sky, *Paul Bowles stayed in remote pensions, where he often wrote in bed.*

8, 9. *Known for his outrageous tales, the artist Brion Gysin (above) experimented with drugs and made frequent expeditions into the Sahara. Tangier socialite Countess Phyllis della Faille (below) lived in a disordered villa where goldfish swam in the bathtub and chimps sat at the dinner table.*

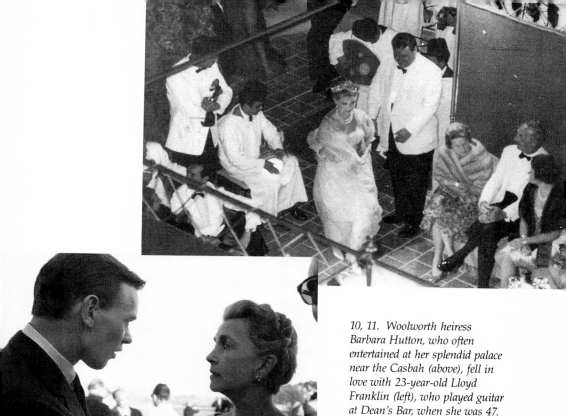

10, 11. *Woolworth heiress Barbara Hutton, who often entertained at her splendid palace near the Casbah (above), fell in love with 23-year-old Lloyd Franklin (left), who played guitar at Dean's Bar, when she was 47.*

12. *Fond of tweed jackets and silk dressing gowns, Paul Bowles (above, in 1956) seldom traveled lightly. According to a friend, he once brought a suitcase full of ties on a trip into the desert.*

13, 14. *(Above, left) When Allen Ginsberg (center) returned to Tangier in 1961, he had a reunion at the Villa Muniria with Paul Bowles and William Burroughs (right), who brought along acolyte Ian Sommerville (above, right).*

15. *(Above, center) In 1957, William Burroughs (in safari jacket) posed for Allen Ginsberg on the beach with Peter Orlovsky (left) and Jack Kerouac (center).*

16. *On the roof of the Villa Muniria, where friends including Alan Ansen (above, right) helped him type the manuscript of* Naked Lunch, *William Burroughs did a takeoff on a strangulation scene from his book.*

17, 18, 19. *A dissolute British blueblood, Michael Portman (above, right) was staying with Burroughs when Ginsberg returned to Tangier with Peter Orlovsky and Gregory Corso (at right) in 1961. Although Allen wanted William and Peter (below, in 1957) to be friends, the two could barely tolerate one another.*

20, 21. *In 1964, Tangerinos including Jane Bowles, William Burroughs (in skullcap), and Paul Bowles were photographed by* Esquire *in a Tangier café (above); Burroughs (with son Billy, left) produced a "cut-up" text for the magazine's photo essay on the city's expatriates.*

22, 23. *The novelist Alfred Chester (at right, and in his wig, below, with the poet Edward Field) came to Tangier in 1963. Extravagantly paranoid, he convinced himself that Paul Bowles wanted to kill him.*

24. *Although Brion Gysin (right, on a Tangier rooftop in 1966) shunned William Burroughs while he was a junkie, the two later became collaborators. Paul Bowles, among others, took a dim view of the writing experiments that the two conducted: "Anyone who came in contact with Brion," he said, "fell ten years behind in his career."*

25. *The second son of the 15th Earl of Pembroke, the Honorable David Herbert (above, in his villa on the Mountain) shared Jane Bowles's taste for wicked gossip.*

26, 28. *After he became distanced from the painter Ahmed Yacoubi, Paul Bowles (far right, in 1959) became the mentor to the Moroccan storyteller Mohammed Mrabet.*

27. Brion Gysin's friend Felicity Mason (right) had a romance with his protégé Hamri, who was a painter.

29, 30, 31, 32, 33. *In August 1967, a frail, anxious Jane Bowles was followed for a week by* Life *photographer Terence Spencer. She made an appearance at a party given by Princess Martha Ruspoli (above, right) accompanied by Cherifa (above, left, and at left, in sunglasses), as well as her husband (opposite page, top). With Paul, she attended a dinner party at David Herbert's house (opposite page, center) and a fête given by Joseph McPhillips (third from right on opposite page, bottom). Weeks earlier, she had undergone electroshock therapy in Spain.*

34, 35, 36, 37. Moody, mercurial, Jane Bowles (in 1967, with publisher Peter Owen and his wife, Wendy) was "constantly giving off different lights and glints, like a prism," said one friend. "She could look incredibly glamorous one moment, and like the worst housewife in history, the next."

38. *In her black* litham *and* haik, *Jane's companion Cherifa looked like "a terrorist," as Paul Bowles put it. Said Bowles, "She* was *a terrorist."*

39. *Yvonne (left) and Isabelle Gerofi (center), who managed the Librairie des Colonnes, were among Jane's closest confidantes. Like many of her friends, they loathed Cherifa. "Jane was always afraid of her," said Yvonne.*

40, 41. *In the years after Jane's death, Paul Bowles admitted that his wife had kept him from becoming a recluse. "I think I lived vicariously," he said.*

ing to do with foreigners who wanted to examine the native culture. After Rabat had turned him down, Paul had persuaded the American embassy to issue an impressive document bedecked with seals, stamps and signatures. The certificate was enough to satisfy the governors of most provinces, but some caïds branded the visitors as opportunists and sent them on their way. "These men seemed to consider us part of a conspiracy to present Morocco as a . . . land of savages," Paul remembered. "It was they themselves who used the expression *une musique de sauvage;* feeling as they did about it, they could be expected to consider it their patriotic duty to see to it that the shameful sounds made by their countrymen did not reach alien ears."

As Wanklyn told it, the calculating Larbi (who spent much of his time smoking *kif* and drinking Scotch) often took advantage of the fact that their welcome was uncertain. "He did more to complicate our lives than anything else; he always seemed to be on the point of trying to blackmail Paul, and Paul seemed to be teaching him how to do it," he said. "Since half the authorities were worried that we would make fun of them, that faction could be appealed to in order to scuttle the expedition."

Aside from trying to placate the locals, Paul and Christopher were obliged to endure lamentable food, primitive lodgings and long hours on dust-choked roads. The heat was often suffocating, and when they could they began their journey before dawn. Since their tape recorder could be used only on 110-volt AC current (a scarce commodity), they devised complex schemes to record remote tribes. "In Tamanar," Paul remembers, "the only generator supplying what we needed belonged to an irascible Frenchman who would not even discuss allowing us to use it. We had to go back to Essaouira and wait three days for the musicians to be shipped to us from Tamanar by truck." Only occasionally did they offer money in payment to performers; instead, they carried loaves of sugar and handed out chunks as gifts.

On their foray into the Rif, where they hoped to record the musicians of the Beni Snassen tribe, Bowles and Wanklyn were serenaded at dinner by the sound of French bombs exploding near the Algerian border. As Paul remembered it, the diners in the garden of the Hotel Terminus near Oujda ignored the earth-shaking detonations, and the waiter shrugged off his inquiries about the noise. "During dessert," Paul reported, "there was a long string of machine-gun fire not more than half a mile distant, in Oujda itself. 'What's that?' I demanded. The waiter's face did not change. 'I didn't hear anything,' he said. All kinds of things happen in Oujda nowadays, and no one asks any questions." That same evening, Bowles came down with a fever; after three days in bed, he finally had a meeting with the governor's secretary, who declared that the Beni Snassen had no music, and sent the party on its way.

For all of their discomfort, Bowles and Wanklyn managed to find magnificent performers and to witness scenes that were pleasantly surreal. At Taza, they recorded popular songs performed by a twelve-man ensemble that included eight riflemen firing their weapons as a rhythmic accompaniment to the music. In Meknès, they found a Sephardic Jewish colony where services were sung in both Hebrew and Arabic, in the florid *andaluz* style borrowed from Spain in the fifteenth century. They recorded a group of Gnaouas whose vocalist was an ancient Sudanese who had migrated by foot across the Sahara in his youth; and they tracked down Beni Bouifrour musicians who played the rare *zamar*—a double-reed instrument with two bull's-horn resonators.

Although government functionaries were often wary of the Nazarenes, the performers were usually delighted by the attention. Said Wanklyn, "I remember a tribe that we recorded somewhere in the mountains near Azilal; the musicians were marvelously dressed all in white, with white turbans. The women had brightly colored scarves over their heads and, of course, jewelry; they were dancing and moving as the musicians played. We played the tape back for them afterwards, and the musicians were rolling around on the floor in ecstasy and delight, laughing and thumping each other. It was great fun."

In October, after they had traveled nearly twenty-five thousand miles in pursuit of the Ait Ulixxek, the Beni Touzine and the Temsaman, Paul received a letter from the Moroccan Ministry of Foreign Affairs requesting that he suspend his "ill-timed" project. Advised by the American embassy that he should simply carry on quietly, he continued until December, when he was sent a sterner communiqué ordering him to halt. From that point onward, it seemed, the Ministry of the Interior would have to give its approval to anyone who wanted to record tribal music. Although Bowles would be unable to tape some of the music he had hoped to collect in the steppes along the Algerian border and the Tafilalet and its oases in the southeast, he had captured more than sixty hours of music from twenty-three towns and villages—a splendidly diverse sample of a genre about to be corrupted by the world of Coca-Cola and Radio Cairo.[1]

That year, William Burroughs was having his own problems with the Moroccan government. During an April expedition to Tangier, he had been caught up in a scandal triggered by one Captain Stevens, a hapless character who had been part of the smuggling crowd. A crony of Paul Lund (himself an ex-con who faced life imprisonment if he returned to England), Stevens had managed to get himself arrested in the Socco Chico for possession of a half-kilo of opium. "On his idiot person," in Burroughs's words, he had been carrying a letter from William to Lund in which he proposed a plan for exporting *kif* hidden in camel saddles. Under police questioning, the desperate Lund had fingered Burroughs, saying that he was an opium baron who had conspired with Stevens to smuggle narcotics to France. The notoriously inefficient Tangier police had failed to discover that this Paris-based drug lord was actually haunting the Café Central, and William had managed to slip out of town on a packet boat before they closed in. Still, he knew that the Moroccan authorities had his Paris address, and that the French police were likely to hear of the camel-saddle scheme.

In May, while William was still living at the Beat Hotel, as it was called, the boom had lowered; a squad of gendarmes raided the firetrap (where Brion Gysin was a neighbor), found a gram of hash in his room and placed him under arrest. The Lund affair, it seemed, would have to be explained. "Telegram from Interpol relative to the Stevens case," Burroughs reported to Ginsberg. "God knows I have no connection with those sorry, stupid *bastards.* But it does look bad to the judicial eye. . . ." By September, he had been brought into court in Paris for a preliminary hearing, and October found him preparing for a full-fledged trial.

As much as the entanglement might have annoyed him in the

past, however, Burroughs was able to approach the inquisition with a certain equanimity. The previous year had brought about a dramatic change in his status as a writer: Just as he had abandoned hope that his novel would ever see print, his work had sparked a literary firestorm. No longer an *hombre invisible,* he was now regarded in certain quarters as an *homme des lettres.*

The turnabout had begun when a *Naked Lunch* excerpt submitted by Ginsberg had appeared in a literary magazine subsidized by the University of Chicago: University authorities had suppressed the next issue (which was to have featured more of William's graphic routines, as well as work by Jack Kerouac), and student editors Irving Rosenthal and Paul Carroll had printed the offending material in an outlaw journal christened *Big Table.* The magazine had been impounded at the Chicago post office on the grounds that it was obscene, and the ensuing censorship controversy had been loud enough to be heard in Paris. In June 1959, Olympia Press publisher Maurice Girodias—who had rejected the portion of the novel that Ginsberg showed him in 1957—had decided to have another look at Burroughs's work. With Gysin and Sinclair Beiles, an Olympia editor who was an erstwhile Tangerino, Burroughs had quickly assembled a final version of the anarchic manuscript and given it to Girodias. At the end of July, the Olympia edition of *Naked Lunch* had appeared in bookstores in Paris. Soon afterward, Grove Press had bought the rights to publish the novel in America, and publishers in Germany and Italy were offering up their own advances. In Paris, at least, Burroughs had created a sensation; even the introduction to *Naked Lunch*—an essay in which he described reaching "the end of the junk line" in Tangier—had been published in the respected *Nouvelle Revue Française.*

That October, when William went to face the three judges who were to rule on his drug case, he was accompanied by Maurice Girodias's own *avocat*—a man who, to Burroughs's delight, was called Maître Bumsell. Bumsell cautioned Burroughs to stand up when he was addressed by the court and to remain sober on pain of death. "He said, even if *they* laugh, don't you ever laugh. Don't ever laugh! That's the worst thing you can do!" remembered Burroughs, who managed to get through the confrontation without cracking an incriminating smile. Arguing that his client was a scholar who had simply consorted with the wrong crowd, Bumsell read parts of William's *Naked Lunch* preface to the court ("Look down LOOK DOWN along that junk road before you travel there and get in with the wrong mob"). Apparently impressed with his credentials, the French judges handed Burroughs a suspended sentence and a token fine of eighty dollars. Being a man of letters, it seemed, was going to have its rewards.

While the crusade against individual expatriates had been called off, the attempt to remake Tangier was gathering momentum in the fall of 1959. Late in October, the Sultan (now known as King Mohammed V) abruptly canceled the charter that he had granted to the International Zone after he returned from exile. Within six months, bank accounts would be frozen and the city would lose even the slim advantage of its free market in foreign exchange. Three hundred banks of various descriptions were still in operation that fall, but no more than fifteen were expected to weather the panic that was setting in. Already transferring its operation to Geneva, the conservative Moses Pariente Bank was telling its customers to exchange Moroccan money for a more stable currency and spirit it out of town. The *zahir,* it seemed, was a final blow aimed at the tainted city that Rabat was determined to reclaim.

The development was so dramatic that foreign periodicals weighed in with a wave of elegiac stories about the port once known as "wicked Tangier." In its November 2 issue, *Time* lamented: "One by one they were disappearing or going straight—those worldly cities that make so glamorous a backdrop for TV thrillers. Now it was the time of Tangier. Along the gleaming Boulevard Pasteur the luxury shops were empty, and the innumerable stalls of the city's money-changers were closed in protest. . . . Now, it seemed, Tangier was scheduled to become, economically as well as politically, just one more Moroccan city. In the cafes of the North African seaport last week, gloomy Tangerines discussed the latest calamitous rumors."

Writing from Barcelona in December, the American syndicated columnist Robert Ruark spared no overstatement in his paean to the "the rowdy, rollicking old days when all the international nogoodniks flocked to the city of evil where Hercules once dwelt." Wrote

Ruark, "I never thought it would happen to Tangier . . . what was once possibly the most wicked city in the world has become practically a Boy Scout camp. I went there by accident back a dozen years or so and in those days you could buy a murder for five bucks. You could buy a female slave if you wanted one. . . . It was a dull day when somebody didn't drown a countess, or a steady habitue of Dean's bar didn't 'disappear away,' as one Australian ex-patriot [sic] used to put it. . . ." Now, he sighed, "I don't even suppose you could buy a slave girl any more."

In January, Paul Bowles picked up the theme in a letter written to Charles Henri Ford. "Most people have left Tangier, and more and more are leaving each week. Shops are closing, there is a bad economic crisis, the Moroccans have no work and have become criminally inclined as a result. Since Moroccans are not supposed any longer to know Europeans personally, no one has any Moroccan friends. . . . The next step is to get rid of all non-Moroccans en masse." Added Bowles, "The only reason for being here now is the fact that one is here and it takes energy to find a new place to settle."

As it happened, Bowles's tone reflected not only his impatience with Tangier but his own restlessness. With the dank winter setting in, there seemed to be no escape from the claustrophobic female world in which he and Jane lived. His male clique was breaking up: Burroughs was in Paris with Brion Gysin, and Temsamany (who had sold the Jaguar that Paul had given him) had left to find work in Germany. Shaken by the recent scandal, Yacoubi had taken a girlfriend—a woman whom he soon would marry. Bowles plotted out a month-long trip to the Sahara and the Atlas Mountains, but nothing seemed to curb what Burroughs had christened the "stasis horrors." When he returned to Tangier in April, Paul sent a telling report to Lilla van Saher, an erstwhile actress who was in Tennessee's orbit. "You want to know about me?" he wrote. "What is there to write? Next to nothing. I live here . . . with Jane and have no friends at all. It's not possible for anyone to come here because Cherifa is here and doesn't permit any Moslem to enter. . . . It's a dull life and the days pass very slowly and the nights even more slowly." Adding that he hoped to go away in order to begin a new book, Bowles declared that writing was out of the question while he was at the Itesa: "I can't work here in this place, with three women servants living and quarreling with each other and with Jane outside my bedroom door," he told van Saher. "It is impossible even to take a walk after dinner because we live outside the town and there are a good many attacks in the streets, and absolutely no police protection. So no one goes out, save in cars, and I no longer have a car. I read the paper and get news on the radio and wait for time to go by so something can change. . . ."

Almost three years after her stroke, Jane herself had reached a kind of plateau: Despite the British doctor's prognosis, her vision had improved, and she had recovered much of her spirit, if not her stamina. Friends like Gallagher (who was also at the Itesa) noticed that she tired easily, and that a single glass of wine could leave her unsteady. Reading and writing still required an enormous amount of concentration; adding and subtracting were impossible, and she constantly turned to Paul for help with bills and letters and bank books. For all of that, she could still wield the humor that her admirers found so endearing. With Gallagher, she made fun of the aging expatriates who remained in Tangier; the town, she said, had become "an elephant's graveyard." In a letter to Libby Holman, she discussed her trouble dealing with names and numbers: "I don't think it would take more than six months to relearn the whole multiplication table," she wrote. "It is very funny but not bad, because I know what I need to know, and then can have someone else do the work. Some women are bad at computing even without strokes, and they are not as charming as I am."

Under the circumstances, it was easier for Jane to focus her attention on the details of domestic life than to invite the torture of trying to work. When she was with friends like David Herbert, she fretted over Paul's diet—worrying half-seriously about what he was eating on his long excursions and turning that obsession into a joke. Said Herbert, "We were talking when he was on one trip and I asked her how he was; she said, 'Darling, he's doing very nicely on gazelle.' " Remembered Gallagher, "She said, 'Paul will eat anything you put in front of him, but he only wants hamburger.' I often saw her during the cocktail hour, and after one glass of wine it was always, 'I've got to go fix Paul's hamburger.' But she would laugh as she said it."

The London-based poet Ruth Fainlight came for a long visit in the winter of 1960 with her husband, the novelist Alan Sillitoe. Through acquaintances who lived in Tangier, she met Paul and Jane, who helped the two find a flat in the Itesa. During the four months that the Bowleses were her neighbors, Ruth became extremely attached to Jane; the two shared not only a quick intelligence but a fine sense of irony about their roles as females. To Fainlight, Jane's intense preoccupation with cooking and shopping and menu planning seemed, in some ways, to be an absurdist take on the part of hausfrau.

"She talked about Paul a lot—she presented herself very, very purposefully as a married woman. . . . She'd say, 'Oh my God, I've got to do this errand and this errand,' and then she'd just snort with laughter at herself," said Fainlight. "She was a combination of anxiety and panic on the one hand and then fiendish humor. . . . She would say, 'Everyone get into position.' It was a combination of glee and real anxiety." Jane, she said, derived at least some satisfaction from stage-directing her household: "This sort of intense concentration on all the minute domestic practicality—I think it had a more existential [purpose] of convincing her that she had a function."

As Fainlight remembered it, Jane's two-bedroom apartment (which had a small enclosed terrace and a pleasing view of the countryside) was dim and cozy; furnished, like Paul's flat, in the Moroccan style, it was headquarters for a cast that included Jane's Spanish companion, her Moroccan cook, the prodigal Cherifa and various members of Cherifa's family, who dropped in at will. The compact kitchen (where Jane sometimes presided) was often filled with the fragrance of couscous or baked beans or jugged hare. Meals were taken around a *taifor* surrounded by plump cushions, and the Bowleses' parrot Seth provided a shrill counterpoint to the proceedings. The ambience, said Fainlight, was that of "a very relaxed harem"—one that was controlled by the indomitable Cherifa. "I remember going over there one day when it was very hot, and Cherifa looked like the proletarian hero in one of those films made in France in the twenties—she was wearing a pair of navy blue boxer shorts and a sort of singlet, an undershirt, and a cigarette was sticking out of the corner of her mouth like she was a truck driver," said Fainlight. "She was slouching around like Marlon Brando, and it was so *amusing,* you know, and she was obviously camping it up to the hilt. She would put her djellaba on top of it and there would be this Moroccan woman, but underneath there was this Marseilles tough. I think this amused Jane; it might well have frightened her, also—there was that potential."

Although Paul detested Cherifa—who had said more than once that she wanted to kill him—he usually came to Jane's apartment in the evenings. When he arrived, friends like Isabelle and Yvonne Gerofi were often lingering with Jane over whiskey. "Paul would come into the flat of Janie and close the door with vigorous energy, which was funny because he was so quiet; he was always telling about something he read in *Life* or *Time*," said Isabelle. As she remembered it, his accounts were usually about death and destruction. "The things he told were awful things . . . and Jane would become upset because of this," she said. "It was a special atmosphere. The bad news of *Time* magazine . . ."

Fainlight's impression was that the Bowleses shared an "anarchic glee" over dire news, and that rather than tormenting Jane, Paul was merely commiserating with her. "In any relationship, you sometimes see one person quite intentionally and maliciously playing on the fears and paranoia of the other, but I never saw him doing that," she said. "He was exceptionally correct and considerate with her. They both had this sort of gusto for awful things, and I think that was a deep link between the two of them."

As much as Paul complained about Jane's capriciousness, he still took pleasure in her ability to astonish. Years later, he remembered an afternoon at Jane's when she provoked a quarrel with a close friend; a man who adored eating and who was sensitive about his weight, Jane's confidant had been dubbed "Fatty" by the ruthless Cherifa. Said Paul, "He was coming for tea and he was late. The maids and Jane and I were all sitting around waiting and talking, and suddenly he appeared. When he came in Jane said, 'Ah, good, here's *Fatty.*' He shouted, 'That's the last straw,' and he went out and slammed the door so hard I thought he was going to break it. She always called him Fatty behind his back, and I guess she forgot . . . he'd never heard it." Jane, he remembered, felt absolutely no remorse, and the Bowleses giggled together over the scene. "I said, 'What's the matter with him?' I didn't know; it didn't even occur to me that it was because of that word. Jane laughed and laughed. She always did that when everything went wrong."

But if Jane exhibited a streak of sadism, she could also be oddly maternal. Tamara Dragadze, the youngest child of her friend Sonya Kamalakar, had just turned twelve when her parents migrated to Tangier and were introduced to the Bowleses. During the early sixties, the precocious teenager sometimes met her mother at Jane's after school, and she did her homework in the bedroom while the grown-ups finished their tea. To Tamara, the household was a welcoming place, and Jane herself seemed like a glamorous aunt. "She had an extraordinary sense of fun; I adored her," said Dragadze. "She was always beautifully dressed—all right, not in the latest fashion, but she was very clean and neat—and she cooked beautifully and so on. There was always a place laid for my tea there, and it was sort of extraordinary chaos. Cherifa would lecture me and say, 'She must do her schoolwork, she must eat properly.' There were very few children who mixed in the artistic circles in Tangier, and because my mother took me everywhere, Jane and Paul were confronted with this child of twelve. Now that I think back on it, I think they both treated me the way they would have wanted to have been treated."

Tamara was convinced that Jane was attracted to Sonya in part because she was a married woman with a young daughter. "In addition to being rather bohemian," she said, "we were an ordinary family—a mommy and a daddy and a child. Mummy had a great sense of humor and sense of occasion, as did Jane, but she also kept a very rigid schedule as far as I was concerned. In some ways, she was very square, and I think that Jane yearned for the normality that she represented."

For a woman who played up the farcical aspects of domestic life, a friend like Sonya Kamalakar seemed indispensable. Over the years, both Paul and Jane developed a fascination for Sonya, who served nasturtium sandwiches for tea and plied her guests with talk about "the belly" (as she pronounced ballet). But while Jane appreciated Sonya for her ability to handle her assignment—to "get into position"—she also recognized her as another figure who might have emerged from her own fiction. Said Christopher Wanklyn, "I always felt that Sonya was an invention of Jane's; she took such huge pleasure in Sonya's presence and Sonya's own eccentricities. It wouldn't have been the same if Jane hadn't been there to form her, as it were."

A short, luxuriously plump woman with black hair and arresting green eyes, Sonya was the daughter of Georgian nobles who had fled to Europe just before World War I. In her mid-forties, she had the aspect of an Eastern princess; flowing saris were the rule, and every gesture was extravagant. To Bowles (who saw her as "a tomato with toothpick legs"), she seemed to be deliberately self-mocking. Said Paul, "She was ridiculous, but I often thought she meant to be—as if she realized she was ridiculous and it would look better if it seemed she did it on purpose."

Educated at a white-glove girls' school in England and trained as a concert pianist, Sonya had married a musician when she was young. "She was a great Bohemian," said Dragadze. "He was a café politician as well, and they moved in very left-wing circles, along with people like George Orwell and D. H. Lawrence." Her marriage ended after World War II, and she met Narayan Kamalakar, an Indian scholar who had studied ballet in London and philosophy at Cambridge. A tiny, sad-eyed man who was dwarfed by the ample Sonya, he immediately fell in love. "His own mother had been one of the first women in the world to be a surgeon—she was a Brahmin who married a prince," Dragadze said. "She divorced his father, and she had little time for her children. He probably saw in Mummy a mother figure that he missed. She had three children, and she was fascinated by the East."

After they wed, Sonya and Narayan had moved to Paris, where Kamalakar had found a job with UNESCO. "It was a very stable time in our lives," remembered Dragadze. "I went to school; Mummy went around with various sculptors and artists, and sometimes in the afternoons I'd go with her sketching. There was a large Georgian colony there, and so I went to Georgian dancing lessons and my mother became their regular musician, playing for all of their concerts and things."

The idyll had ended when the couple met a smooth-talking Englishman who invited them to join a scientific expedition that allegedly was convening in Morocco. "He said he was getting together a group going around the world, with twenty-two members, including a tutor for the children, and he produced these contracts that he had with a newsreel for making films," remembered Dragadze. "My parents thought this was a wonderful opportunity for me to see the world, and they decided to blow their lives in Paris up in flames."

After turning the better part of their savings over to their new acquaintance, the Kamalakars had headed to Agadir, where they were to join the expedition en route. "We got off the bus and we were taken to a campground with one tent—it was this man and his family and nobody else. He said that there were other members of the expedition in Marrakech, but we got there and found none of the people we were supposed to find. In short, we had been completely conned," she said. "We were absolutely desperate; we got ourselves to Rabat and tried to seek redress through the British consulate there, but in fact Mr. Delmar, as he was called, had managed to leave very little trace. My parents had no idea how to hire a lawyer or to pursue the man."

Unable to return to Paris, the Kamalakars had headed for Tangier. For the first few days, they had camped on the beach in the tent that Delmar had given them; after Narayan found work, they had managed to find a cottage on a lush estate high above the sea. By 1960, they were still living hand to mouth, "expecting every moment to go somewhere else," as Dragadze put it. "Daddy did all sorts of odd jobs; he taught British culture at various places and sort of thought up mad schemes. My parents were both fantasists in a way, as far as earning bread and butter, and so we were in great financial straits compared to everybody else in Tangier. My mother was humiliated by the circumstances, but you know how the crumbling aristocracy can carry on; we managed to have servants, and she found a discarded tea trolley in the souks and rolled it out whenever we had guests."

Disturbed by the worldliness of his neighbors, Narayan held a weekly salon in which Tangerinos gathered to discuss Annie Besant or the Hindu Vedas or the Book of the Dead. Said Dragadze, "My father thought that European Tangier spent too much time thinking about who was sleeping with whom, and that once a week they should leave behind their stupid ephemeral obsessions. People would gather in our garden on a Saturday afternoon and he would ring a bell and they would have to sit quietly for one minute and not open their mouths. Then he would ring the bell again and somebody would volunteer to read a chapter of a book or a long poem or whatever. They were nearly all books to do with philosophy or religion, and he came into his own because he was a Cambridge-trained philosopher. It was very structured, and if people got off the track he got them back. But things were never too ardent or too serious; all sorts of people came, and there was always the comic relief of my mother making dreadful jokes."

After one reading, an ethereal young American living in Tangier with her poet boyfriend had presented her hostess with a nugget of *majoun* wrapped in silver paper—a gift that was intended to shock Sonya, who disliked drugs and drink. Instead of registering disapproval, Sonya had merely thanked her benefactor and tucked the lagniappe into her biscuit box. On a day when the family was due at the Bowleses' for dinner, Tamara came home from the lycée to find her mother having tea with two women whom she found particularly boring. Feeling abandoned, she made a foray into her parents' bedroom, where she opened the forbidden box. "I found the *majoun,* which looked a bit like marrons glacés, and I took a bite," said Dragadze. "I thought, 'It tastes a bit odd,' but I finished it and I told myself, 'This will upstage these bloody boring people.' "

When the Kamalakars reached the Itesa that evening, the drug was beginning to take hold. "We had gotten a lift with these old ladies who had a car, and as we got in the car I started to get very hot," she said. "My arms and legs felt like they were burning. When we arrived at Jane's flat, I said, 'Mummy, I'm going to die, call the doctor.' And she looked at me and said, 'You've been in my *kif!*' because my eyes had by that time dilated."

Tamara's plight threw Jane and her household into hysterics. "Jane got in an awful panic, and someone—Cherifa or the woman servant—made this enormous pile of bread and butter, and a pot of mint tea, and said I had to finish both. I remember one of them singing a Moroccan song and clapping and dancing round me, but I was so totally out of control that it was very much like having malaria or something. Finally they said, 'Go in Jane's room and don't come back until you calm down.' It was very funny, because everyone was panicking. Neither Jane nor my family knew what to do."

When Tamara groped her way back into the living room and announced that she couldn't lie still, someone thought to summon Paul. Although he took pleasure in spooking other *majoun* eaters, he managed to banish her horrors and make her feel more like Alice in Wonderland than a plague victim in a Poe story. "He came in and took over," said Dragadze. "He took me downstairs with him, only me, and he sat me down and calmed me. It was a great present, because I had him all to myself; he had always been nice to me, but aloof. He told me, 'While it lasts, you'd better enjoy it.' He played music and asked me to tell him what I thought it was about, and he gave me things to eat and drink. He was just there, just the way one would love to have somebody older."

Chapter 16

As the summer of 1960 drew to a close, two lavish celebrations served as welcome distractions for those who had decided that Tangier was moribund. Late in August, King Mohammed V descended on the city and was greeted with great rejoicing: Thousands of shouting Tanjawis turned out to watch the royal procession, and battalions of smartly uniformed soldiers marched through streets lined with red-and-green Moroccan flags. In a letter to his mother, Paul Bowles reported that the event had raised wild hope among the natives struggling for economic survival: "The whole town is crammed with Moroccans from other parts of the country, come to see the Mouloud[1] being observed under the auspices of the Sultan," he wrote. "The people still seem to believe he can do something to bring back prosperity to Tangier, but nothing is going to bring back all the Europeans who have taken their capital elsewhere; every fourth or fifth shop or bank is empty, with 'To Let' signs on it. . . ."

Against that background, the gala staged that month by Barbara Hutton seemed an anachronistic exercise in glorious excess. A reminder of the days when Tangier had been awash in ill-gotten gains, it brought a rush of excitement to the subdued city. For weeks, the remaining strivers talked of nothing but the ball; those who had been asked engaged in luxurious debates about what to wear, and unfortunates whose invitations had not arrived threw themselves at the feet of David Herbert, who had drawn up the guest list. Tangerinos who kept track of such matters noted that neither David Edge (Herbert's putative rival) nor any of his friends seemed to have been included. The Bowleses, of course, were high on Herbert's list, and "Jane was busy for a week trying to arrange her clothes," as Paul reported to his mother. "Every hour there were telephonic consultations, and [she] changed her mind at least twenty times about going and not going."

On the fog-shrouded evening of August 29, two hundred guests and thirty gate-crashers (some clutching purloined invitations that had cost twenty thousand francs) made their way through the Casbah, which was jammed with gaping spectators. Blazing white and bathed in floodlights, Sidi Hosni had been done up "like a palace ready to receive a Sultan in *The Thousand and One Nights*," as Bowles described it. The scents of jasmine and hibiscus wafted through candlelit enclaves full of treasures including rare Oriental rugs, rock-crystal plates studded with rubies and the immense red velvet tapestry that had belonged to a fifteenth-century maharajah; encrusted with pearls, rubies and emeralds, it was set off by matching jeweled harem pillows. Waiters dashed about with trays bearing oversized lobsters and salmon imported from Scotland, and the sound of popping corks punctuated the babble of French and Spanish and Italian. A company of flamenco dancers performed with a Spanish guitarist in a large courtyard, and a concert pianist serenaded guests from a hidden balcony. Native musicians with lutes and hand drums held forth in a cushion-lined room where one could watch dancing boys, and a jazz orchestra played Latin American music in a gilded pavilion on a rooftop terrace.

Members of the Moroccan secret police mingled with the guests who wandered about the maze, admiring the intricately carved walls and the jewellike tiles and the solid gold clocks from Van Cleef & Arpels. The art collection was dazzling—Kandinsky, Klee, Dalí, Braque, Fragonard and Manet, all hung in salons that were spectacularly overdone. (Recently redecorated, the house was "very Hollywood," in the words of one observer, "like the sort of thing you'd see in the old days with Rudolph Valentino.") The determinedly paranoid Jane was uneasy about being amid such riches; when she and Paul went to inspect the Million-Dollar Tapestry, as it was called, she perched on one of the glittering cushions until he announced that a large emerald seemed to be missing from one section of the hanging. Jumping up immediately, she said, "Let's sit somewhere else."

To Paul, the ball seemed a carefully staged fantasia in which natives appeared chiefly as extras. From the highest terrace (where a company of Moroccans in slave costume sifted wax in careful patterns over the dance floor) one could see the houses that belonged to Hutton's neighbors—each façade newly whitewashed and illuminated for the occasion. Later, he observed:

> The floodlighting of their dwellings makes it clear that these are meant to be a dramatic backdrop for the party, and indeed nothing in the house itself strikes me as being nearly so theatrical in effect as this unexpected view of the quarter. . . . As I examine the nearby roofs and my eyes grow used to the relative darkness of the night, I see that we are surrounded by staring Moroccans on all sides. Some are rolled in blankets, lying on mats, some are leaning out the tiny windows, some are just sitting cross-legged on their terraces under the moon. They don't seem to be talking to one another, and it is obvious that in order to miss nothing they are going to stay where they are until the party is over.

What Hutton's neighbors couldn't see was the hostess herself—a rail-thin woman of forty-seven sitting in a secluded part of the terrace, receiving friends from a brocaded throne embellished with spears and feathers. With her oversized bijoux and golden hair, she looked from a distance like a cinematic version of a princess, and that was precisely the way she wanted it. As Bowles noted, "She liked everything around her to show an element of the unreal in it, and she took great pains to transform reality into a continuous fantasy." In fact, it was said that she disapproved of *The Sheltering Sky,* and that she refused to allow the book in her house; bleak and brutal, it had nothing to do with the romantic Morocco that she knew.

In the years since she had bought Sidi Hosni, Barbara Hutton had spent much of her time pursuing pleasure. For the woman who had inherited over $28 million at the age of twenty-one, self-restraint was unthinkable, except when it came to refusing food; moderation, she said, was "a bore." She had spent giddy sums on clothes and jewels and parties, and she had moved about ceaselessly—alighting with her entourage in Paris, Cannes, St. Moritz, San Francisco, Madrid, New York and Tangier between jaunts to Japan and Mexico. Although her recklessness was beginning to catch up with her, she liked to dance until dawn, and she drank with abandon; heavily dependent upon caffeine, cigarettes and an array of drugs, she kept herself on a kind of anorexic high—even at her own banquets, she could sit at table without touching a scrap of foie gras.

Despite her efforts to keep them at bay, Barbara still was on intimate terms with boredom and depression. Plagued by mood swings, she was a hard-core hypochondriac who consulted endlessly with physicians but refused to see a psychiatrist. During the fifties, she had played the wan heroine through crises including an ovarian tumor and a damaged intestine (both of which required operations) and at least two suicide attempts. Perpetually insecure about her looks, she had turned to plastic surgery in 1957, when she underwent both a partial face-lift and an operation to reduce her generous breasts. Typically, she had made no effort to keep the procedures a secret: On a late-summer afternoon at Sidi Hosni (where Herbert's friend Ira Belline was her housekeeper) she had been gossiping with David and Ira when she suddenly asked whether they knew about her breast reduction. Telling Herbert that she wanted him to see how "lovely and small" her bosom was, she had unfastened the top of her dress to display her surgeon's handiwork.

None of Barbara's dramas had gone undocumented, of course, and she was unable to make the slightest move without stirring up the press. Even in Tangier—the city that she regarded as a refuge—she received a torrent of mail from strangers. Although she often walked the streets without being stopped, she sometimes drew verbal attacks. "When we went into the Casbah together, young Europeans sometimes turned on her," said her friend Ruth Hopwood. "I was walking home with her once when two beatniks came up to her and said, 'Fuck you, Barbara.' She got a lot of that, but she took it with great dignity."

In the popular imagination, Barbara was a self-absorbed neurotic who insulated herself with her money. To those in her inner circle, however, she was more complex. "She wasn't stuffy," said Hopwood. "She was rather bohemian—she liked contrast." Although she had created a kind of dream world at Sidi Hosni, Hutton was eager to know what went on outside its gates: She gave parties for the Tangier police and her neighbors in the Casbah, and she went with friends to waterfront dives like the Mar Chica, as well as to tearooms like Madame Porte's.

As loyal as they were, close friends found it difficult to be with Barbara for weeks on end. "She literally turned day into night," said Hopwood (whom Barbara had invited to live at Sidi Hosni). "She slept all day, and it made it a little difficult for the rest of us because we all had to go around on tiptoe. She woke up at six or seven raring to go, and she liked to sit under the fig tree on the patio and drink champagne until four in the morning. Some of her friends were quite exhausted: [My husband and I] put a lock on our bedroom door when we wanted to get a good sleep."

The devoted David (who slept under the same roof with Hutton only when they were traveling) was inclined to downplay her eccentricities. As he told it, she was given to staying up through the night "only during those awful [drinking] bouts. . . . It was an illness, really, drinking," he said. "She may have done that for a week, maybe ten days; then she never went to bed at all. It was hopeless."

Although some intimates pegged her as a chronic alcoholic, David contended that Barbara's problem surfaced only intermittently. "There were many months when she didn't drink at all; you never knew when—it was just bang—and then she drank champagne, champagne, champagne. Then she came out of it, absolutely as though nothing had happened. She would have an enormous breakfast of sausages and mash, and go on her way.

"Even when she was drinking," he said, "she never became

common. She never lost her status as a lady. On one occasion I introduced her at a party to Prince William of Gloucester: Barbara was tight, but not awfully so. She dropped a curtsy and fell flat on her face. She refused the Prince's offer to help her; she said, 'No, I must do this myself.' She tried it again and she did it perfectly. It was extraordinary."

While champagne may have been her anodyne of choice, romance had always been Hutton's favorite intoxicant; after six marriages, she was still struggling to find the perfect companion. A self-styled poet, she wrote rapturous odes to idealized lovers and published them privately in volumes like *The Wayfarer*, which appeared in 1957. Long-term relationships didn't suit her; always seeking the *coup de foudre*, she went through partners with blinding speed, rejecting each one as soon as the intoxication had evaporated. "She was always having upheavals," said Ruth Hopwood. "Her old governess said, 'Ah, madame, you may be sure of one thing: With Barbara, every man is eventually going to be kicked out.' She was like a sixteen-year-old girl who had a crush, and she woke up from the crush and wondered why things weren't the same. I think it was always harder on the men than it was on her—they would age visibly. Barbara would simply plow on and then she'd collapse a bit."

Since installing herself at Sidi Hosni, Hutton had kept herself occupied with a dizzying series of romantic entanglements. In the aftermath of her 1950 separation from her fourth husband, Prince Igor Troubetzkoy, she had taken up with Henri de La Tour d'Auvergne, a wellborn Parisian broker. That dalliance had been followed by her December 1954 marriage to Porfirio Rubirosa, the Dominican playboy-cum-diplomat who had cut a wide swath through café society before he encountered Barbara. After dismissing Rubirosa (who had received a reported $3.5 million in cash and gifts by the time their fifty-three-day marriage ended), she had kept company with a twenty-eight-year-old American whom she met in Morocco; later, she had had a fleeting encounter with the actor James Dean. In the summer of 1955, Barbara had rendezvoused in Tangier with the German tennis player Baron Gottfried von Cramm, and under the spell of the Casbah they had embarked on an affair. Although Cramm (like certain others who captured Barbara's fancy) was said to be a homosexual, she had taken him as her husband in Paris that November. Their de facto separation had come less than two years later; and while the divorce did not become final until January, 1960, she had wasted no time mourning the breakup. From 1958 on, she had been seen most often in the company of the handsome Jimmy Douglas, a loyal friend who was eighteen years her junior.

By the summer of 1960, Douglas had taken his leave and Hutton was ready to audition another companion. It was David Herbert who introduced her to Lloyd Franklin, a young musician who had appeared in Tangier a few months earlier. A free spirit who had seen duty as a trumpeter in the British Royal Guards, Lloyd had been traveling through France and Spain with a backpack and a guitar, playing and singing "like a medieval troubadour," as David described it. When he presented a letter of introduction from a mutual friend, Herbert had asked him to lunch; taken with the attractive newcomer, he had introduced him to Joseph Dean, who hired him to sing at his bar. Soon, David had begun inviting Lloyd to his dinner parties, and Hutton was on hand one evening when Herbert asked him to play.

As David told it, Barbara was talking with the American ambassador when the tall, blond Franklin (in a white dinner jacket borrowed from his host) picked up his guitar. "Suddenly, her eyes turned, and she took in Lloyd, and I don't think she took her eyes off him for a moment," he remembered. "At the end of the evening I said, 'Barbara, would you be very sweet and give Lloyd a lift home, he hasn't got a car.' She did and I didn't hear from them for four days, and when they finally called he was living with her. It was the most extraordinary change—Barbara was so happy with him."

Madly infatuated with the strapping Lloyd (who, at twenty-three, was a year younger than her son, Lance), Hutton began trotting him out in public, triggering a storm of gossip in scandal-starved Tangier. It was said alternately that Lloyd was a common gold digger and that he was the illegitimate son of a duke; that Hutton had given him cars and clothes and polo ponies and that he would be back on the street when she came to her senses. The stories immediately reached the States, and gossip mavens began serving them up with glee. In her dispatch about Barbara's August ball, the syndicated columnist Suzy reported archly that "Barbara's newest" was a "simple, kindly boy [who] has been her refuge and her strength." Such sniping was hardly new to Hutton, of course, and that season she staged a succession of fêtes that drew even more attention to the interesting development at Sidi Hosni. After the party in August, she gave an enormous ball at which guests were asked to appear in drag. Herbert showed up as a peasant girl, Lloyd turned himself out as a curvaceous Jean Harlow and Hutton herself dressed as Peter Pan.

As the romance continued, it became apparent to Barbara's friends that while he may have been willing to accept her largesse, Franklin was hardly a classic fortune hunter. (Neither was he a duke's son; according to one friend, he had been raised by middle-class Londoners who adopted him as an infant.) Sweet, passive and completely lacking in worldly ambition, he impressed most observers as being utterly devoted to his benefactor. "He wasn't after her money at all," Herbert asserted. "He really loved Barbara."

"Lloyd was a simple, straightforward lad who found himself caught up in a train of circumstances," said Tessa Codrington Wheeler, who became a close friend over the course of several summers. "He was a bit boring—I don't remember any wittiness or wonderful conversation—but he was a nice person to have around. He was one of those characters whom things happen to. There was no question of him conniving to get Barbara—she just picked him up by the scruff of the neck like you might pick up a puppy."

In the fall of 1960, Barbara packed up her new paramour and took him on her travels. Before they returned to Sidi Hosni the following summer, she and Lloyd would visit all of her old haunts, and the ennui-stricken Mountain set would be taking bets on whether the guitarist from Dean's was destined to become Hutton's seventh husband.

Although Tangier had lost its appeal for the fast-money crowd, the winter of 1960–61 was enlivened by the appearance of a new crop of expatriates. Heading to the fading port in hopes of discovering the mysterious East, hipsters like the ones whom Jack Kerouac had encountered at the Muniria were settling near the Socco Chico, where rents were low and *kif* was abundant. Young, bumptious and unkempt, they adhered scrupulously to the dress code that prevailed on Eighth Street in Greenwich Village—jeans, sandals and unwashed hair that gave them the look of prophets. And while they were inspired by *On the Road* and *Naked Lunch* (an underground sensation that had yet to be published in America), few of the amateur bohemians had literary ambitions; it was enough simply to drift along in a *majoun* haze, savoring the sense that they were beyond the reach of reality.

A few Tangerinos found them amusing, but most expatriates were horrified by the interlopers; to David Herbert's friends, they seemed ambassadors from a world that had lost all sense of decorum. For their part, the Bowleses were dismayed; still frightened of being deported, they regarded the group as provocateurs who could trigger another campaign against Nazarenes. As William Burroughs remembered it, Jane Bowles informed friends that she and Cherifa were cooking up a spell against them: "She said, 'I don't want to really hurt them, just make them a little sick so they'll go away,' " he said.

In a letter to his mother, Paul reported that the newcomers were an alarming sight: "The Beatniks have invaded Tangier at last. Every day one sees more beards and filthy bluejeans, and the girls look like escapees from lunatic asylums, with white lipstick and black smeared around their eyes, and matted hair hanging around their shoulders." By his account, they had been drawn by the presence of Burroughs's circle, whose members were now regarded as elder statesmen: "The leaders of the 'movement,' " he wrote, "have moved their headquarters here. . . . Allen Ginsberg, Gregory Corso and Burroughs are all established in Tangier now, sending out their publications . . . [and] the residents have been outdoing themselves giving parties. . . ."

Burroughs, in fact, had landed in Tangier that April. To those who had known him in 1959, he was almost unrecognizable; once a mere drug-crazed eccentric, he had become a dissolute dignitary whose novel was a succès de scandale. Discovered by the American press when *Naked Lunch* made its splash in Paris, he had been introduced to the readers of *Life* as a cadaverous seer who smoked Old Golds and inhabited a flophouse on the rue Gît-le-Coeur. The buzz had spread quickly, and the Beat Hotel had become an important stop for hip pilgrims, literary disciples and opportunists of all descriptions. Christened "Rimbaud in a raincoat" by the British writer Kenneth Allsop, William had been asked to dine with Samuel Beckett and drunk himself into a stupor at a party given by James Jones.

For all of that, the most important element in his life was not his notoriety but his spiritual bond with Brion Gysin. ("At that point," said Bowles, "Burroughs and Brion were like the same person.") Under Gysin's influence, he had begun to style himself as a sorcerer's apprentice: He had practiced meditation and hypnosis and mirror gazing, and he had fallen under the spell of Hassan-i-Sabbah, an eleventh-century Persian mystic who founded the cult of the Assassins. The Old Man of the Mountain, as Gysin called him, had shut himself away with his books and his adepts in a high-altitude citadel called Alamout; according to legend, he had held sway over his followers by feeding them hashish—a concept that had enormous appeal for the ambitious Brion. Like Hassan-i-Sabbah, Burroughs had removed himself from the world; obsessed with the subject of mind control, he was steeped in paranoia. Life in America, he decided, was an illusion created by image banks controlled by the FBI, the CIA and the morgue at *Time.* Despite his earlier assertions about wanting to consort with women, he had concluded that females were she-devils who should be eliminated at all costs, and that even male comrades should be subjected to cold scrutiny. To the remaining friends who passed muster, Burroughs had begun quoting a bit of pertinent wisdom from Hassan-i-Sabbah: "Nothing is true," he said, "everything is permitted."

Bound together by their intellectual passions, William and Brion had forged an aesthetic alliance that continued to thrive. Their joint mission was exploring the cutup—a collage technique that Gysin had hit upon when his Stanley blade sliced into a layer of newspaper while he was preparing a mount for a drawing. Deciding that the strips of text would make an amusing mosaic, Gysin had rearranged the newsprint into a nonsensical pastiche; and although its creator had seen the construction as a kind of game, Burroughs had been struck by its literary potential—here, he decided, was "a project for disastrous success." While William was still at the Beat Hotel, the two had gone into a creative frenzy; extracting and combining shards of text from Shakespeare, St. John Perse, Aldous

Huxley and the New York *Herald Tribune,* they turned out word salads that they believed to be the embodiment of a new aesthetic.[2] Asserting that "writing is fifty years behind painting," Brion had begun plotting out manifestoes and making pronouncements about "artless art" and "rubbing out the word." Words, he claimed, belonged to no one, and they could be appropriated as raw materials by any artisan who was sufficiently bold.

After setting himself up in his old room at the Villa Muniria, Burroughs had begun working on a manuscript that he had brought with him from Paris—constructing a dadaistic narrative from routines and notes and *Naked Lunch* outtakes. Splicing random bits together, he typed up the found prose and chortled over the unexpected juxtapositions. ("Cold metal excrement on all the walls and benches, silver sky raining the metal word fall out—sex sweat like iron in the mouth. Scores are coming in. Rate shoe. Pretend an interest," read one paragraph.) Caught up in his experiments, he paid little attention to his surroundings; instead, he burrowed in with a supply of *majoun* and shielded himself behind Michael Portman and Ian Somerville, the myrmidons who had followed him to Tangier.

A beautiful black sheep born into the family that owned much of London's West End, Mikey Portman was an arrogant idler lost in drugs and alcohol. Reckless, self-destructive, the eighteen-year-old had turned up at Burroughs's door after reading *Naked Lunch,* and he had shadowed him ever since. To Mikey, William was a prophet whose every utterance was sacred; by the time he reached Tangier, he was affecting Burroughs-style trenchcoats and aping his distinctive drone. Although William had developed a perverse connection to the insistent Mikey, his strongest relationship was with Somerville—a high-strung specimen whom he had met in a Paris bookstore. A gifted mathematician and computer scientist, Ian was a scholarship student at Cambridge; he had moved into the Beat Hotel in 1960, when William had hired him to stay by his side during another apomorphine cure. Drawn by his well-trained mind and ready humor, William had appropriated the nineteen-year-old as a lover, as well as a nurse. Unlike the dissolute Mikey, Ian was shy, fastidious and analytical; with his gaunt frame and copper hair that "stood up as though electric currents were shooting through it," as one observer put it, he often seemed like a creature about to take flight. Instead of merely parroting Burroughs, Ian had been anointed as a collaborator. In Paris, he had helped Brion stage light shows, tape-record cutup texts and design a stroboscope christened the Dream Machine, and he had worked with William on photo collages spawned by his obsession with the cutup. Like Mikey, Ian had become a permanent fixture in William's life—one who would leave little room for other comrades.

From the moment Allen Ginsberg got off the boat in Tangier, he knew that William had undergone a metamorphosis. Separated from Burroughs since their 1958 visit in Paris, he had been hoping for a gala reunion when he and Peter Orlovsky headed to France in March 1961. Instead of finding William at the Beat Hotel, however, he had been met by the overpowering Brion, who filled him in on their conspiracy theories and "whispered to me [that] Burroughs went away because he didn't want to see me," as Allen reported to Jack Kerouac. Eventually, William had written to invite Allen to Tangier, but the communiqués had been terse: Gone were the intimate tone and the sense of longing; now, Burroughs sounded like an automaton. Giving Allen a preview of his new persona, he informed him that he had reconsidered his role as an artist: "All novelists of any consequence," he declared, "are psychic assassins in the truest sense. . . ."

Although Allen had sent a wire asking William to meet the boat that he and Peter and Gregory had taken from Marseilles, Burroughs was "sitting at home oblivious to our arrival," as Allen put it, when they docked in Tangier. At the port, the three had been stopped by the Moroccan police, who pointed out that Corso's passport had expired. Weeping, screaming at the American consul, Gregory had been kicked down into the ship's hold and kept under guard until it headed south to Casablanca. Leaving Peter on the dock with the baggage, Allen had stayed on board to look after the hysterical captive, who spent the night on a bed of straw.

After Allen rescued Gregory with the help of embassy officials in Casablanca, the two had made the bus journey back to Tangier. There, he told Jack, Burroughs proved to be "rather indifferent to all our dreary hegira. . . ." Asking, "Who are you an agent for?"

William mirrored the detachment that Ginsberg had seen in Gysin. "Bill," wrote Allen, "had declared independence from all passions, affections, mayas thought & language & was sitting around listening to the messages of static on transistor radios & staring at strobiscopes [sic] & taking photographs of photographs of his own & making super collages. . . . he'd sit and stare at [photos] & point out interesting blobs & ghosts & phantoms . . . [while he tried] to track down the original master Agents of the cosmos who were using us humans as TV screens to project their schemes." To Jack, Allen confessed that Burroughs was "so inhuman it scared me."

It seemed to Ginsberg that much of the problem was William's involvement with Brion, whom he pegged as an aesthetic con man. Unimpressed with the cutup, he was convinced that Gysin had sold Burroughs a bill of goods, encouraging him to apply the method not only to prose but to his own emotional attachments. Steely, methodical, Burroughs began to dissect everything Ginsberg said—giving him the "hyperanalytic cold shoulder," as Allen described it. "Bill was tracing along word lines to determine people's missions," Ginsberg remembered. "He thought that I was an agent of Lionel Trilling; because I was a public figure, he thought I had been absorbed or co-opted. With all the hashish, the *majoun,* he had become hypersensitive—suspicious not in a paranoid way but in an acute, analytic way of looking at subtexts."

Allen's discomfort was heightened by the fact that it was impossible to see William alone. Encamped with Peter and Gregory in the Hotel Armor's ramshackle penthouse, he was reluctant to visit the Muniria without making an appointment, since Ian and Mikey had made it clear that drop-ins were unwelcome. To Jack, Allen complained about the "little English boys" who were "scampering and skipping behind [Bill's] elbows like demons." Mikey, he reported, was particularly troublesome—"an angelic looking narcissistic young english lord who sat and simpered." And while Ian was brighter, he had a nervous giggle that never ceased. It was difficult for Allen to accept that these two had replaced him in Burroughs's affections; although he still had no desire to be William's lover, he cherished their "old amity," and he was wounded.

Soon after their arrival, Allen, Peter and Gregory joined Paul Bowles, Alan Ansen, Burroughs and his companions for a picture-taking session in the overgrown garden at the Muniria. Wearing a fedora and a dark shirt buttoned to the neck, a *kif*ed Burroughs leveled a stare at Ginsberg's camera. Behind the shadowed eyes and the compressed lips, there was an astonishing vulnerability; for all of his guardedness, he had the look of a lone wolf afraid of the world outside his lair. In a group shot, William was a sepulchral figure standing behind the smiling Allen, clutching his own camera as if it were a weapon. Peter (who already had felt the weight of Burroughs's disdain) sat at one side, hidden behind glasses and a thick fringe of hair; at the opposite side stood an aloof-looking Ian. Sitting on the concrete in front of Corso was Bowles—squinting, sun-browned, braving the hot sun in an impeccable white suit.

Although he complained about the "Eighth-Streetniks" in the medina, Paul had welcomed the invasion of the Burroughs set. Whenever they descended on his flat at the Itesa, the Beats created a perverse boys-club atmosphere that was a bracing change from the scene at Jane's. Not that he was interested in belonging; as always, he withdrew and watched his visitors as though they were characters in someone else's short story. Peter, he decided, was a gabbling amazement; Mikey was a hopeless doper and Ian was an insecure savant who went on about mathematics when he had smoked enough *kif*. Allen was an intellectual who shared his own interest in altered states of consciousness, and Burroughs was full of crackpot notions culled from Brion. "Bill was always talking about what he could do with his mind," said Bowles. "He claimed he could put himself in a certain frame of mind whereby he could become invisible. He and Brion believed that they could travel to other planets, and I don't need to tell you that I didn't—there was enough fantasy around without subscribing to science fiction."

Bowles pegged the cutup technique as one of William's follies. Writing under the influence of *majoun* was one thing; creating non-sensical prose-blocks was another. To Paul, the method seemed a diversionary tactic, at best. "I didn't consider it to be literature," he said later. "Of course, Brion would say, 'You can *make* it literature,' and Burroughs always said it was viable in the hands of a master—with the implication that he was the master." Dogged in his attempt to win converts, William constructed cutups from sections of *The Sheltering Sky* and demonstrated his tape-recorder method for Paul:

After reading odd paragraphs into the machine, he ran through the tape, cutting in at random with new selections. (Paul admitted that Burroughs managed to establish his own voice even when the material made no sense: "When he played it back, the tape still sounded like the prose of William Burroughs and nobody else," he remembered.) Everything, it seemed, was considered grist for the surrealist mill: A tape of music that Paul had recorded was slowed to one-quarter speed, so that it sounded like static, and Burroughs used it to set the mood when he was working.

When he wasn't proselytizing about the cutup, William was plying Paul with the theories of Wilhelm Reich, who claimed that the blockage of "orgone energy" was the root of all psychic ills. In the garden of the Muniria was the coffinlike "orgone energy accumulator" that he had built according to Reich's specifications; and on a chilly night, he finally prevailed upon Paul to try it. It was a decidedly unpleasant experiment—Bowles closed himself into the pitch-dark device and "almost froze to death," as he reported it. Although Burroughs told him that the orgone treatment required at least an hour, he gave up after twenty-five minutes. "He said, 'Did you feel anything?' " remembered Paul. "I said, 'No, just a lot of cold.' "

A month after the Beats arrived, Bowles made a short trip to Marrakech, where he and Christopher Wanklyn had taken a house in the native quarter. From there, he sent a postcard to Ginsberg, describing the "huge casual pageant" in the Djemaa el-Fna and suggesting that he come along on the next excursion. For Allen, the prospect of escape was alluring: Aside from his difficulties with William, he was now trying to salvage his relationship with Peter. Burroughs and his boys had set upon the hapless Orlovsky; mocking him mercilessly, they had baited him about his relationships with women and provoked arguments that left him hoarse. Stricken with dysentery that led to a mild case of hepatitis, Peter had taken to his bed and told Allen that he wanted to go to Istanbul without him. Sitting at the Café Fuentes a few weeks later, waiting for his lover to emerge from a whorehouse, Allen had thought of their seven years together and begun to weep.

With Peter still recuperating in Tangier, Ginsberg and Bowles headed for Marrakech on July 17. While they were en route, the medina was swept by a fire that consumed hundreds of bazaars. On the evening of their arrival, Paul, Christopher and Allen stood on their rooftop terrace and watched shopkeepers sifting through the ruins. Feeling lost, Allen allowed his hosts to arrange an assignation with a Moroccan boy—an experiment that left him with a case of the crabs and a heightened sense of isolation. "They told me how to behave and what to give him—not money, but presents," he remembered. "I was uneasy, and I didn't feel spiritually attracted—I always liked lovers you could talk to rather than going through discreet courtships and swift consummations."

In Allen's absence, Peter spent much of his time with Gregory, who alternately quarreled with him and tried to help mend his rift with Burroughs. A hard-drinking street fighter who had devoured the classics while he was behind bars, Corso, thirty-two, had been a great success among the avant-garde in Paris, where Maurice Girodias had published his novel, *The American Express.* In Tangier, he was immersing himself in his poet-maudit role—losing impressive sums at the casino with Francis Bacon and presiding at parties where "kids would just sit at our feet and talk, and we [would] wander from room to room," as he remembered it. Undoubtedly hoping to shock the locals, he accompanied Peter and Alan Ansen to the Kamalakars' Saturday-afternoon teas, where Ginsberg had been asked to read "Howl" and Ansen weighed in with a reading of the Gospel of St. John. With the abandoned Peter, Gregory closed in on Sonya's daughter Tamara Dragadze—by then a fetching seventeen-year-old with auburn hair and milk-white skin. Both told her stories about their deprived childhoods: Orlovsky talked about living with his impoverished family in a converted chicken coop, and Corso pitched himself as a soulful orphan who had fended for himself on the streets of New York City.

Although she was guarded carefully by Sonya (who, like a Moroccan mother, set great store by her virginity), Tamara was allowed to spend time with their satyric visitors. "I went with them to a Turkish bath that had been hired by Europeans for the evening, and my mother gave me strict instructions to keep my bikini on underneath the towel," she remembered. "Gregory said, 'Doesn't anything turn you on?' " Allen had been at the *hammam* as well, and he had added, "Look at that nude man, doesn't that do it?" Remembered Dragadze, "I said, 'I see that in statuary all the time.' Actually, they were all very kind."

Writing to his girlfriend Janine Pommey in July, Peter reported that he was about to leave for Tamara's birthday party, where he planned to present her with a drawing that he had made on the beach. "Rapped it in newspaper & on the frunt it shows the russian dancer Nureyev who recently deflected to France—a picture of him with headlines above his head . . . Nureyev: 'I'm a dancer, not a Pliitician'—this girl wants to be a actress & has been dancing since she was walking so I thought it a good cober for a bithday presidant—" He also confided that he was upset about the standoff with Burroughs: "Me and Bill B. don't get along," he wrote. "To maney blocks & pre concieved attitude he has about me. Thinks I'm a dope . . . dont even read my peotry. . . ."

When Allen returned to Tangier at the end of the month, the unhappy Peter told him that he was ready to ship out for Istanbul. As they parted, Orlovsky predicted that it would be years before they saw one another again. Ginsberg felt lost; with Burroughs on the offensive and Peter going into the world alone, there was nothing that he could take for granted—including his calling as a poet. In his journal, he noted, "As I am 35 and half my life now past, I have no sure road ahead, but many to choose from, and none seem inevitable."

Sorely in need of allies, Ginsberg was heartened when Timothy Leary appeared in Tangier. Late in 1960, he had visited the psychologist at Harvard, where he was researching the effects of psilocybin, a hallucinogen extracted from the *Psilocybe mexicana* mushroom. Under Leary's supervision, Allen had taken a generous dose, and it had triggered a dizzying sense of omnipotence. Exhilarated by the experience, he had become a front man for Leary—plotting to introduce the drug to writers, artists and intellectuals who would endorse the idea of mind expansion. He had given Leary's pills to Thelonious Monk, Robert Lowell and Jack Kerouac; now, he was determined to convert Burroughs. Although he had been lukewarm about psilocybin when he tried it in Paris, William had promised to come to Cambridge in the fall for Leary's symposium on psychedelic drugs.

When Leary arrived at the Hotel Armor, Ginsberg was nowhere in evidence. Instead, he saw Burroughs himself—"a thin stooped man . . . accompanied by two handsome British boys," as he remembered it. Sitting in an outdoor restaurant while they waited for Ginsberg to return, Leary and Burroughs drank gin and went over the plans for the trip to Harvard. By Allen's account, William "knew more about drugs than anyone alive," and Leary was eager to get him in his camp; he had formulated a grandiose plan that included "turning on" world leaders like John F. Kennedy, and he needed all the expert testimony he could get.

That evening, Leary had dinner at the hotel with Ginsberg, Ansen, Corso and Burroughs and his shadows. Afterwards, the group adjourned to William's unkempt room, where three radios created a symphony of static. Leary distributed his pills, and Burroughs took an enormous dose and lay back on his bed, with Mikey and Ian sitting over him like a pair of sinister angels. Allen and the others walked out into the garden, where the night was soft and warm. The Royal Fair had moved into town, and they could hear seductive music drifting up from the fairgrounds.

After a time, the psilocybin began to take hold, and everyone took deep breaths and looked at one another. "Alan Ansen and Gregory were grinning," Leary remembered. ". . . We floated down the steps to Allen's hotel then up to the patio in front of his room. The city below us was a glittering carpet. Lanterns shone from the rigging of ships in the harbor, and the carnival rollicked by the water's edge." For Leary, it was an ecstatic experience: "We were all in the highest and most loving of moods," he wrote later. ". . . Ansen couldn't believe it. He kept laughing and shaking his head [saying], 'This can't be true. So beautiful. Heaven. But where is the devil's price? Anything this great must have a terrible flaw in it. It can't be this good.' "

Back at the Muniria, the mood was a bit darker. When Leary and Ginsberg went to fetch Burroughs on their way to the fair, they found him in a state of quiet terror. As the door creaked open, they saw the pale, drawn William leaning against the jamb, staring like a man roused from his deathbed. According to Leary, he sounded as though his speech had been subjected to the cutup: "I'm not feeling too well," William told them. "I was struck by the juxtaposition of purple fire mushroomed from the Pain Banks. Urgent Warning. There are many hostile territories in the cerebral hemispheres. I think I'll stay here in this shriveling envelope of larval flesh [and] take some apomorphine."

Although Burroughs never developed a taste for Leary's mushrooms, he was taken with his ideas about manipulating brain function. Claiming that psilocybin could supplant poetry by delivering aesthetic pleasure more efficiently, Leary argued that words and images were passé. Humankind, he said, was on the brink of a new "superconsciousness" that would render the artist obsolete. For William—who had told Allen that poetry was "finished"—Leary's notions about subverting the ego made perfect sense, and during the next few days he appropriated him as a confederate in his debates with Allen.

For his part, Ginsberg felt cornered; without Peter, he found it impossible to defend himself against both Leary and Burroughs (who had pointedly neglected to read "Kaddish"). Overwhelmed by the assault on his identity as a poet, he was seized by episodes of vomiting. In a letter to publisher Barney Rossett, he thanked him for sending an issue of *Evergreen Review* and added, "The review of 'Kaddish' was laudatory enough but since I no longer know who Allen Ginsberg is and in fact hate the identity it was golden ashes. . . . I am sort of shook up & wondering what next. . . ." To Peter, Allen reported that he was so disoriented that, after doing mushrooms, he had kissed Jane's friend Pamela Stevenson on the Boulevard Pasteur. "I think I will start chasing girls again," he said.

As unhappy as he was, Ginsberg remained loyal to both Burroughs and Leary. "I think Bill & Leary at Harvard are going to start a beautiful consciousness alteration of the whole world," he told Peter. With Allen's help, Leary wasted no time in making connections in Tangier; he went gambling with Gregory and Francis Bacon, and he visited Ahmed Yacoubi at his studio. With William and Allen and their entourage, he made a pilgrimage to the Itesa to see the Bowleses. There, they were treated to the spectacle of one of Mikey Portman's friends going into a *majoun-* induced panic. By Allen's account, he, Leary, Paul and Jane tried to quiet the victim by holding his hand, but Burroughs and Portman were too drugged to notice what was happening. As a parting gift, Leary gave Paul a vial of psilocybin.

When their visitor left for a conference in Copenhagen on August 2, the dispirited Allen tried to repair his relationship with Burroughs. William agreed to a tête-à-tête, but Portman refused to leave them alone; he hovered outside while they talked in William's room and then trailed along when they went for lunch. Still, Allen began to see that William's connection to his acolyte wasn't as strong as he had imagined: When Mikey was out of earshot for a moment, William said, "He's too *dependent* on me, that's his problem." Ginsberg decided that, as cold as he was, Burroughs hadn't lost his humanity; caught up in his "Zen-cut-up assault on identity," he had simply transformed himself into a tough-truth merchant. In a dispatch to Kerouac, Allen claimed that William's attack had served its purpose: "It really shook my self-confidence and that's a good thing too because why cling to self-confidence." Although he confessed that he had "resented him operating . . . on old friendships," he told Jack that he had come to see Burroughs as a great guru. "What a hero!" he said. "What a grim prospero!"

For all of that, Allen's attempt to put the best face on things was only half-successful; deeply shaken, he was unable to write a line of poetry. With Burroughs and his companions plotting an excursion to London, he began making plans to continue his journey alone. Before the end of the month, he sailed for Athens—feeling that he was leaving behind something that was irreplaceable.

For the Mountain crowd, the summer's dramatic climax came when Barbara Hutton returned to Sidi Hosni with the ex-guardsman who had played guitar at Dean's Bar. Together, the heiress and her twenty-four-year-old lover had sparked gossip in Venice and Paris and New York; now, it was Tangier's turn to talk. With another lavish ball scheduled in August, old-line Tangerinos were in a delicious frenzy; at Porte's and Dean's and the Parade, there was a steady buzz about the soirée and about Hutton's best-known houseguest.

In the days before the ball, café society descended upon Tangier en masse; more than two hundred partygoers were imported at

Hutton's expense, and another hundred hopefuls registered at the Minzah and sent flowers to David Herbert, who once again was fine-tuning the guest list. Those who had received the gilt-edged invitations early on included Herbert's close friends—among them, Cecil Beaton and Princess Lala Fatima Zora, a fashionable Moroccan royal. Lloyd's of London, which insured Sidi Hosni, reportedly had warned that the floors would give way if more than 150 guests collected in one area, and security arrangements were stepped up— eight members of the Tangier police force were hired to discourage gate-crashers, and a sharp-eyed secretary was assigned to examine invitations at the door.

Few of the Wrong People made it into Sidi Hosni on the appointed evening, but Hutton's guests might have been happier if they had. As a member of "the global glitter set" reported it to the New York *Daily News,* the fête had been painfully subdued. "Many attractive girls were excluded, maybe because Babs' boyfriend, Lloyd Franklin, had been in love with a lot of them and didn't want to be reminded," wrote *News* columnist Nancy Randolph. "The music, from Madrid, was too dreary. Cecil Beaton, Britain's royal photographer, said, 'It's half-empty, like a Cunard crossing in the wintertime.' "

Guests had been asked to assemble at ten-thirty, and for the first hour "a hundred ill-assorted people of all ages wandered aimlessly from room to room wondering when the hostess would appear to greet them," as Beaton remembered it. World-weary sorts sat about making delicate little digs, and the restless Beaton was "trapped by consuls' wives or ex-ambassadors." Rescued at last by David's friend Ira Belline, he was taken to a vast terrace that had been transformed into a dreamlike tent camp: All of the Casbah, it seemed, had assembled on the nearby rooftops for a glimpse of the orange and crimson tents that were surrounded by brilliant cushions and mannequins fashioned from flowers. An explosion of flash-bulbs marked the presence of the hostess, who was enthroned inside in a silken tent overflowing with gladioli. Wearing a dress heavily embroidered in diamonds, the magnificent diamond-and-emerald fillet that had belonged to Catherine the Great and a string of enormous pearls, Barbara looked to Cecil like "a little Byzantine empress-doll." As Beaton described it, she was receiving guests "as if she was in reality playing a scene on the stage." Every gesture was studied, every bit of coquetry, exaggerated; while she seemed "oblivious to the stares" of her guests, she was artifice itself, to Cecil's eye. As the evening progressed, Barbara mellowed a bit, but the performance (and the flow of champagne) never stopped; by the end of the party, said Cecil, she was "too euphoric to be able to communicate except by pantomime."

In fact, it had been a heady year for Hutton and her young consort. Barbara was still in the throes of her infatuation, and friends like Herbert were convinced that this time there would be no breakup. Declaring herself to be "one of the happiest women alive," she was demonstrating her devotion by spending lavish sums on her lover. Along with more traditional gifts (which reportedly included an MG and a Rolls-Royce like her own), she arranged to install a $2,500 underground irrigation system at the Tangier Polo Club. Already the owner of a dozen choice ponies, Lloyd soon would take possession of the house and stables that she was building for him beside the polo grounds. Despite the change in his fortunes, he still seemed immune to hubris. "He had some rather ordinary friends, naturally, but he kept them after he met Barbara," said David. "She had them all to her house and invited them to her parties; she hadn't got *that* much snobbery."

As Herbert told it, Hutton was on her best behavior when Lloyd was by her side. With Ira Belline, the three made a tour of Morocco by car, stopping in Fez, Meknès, Ouarzazate, Taroudant and, finally, Marrakech. "It was the most heavenly trip I'd been on," remembered David. "Barbara wasn't drinking at all, and she was absolutely wonderful. We were in two cars, with no entourage of any sort, and we were received by all of these marvelous Pashas. Every morning she was always downstairs before anyone else, sitting on her suitcase on the chair in the hallway—looking so perfect, like Lillian Gish in a film. Totally unspoiled; she had no maids, no servants at all. I got a totally different picture of her on that trip."

To her public, however, Hutton was still a debauchee entrapped by her own delusions. In February 1962, *Life* published a

pensive portrait taken by Beaton at Sidi Hosni. Seated in an elaborately tiled room with the sun streaming in at her back, Barbara was
wearing her emerald tiara and "plucking at a Moorish lute with
queenly casualness"—looking for all the world like a creature
whose feet had never touched the ground.

Chapter 17

Like his wife, Paul Bowles had a trick of portraying their lives together as a kind of black comedy. In the fall of 1961, he reported to his mother that he and Jane were mourning the demise of Babarhio, the parrot whom he had taken into the Sahara while he was writing *The Sheltering Sky:* "He was always loose, as you remember, and might easily have picked up something poisonous, like DDT or lead," he wrote. "Very sad, since I had had him for fourteen years and was very fond of him. Cherifa came down one evening at nine o'clock and merely announced that he was dead. And so he was, in rigor mortis, on the bathroom shelf. . . ." A few months later, he noted that Jane herself had been feeling poorly; dosing herself with "a good many things each day, on the doctor's orders," she had had an alarming reaction to one of her medications. Reported Paul, "She is covered with serious-looking eruptions which come out in great welts, all over her face. So she is wearing a Moroccan veil, and claims she is going to wear it tonight when she gives a couscous dinner to a group of American journalist women from Germany. . . . I don't know how they will take it."

After dropping the veil, Jane felt energetic enough to engage in a new flirtation. She settled on a peripatetic Englishwoman who had written several novels—an affected blueblood whom Paul found appalling. Years later, he described "Lady Anna"[1] as a stentorian alcoholic who was "absolutely crazy." Said Bowles, "You couldn't believe it—she was very decided, and she looked like one of the statues on Easter Island. Again and again I was trapped into having dinner with her; she would suddenly announce, 'I shall now tell you my experiences with E. M. Forster,' and all I could do was turn sideways and pretend I wasn't at the table. Her mother was peculiar, too; she came to visit one Sunday, and she seemed perfectly normal when we all had lunch with her. On Tuesday, we heard she had gone over to Gibraltar and committed suicide at the Rock Hotel. Blumph."

As much as Paul disliked "Lady Anna," he had no trouble understanding Jane's attraction to her. "She was unlike anybody else, and that was what made Jane like her, of course. Jane used to say to me [in a conspiratorial whisper], 'She's ghastly, isn't she, she's awful.' I'd say, 'Well, no, she's not *awful.*' Jane would say, *'Oh,* I think she's ghastly. That meant, 'I like her.' "

To the poet Harold Norse (a Beat Hotel alumnus and Burroughs crony who had joined the dropouts in the medina), the Bowleses' was a "Charles Addams household" whose occupants were perfectly suited to life in Tangier. Norse observed that both Jane and Paul "seemed to be enjoying themselves immensely . . . at the mercy of superstitious illiterates who could not read a word they wrote."

Many of those who knew the Bowleses felt compelled to choose sides, and Norse was no exception. Like Brion Gysin (whom he had known in Paris), he took a dislike to the demanding Jane; to his eye, she was a "small, lame, morose, anxious woman [who] led a claustrophobic, hothouse existence." A petulant masochist who felt that Paul had eclipsed her as a writer, the Jane whom Norse described was jealous of Paul's friends and complained that visitors came only to see her husband. As Norse told it, Paul's attempts to mollify her were seldom successful; after a tantrum, "[Jane] would sulk awhile with a look of defiance, her crippled leg protruding straight out in front of her, as she'd slouch against the wall like a disgruntled waif, peering at a hostile world from behind horn-rimmed spectacles," he remembered. "Having vented her irritation on the subject of being abandoned by everyone, she'd watch Paul intensely, both of them puffing cigarettes, and then he would broach the subject [of] what they would have for dinner." Assuming "the rapt expression of players in a game of chess," the two would debate the question until Norse felt like fleeing. To their visitor, it seemed a "bizarre ritual [that was] carried to the point of absurdity"—and one that gave Jane enormous pleasure.

Others who visited the Bowleses that year found themselves in a setting that (like Jane's fictional terrain) was defined by cryptic jokes and domestic intrigue. An intense young Princeton graduate who became an English teacher at the American School, Joseph McPhillips III was introduced to the two just days after he arrived in Morocco. A strong-willed Southerner whose literary tastes ran to André Gide and Ezra Pound, McPhillips was impatient with the clubbiness at the Itesa. "It was all so precious," he said. "It was all about finding some meaning in some little joke between Jane and Paul about some dish that Cherifa had cooked—the little giggles about the fact that one of the parrots had bitten someone's hand and what Janie said about the biting of the hand or that Cherifa had let out a scream at the wrong time and burnt the eggplant. It all seemed like nonsense. Maybe I wasn't sophisticated enough to know what was going on, but they seemed to have done a retreat, and I wasn't at that point interested in retreats."

As the months went by, McPhillips and John Hopkins, another wellborn Southerner who taught at the American School, were drawn into the Bowleses' orbit. "You would only be in Paul's group or in Jane's group, and we were in Paul's," remembered Hopkins.[2] "Jane's included people who fawned over her and went to the market with her—she had to be helped around. She was terribly amusing, but Paul was easier to know—he was more accessible, and you could talk to him more easily. Every time you went to his house you'd find an assortment of bizarre characters—including some guy who was lying on the floor, stoned out of his mind, whom Paul would introduce languidly. He said no to no one."

The more time Hopkins spent at the Itesa, the more he came to appreciate the subtleties of Paul's character. "Paul loves to play games," he said. "When you'd go to his house and smoke a lot of dope, he'd put on real spooky music that would make you want to cut your throat. He'd know it if you felt the least bit paranoid. But then he'd put Fats Waller on at the end to cheer you up. He was like a scientist who'd have you under a microscope."

Although they felt more comfortable at Paul's, the two sometimes went to Jane's flat for dinner. As Hopkins remembered it, the scene was always lively; there was an abundance of laughter, and even the severe-looking maid, Aicha, cracked jokes between courses. The winy camaraderie at Jane's was a marked contrast to the introspective cannabis high that prevailed at Paul's flat. "That was the difference between the two," said Hopkins. "Jane was a drinker, and Paul was a *kif* smoker."

After he had gotten past the Bowleses' cliquishness, McPhillips began to see Paul as a generous spirit who introduced newcomers to Moroccan culture and encouraged young writers like Hopkins, who had begun to write fiction. Jane, he decided, was a vulnerable creature with "a profound sympathy for the underdog, the female," as he put it. "Every time I saw her, something would rise up in me; I felt a tremendous tenderness toward her," said McPhillips. "I felt that she was stricken—she'd been crippled by the stroke, but there was also a sort of spiritual hurt within her. You wanted to comfort her, put your arm around her. And in no way do I mean she was helpless; she was a very tough lady. But at the same time there was a gentleness and humanity about her that I found deeply moving."

Others, however, decided that Jane and Paul were supremely selfish. One writer who came to know them after he migrated to Tangier that year described their behavior as "self-indulgent eccentricity lived at other people's expense." Years later, the expatriate (who asked to remain anonymous) noted that both Paul and Jane were "basically spoiled children of the thirties. Their world, he said, "was entirely inner-focused and unreal." He noted that Jane in particular relied on a kind of denial that he found off-putting. Not long after they had met, he said, he encountered the Bowleses on a ferry crossing from Spain, and she began to insist that they make plans to rendezvous in Tangier. "She said, 'Now, look, we never see you, you always hide away,'" he remembered. "'You are not getting off this ship before I know when you are coming to see us.' I said, 'All right, Janie, if you insist.' She said, 'I always go to the Minzah pool with David [Herbert]—you come and see me there tomorrow, and we're going to make a dinner date.' So I turned up and we made a date.

"On the prescribed evening, I arrived at Jane's flat and two visitors were sitting there, talking very animatedly. They were all dressed up to go out, and Janie said, 'Oh, oh, oh. . . .' She immediately went through her act—the thing where she 'wasn't responsible' for what had happened. It seemed that they were all going to dinner at David's; she said, 'Oh, phone David, I'm sure he'd be glad to have you,' and then she left the room. I walked out and I never, ever, made any dates of any sort with her again."

To her unexpected visitor, Jane's behavior seemed entirely in character. "It was so symptomatic of how she would do whatever she wished and be very clear in her mind about it and then suddenly, here was the great pretense, the retreat into innocence," he said. As he told it, she had learned to use her frailty as a smoke screen. "She became her own victim," he said. "That whole life— that attention-getting, mischievous behavior—so many people saw it as the empress's new clothes."

By 1962, physical setbacks had become a constant for Jane Bowles. Although she had recovered some of her strength, she had been plagued by a series of minor ailments, including shingles and a hernia that required surgery. In an April letter to Libby Holman, she joked about the state of her body: "Since my operation I have a crooked stomach and am thinking of having it made straight [again]," she reported. "I think it's the surgeon's fault and so I should be able to get it done for almost nothing, but who knows. I don't know what to do because a woman of depth should not think about her stomach after fourty-five. . . ."

Paul, as always, urged her to try to lose herself in work. After she received a $3,000 grant from the Ingram Merrill Foundation, she made fitful efforts to construct a new play, but there were distractions at every turn; in the end, most of her energy was channeled into stage-directing her harem. When she did manage to write, the words came no faster than they had before: With her impaired sight and damaged hand, it was a challenge to finish a simple letter, much less to create characters and set them into motion.

Believing, on some level, that she was doomed, Jane began to give herself over to her role as an invalid. From time to time, Paul would find her pacing about and wringing her hands, repeating the line from Kafka that he had used as an epigraph in *The Sheltering Sky:* "From a certain point onward there is no longer any turning back. That is the point that must be reached." As always, Paul would tell her that the quotation had nothing to do with her own life. "Why did you use it, if you didn't believe it?" she would ask.

Jane's friend Ruth Fainlight was in Tangier that season with Alan Sillitoe and their baby, David, and she witnessed Jane's frustration. "I showed her the poems that I was working on, and we talked about them; she was hardly writing, and she was very unhappy about it, so her part of it was to say how awful it was that she couldn't write," said Fainlight. "Maybe it happened two or three times—she would show me something, and she was sort of quiet, hesitant. She would say, 'Look, this is all I can do.' What she meant was the fact that she couldn't spell properly and she couldn't overcome the problems caused by the stroke. Just the actual physical difficulties of putting pen to paper were enormous." To Fainlight, Jane seemed a valiant figure; despite her pain and her fear and her phobias, she kept trying, and she was the first to laugh at her own absurdity. "Everything was difficult for her," she said. "There was always that underlevel of anxiety and panic. But she did make a great effort; she was so gallant and so witty. I felt very sisterly towards her."

The Bowleses' friend Edouard Roditi believed that aside from her stroke, Jane was hampered by a growing sense of isolation. An urbane creature who required a sophisticated audience, she was stranded in an outpost where there were no theaters, no critics, no avant-garde circles—nothing to sustain her creative momentum. Said Roditi, "A great deal of Jane's trouble, I think, was that she'd been uprooted. All of her writing was about America, and her real identity was to hang around parties and be the 'Kike Dyke,' as she named herself. And being torn away from that she felt at a loss. She was less and less capable of writing, and eventually she couldn't have cared less about it."

*   *   *

Jane, of course, had always said that she felt islanded in North Africa; as early as 1948, she had confided in a letter to Holman: "We live on visitors coming through." When admirers like Libby were on hand, Jane could commune with others who had made a mark in the world—people whose lives were played out against a broad canvas, and who saw her as a serious writer. She could give ironic performances in the role of hostess—making fun of herself the way she did when she informed Charles Gallagher that she had to dash home "to fix Paul's hamburger"—and know that her visitors got the joke. She could also step into the role of surrogate mother—a part she had always loved.

Thankfully, the summer of 1962 brought visitors including the devoted Tennessee Williams, who had written to ask Paul to find him a cottage near the beach. Distraught over his recent estrangement from Frank Merlo, he was accompanied by a traveling companion—a young poet who had helped him to transport suitcases, typewriter and scripts to Tangier. Physically and psychologically depleted, he was seeking solace that season in double martinis and "crazy pills," as he called them. At work on *The Milk Train Doesn't Stop Here Anymore,* which was to begin tryouts in the fall, Tennessee brought little energy to the task of writing; without Frank, he felt himself to be adrift.

Later, Williams remembered, "It was a curiously difficult summer, both for me and my new companion. . . . Despite the charm of the little white house and of the beautiful poet, I was beset by inner torments, the most explicable of which was an inability to talk to people. There was a good deal of social activity that summer in Tangier . . . but at cocktail parties and suppers I sat in silence that was seldom broken. Even with the young poet I could barely communicate except in bed."

As always, Jane took Tennessee in hand, escorting him to Porte's and the Parade and inviting him to the Itesa. To his mother, Bowles reported: "Jane as usual feels very responsible for his welfare, and she's been helping him get settled in. . . . Having finished arranging Tennessee's problems, [she] is now busy doing the same for the Sillitoes, who were here a year and a half ago."

At her flat, Jane arranged dinners that included all of her

charges—Tennessee and his companion, Fainlight, Sillitoe and their tiny son. "Jane was making these meals with Cherifa, and she took us all under her wing," remembered Fainlight. "I was in this odd state, having finally produced a child, and we were a jolly little family group with Tennessee holding my baby on his lap and looking at this child with fascination. I remember so distinctly because he was flushed and moved and excited—he *loved* this little baby."

Being in Jane's company, it seemed, had a therapeutic effect on Tennessee. Years later, he remembered that the two had been together one afternoon during the worst of his depression and he had told her, "Janie, I can't talk anymore." As he reported it, "She gave me one of her quick little smiles and said, 'Tennessee, you were never much of a conversationalist.' For some reason," he added, "perhaps because it made me laugh, and laughter is always a comfort, as Janie was also a comfort, this answer to my anguished confession was a relief for a while."

By one account, the bond between Tennessee and Jane was so strong that it triggered Paul's competitiveness. Harold Norse, who had shared quarters in Provincetown with Tennessee during the summer of 1944, remembered being taken aback when Bowles complained about their visitor. As Norse reported it, he said, "Tennessee doesn't come here to see me—he's only interested in Janie. He wouldn't even bother to come to Tangier otherwise. They positively *adore* one another." Added Norse, "[Bowles] commented peevishly that they had an almost mystical union, believing that they alone among American writers possessed a rare poetic sensibility." Paul, he said, dismissed that lofty notion; instead, he told Norse, his wife's alliance with Tennessee was "an alcoholic *participation mystique.*"

In fact, Tennessee did have more in common with Jane than with Paul; both wildly vulnerable, they spoke a language that was foreign to the dispassionate Bowles. Tennessee had never shared Paul's appreciation for Moroccan culture, and he had declared Tangier to be impossible—"just like Miami Beach thrown in the middle of some ghastly slums," as he described it to his friend Maria St. Just. Like Jane, he preferred alcohol to exotica like *kif,* and the one time he tried *majoun* he went into a panic. "He said, 'I can't control my thoughts!'" Bowles remembered. "'I can't let all these meaningless thoughts flit through my head—it makes me nervous.' "

For all of that, Tennessee admired both the Bowleses, and—unlike others—he had never felt compelled to choose between them. Empathetic, intuitive, he saw the generosity that lay beneath Paul's Edwardian reserve, and he found his eccentricities endearing. For Tennessee, Morocco was on the map only because Paul had put it there. After one uncomfortable visit to the Bowleses, he had written a dispatch to St. Just in which he discussed the horrors of the rainy season, and then added, "I miss [Paul] a lot more than I do Morocco; he will always be more interesting than any place he inhabits."

That summer, Paul was spending long hours on a collaboration that Jane quickly pronounced a waste of time. On Merkala Beach—a secluded bit of shoreline about a mile from the Itesa—he had met a young watchman called Larbi Layachi, who was guarding the entrance to a deserted café. An illiterate raised in desperate poverty, Layachi had served a prison sentence for selling *kif;* feeling himself to be an outcast, he was content with his solitary post on the beach. Although he was "singularly quiet and ungregarious," in Paul's words, he soon became a visitor at the Itesa, and he gradually had opened up to his host. One evening, their conversation had turned to filmmaking, which Layachi believed to be vaguely sinful, involving, as it did, a departure from the truth. Explaining that it was no more sinful than telling stories in the marketplace, Bowles had talked about his own work, explaining to Layachi that his books were collections of stories "like *The Thousand and One Nights.*" Excited by the notion that making up stories was not synonymous with the wicked act of telling lies, Layachi had announced to Paul that he, too, wanted to "make a book." The next evening, he had astonished Bowles by sitting down and inventing a flawlessly crafted tale that sounded as though he had rehearsed it for weeks.

Paul immediately had decided that he wanted to hear more, and the two had begun to meet several times a week. After smoking a few *sebassa*[3] of *kif,* Layachi would sit in front of Paul's tape recorder and tell his stories in Maghrebi, as Yacoubi had done. Bowles transcribed them, translated the text into English and then went over the transcript with him word by word. The tales needed almost no editing, for Layachi had a flawless ear; as Paul observed, "The good storyteller keeps the thread of his narrative almost equally taut at all points. This [he] accomplished, apparently without effort. He never hesitated; he never varied the intensity of his eloquence."

Based on his own life, the novel that Layachi spun out was spare and compelling. Forced to shift for himself after he was separated from his mother at the age of eight, his narrator is a stoic who stays alive by tending sheep and laboring at a sawmill. Arrested and tortured by the secret police when he attempts to sell *kif,* he is imprisoned for ten months in the jail at Malabata (where he encounters the notorious Marnissi, still serving time for his rampage through the medina). Unable to make a living after he is released, Layachi's protagonist is jailed a second time when he is caught stealing copper wire from a warehouse. After months of forced labor, he is put into solitary confinement; there, he attempts to hang himself, but Allah intervenes. When he finally is set free, he finds work as a houseboy for Nazarene homosexuals who pay him only sporadically.

Layachi asked that Bowles "give [the manuscript] to the book factory in your country," and Paul sent an early chapter to a magazine called *Second Coming,* which quickly accepted it. Layachi was delighted, and Paul dispatched another installment to *Evergreen Review,* which had published Yacoubi's stories. That, too, was accepted, and on the strength of those chapters, Grove Press editor Richard Seaver wrote to offer a small advance for the finished volume.

Over the summer, then, Bowles and Layachi (who had been hired as a cook for Tennessee) met nearly every day to go over his translations. And while Paul was pleased to have unearthed such talent, Jane couldn't see the point; she argued that he should be producing his own pieces rather than transcribing Layachi's fantasies, and told him that the book was draining his creative energy.

In fact, Bowles had been producing essays and short stories all along. At that moment, two collections of his work were being readied for publication: The first was a group of travel essays written for *Holiday* and other magazines, and the second was a selection of stories in which he explored the mysteries of cannabis. Both portrayed North Africa as a realm that refused to yield its secrets to Nazarenes, and both revealed Paul's skill as an interpreter of exotic cultures.

The British publisher Peter Owen had proposed the book of travel pieces, which were to be published as *Their Heads Are Green and Their Hands Are Blue*. Paul had taken the title from Edward Lear's "The Jumblies"—a poem that suggested his own delight in alien creatures:

> Far and few, far and few
> Are the lands where the Jumblies live;
> Their heads are green, and their hands are blue
> And they went to sea in a Sieve.

In the introduction to the volume (which included essays about his travels in Ceylon and Turkey and Latin America, as well as the Sahara), Bowles wrote, "Each time I go to a place I have not seen before, I hope it will be as different as possible from the places I already know." Noting that it was increasingly difficult to find Jumblie-lands in a pristine state, he lamented the fact that bizarre sights and curious customs were more elusive than ever. "Jumblie hunters," he complained, "are having to increase the radius of their searches and lower their standards. For a man to qualify as a Jumblie today he need not practice anthropophagy or infibulation; it is enough for him to sacrifice a coconut or bury a packet of curses in his neighbor's garden."

Paul's stories about the realms that one could visit only with the help of *kif* were to be published by Lawrence Ferlinghetti, whose City Lights Books had issued *Howl and Other Poems*. It was Allen Ginsberg who hit upon the notion of presenting the tales together; convinced that they would work splendidly as a book, he had written repeatedly to suggest that Bowles offer them to City Lights. Pleased with the stories—which seemed wonderfully au courant— Ferlinghetti had agreed to Paul's request that the word "Morocco" appear neither on the book jacket nor in any publicity material. ("Anyone who knows the region can infer from reading the stories that the country is Morocco, but that's not the same as using the word," noted Bowles. "Moroccan diplomats take offense easily.")

Paul had suggested the title *A Hundred Camels in the Courtyard*—a reference to his favorite Moroccan proverbs which asserted, "A pipe of *kif* before breakfast gives a man the strength of a hundred camels in the courtyard."

The four stories in the City Lights volume were unlike anything else Bowles had ever written. Set in "a land where cannabis, rather than alcohol, customarily provides a way out of the phenomenological world," as he described it, all had been composed while he was under the influence of *kif.* His protagonists were all Moroccans like Layachi, and they used the drug as he did—not as an intoxicant, but as a means of breaking down the barriers of logic and reaching another level of consciousness.

Of course, Paul had always been fascinated with the role of cannabis in African society. In a piece written for *Kulchur* (a quarterly popular among the Beat set) he had described the straightforward manner in which Moroccans approached the drug: "In the wintertime," he wrote, "a family will often have a 'hashish evening': father, mother, children and relatives shut themselves in, eat the jam prepared by the womenfolk of the household, and enjoy several hours of stories, song, dance and laughter in complete intimacy. 'To hear this music you must have *kif* first,' you are sometimes told, or: 'This is a *kif* room. Everything in it is meant to be looked at through *kif.*'" As he explained it, the Moroccan attitude about *kif* was the obverse of the prejudice that prevailed in cultures where alcohol was the drug of choice and cannabis was deemed "a social menace." Wrote Bowles, "The user of cannabis is all too likely to see the truth where it is and to fail to see it where it is not. . . . Obviously few things are potentially more dangerous to those interested in prolonging the status quo. . . ."

Bowles's ideas about cannabis struck a chord among the dreaded "Eighthstreetniks," who had been primed for the message by Ginsberg and his allies. Published in July, 1962, *A Hundred Camels in the Courtyard* established Bowles as the patron saint of barefoot expatriates and drew a fresh wave of pilgrims to the Itesa. And while he continued to complain about the strangers who turned up at his door, he also continued to let them in. "People used to literally sit in queues outside his flat because he didn't have room for them all," said Tessa Codrington Wheeler. "You'd see people gazing into space and hoping Paul was going to tell them how to write the greatest novel of the twentieth century. Poor Paul—he was so polite—always the same boring questions: 'How do you get your ideas?' We all thought he was just amazing—the fact that he had smoked dope for so long . . . living in that flat and knowing all of those important people. It all seemed terribly glamorous."

"I don't know whether it was the result of any one book, but it must have been," Bowles said. "People began coming more and more, and [magazines] published stories in which interviewers said, 'I smelled the *kif* before I went inside. . . .' I remember opening the door one day and this man said, 'You Paul?' He said, 'Hey, man, can I park my gear in your pad?' That was all I needed."

Jane, of course, felt besieged. Although none of the newcomers were asking for her, she did what she could to discourage them— telling Aicha to dispatch those who found their way to her flat and asking "Who *are* you?" when they telephoned and asked for Paul. "It bothered her very much," Bowles said. "She was very paranoid about [the strays]; she said if I let them in the police would come in and I'd be accused of dealing or smoking *kif*."

The New York *Herald Tribune*'s John Crosby was among those who found his way to the Itesa in August, 1962, and he quoted Paul at length in two columns. Bowles's themes were familiar ones— Tangier was being despoiled by Western culture, and the future looked bleak indeed. The fast-money crowd, he said, had been replaced by slovenly artistes who arrived on Yugoslav freighters, and the change was hardly an improvement. "The *Village Voice* runs ads for cheap houses in the Arab Quarter," Bowles told Crosby. "Now, they come here to speculate, not in money, but in the metaphysical conditions in North Africa. They come here to paint and write. Most of them don't make out here because it takes more perseverance than they possess." Noting that "Tangier has an international reputation as a place to go to pot in," Crosby observed that Bowles was among the rare Tangerinos who seemed to have prospered there. Paul claimed that many of Tangier's exiles had never had a chance; "Tangier doesn't make a man disintegrate," he said, "but it does attract people who are going to disintegrate anyway. Life is so easy here, so cheap and the climate is marvelous. If you're going to go to hell, you can do it here more cheaply and more pleasantly than in Greenwich Village."

Crosby made expeditions into the medina as well, and there he met newcomers like Ira Cohen. An irrepressible New Yorker living in an extravagant hideaway known as the Bat Palace, the twenty-five-year-old poet gave the columnist his own perspective on the mysterious East: The day he arrived at the port, he said, "A man comes up to me and throws two black socks on the ground—bam! bam!—like that. Out of the socks come two snakes sticking their little forked tongues out at me. Then the man puts a big spike up his nose. Well, I was impressed. Why not?" The gregarious Cohen took Crosby to visit neighbors including John and Natasha Dougherty,[4] who had come from America with their two little boys. Although it had its own charm, their thirty-dollar-a-month house was virtually empty, and Crosby reported that the children slept on mats on the roof. An aspiring writer who favored sandals and dirty canvas trousers, Dougherty worked on a typewriter set on a crate in the living room. While the others passed a joint, their host read a passage from his latest work: "Out of the vortex, the entrails spilling red, stars like diadems exploded, purple green, curving and tearing the eyeballs like vomit into dissonance. . . ." In his column, Crosby explained: "That's kif writing, like kif talk, full of sounds and smells and visions and incoherence. There's a whole literature of it being turned out on egg crates in Los Angeles and Greenwich Village and the Arab quarter of Tangier. . . ."

On rare occasions, Bowles himself ventured into the houses where Cohen and his cohorts were conducting their literary experiments. He found the Dougherty family to be particularly curious. Later, he said: "Natasha [seemed to be] a crazy woman; she looked like you imagined one of Dostoyevsky's peasants would look. She dressed in rags tied with rope—old jackets, sweaters, bathrobes in layers. She was of Russian descent, and she had a *matroyoshka*-doll face. It was a very strange household; the children would get hashish with their oatmeal in the morning to make them quiet during the day—they would whisper and play their games on tiptoe because they were so high. I went to see them one evening and found John in the darkened living room; I had to lie on the floor, which he was doing. We started talking about Brion Gysin, and suddenly there was a [sepulchral] voice from the corner—'Brion is Brion.' I was startled; I said, 'Who was that?' He said, 'That was my wife.' Well, it was pitch dark and I hadn't seen her at all. I was glad to finally get out."

Cohen himself remembered that life in the medina had its share of dramatic tension. Everyone, it seemed, used *kif,* and the paranoia levels were stratospheric. "There was a whole mystique about Tangier that was created by newspapers with lurid headlines about drugs, and there were people who tried *kif* and were not prepared for it," he said. "There was the intrigue of the Moroccan hustlers, and the thing about people speaking in different languages—people would sit in cafés getting stoned, and they would hear someone say something in Arabic and imagine that they had said something [menacing] in English. . . ." Aside from that, he noted, there was a certain competitiveness between poor Tanjawis and impoverished expatriates. "It was a very hard place to get any money," he said. "People regarded everything from a used shoelace to an empty tube of toothpaste as having a value, and although Moroccans can be very hospitable, they can also take you for everything you have—if you're just walking around with too much, they can kind of equal out the balance. Most people were hit on constantly if they had anything at all."

Still, as Burroughs and Ginsberg and Kerouac had discovered, one could live in Tangier for almost nothing—trusting in fate when the check from home failed to arrive at the appointed hour. Cohen kept himself alive on the equivalent of fifteen cents a day, scouting out hole-in-the-wall restaurants that sold *harira* for a few pennies and haggling energetically with shopkeepers. "I remember going to John's when he had nothing to eat; he was feeling desperate," he said. "I had very little money—less than a dollar in Moroccan currency. It occurred to me that we should go in together and make a big pot of soup. We did, and we all ate sitting on his floor. John was wearing his overcoat, and he hadn't shaved; it was like something from skid row."

By Paul's account, Dougherty was among the pilgrims who came to him to borrow money. "I was the Itesa bank," he said later. "I didn't like to lend money, but various people came to me because they knew I had it. John's father sent him money every month, and as soon as it came the hucksters were waiting; they'd say, 'I've got a wonderful load of Timbuktu purple or something—Congo brown.' They'd say, 'It'll only cost you forty-five hundred francs.' He spent all his money on drugs, and then he'd come to me."

In August, Paul sent news of the post-Beat scene to his friend Charles Henri Ford: "I see Alan Ansen now and then," he reported. ". . . Jane and I went to a party on his roof a month ago. He declaimed a poem about Mayakovsky under hashish. . . . I mean Alan was under. There was a contingent of Negro sailors from an American warship stationed in the harbor. They went for the *kif,* and strangely enough, for the poetry, too. Then Alan went into Greek; they went for that, too. Then Jane and I went. . . ."

To Ginsberg (who was traveling in India), Paul dispatched a chatty letter reporting that the surrealist poet Ted Joans was in town, "working on something with Ahmed," and that Gregory Corso had come and gone. Tennessee, he said, had heard his recording of Ginsberg reading "Howl" and "pronounc[ed] it magnificent." As Paul described it to Allen, it had been a frenetic season:

Tangier is full of people because the King[5] is living on the mountain in his palace. Large American cars rush through the streets and there are police on every corner. Members of the royal guard walk hand in hand along the boulevard, and a group of Reguibat [tribesmen] now wanders about, looking lost, trailing their long blue garments behind them. They have been imported by Miss Hutton, whose guests they will entertain day after tomorrow at the annual ball she gives. Jane has decided to go, but to stay away from the room with the jeweled tapestry and the sofa-cushions. Also not to go into any part of the house directly under the terrace on the roof, for fear of being crushed when the house caves in. Last year she worried about it for a few weeks, until she discovered that our names had been crossed off the list anyway. But this year she is buying a series of evening gowns and matching accessories, and that of course augments her anguish, since she can't decide what to wear. . . . There are only two more days to go, and then she can settle down and go quietly mad planning the trip to New York, which takes place on the sixth of September, God forbid.

As it happened, the Bowleses were venturing back to the States to visit their aging parents; Jane was to rendezvous with her mother, Claire, in New York, and Paul was to see Claude and Rena in Gulfport, Florida, where they had bought a house. After undergoing another hernia operation in midsummer, Jane was indeed showing signs of wear; before leaving Tangier, she sent an urgent note to Libby Holman, outlining her travel plans and imploring her to remember that Claire had not been told about her recent illness. The surgery, she said, had done little to improve the look of her body: "My stomach is a mess when I undress, so I am not going to undress."

Once they were in America, Paul kept moving—staying for a few days at Holman's Treetops, then shuttling to her townhouse, then lodging with Oliver Smith and, later, his friend John Goodwin. By early October, he had reached Gulfport, where he found the Old Bowleses to be forgetful and "smaller than I remembered them," as he put it. With the Cuban missile crisis growing more acute, the three shared an agreeable sense of dread; by Paul's account, Rena said somberly, "We'll be the first to be hit," and added, "All I can say is, I feel terribly sorry for the young people growing up today. What chance have they got? They're beaten before they start."

Asked to write the score for *The Milk Train Doesn't Stop Here Anymore*, which was to open on Broadway at the first of the year, Paul returned to New York in November. There, he found that Jane had made the most of her time away from Tangier; aside from seeing friends like Libby, Lyn Austin, Katharine Hamill and Natasha von Hoershelman, she had been reunited with the formidable "Lady Anna," who had gone to the States months before. In her company, Jane was apt to drink steadily, and Paul did what he could to separate the two. Although he was obliged to stay on, he persuaded Jane to sail back via Gibraltar on November 14. She had begun to work fitfully on another play, and he argued that she could make more progress if she removed herself from temptation.

Once she reached Tangier, of course, Jane declared herself to be blocked. In a letter to Paul, she complained about the "mess" of her daily life, saying it was impossible to concentrate when everything was in disorder. On December 11, he wrote back, entreating her to ignore the distractions:

> I was sorry to hear that as you put it, everything has got to be a mess in Tangier and therefore you haven't worked. That was the very thing we were making great resolves about while you were still here—that you wouldn't *allow* the mess-tendency to take over, because . . . that has been exactly what has got in your way. Of course everything's a mess, but *please* forget the mess now and then each day, because otherwise you won't ever work. The mess is just the decor in which we live, but we can't let decor take over, really. I know you agree in principle, but does that help you to leave the mess outside regularly for a while and get inside to work? Also I know it's easy to talk about and hard to do, but pretend you really live here in New York instead of there, and it might help. I mean, that you're only over there for a short while, and not permanently. . . .

While Paul himself was working steadily on the music for Tennessee's play, he also managed to make the rounds in Manhattan. That month, he looked in at Random House, recorded his short stories *The Delicate Prey* and *A Distant Episode* for Spoken Arts Records and called on Richard Seaver at Grove Press. In a letter to Ginsberg, Paul reported that Seaver was "worried about official reaction" to the Grove edition of *Naked Lunch,* although the publishing world was buzzing about Mary McCarthy's rapturous review. ("The bitchy ones say: A kiss from the Angel of Death," Paul noted.)

It was at a dinner party that Paul encountered a fiercely talented, dazzlingly eccentric writer called Alfred Chester. Born in Brooklyn, the deliriously ambitious Chester had seen duty as an expatriate in London and Paris and Piraeus before alighting again in New York, where he became an exuberant presence on the literary scene. At thirty-four, he had sold short stories to *The New Yorker* and written an arresting first novel, and he was offering his irreverent opinions on books in the *Herald Tribune, Partisan Review* and *Commentary.* Sharp and funny and incisive, he had amassed an impressive number of enemies, as well as admirers, and he had been pegged by *Esquire* as a writer to watch. In fact, it was impossible to ignore him: Pasty-faced, gut-sprung, he wore a badly fitting red wig that gave him an air of rakish absurdity. For all of that, he was a curiously seductive figure, and he inspired passionate devotion among friends like Susan Sontag and the poet Edward Field. As a connoisseur of marginal characters, Bowles was delighted with Alfred; the two saw each other several times, and he decided that Chester was "great fun." Before he left, Paul suggested that he come to visit him in Tangier.

Bowles left for Morocco in January, and when he arrived he immediately took up his work with Larbi Layachi. It seemed that Seaver (who planned to submit the novel for an international award called the Formentor Prize) had asked for the manuscript by April, and there was still a great deal of translation to be done. He also faced the task of buoying Jane, who continued to agonize about her new play; she had lost her bearings again, and it was impossible for her to tell whether she was proceeding in the right direction.

With Paul urging her on, however, she kept trying. In a letter to Ruth Fainlight (who had left for London), she confessed, "Things are going badly for me. My work has come to a standstill although I tried again this morning to start off on a new tack (spelling?). I did not scrap everything I had written but typed up the first eighteen pages of which I showed Paul ten. Paul was pleased and said it sounded like myself and not someone else but he would have liked to see more. I would like to see more myself but I seem to have come to a dead end." Telling Ruth that she missed her terribly, Jane reported that she had felt particularly isolated of late: "I have only David occasionaly, (spelling), and Ira Coh[e]n and Isabelle [Gerofi] and every now and then as a great sexy treat—Mrs. [Marguerite] McBey.[6] I went to a fashion show at the Hotel Rif with Mrs. McBey and Veronica. One of the boys belonging to the cuban couple— Irving—loathes me." Added Jane, "I have a feeling that I am going to be more and more hated as the years go by."

When Libby Holman came for a visit, Jane welcomed the diversion, and she devoted every second to the task of trying to entertain her. It was not an easy assignment: Increasingly unhappy with third husband Louis Schanker—a hard-drinking, ill-tempered artist whom she had married in 1960—Holman was in the throes of a depression. The jealous Schanker couldn't abide the Bowleses, and he and Libby began to quarrel. Paul decided that he was a boor who treated her abominably; later, he remembered Schanker snarling, "What the fuck do you want now?" when Libby objected to his rattling the newspapers at breakfast. After they had gone, Jane told Fainlight that she felt drained: "Libby Holman was here with her abstract Painter fisherman husband and she did not want to meet anyone nor go anywhere—so we stayed closeted for ten days," she reported. "I did not write either letters or plays of course as you know. Her departure left me feeling sadder even than I had felt when she came and I am still trying to recover."

As always, however, Jane managed to find distractions. In May, 1963, Paul took a house in Asilah, the cool white port about thirty miles down the coast. After he settled into his new quarters, she began to make the hour-long commute with Cherifa at least once a week, wedging herself (and her stiff leg) into crowded buses and dragging along burlap bags laden with provisions. In theory, Bowles could have looked after himself—or arranged for someone else to do the marketing. But Jane had to have a mission, and she savored the absurdity of it all. That summer, she wrote to Ruth, "My life has turned into a veritable farce, shlepping between Arcila [Asilah] and Tangier as I do, and if I did not find it humorous I would weep."

Chapter 18

The town that Tennessee Williams had taken as a model when he wrote *Suddenly Last Summer*, Asilah was an appealing retreat for Tangerinos weary of hipsters and tourists. Few intruders found their way there, and the place had the slumbrous sensuality of a Greek fishing village—the air was sharp and salty, the light was strong, and there was an abundance of brown-skinned boys. Outside the ramparts was a moat surrounded by olive groves; inside were cobblestone streets that snaked through a medina where whitewashed houses were shuttered against the heat, and where the sound of the waves was an agreeable accompaniment to the shrieks of the seabirds and the songs of the muezzins. At dusk, one could watch the sun set flamboyantly over the Atlantic and imagine that the idyll would last forever.

In the summer of 1963, Paul Bowles was devoting himself to the task of playing the disaffected writer-in-exile. He had chosen a hideaway that was suitably exotic: Built into the seawall, his house was filled with Buddhas and baroque pieces that its Indian owner had brought from Bombay, and it had the kind of drama that was missing from his Spartan flat at the Itesa. With Larbi Layachi to serve as houseboy and Jane to fret about the food, he was free to contemplate the state of the world—and to write cynical dispatches to those still in the thick of it. In a letter to Charles Henri Ford, he declared, "The only way to live in Morocco now is to remember constantly that the world outside is still more repulsive." To Random House editor Joseph Fox, he sent communiqués pronouncing himself to be hopelessly at odds with America, where writers were "persecuted and forced to remain outside." After sixteen years as an expatriate, he said, he had all but lost contact with colleagues who had chosen not to flee; in response to Fox's request that he nominate candidates to provide book-jacket quotes for *Their Heads Are Green and Their Hands Are Blue,* he wrote, "I can't think of anyone anywhere who would be interested in seeing the book, which is why I haven't replied. . . . Each decade I know fewer people. By 1980 life will be perfect."

The truth, of course, was that Paul was a cult figure whose pull could be felt even from Asilah. *The Sheltering Sky* had never lost its mystique, and acolytes were eagerly awaiting Layachi's book, *A Life Full of Holes,* which was to be published in August. New characters entered his life every day; for a man who claimed that he craved solitude, he was astonishingly accessible. In July, he sent a letter to his mother reporting that since leaving Tangier, he had been besieged: "Constant arrivals here at the house of friends, acquaintances, and even completely unknown individuals, have been getting in the way of my plans to write [you]," he told her. "As usual, the arrivals of summer in Tangier are heavy. *Esquire* sent a photographer who took over a hundred color pictures of me, and *Newsweek* sent a reporter who wanted to talk. And people arrived from London in two contingents, while Jane and three servants rushed around to provide food and drinks. . . ."

Still addicted to intrigue, Paul had upped the stakes that spring by urging Alfred Chester to join him. The two had been corresponding since January, and Alfred had developed a fascination for Paul. He also was ready to uproot himself; although he was being courted by every magazine editor in Manhattan, he wanted to concentrate on writing fiction, and he liked the notion of running away to Morocco. In May, he had reported to Bowles that Random House had offered an advance for his novel and a short-story collection,

Maurice Girodias had promised to pay him for a new edition of his 1957 pornographic potboiler, *Chariot of Flesh,* and he had enough money to get himself to Gibraltar. Although he wasn't certain how long his windfall would last, he declined Paul's invitation to stay with him and turned down his offer of a loan; instead, he asked Bowles to look for modest quarters where he could live with his two wild dogs. Not only did Paul agree to help him find a house, but he enlisted a young fisherman called Dris to serve as his suitor.

Years later, Bowles discussed his matchmaking experiment in a letter to the poet Edward Field, who was Alfred's closest friend and literary supporter. "The first time I met that young man [Dris], I decided never to have anything to do with him. He struck me as bad news, and I admit I was afraid of him," he wrote. "His conversation consisted solely of accounts of assaults he had made on European men, and this seemed to me a very bad sign. So (this may sound like a non-sequitur) as soon as Alfred wrote me he was definitely coming to Morocco, I began to coach Driss on how to behave with him. I'd tell him all I knew, and what I surmised, about Alfred. Reason for that behavior: I was curious to see what would happen."

In fact, Paul couldn't have chosen a better subject for his experiment. Paranoid, unstable, Chester had flirted with madness, as Jane had, but the courtship had been more serious. In New York, he had made his name as a provocateur: Feuds, lawsuits—he adored conflict, and he could bring out the worst in his opponents. Haunted by the sense that he "existed only as a sequence of behaviors," he was convinced that the character who was Alfred could disintegrate at any moment. Indeed, the signal flares already had made their way to the surface; during the late fifties, when he was at the *Paris Review,* he had made a sleepless journey from Luxembourg to Paris, believing that he was being pursued by a diabolical stranger who later disappeared. In 1960, when he was at the MacDowell Colony in New Hampshire, Alfred had begun to hear voices, and he had managed to have himself expelled after being abusive to his neighbor, the anthropologist Hortense Powdermaker.

Triggered by a childhood trauma, self-hatred was Alfred's leitmotif. At seven, he had suffered an illness that robbed him of his hair, and he had developed a profound sense of shame about his bald head and browless face. Mirrors had become instruments of torture; at the yeshiva and on summer trips to the Catskills, the curious gazes had burned straight through him. When he was fourteen, his mother had taken the pale, round Alfred to an expensive wigmaker in Brooklyn, and he had been fitted with a hideous hairpiece. He hated it from the moment it touched his head; later, he remembered: "It was like having an ax driven straight down the middle of my body. Hacked in two with one blow like a dry little tree. Like a sad little New York tree."

At New York University and at Columbia, Chester had learned to use his cleverness to eclipse his looks, but his shame was immutable; although he was extraordinarily open about other matters, even close friends had learned never to mention his baldness. ("I could bear no references to the wig," he confessed later. ". . . It was like some obscenity, some desperate crime on my head.") Becoming a writer had seemed the only route to salvation, and he had made his mark early on. His novel *Jamie Is My Heart's Desire* and short-story collection *Here Be Dragons* were published by André Deutsch when he was twenty-six, and he was buoyed by the hope that fame would descend on him at any moment.

Before he left New York to join Paul Bowles, Alfred arranged to rendezvous in Gibraltar with Field (who was in Europe on a Guggenheim) and Neil Derrick, the novelist who was Field's companion. On June 10, he wrote a note to the two describing the bon-voyage party at his Greenwich Village apartment. By Alfred's account, it had been a lively occasion, indeed: "I learned today that I did the following things," he reported: ". . . bit Muriel's finger nearly to the bone, smacked Jay, bit Dennis' upper arm so hard that he's been in pain since, smashed Walter's precious tea cups, tried to jerk off Jerry, threw a Bloody Mary at D. and then threw him on the floor and later tried three times to push him out the window . . . put my hand on the cunt of a girl named Sally [and] squeezed lime juice in everyone's eyes. . . . After the party I went out and picked up a gorgeous Puerto Rican."

Along with his books, a new powder-blue jacket and his disreputable dogs, Chester sailed from New York later in the month. After he met Field and Derrick, the three crossed the Straits by ferry and commandeered a taxi for the trip to Asilah. As soon as they arrived, the party descended upon Paul Bowles, who took them to the beach.

Later, Field remembered that there had been a striking intensity about the scene by the water's edge: "The fishing boats had just come in; all the fishermen had the fish in great boxes on the sand, and the villagers had come down to watch—it was all very lively," he said. "We looked down across the beach and this tall fisherman came across the sand, holding a great fish in one hand. He was nineteen years old, very handsome in a ferocious-looking way. Paul introduced him to Alfred, and that was Dris."

By Field's account, Chester was impressed, but not smitten. Despite his looks, he had managed to attract a succession of lovers, and he had grown used to being wooed. Attended by high drama (and often, low comedy), his affairs were relentlessly theatrical; he needed someone who could scream like a fishwife and make love like a gigolo—someone who could make him feel rhapsodic. In the beginning, at least, it was impossible to tell whether Paul's Moroccan could meet the challenge.

On their first evening in Asilah, Alfred and his friends stayed at Bowles's aerie. Jane and Cherifa had come down from Tangier; Larbi Layachi was padding about in his djellaba and bringing drinks to the terrace, where they all sat swatting mosquitoes. To Field, the household seemed vaguely unsettling. Cherifa announced that she had a paper certifying that she was a virgin, and Paul himself barely spoke. "It was very hard for me to understand him," Field remembered. "Also, the way he lived was strange—he wouldn't eat any of the local food. Everything was canned, because he'd had typhoid a couple of times." Jane, he said, seemed "very sophisticated, in an understated way. That little laugh she had was so devastating—she was *so* clever and glib. She could wipe you out, and she made me feel unutterably clumsy and stupid."

Alfred himself felt an immediate kinship with Jane. Aside from the fact that he could thrust and parry as deftly as she could, he, too, was a paranoid original who saw himself as a freak; if she was "Crippie the Kike Dyke," he was a homosexual Jew who loathed his hairless body. Like other needy creatures, he had a talent for finding sympathetic souls, and he zeroed in on Jane with the skill of a wide-eyed "orphan" cadging coins in the souk.

After a few days, Field and Derrick returned to the comforts of Paris, and Alfred moved with his dogs into a ramshackle rented house not far from Paul's. Dris swooped down immediately, offering sly caresses and rank flattery in broken Spanish. So, too, did an enterprising young neighbor called Hajmi, who was "gorgeous but unbelievably boring," in Alfred's words. By the middle of July, his swains were locked in mortal combat, and Chester was in heaven. In a letter to Field he reported, "[Hajmi] banged on the door for hours last night while D. and I were [making love] and I think that D. has gone to beat the shit out of him. I feel like Carmen."

Soon a regular at Paul's house, Alfred began to make friends with Larbi Layachi. Now a husband and father, Bowles's protégé gave Alfred advice about handling his Moroccan beaux—cautioning him about black magic and explaining that "love affairs between Christians and Moslems are wars." Paul's perspective on the subject was eminently practical; when Alfred told him that Dris had talked about moving in and running his house, he observed that "[Moroccans] feel like Moslem women when they go to live with a foreigner," as he reported it to Field. "[He said that] they expect to be taken care of completely, and in exchange they take care of you completely."

Aside from playing Carmen, Alfred was picking up Moghrebi and taking stock of the little port that Paul had chosen as a retreat. Asilah was alive with a sort of exoticism that he loved: The entire town, it seemed, came to a halt on circumcision day, when two hundred and fifty boys were paraded on horseback into a mosque where a team of barbers did the honors. When the ritual had been completed, members of the Hamacha cult performed trance dances in the square, leaping about in ecstasy and gashing themselves with rocks. (To Field, he wrote, "Dris' father is a leading member [of the cult]. He is a cherif. So is Dris. This obviously makes me a cheriffa.")

Bowles was happy to introduce his visitor to the more primitive aspects of Moroccan culture. "We're going to have a special session of the Djelala cult tomorrow night," Alfred told Field in early August. "Aicha, the cleaning woman, is high priestess, a witch noted for black magic and murder. Her husband is high priest. Paul is agreeable to having it at his house since non-Moslems can never get into the thing when it goes on in a Moslem house. . . ."

With its lurid rites and delicious drugs and aggressive boys, North Africa seemed like paradise to Alfred. In Morocco, there were no moorings; one could cast off self-consciousness and float through languid days and sybaritic nights. Here, he decided, was a new life—one where the past had no meaning, and where the future seemed impossibly remote.

But if Alfred had a giddy sense of being in Nirvana, he also felt vertiginous. Cannabis stoked his paranoia, and he often drank cognac while he was *kifed*—a practice that Bowles deemed foolhardy. An experiment with *majoun* sent him into an anxious frenzy; after Dris brought a chunk as a present, he consumed a healthy portion and decided that he had been poisoned. He took little interest in other expatriates; except for Paul and Jane, he deemed them a dreary lot. And while *Esquire* and *Show* had asked for articles about Morocco, Alfred felt invisible in a setting where there were no phone calls, no convivial lunches with admiring editors. At times, he was struck by the sensation of being utterly displaced; as he described it to Field, "There is no one or thing around to establish my past. Even the dogs seem vague to me."

When *A Life Full of Holes* reached the bookstores in August, Alfred wrote an evocative piece for *Book Week* about Larbi Layachi (whose nom de plume was Driss ben Hamed Charhadi). Aside from portraying "Charhadi" as a wise, tender, pious sort who struggled to support his young family, he described the hypnotic power of Morocco itself. In Asilah, he wrote, the air "[is] thick as honey, and as your body swims through it, your spirit begins to fall asleep." Soon, he said,

the sense of self you arrived with, the great American city you so recently left, your ambitions, your memories, your friends—they too have started swimming in the air. They seem to have come unanchored from you, gotten loose. They bob around, and soon they float lazily away, like balloons on a windless afternoon. You watch them go and you feel an odd vestigial grief or fear, but also a certain relief. They are you, and they are drifting away, disappearing. There is no longer any tomorrow to waken to: there is only the heavy aimless sleep called Now.

For Alfred, being adrift was both exhilarating and terrifying. Every sensation was heightened; every event took on a hidden meaning. With few worthy sparring partners on the scene, he began to focus his energy on Paul Bowles. After a few weeks, he decided that, instead of being a coolly glamorous eminence, Paul was a "dried-up old Dr. Schweitzer" who had closeted himself in a colony where he could control the unfortunates who fell into his orbit. To Field, he complained that he felt "more and more like a prisoner" in Paul's presence. "He . . . really wants to own me," Alfred wrote. "He is so used to owning people and things here. He keeps saying 'they' about the Moroccans, even when he means 'he.' Like Larbi says something and Paul delivers a comment on 'they' to me. He is incapable of a conversation. To tell the truth I loathe him." In a letter to Harriet Sohmers, a close friend who lived in New York, Chester claimed that Paul was "kifed out of his mind most of the time, and . . . terribly unhappy."

As Bowles undoubtedly had observed, it took only the slightest provocation to send Chester into a tailspin. At some point that summer, he went to Paul's to borrow blankets, and Paul refused. Alfred decided that he was being persecuted, and that Paul had told the handful of expatriates in Asilah to spurn him. Typically, he held on to the grudge until it festered; one evening, when he was sitting alone on the ramparts, he was spotted by an acquaintance named Norman Glass, who caught the full force of his anger. A British-born translator who had met Alfred at Bowles's house, Glass found him in a fractious mood: "Snarling, growling, barking, snapping, spitting out his words," as Glass described it, Alfred demanded to know why he had been avoiding him. Glass was startled; later, he remembered that Chester had "left me wondering whether his animosity was directed against the topic at hand, himself, me, or the entire world. Clearly, however, he was talking under pressure; he was tormented and did not enjoy the sound of his own voice. At times, oblivious of my company, he would interrupt and answer himself, leaping from one subject to another in wild ellipsis."

As Glass told it, Alfred was obsessed with the subject of Paul Bowles, and he continued to cross-examine him about whether Paul meant to turn him into a pariah. Assured that Bowles had said nothing in particular about him, Alfred had calmed a bit and said, "So he just talks about the mineral silence of the Sahara, I suppose, and plays those Cecil Taylor tapes. How very dull. . . ."

Like others, Glass found that Chester could be wonderfully amusing when he was rational. The two began meeting for tea, and Alfred introduced him to Dris, who was living with him in his cramped quarters. Glass noted that Alfred and his illiterate companion had almost nothing in common (aside from a boundless supply of sexual energy) and that their relationship was peculiarly volatile. Already, Dris had seen his Nazarene erupt into violent tantrums, and he bragged that he and Alfred were "the two craziest people in the whole of Morocco."

On an afternoon in early September, Glass happened to walk past Chester's house after visiting Paul Bowles. Leaning out of his narrow window, Alfred called down and invited him in for tea. He seemed agitated, but his visitor had no idea what had set him off. When their conversation turned to Larbi and *A Life Full of Holes,* Glass (who was interested in translating a French novel) reported that he had just been quizzing Paul about the business of doing translations. He told Alfred that Bowles had given him a detailed account of his financial arrangements with Larbi and with Grove Press. While Glass could recall only a fraction of what he had said, Alfred insisted that he report just what Paul had told him. "I began what was bound to be a garbled if not erroneous account of the financial procedure," Glass remembered. "Before I had dealt with even a third of the clauses, Alfred sprang suddenly to his feet. He was transformed by rage. He grabbed hold of a footstool and hurled it to the other end of the room. 'Come on,' he roared, 'I'm going to get him.' "

According to Glass, Alfred stalked down the street to Paul's, where he pounded on the door like a man possessed. Glass followed him inside, where he witnessed a barely coherent tirade against Paul. "Evidently," he reported, "[Chester] had used the scraps of information about the contract as a pretext for a showdown which he had been hatching for a long time, perhaps ever since Bowles had failed to provide him with the blankets." At first, said Glass, "Bowles remained alert, calm and silent," but he finally told Chester to leave the house.

Years later, Paul himself described the incident as though it had been utterly trivial: "Alfred," he said, "decided that I was cheating Larbi Layachi out of money because I translated his book. Larbi knew how much money I'd gotten—I gave it all to him. But Alfred decided I'd gotten much more. He came to [my house], bringing a witness, to officially denounce me."

A few days after Alfred's outburst, Paul sent a note to Ira Cohen, who had asked him to contribute to a literary magazine that he hoped to publish and who knew both Glass and Chester. In it, he reported, "Unfortunately I gave the copy of the story for you to Norman [Glass], to take back to [Tangier]. Whether he will or not is another question, since we just broke off diplomatic relations for all time. If he comes back here I'll throw him out. I've finally had enough of his nonsense, as well as that of his friend Alfred Chester. I'm arranging to have them both bumped off in Tangier, incha'Allah." Added Paul, "What a shame all these people have to be born and give forth their stench to an unsuspecting world! But now that they exist, one has to do something about cleaning the place up, obviously."

In a letter to Edward Field, Chester offered his own version of the contretemps: "I finally had a great fight with Paul, drove him to a tantrum, he smashed things all over the house, and I threatened to expose him to the world. He has been a monster in my life here. He wrote a letter to Ira Cohen saying he was making arrangements to have me 'rubbed out' in Tangier. Il est fou."

As Ira Cohen told it, Paul eventually admitted that Alfred had provoked him into losing his temper (if not "smashing things all over the house"). Reported Cohen, "Paul told me that it reached a point where he picked up a plate and threw it on the ground and broke it. He said, '. . . And I pride myself on never showing an emotion.' "

Although Alfred had proven himself as a scene maker, his relationship with Paul survived—perhaps because there was always the prospect of a repeat performance. Within weeks, he was back at the Bowleses', practicing his Maghrebi on Larbi and delivering progress reports about his relationship with Dris. Paul's plan, it seemed, had taken an unexpected turn; Alfred pronounced himself to be wildly in love, and by his account he had "taken vows of always and fidelity and so on." When he broke the news that he and Dris were "married," Paul was shocked. Later, he said that he had suspected that Alfred was deluding himself about his relationship with the young Moroccan. "I didn't know whether to believe him," Bowles said. "I don't know whether you should [ever] believe people when they say that they're in love."

Chapter 19

The summer of 1963 brought William Burroughs back to Tangier with his twin shades, Ian Somerville and Michael Portman. After long months in London, Burroughs needed a new perspective; Paul Bowles had sent ominous reports about the dropouts in the medina, but it was hard to find another haunt where a libertine could live so well. America was out of the question: Although *Naked Lunch* was still a sensation, the literary scene in New York made Burroughs queasy and his visit to Boston had been a disaster. (Timothy Leary, he decided, was "a horse's ass" who was pushing poison.) The rue Gît-le-Coeur had lost its appeal when the Beat Hotel was sold to Corsicans, and while Allen Ginsberg had gone to seek his fortune in India, William didn't require anything so demanding. At the very least, Tangier offered fine weather, decent *kif* and an interesting assortment of misfits.

Early in July, Burroughs found a house on the Marshan that was "straight out of the Arabian Nights," as he described it. Embellished with mosaics, the two-story villa on the Calle Larache had a leafy balcony and a flat roof where one could lie back and watch the stars. There was a garden in the back, and off the dim kitchen, an Arab-style toilet. Upstairs, Burroughs installed an orgone box where he could smoke *kif* before dashing back to the typewriter. Still infatuated with cutups, he had constructed a disjointed novel called *Nova Express* (parts of which, he said, had been dictated by Hassan-i-Sabbah), and he was churning out new montages. On his tape recorder was a sped-up version of Brion Gysin reading one of his favorite word-salads; a construction based on the phrase "I come to free the words," it had a hypnotic effect on callers who happened to be *kif*ed.

Once he was in place, Burroughs dusted off his complaints about Tangier—saying that the city was dead, that only the halt and the lame were still clinging to the raft. Even so, he managed to find amusement; he looked in on locals including Sonya and Narayan Kamalakar, as well as on comrades like Alan Ansen, who was back at the Muniria. In the medina, he found a crop of newcomers, including the poet Ted Joans; Irving Rosenthal, a *Big Table* alumnus who had helped edit the Grove edition of *Naked Lunch;* and Mark Schleifer, an erstwhile *Kulchur* editor who was lodging in the Bat Palace with Ira Cohen. Since Bowles gave no sign of stirring, Burroughs made a pilgrimage to see him in Asilah. There, Paul introduced him to Alfred Chester, who was terrified that William had read his supercilious review of *Naked Lunch* in *Commentary.* (Titled "Burroughs in Wonderland," it depicted the author as a latter-day Alice who fell down the "rabbit hole [of] heroin.") In fact, William hadn't seen the piece, but he decided that Alfred was a rare specimen.

If Tangier seemed anticlimactic to William, there was no dearth of drama in his own household. Still steeped in drugs and alcohol, the dependent, destructive Mikey was often at odds with the jittery Ian. Competitive with each other and territorial about William, the pair created a kind of static that settled in like a low fog. Suspicious of their Nazarene neighbors, the Tanjawis on the Calle Larache began to monitor their every move, and urchins pounded on the door at all hours.

In midsummer, the plot took an unexpected turn with the arrival of William Burroughs III, who had seen his father just three times since 1953. In Palm Beach, where he lived with Mortimer and Laura Burroughs, Billy had created a commotion when he accidentally wounded a schoolmate with his grandfather's .22. Already experimenting with drugs, the sixteen-year-old was a truant who regarded William as a glamorous stranger—an adventurer who lived the most romantic of all possible lives. He, too, wanted to be a writer, and Burroughs had done what he could to encourage him; from London, he had sent Billy a copy of *The Sheltering Sky* —a novel that he knew would appeal to a brooding adolescent.

After rendezvousing with Billy in Lisbon, Burroughs flew with him back to Tangier. On their way to the Marshan, father and son stopped in at the Parade Bar. While William huddled with Mikey, the stocky teenager was sized up by one of the regulars (or "accosted by an aging fag," as Billy remembered it). By Billy's account, his admirer informed him that "half the old Tangerines knew you were coming and wondered what you looked like," and added a graphic comment to indicate that he had passed muster.

When the party arrived at the house on Calle Larache, the electricity somehow had failed, and it was dark. Searching the rambling villa with a flashlight, Burroughs finally found a place for his son to sleep. When Billy woke the next morning, Ian was sitting on his bed, "looking at me like a loving mother," as he remembered it. After a bit of small talk, Ian clasped Billy's hand and tried to guide it into his lap. He resisted, but Ian took the rejection gracefully; the next day, the two went together to the Grand Socco, where he helped Billy select a *sebsi* for smoking *kif*.

To a boy raised among the Posts and the Dodges in Palm Beach, Burroughs's Tangier was thoroughly alien. Accustomed to strict discipline, Billy found himself in a setting where anarchy prevailed; he was free to dip into William's mason jar of *majoun* or to sit until dawn at dives like the Dancing Boy Café, and no one seemed concerned about where he was at any given moment. The wailing of the muezzins seemed unearthly, and Arab customs, unfathomable. Oblivious to the fact that the rooftops were off-limits during the daytime (when they were considered women's territory), Billy went up for air one afternoon and scandalized the neighbors; for a week, Moroccans flung mud at Burroughs's door. Since William often closeted himself with his collages, Billy passed the time sitting through French movies dubbed in Maghrebi or wandering on the sea cliffs, smoking the *kif* that Mikey had given him.

Burdened by guilt over Joan's death and his own long absence, William tried to make contact with the stranger who was his son. Billy, however, was out of reach; laconic, unresponsive, he seemed to have inherited Burroughs's ability to detach himself from his environment—particularly when he was in distress. By William's account, their conversations were "strained and off-key," as though they were on a long-distance call with a bad connection. At night, he could hear Billy playing his guitar in the bedroom next to his, and he felt profoundly melancholy.

When the fall term began, Burroughs enrolled Billy at the American School (where Ezra Pound's son Omar had taken the job of headmaster). Although it had an excellent reputation, the school could do little for Billy, who skipped classes and sat daydreaming in the library. "He was very cut off, very noncommunicative," said Joe McPhillips, who taught English that year and had come to know Burroughs. After a few weeks, Billy dropped out, and William was at a loss. Discipline, of course, was beyond him, and his reunion with his son had become a trial.

While Burroughs and his mason jar of *majoun* had escaped the attention of the authorities, Tangier's post-Beat pilgrims had been less fortunate. Since few took the trouble to be discreet about drugs, they were testing the patience of the police, and their Tanjawi neighbors were using them as pawns. Native dealers sold *kif* to the young expatriates and then turned them in to detectives; after the contraband was confiscated, it was returned to the informants, along with a reward. Hipsters who escaped that trap were being caught up in periodic police sweeps; bursting into their houses in the medina, the authorities were rounding them up, shaving their heads and shipping them out of Morocco.

Oddly, the interlopers often headed back to the Casbah even after being deported; falling into the hands of the police was seen as a minor inconvenience at worst, and some even regarded it as an adventure. Old-guard Tangerinos savored a story about a mad poet who was arrested on a drug charge and declined to leave prison after friends raised bail money; deciding that being held in a Moroccan jail was the ultimate degradation (and hence, a mystical experience), he refused to accept the services of a defense lawyer. In the end, the government had decided that it was too expensive to keep him, and he, too, had been bounced from the country.

Although members of the Mountain set developed crushes on the occasional beatific specimen, they were dismayed by the flamboyant newcomers. It was impossible to know how far the authorities would go, and expatriates who remembered the purge of 1957 realized how quickly the winds could change. Like all true escapists, however, they were happy to seize upon any bit of excitement that would keep them from dwelling on the unpleasantness. Fortunately, they had to look only as far as Sidi Hosni to find a delicious tempest; Barbara Hutton, it seemed, had finally grown weary of Lloyd Franklin, and *tout* Tangier was watching the changing of the guard.

The upheaval had begun some months earlier in Marrakech. During a trip with David Herbert, Franklin and Ira Belline, Barbara had been introduced to Raymond Doan, a half-French, half-Vietnamese mining engineer who had a passing acquaintance with Belline. Fine-boned and ethereal-looking, the forty-seven-year-old Doan styled himself as an artiste, and he had taken an immediate interest in the profligate Barbara. He had invited Hutton and her party for tea at his house (where his French wife had greeted them in curlers), and he had shown them dozens of his paintings of Moroccan street scenes. Before making her escape, Hutton tactfully had bought one of Doan's works to take back to Tangier.

While Barbara had seemed unimpressed with Raymond Doan, the eminently practical aesthete behaved as though he had been struck by a grand passion; after she returned to Sidi Hosni, he had plied her with poems in which he declared eternal love. For a woman inundated with letters from anonymous suitors, such a tribute was hardly remarkable, but it seemed to have its effect on her. When Doan arranged a one-man show at the Tangier Casino, Barbara not only made an appearance but bought every last painting. To those who knew her, the gesture was clear—she was ready for a diversion, and Lloyd Franklin was on shaky ground. Remembered Ruth Hopwood: "She had just gotten tired of Lloyd—she was bored with him." Typically, Hutton wasted no time breaking in her new consort; by the end of the summer, Doan had joined her entourage, and Franklin was de trop.

As unlikely as the romance may have seemed, it did follow a certain logic. By Barbara's reckoning, her effusive new beau offered a great deal that Franklin couldn't. Poetry was the way to her heart, and she had a passion for all things Oriental. An enigmatic sort who described himself as a spiritualist, Doan knew precisely how to appeal to her overheated imagination. He also was mature enough to play the role of helpmate; even with six ex-husbands to her credit, Barbara wasn't prepared to give up on matrimony, and she had always said that Lloyd was far too young to marry.

Accustomed to seeing Hutton discard one lover after another, most of her friends welcomed Doan into the fold. Herbert, however, was distraught: Lloyd had been his candidate, and he believed that Franklin truly loved the capricious Barbara. Furthermore, he suspected that Raymond and his brother Maurice (a sybarite who also had settled in Marrakech) meant to take advantage of her. Convinced that the elder Doan had masterminded Raymond's campaign to snare Barbara, Herbert went to her and told her that Maurice had written the billets-doux that Raymond had sent. It was not what Hutton wanted to hear; she had known David since her debutante days, but she made it clear that the friendship was over.[1]

Years later, Herbert observed that the lovestruck Hutton had found it impossible to direct her anger at the Doans. "Poor Barbara; she was taken in by those poems," he said. "Maurice, the older brother, had written all [of them]; the other was too illiterate. But she believed in him. When I told her it was lies and told her the true story she said, 'David, you've ruined my life.' "

In a town where there were no secrets, the news from Sidi Hosni traveled quickly. Society columnists went on the alert; Raymond Doan was pegged as the man who had captured the aging Huttontot, and Lloyd Franklin as the runner-up who had been well rewarded. On September 16, 1963, Suzy reported in the *New York Mirror* that Barbara had been as generous to Lloyd as to her other cast-offs. As she put it, "The troubadour is having a luxurious bachelor flat made ready in Paris, can lay his hands on bundles of cash right this minute, is planning a safari in East Africa, owns a string of polo ponies and a splendid stable to keep them in, nips about the world in a private plane, has his very own Rolls-Royce with his very own crest . . . lives in a beautiful North African bungalow while an even finer place is being built for him and has set up his mother and family in the restaurant business. Isn't it absolutely marvelous what you can do with a guitar?"[2]

Taken with the idea of having an exquisite Oriental as her husband, Barbara began setting the stage for her seventh marriage. In October—while the inconvenient Madame Doan went about the business of obtaining a divorce—Hutton and her attendants traveled in state to Rabat. There, Barbara made a visit to the Laotian embassy, where she announced that her fiancé required a title and offered up a fifty-thousand-dollar bounty to anyone who could transform him into a noble. Before her party moved on to Marrakech, Hutton's consort had become Prince Raymond Doan Vinh Na Champassak, and an "aristocrat" who worked as a clerk at the embassy was counting his windfall. For Tangier's most extravagant dreamer, an acquired title was every bit as useful as a real one, and the promise of becoming a princess was enough to stave off—if not vanquish—the neverending problem of ennui.

Back from Asilah by the middle of October, Paul Bowles had no sooner settled into the Itesa than he began planning a long trip to the south. Undeterred by the border clashes between Morocco and Algeria, he decided to go with Jane and Christopher Wanklyn to Tafraoute—a palmy outpost in a valley that was about seventy-five miles from the frontier. They arrived in the almond-pink town at the beginning of November, and Paul found the atmosphere to be congenial; not only did he encounter drummers and dancers staging a dramatic *ahouache*,[3] but late at night he could hear savage skirmishes between the jackals that came down from the Anti-Atlas and the mongrels that stalked the marketplace. Each day brought pleasantly gloomy reports about the face-off with Algeria, and there was every reason to think that the fighting would continue.

Always skittish in the countryside, Jane was ready to return to the tranquillity of Tangier after just two weeks. Driving north through the High Atlas, the party descended to Marrakech, where they were to stay for a night at Wanklyn's house in the medina. When they arrived, his aide-de-camp, Boujemaa (a storyteller of some repute), greeted them with a stunning piece of news—the President of the United States, he said, had been shot dead. This was too disturbing for even Bowles to believe; as he described it later, "[it] sounded too Moroccan to be anything but an invention."

In Tangier—where events in America had always seemed decidedly unreal—even the most detached expatriates felt a chill when they heard about the murder of John Kennedy. Holding forth at the Parade Bar, William Burroughs announced that the idealistic JFK had "scared the shit out of America, and they had to bump him off. Oswald's bullet," he said, "is the beginning of the end." As a follower of Hassan-i-Sabbah, William was fascinated with the assassination; here was proof that the forces of evil had seized control of the universe, and that Armageddon was around the corner.

Alfred Chester was also willing to believe the worst. After the Bowleses returned from Marrakech, he spent an afternoon with Jane in the Socco Chico, eating *pinchitos* and savoring the disturbing development. "[Jane] says everyone on earth knows the Kennedy thing is a fascist plot," Alfred reported to Edward Field. "I knew it all the time and it is scaring me. . . . It makes me nervous like some gigantic web covering the world. . . ."

Since October, Alfred had been living in a faded villa on Sidi Bujari, a quiet street between the Marshan and the Mountain. Money was short, but he had found a flat with three rooms, two bathrooms and a terrace, for just thirty dollars a month, and it was big enough for his dogs and the overgrown Dris (who, he said, ate "like a Great Dane"). Although he was delighted with his new quarters, Alfred was lukewarm about the beatniks and refugees who lived on the Mountain. "It would be a perfect place if there were people here one liked," he told his friend Harriet Zwerling. "But everyone is so fucked up and mostly boring. . . . It's sort of a strange life that mustn't be questioned too closely or it all falls apart."

To Edward Field, Alfred reported that Tangier was only slightly more stimulating than Asilah. When he wasn't working, he said, he spent time with Jane or Norman Glass or Christopher Wanklyn, who had promised to take him to Marrakech. "Occasionally I see the people from the Bat Palace who are so far gone on drugs it's mostly impossible," he wrote. ". . . I had them all over on Saturday for snake *tajine,* stewed that is, a specialty of Dris'. [Ira Cohen's girlfriend] Rosalind [Schwartz] was all squeamish about it, which was ridiculous as she once Southern-fried a dead bat and they all ate a piece of every part of it." The good news, he said, was that William Burroughs seemed less malign than he had at first: "I feel sort of sorry for him," Alfred observed, "though I think he's a monster." And as for Paul Bowles, he said, "I saw [him] for a minute while he was putting up his goodies from Marrakech. I hate him. . . ."

As vigorously as he mocked his neighbors, Chester reserved the real venom for himself. That fall had seen the publication of Susan Sontag's novel *The Benefactor*—an event that had been traumatic for the relentlessly competitive Alfred. He had always been ambivalent toward Sontag; he had nominated her as his successor when he abandoned his post as drama critic at *Partisan Review,* but he was convinced that she maintained their friendship only to appropriate his ideas. Now she was establishing her presence among the avant-garde, and he was living in the shadow of Paul Bowles. Clinging to the notion that he was a failure, Chester took little comfort in the fact that *Behold Goliath,* his new collection of short stories, was to be published in April. When he received the galleys, he pronounced the book an embarrassment, and he ripped through a series of revisions.

Alfred's self-hatred was heightened by the fact that he could barely support his "idiotic menage," as he called it. By late December, he had run through his small advance from Random House and was desperate for a check from Maurice Girodias. He sent a telegram to his mother pleading for a loan, but she responded with silence. Since there was no wood for the fireplace, he stoked himself with *kif* and codeine in order to turn out an essay for *Commentary.* In a letter sent to Field on December 20, Chester reported, "I've been starving lately. I sent Dris back to Asilah on Sunday as there was no point [in] both of us starving, though he obviously loves me better poor than rich. He cooks beans in a variety of gorgeous ways and he wants to go on eating them so we can have money for other things, like the pair of shoes I've been promising him since July. . . ." Saying that he loathed his short stories, Alfred added, "I simply can't work under these circumstances. . . . I am worn out with my own judgments of myself. I am thirty-five and still begging. Why don't I just get a job? Why don't I just forgive myself my past? Even that I can't do. I just go on living all my sorrows and shames."

Increasingly anxious, Alfred went to the American consulate to telephone his mother in Brooklyn. "I waited two hours to get the call through because mama kept picking up the receiver and hanging up as soon as she heard Morocco calling," he told Field. "I think she was afraid I might be dead. Finally she answered and just yelled and said she wasn't going to send me anything. . . . I kept saying in a subdued way, 'Do you want me to die here?' and she said, 'Do what you want.' I hung up on her as I couldn't think of anything to say and it would have been embarrassing to shout with all the embassy people hanging around."

In the midst of the crisis, it was Jane Bowles who appointed herself Alfred's protector: Financially independent after inheriting thirty-five thousand dollars from an aunt, she was able to lend him small sums and to take him to a doctor when he contracted a painful eye infection. She prevailed upon the Gerofis (who still managed the Librairie des Colonnes) to advance the money owed by Girodias, and she comforted him when he fretted about Dris deserting him on grounds of poverty. "Jane says Moroccans love [it] when their Nazarenes go broke," Alfred reported to Field. "It makes them equal, she says."

Dris, in fact, had been spectacularly loyal to the mercurial Alfred; apart from the fact that it was considered a coup to have a Nazarene as one's benefactor, he seemed genuinely to care for Chester. Over time, the two had fallen into a pattern that was comfortable, if slightly bizarre. By Norman Glass's account, he had been sitting in the Grand Socco late one evening when Alfred rushed by in a fury; Dris, it seemed, had broken his curfew, and Chester was about to haul him home. As Glass remembered it, "Dris emerged from the cafe with his head bent low, while Alfred followed, punching him repeatedly. 'Don't do it here! Don't do it here! Wait till we get home!' Dris pleaded. . . . 'But of course I had to do it there,' Alfred explained to me the next day. 'If I'd waited till we got home, he'd have started with his Rudolph Valentino voice: "*Alfredo, que tienes, mi amigo?* . . ." and all my anger would have melted.' "

Between fights, Alfred had been blissfully happy with Dris. The young Moroccan was moody enough to be interesting, and their lovemaking was so ardent that even Chester felt satiated. (In a letter to Field, he reported: "Sometimes I get panicky, really deeply frightened by all this sex. His ease though is reassuring. In the middle of it all last night he began singing me an Arabic love song. . . .") To Alfred, the hulking Dris seemed a tender innocent; he brought presents after visiting his family in Asilah, and he promised that they could live on his income as soon as fishing season began. A born romantic, Chester called Dris "Heaven" or "My heart's beloved," and he waxed rhapsodic about the way he looked in his white djellaba.

Acutely sensitive to Alfred, Dris did everything he could to help keep his demons at bay. At the end of January, as the deadline for his *Commentary* piece on Jean Genêt was approaching, Chester edged into a panic; determined to make his essay as trenchant as Sartre's *Saint Genêt, Comédien et Martyr* (which he had read twice), he laid in a supply of Dexedrine and sat at the typewriter for long hours, discarding page after hard-fought page. At night, he tried to take the edge off with whiskey and *kif,* but his mind kept racing. "It is eight P.M. and I've been at the Genêt since eight in the morning and yesterday and forever and it is supposed to be there this week and I'm exhausted," he told Field on the twenty-ninth. "It gets more and more brilliant, but I hate it more and more." Seeing that he was in pain, Dris decided to intervene. One night, while Alfred was at the typewriter, he heard chanting coming from the direction of the hearth. Looking up, he saw Dris "stripped to the waist and swaying in a trance by the fireside," as he reported it to Norman Glass. By Alfred's account, Dris had used fresh blood to write incantations on eggshells that he had placed before the fire; murmuring in Maghrebi, he refused to explain what he was doing until the ceremony was over. Finally, Dris told Alfred that he had worked a spell for him—he not only had arranged for Alfred to meet his deadline but had instructed his editor to pay him twice as much as he had been promised.[4]

Alfred did finish the column on Genêt, but his anxiety abated only slightly. Continuing to rely on Librium and Dexedrine as well as *kif,* he felt increasingly disoriented; he had no internal gyroscope of his own, and there was nothing in Morocco to give him his bearings. In a piece written that season for *Show,*[5] he described Tangier as a place where it was impossible to resist the siren call of insanity:

The winds fly in from all directions, sometimes hot and violent skimming off the desert, sometimes cool as grass. Driven mad by the Atlantic, the Straits of Gibraltar and the Mediterranean, the air comes on like Ophelia or Lucia; it sings and it rings and it tosses flowers around; it is a berserk coloratura that tastes like stained glass. Your blood goes lunatic. Not even Greece has this wild drunken sky and this sunlight falling like diamonds. Not even Greece has the blue of Morocco, nor the white. Here, these colors hypnotize. They stun you, catch you, hold you, refuse to let you go. . . .

There is a terminal feeling here for the Nazarene: it feels like destiny. It feels as if you've been summoned here. When you're smoking kif, you imagine that the friend who told you to come here was the devil's advocate. You imagine he went all the way back to New York with no other purpose than to bring you back here. Like the saints and the black magicians, he spat in the palm of your hand and thereby passed on his good or his evil. Under kif, everyone becomes part of the network. Friends, lovers, all of them are agents of another power. Only you are in the dark. They are all surgeons and Morocco is the table over which your helpless soul is spread.

Early in 1964, Alfred Chester careened from one mad scheme to the next, unable to distinguish between ideas that were inspired and those that were truly unhinged. Like Jane Bowles and William Burroughs, he had a sense of humor that was difficult to read; he was, by turns, deliriously funny and deadly serious, and one never knew when he was casting himself as a character in a farce. Even Alfred sometimes lost track; in the light of day, he often was appalled by notions that seemed brilliant when he was *kif*ed.

Finally at work on another novel, Chester decided in February that he wanted to free himself from the drudgery of writing on deadline. In a dispatch to Edward Field, he reported that he had given Dris five hundred francs to pay the witch of Asilah to cast a spell on his mother. He also confided that he had embarked on a search for patrons; if Jane could accept money from admirers like Tennessee Williams, surely he could do the same. Already, he said, he had written letters to Jacqueline Kennedy and to Rex Henry—one of Jane's own allies, "a local millionaire who thinks I'm great," as he reported it. ("Jane will have another stroke when she hears about it, as he is her millionaire," he added. "But she has so many I don't see why it should matter.") And while Alfred thought at first that his strategy made sense, he changed his mind as soon as he finished the missives. "I'm scared," he told Field. "It really scares me. . . . I mean, imagine writing a letter to Jacqueline Kennedy. Don't you think I'm crazy?"

As the publication date for *Behold Goliath* drew nearer, Alfred's hysteria reached its peak; he was convinced alternately that the book would sink without a ripple and that the entire world would read it and brand him an impostor. Seized by the fear that Random House would do nothing to promote his stories, he implored his editor to order new jacket copy and to place ads in the *Post* and the *Times* and the *Tribune.* He petitioned both Burroughs and Bowles for quotes, and he resolved to ask Random House to fly him to New York.

While his mind was still spinning, Chester fell into a labyrinthine contretemps that involved Paul, Jane and the ambitious Ira Cohen, who was about to publish a literary magazine called *Gnaoua.* Cohen had culled pieces from writers including Bowles, Burroughs, Allen Ginsberg and Brion Gysin, and he had asked Alfred to help proofread the material. The intrigue began at the end of February, when Cohen's friend Irving Rosenthal came back to the Bat Palace after a visit with Paul Bowles; angry with Paul for reasons that remained obscure, Rosenthal insisted on making a change in the story that he had given Ira. In a line that read, "Some of the campiest queens I've known had cocks drier than an Arab's mouth caught between Tafraoute and Taroudant with kif and without water," he substituted "Paul Bowles" for "an Arab." The tale went out through the beatnik grapevine, and Paul (who also had agreed to help with the proofreading) went straight to Rosenthal's story when Ira showed him the galleys. "He read the line and then he recoiled," Cohen remembered. "He looked up at me and said, 'You aren't going to print this? . . . Jane won't like it.' "

Torn between his fear of Irving and his respect for Paul, Ira went into a frenzy of indecision. When he asked for Alfred's advice,

Chester suggested that he simply let Paul have his way. Hours later, however, he came up with a plot that sounded like something from a bad detective novel: He informed Ira that he planned to tell the Bowleses that if they paid him ten thousand dollars, he would arrange for the line to be deleted; if they failed to comply, he would "expose them," as he put it. Alfred knew that Ira still had the note in which Paul joked about having him "rubbed out," and he said that he would threaten to offer it to the American consul as proof that Paul was plotting his murder. "Alfred said, 'You're going to take half the money or else,' " Cohen remembered. "He was coming on with an Edward G. Robinson imitation. It was quite funny."

At some point, Cohen realized that Chester wasn't joking. He tried to reason with him, but Alfred had his own agenda: He snatched Bowles's letter from the Bat Palace and arranged a rendezvous with the unsuspecting Jane in a public park. With Dris at his side, Alfred gave her the ultimatum; as Cohen told it, he said, "I'm going to come right to the point—ten thousand dollars or else. Otherwise, Ira's going to print that line." Jane was aghast; according to Cohen, she said, "But Alfred, I love you." Said Cohen, "Alfred told her, 'Don't give me any of that shit—ten thousand dollars or else.' Jane just couldn't believe it; they left her standing in the park."

In his agitated state, Alfred began to believe that Paul was serious about having him killed. As he explained it in a dispatch to Edward Field, "The people here . . . are not like the people we've ever known. Bill Burroughs, as you know, murdered his wife. Jane's best friend Libby Holman murdered her husband. . . . Paul and Jane are poison." Convinced that he could be assassinated at any moment, he mailed copies of Paul's letter to Field and Norman Glass (who was in Italy). "Naturally I want to get out of here as fast as possible," Alfred told Glass. ". . . I'm scared to be alone a minute now." He followed that communiqué with a wire begging Field to fly to Tangier and save him from Paul and Jane. "Afraid," he said. "Don't fail me, afraid."

When the wire reached New York on March 3, Field telephoned Jane Bowles, who seemed determined to keep the story from spreading. "Everything is fine," she told him. "Alfred is fine." Still contemplating a rescue mission, Field received a second telegram from Chester on March 4. It read, "Forget other wire. Decided to become a man. Alfred."

Although they tried to downplay the incident, Paul and Jane were shocked: Not only was Alfred more unbalanced than anyone had suspected, but he was perilously indiscreet. That month, he carried out his threat to go to the American consulate with the story that Paul wanted to have him murdered. "He asked for full-time Marine guards to protect him," Bowles remembered. "The consul called me in and said, 'Of course, I don't put any stock in this, but it's my job to investigate.' " The matter was quickly dismissed, but Jane, in particular, was traumatized; after the Yacoubi scandal, she feared that the Tangier police had little patience for such dramas. Instead of dropping Alfred, however, she gave him a lecture about the importance of closing ranks in times of trouble. As he told it, she said that it was "against the rules to snitch on each other," and that alerting the police was "criminal."

That spring, the Bowleses continued to see the quixotic Chester. "They had a very high opinion of his writing, and the fact that he was a good writer excused everything else in their eyes," said John Hopkins, who met Alfred through Paul. Jane kept Chester firmly under her wing, while Paul pricked up his ears: Clearly, this was a new species.

Their protégé reined in his hysteria, but he was quietly terrified; he decided that Paul was campaigning to drive him mad and that Jane wanted him locked away. "We are pretending to be great friends now," he told Edward Field, "but I think we're scared shitless of one another."

When David Herbert gave a dinner for Cecil Beaton in May, Jane prevailed upon him to invite her charge. "She felt sorry for Alfred, but she was impossible," said Bowles. "She introduced him to people who couldn't possibly appreciate him." The occasion made a lasting impression on everyone involved—in part because Alfred became disoriented when he ascended to the Mountain.

The morning after Herbert's soirée, Chester confided to Field that the occasion had been curiously depressing. Although "the dinner was stupendous, and the evening was like paradise, and the garden was starry and full of flowers and huge trees," he said, there had been "no magic," and he felt the need to liven things up. "On the table were huge overblown roses," he told Field. ". . . And I said, smelling the roses, 'They don't smell.' And the Hon. David Herbert said, 'Oh yes they do.' And I said (knowing that Cecil would love it): 'Oh a bit pissy, like not quite clean diapers.' A moment of stunned silence. Then Cecil cued in with a huge guffaw, and then David roared with laughter,[6] and then Jane and Paul came in with a nervous titter (they were identifying with me), and at last [Marguerite McBey]. . . . And I was the star."

Days later, Alfred was involved in a bizarre accident that destroyed his wig. While he was lighting the gas stove at his flat, he managed to set fire to the hairpiece; although he escaped serious injury, the wig melted and he decided not to replace it. For a time, he wore a *tageeya*,[7] but he eventually abandoned the camouflage. Rabidly self-conscious, he carefully monitored the reaction to his bared scalp. When he asked Paul and Jane to lunch after the mishap, they found him in an odd state. "He'd never mentioned the wig, and we weren't supposed to look," said Bowles. "People would say to me, 'Can't you tell it's a wig?' . . . I'd say, 'No, no.' I wasn't observant. When we arrived, Alfred was lying on the floor, and he was completely bald. Later he was furious and said we were snobbish for not bringing it up. I suppose he'd invited us to show us his bald head."

Paul Bowles decided to look for another retreat that summer, and he found one on the Mountain. An isolated property shaded by eucalyptus trees and umbrella pines, it was set on a cliff where one could hear only the rush of the sea below. Furnished sparsely in the Moroccan style, the estate was gloomily romantic; on the grounds were broken marble benches and lianas and reflecting pools, and there was a steep footpath leading to the sea. Although he confessed that he was afraid to sleep there alone, Bowles pronounced the place ideal; at work on a new book, he wanted to distance himself from the distractions at the Itesa.

Begun in the winter of 1964, Paul's fourth novel was inspired by the Poe tales and the pulp thrillers that he had devoured when he was a boy. The story of an American couple destroyed by a psychopath whom they meet in Central America, *Up Above the World* would echo the themes that he explored in *Let It Come Down* and *The*

Sheltering Sky. Like Nelson Dyar and the unfortunate Moresbys, the alluring Day Slade and her husband, Taylor, find themselves in a setting where all the rules have been suspended. Seduced and held captive by Grove Soto (a voluptuary who suspects that they know he murdered his mother), they are plied with hallucinogens and subjected to a form of brainwashing. The disoriented Slades are unable to save themselves, and even their captor becomes a victim; when the elaborate plot takes its final twist, Thorny, the drug-addled beatnik who is Soto's confidant, is planning to destroy him.

In many ways, *Up Above the World* was vintage Bowles: Through a pair of hapless travelers trapped in an amoral milieu, he explored the way in which fate turned on the unwary. This time, however, Paul manipulated his characters from an even greater distance; the impassive Slades were given none of Kit Moresby's sense of doom, none of Nelson Dyar's existential despair. Mere pawns for the diabolical Soto, they were blank slates even before they were dosed with LSD. As Bowles explained it, their story was meant only as a divertissement; the writing itself, he said, had been intended as "a purely pleasurable pastime"—an exercise in creating suspense rather than an exploration of anomie.

While Bowles was on the Mountain crafting his novel, he was also holding court. Jane ferried provisions from the city, and Larbi Layachi came to work as his houseboy. A distraught Tennessee turned up that summer but left in less than two weeks; burdened by the recent death of Frank Merlo, he could take only the most perfunctory interest in Paul or Jane or Tangier. Bowles's regular visitors included Brion Gysin, who had ventured back to Morocco in the spring. Brion often appeared in the evenings with his aides-de-camp, Salah and Targuisti, who conjured up *tajine*s and *harira*.

Gysin had lost none of his powers during his seven years in exile: Newcomers like John Hopkins and Joe McPhillips (who had become Paul's neighbors on the Mountain) saw in him the same charm, the same energy, the same hauteur that had impressed those who met him in the fifties. Still exhilarated by North Africa, he took the younger expatriates on the long trek to Jajouka, where they heard the Master Musicians,[8] and to late-night landmarks like the Dancing Boy. He talked constantly about his sound poems and his cutups, and he had a passion for new ideas. He also exhibited a spontaneity that his admirers found wondrous. Said McPhillips, "I was downtown one day, near Brion's, and I thought, 'Well, hell, I've got to go see him because I've got something very important I've got to ask him. I took the elevator to his apartment and he opened the door and I said, 'Brion, what's the *meaning* of life?' The stupidest adolescent remark—but he just looked me in the eye and said, *'Lumière, mon cher, lumière.'* Instantaneously. Not 'What are you bothering me for?' or 'What's wrong with you?' or 'Did you have a rough night?' He just looked me straight in the face and answered me as I'd asked it."

"I'd heard about Brion before I came to Tangier—he was a myth," said Hopkins. "I was sitting one day at the Parade Bar, where all things begin and end, and there was a man looking at me with very clear green eyes; I was trying to avoid his gaze, but I found out that it was the great Brion Gysin. Then I saw him at Paul's house and I found him fascinating. . . . [One night] there we were all smoking *kif,* and Larbi made *majoun.* We walked out on the cliff to look at the moonlight, and everyone was stoned out of their gourds. We were talking about [why we were here] and Paul said, 'We're here to learn.' Brion said, 'No, we're here to *go.'* "

Desperate for the sort of recognition that Burroughs had received, Gysin was still serving as his aesthetic co-conspirator. Together, they spent hours at William's Spartan penthouse on the rue Delacroix (which he had taken after shipping Billy back to Palm Beach) or at Jay Haselwood's bar. It was Burroughs who presided at the opening of Brion's one-man show in the Ville Nouvelle, and Brion who promoted William's word collages. Even expatriates who found their prose experiments incomprehensible were dazzled by their creative spirit. "So much energy came from being around Brion when he was with Burroughs," said McPhillips. "They had an intellectual rapport that was stunning."

Gysin's own obsession was his Dream Machine, which Ian Somerville had helped him perfect in Paris. Brion subjected what seemed like the entire expatriate population to private demonstrations, but aside from Burroughs no one could see the point. "I went along after school to Brion's; I think it was with Yacoubi," said Tamara Dragadze. "The machine was a turntable with a paper cone around it. It had holes in it and a light inside, and you had to let the light sort of flick across your eyes. You were supposed to see colors and dreams and things, and I didn't see any, and they were all laughing at me." Brion, of course, ignored the naysayers; in Paris, he had shown the Dream Machine to prospective patrons, including Helena Rubinstein, and he told Bowles that he would make a fortune when it was mass-produced.

Paul himself was no more impressed with the invention than he had been with Brion's nonsensical prose. In a letter to his mother, he reported that the Dream Machine "promises a new kick to the juvenile delinquents." Although he said that he found the device absurd, he added, "So far there is no law against such a contraption. If people want to knock themselves out with the alpha wave, they're at liberty to do it, I suppose."

To those who were seeing them together for the first time, Paul and Brion seemed to be on different frequencies. "They were like two old stags in the forest who looked across at one another from opposing mountaintops," remembered Hopkins. "Paul said that Brion had experimented with drugs so much that he'd altered his own personality, and Brion would say outrageous things [about him]."

Jane, of course, had always regarded Brion as a charlatan, and the two barely looked at each other when they were compelled to be in the same room. Over time, Gysin's comments about her became increasingly acerbic. He decided that Cherifa was a castrating bitch-goddess—"the sinister servant you can't get rid of before she gets rid of you"—and that Jane was more unbalanced than ever. Years before, he had said that he admired Jane's writing; now, he dismissed her as "a drag."

Since the beginning of 1964, Jane had weathered a series of upheavals that had left her feeling increasingly unsteady. Aside from her worries about Alfred Chester, she had been beset by anxiety about her work; though she was toiling sporadically over her notebooks, her eyesight was no better, and the shards of the play that she had begun in 1962 refused to fall into place. In March, she had gone into a "death rattle fandango," as she put it, over a lightning revival of *In the Summer House* that was set to open Off-Broadway. After deciding not to leave Tangier to oversee the production, Jane had worried obsessively about the casting and the director and the reviews. Her worst fears had come to pass when the play closed a few weeks after it opened, and she had been heartened only slightly by the favorable response from critics. Her anguish had gathered momentum that spring when Peter Owen, one of Paul's British publishers, proposed to reissue *Two Serious Ladies.* Terrified that the reviewers would devour her, she tried to block Paul's efforts to cooperate with Owen. For Jane, even the pain of feeling like a wraith was preferable to the prospect of facing critics.

Determined to see her novel published in England, Paul had coaxed and prodded until both he and Jane were exhausted. In a letter to Owen, he detailed the battle to get an answer from her; reporting that Jane was paralyzed by the thought of being reviewed, he said that she had complained that "the first publication was already a traumatic experience, and did I want her to have a nervous breakdown, or what? . . . But if I tell her I have written saying she does not want the book published, it will be the greatest explosion of all, and become really bad, and go on for days. Thus, I shan't say I've written. . . . She also made a remark, only once, but one to which I attach some importance, which was, 'And anyway, why should it be your publisher? Why does it have to be yours? Why can't I have my own publisher? He only wants it because of you.' " At the end of the dispatch, Paul admitted that he was vexed by her attitude, which he attributed, half-jokingly, to feminine perversity: "There are opacities that I can scarcely conceive!" he said. "Mysterious depths of ordered irrationality. I constantly find myself being fleetingly astonished that women can speak. They can open their mouths, and perfectly good English comes out, and it's hard to believe. And what they say makes no more sense than what my African Grey parrot says in Arabic. . . ."

At length, Jane agreed to sign the contract, but she wasn't ready to relinquish her distress. Now came the endless debates about whether she should go to England when the book appeared and the worries about being demolished by the press. Ironically, she was able to recognize her own absurdity: In a letter to Libby Holman, she admitted, "I do get worse with the years. David would say, 'tiresome.' " When Jane wrote to Ruth Fainlight in September, she outlined the complex case for making the trip to London, and then added, "I could go on forever about all this, the pros and cons of going or staying here, but I fear that the letter will turn into a fifteen page ganze magilla[9] of, 'if's and but's' which I shall never send and then more months will go by and I will never write; but the letter could be used as a document for some doctor who specializes in states of anxiety." Before it was all over, she said, she would write again about her travel plans. "You may come to dread these tortured letters about tiny decisions," she told Ruth. "I am famous for them or I was when I was famous. . . ."

As disturbed as she was about her work, Jane had reserved at least part of her energy for tormenting herself about her romantic adventures. In 1964, she was involved in one of her most difficult entanglements—this one with Princess Martha Ruspoli de Chambrun, a wealthy French-American expatriate who was separated from her Italian husband. A handsome intellectual who was about ten years her senior, Ruspoli was an old-guard Tangerino who had lived for years in a disordered villa on the Mountain, and who inspired sharply divided feelings among her neighbors. "She could evoke terrible hatreds and great admirations," said Yvonne Gerofi, who had known her since the early fifties. Fearless, domineering, Ruspoli liked to shock; she was known for making outrageous pronouncements and for using her wit to skewer those who were less agile. In a setting where erudition was in short supply, many expatriates found her intimidating; fluent in at least six languages, the Oxford-educated Ruspoli had an impressive store of knowledge about art and music and religion, and she was a self-taught archaeologist who could hold forth about the excavations that she had conducted at the Phoenician ruins near Tangier. At work on a book about ancient Egypt, Ruspoli presented herself as a mystic; she talked about the occult and the Osiris legend and the spiritual aspects of yoga (which she practiced assiduously), and she affected dramatic caftans that set off her blunt-cut silver hair.

Jane found Martha to be dazzling. After meeting her at Sonya Kamalakar's late in 1963, she had asked the Gerofis to invite her to lunch with Ruspoli at their flat on the Boulevard de Paris. Afterwards, she had telephoned to report that she and Martha had had a long talk after they left together. "She was fascinated, and very emotional and very excited and very much in love," remembered

Yvonne Gerofi. "Martha disturbed Jane and excited her, and Jane liked very much to be disturbed. . . . She told us that Martha was 'wicked.' "

Although Martha (who had borne three children) had never displayed a marked sexual interest in women, she and Jane became romantically involved soon after their meeting. "Martha was very curious—the relationship was like an experience for her," said Isabelle Gerofi. "Janie was furiously amorous, and for a short time it was happy. But then poor Janie began to suffer."

As Isabelle remembered it, the relentlessly insecure Jane became possessive, and Ruspoli responded by pulling back. "Martha always told Jane, *Demain,* I'm very busy.' She finally gave an appointment, and she arrived for five minutes and then she leaves, and Janie would be very depressed. She was always hoping, waiting. . . ."

To Yvonne and Isabelle (among others) it was apparent that Martha Ruspoli was not in love with Jane. Imperious and self-involved, she regarded her as an interesting conquest, but she kept her emotional distance. And while it seemed important to her that Jane was an author who was much admired, she professed to have little regard for her writing. "She wasn't interested by the work of Janie," said Isabelle Gerofi. "She said, with disdain, 'Oh, it's just fiction.' Martha doesn't want fiction because her life was fiction; she has no reason to be interested."

In the face of such hubris, Jane felt powerless, but she made no move to break with Martha. Those who saw them together often felt uneasy; it seemed that Jane had taken on the role of victim, and that Martha would destroy her. David Herbert was particularly apprehensive about the affair: "I think Martha was a really wicked woman," he said. "Along with my sister and my cousin I went to her house for drinks, and afterwards I said, 'What will we do now?' My sister said, 'I think I'll go back and have a bath.' . . . Martha was an intellectual snob, so to have Janie in tow was rather wonderful. Janie was a sort of catch for her—even in those days she was considered an intellectual pillar."

According to another prominent Tangerino, the foreign colony was fond of inventing tales about Ruspoli, and the folklore was recirculated when she took up with Jane Bowles. Years later, he said:

"Martha was a silly pretentious beast; she fancied herself rather as a *monstre sacré*, but I think she was in the English sense of the word a monster. . . . The story goes that she actually murdered her Armenian lover. So the story goes—I have no idea whether it's true. But she was supposed to have done the trick that Lillian Hellman did in *The Little Foxes*—[she was moving house] and there he was having a heart attack and she made him carry a piano upstairs. He said, 'My pills, my pills,' and she said, 'I've left the pills in the other house.' Whereupon he died, which got rid of him for her when she didn't want him anymore. That was a Tangier story." And although the fable seemed to have no more relation to the truth than one of Larbi's *kif* tales, it illustrated the fact that many Tangerinos were prepared to believe anything about Martha Ruspoli.

Adept at creating drama, Jane's new lover quickly squared off against the manipulative Cherifa. Although their relationship had become platonic, Cherifa had lost none of her ability to control Jane; by Paul's account, Jane often gave her money after receiving whispered instructions while she slept. Like others in the Bowleses' circle, Ruspoli was convinced that Cherifa wanted to bleed her dry, and she urged Jane to turn her out. In the beginning, at least, Jane refused; although she was afraid of Cherifa, she needed her desperately, and she had never conquered her guilt about taking her away from the grain market. Caught between her two iron-willed companions, she was immobilized, and she clung to her angst as though it were a life raft.

While Jane was unable to help herself, she still had the impulse to rescue friends who were imperiled. Sonya Kamalakar was stricken with cancer that year, and there was little money for her medical care. It was Jane who paid for her treatment in Europe and who comforted the distraught Narayan. At the same time, Alfred Chester had a series of minor crises, and it was the maternal Jane who hovered over him.

In the fall of 1964, Chester was brooding over the lukewarm reception of *Behold Goliath*. Only a thousand copies had been sold, and there was little sign that its author would ever become "gigantically famous," as he put it. Critics had regarded the collection as a curiosity; Theodore Solotaroff had observed in *Book Week* that, with its homosexual satyrs and baby-killers and drag queens, Chester's explicit fiction was likely to shock readers who could stomach nothing stronger than Grace Metalious. Still, he said, the stories had a perverse appeal: "What makes Chester an interesting writer," he noted, ". . . is that he occasionally has the radical insights that both children and deviant adults are known for. He is himself a very curious combination of innocence and depravity—a sort of cross between the Baron de Charlus and Huckleberry Finn. . . ."

For Alfred, it wasn't enough to be pegged as a wide-eyed traveler chronicling his trips down the Styx. A writer who (like Jane) was terrified of being branded an impostor, he found such praise to be faint indeed, and he was stung by a hostile review in *The New York Times.* Although he had almost completed a draft of his second novel, Chester pronounced himself a rank failure. That summer, he often woke in a panic—imagining that *The Exquisite Corpse,* as it was called, would be a source of even deeper shame if it ever saw print.

In fact, Alfred's new novel was more outré, more powerful, more disturbing than anything he had done before. The title was that of a parlor game popular among the surrealists: Each player wrote a word on a piece of paper, folded it and handed it to his neighbor; when the contributions were read in sequence, a poem emerged. Chester's finished novel would have a deliberate disjointedness that suggested that process. Its fever-dream scenes have only a vague relationship to one another, and the story is held together by his baroque protagonists—a group of ensemble players whose identities remain elusive. Masks are important props, and cross-dressing is a recurring motif. Two homosexuals (one a paterfamilias in another life) engage in a sadomasochistic folie à deux, and other mutable characters enact fantasies that are similarly rococo. Through it all, one lost soul repeats, "Who am I supposed to be?" And while the book is often brutal, profane and morbid (a baby, for example, is turned into a "pile of bloody meat" when it tumbles off a roof), it is balanced by surreal humor and a kind of lyricism. Beautifully controlled, it seems to be the work of a writer who has peered into the vortex of insanity but has yet to lose his balance.

With its electrifying images and demented sense of urgency, Alfred's book reflected not only his creative exuberance but his increasing fascination with drugs. Like Bowles and Burroughs, he had discovered that going behind the looking-glass put a spin on his fiction, and he used both *kif* and amphetamines while he was writing. When he wasn't at the typewriter, he experimented with opium and LSD—the drug of the moment in Tangier. In a letter to Edward Field, he described his first trip as a wondrous experience. "I loved it," he reported. "It made me very sick at first, like too much amphetamine, plus making me very nauseous. So I took a cab down to Ira's because I thought I was going to die and then suddenly the Socco Grande turned into a carnival and all the people into freaks, everything in technicolor, Disneyland. I roared with laughter. Ira's palace, with all its tiles and campy furnishings, turned into a box of jewels. . . ." Added Alfred, "I can't wait to do it again."

While he was living in the hallucinogenic world of his novel, Alfred was struggling with real-life complications that included a suit filed against him by Holt, Rinehart. In 1960, he had been given a small advance for a book that he had titled *I, Etc.*, but the novel had never been completed. Although Alfred contended that Holt had "unloaded" him in 1962, its lawyers were pressing him to return the $350. Now, he was faced with the choice of writing a check to Holt or launching a countersuit.

Aside from that distraction, Chester had had several attacks of professional jealousy. Susan Sontag's "Notes on Camp" had appeared that fall in *Partisan Review,* and Alfred not only imagined that she had appropriated his thoughts on the subject but was sorely provoked by the fact that all of New York seemed to be talking about her. He was similarly troubled by the success of Charles Wright, an expatriate whose unorthodox novel *The Messenger* had caused a small stir in America. One of the few blacks in the medina crowd, the moody Wright had attached himself to Alfred, and he brought out his worst instincts: To Field, Chester reported: "[He] throws me into the idea of Big Time and I feel like a failure."

Just before Christmas, Chester and his household went into an absurdist decline. Dris had a debilitating foot ailment that was diagnosed as a bone spur; Alfred suffered an excruciating attack of sciatica in his leg; and his brain-damaged dog, Skoura—whose hind legs were nearly useless—began to deteriorate. "I walk more or less like a cripple," Chester told Field. "So does Dris. He is embarrassed for us to be seen together in public, and so am I a little. Rosalind says all we need is to go out with Skoura and Jane and the scene would be perfect."

Confined to bed for several days, Chester was attended by both of the Bowleses. On December 17, he reported to Field, "Paul and Jane have come over a lot lately and I quite love them now. I feel I finally understand him and the way he has had to organize his life and his mask. He is really my only friend. . . ."

Chapter 20

Cast changes were a constant in the Bowleses' circle, and the close
of 1964 brought several. In December, William Burroughs and Brion
Gysin sailed for New York on the *Independence,* and with them they
took Larbi Layachi. Burroughs was having one of his periodic bouts
of disgust about idiot Tangerinos and sinister Arabs, and he had
been asked by *Playboy* to do a piece on returning to St. Louis as a
cult hero. Gysin, who claimed to have perfected his Dream Machine, had decided to look for a manufacturer who would make him
a millionaire. For his part, Layachi was convinced that he was in
grave danger; the Gallimard edition of *A Life Full of Holes* was about
to make its debut in Morocco, and he was terrified that the authorities would clap him back in jail. Paul Bowles paid for his passage
to America, and he asked friends to look after Layachi when he
reached its alien shores.

No sooner had the Burroughs party left Tangier than Jane's
friend Sonya Kamalakar died of cancer. Jane took the loss badly;
although she often made jokes at Sonya's expense, she was attached
to the Kamalakars, and she dreaded any alteration in the emotional
landscape. After Sonya's funeral, she went into a depression that

deepened when Ramadan came; unable to sleep while Cherifa, Aicha and her small daughter were taking their meals in the dead of night, she used the time to brood.

Paul himself had returned to the Itesa when he finished *Up Above the World,* and he was spending time with a young Moroccan called Mohammed Mrabet. A lithe, handsome cynic from the Rif, Mrabet made his living as a fisherman and a bartender. Original, observant and vaguely menacing, Mrabet was possessed of a short-legged swagger and a limitless ego. He also had the makings of a storyteller; he knew how to hold an audience, and how to build on every bit of drama in his own life. By his account, he had had an eventful time of it; already, he said, he had been taken to America by a wealthy couple whom he met in Tangier, and had made his way back to Morocco after deciding that infidels were decidedly inferior.

On a visit to Paul's flat, Mrabet saw a copy of *A Life Full of Holes,* which had a photograph of Larbi Layachi on its cover. Mrabet knew that Larbi was illiterate, and he laughed when Paul told him that he had written a book. When Paul explained that the stories had been dictated to him, and that Larbi had been paid for his work, Mrabet decided that he could concoct stories that would outstrip anything that Larbi had invented. A few days later, he returned to Paul's, brought out his *sebsi* and spun out a fable with supreme self-assurance. Now Bowles wanted to hear more, and Mrabet was coming several times a week to record his *kif* tales.

Although she usually felt uneasy when Paul took a new pro-tégé, Jane seemed too distracted to focus on the relationship. As *Two Serious Ladies* arrived in the bookstores in London, she went through an agony of suspense before she saw the reviews. Nearly all were laudatory, and she took some comfort in the fact that she had avoided an "English disgrace," as she put it. In a letter to Libby Holman, she allowed: "I guess it hasn't done too badly (prestige at least). . . . The blurb's were excellent and to quote Peter Owen, 'The book is getting a big press here and is being treated as an important book as it deserves.' "

Escaping punishment, however, wasn't enough to help Jane out of her slough. Instead of moving ahead with her own writing, she worried over the fate of Paul's novel (which he had yet to send to his agent). When Claude Bowles suffered a cerebral hemorrhage and her own mother's health began to decline, she and Paul arranged to sail for New York. In a state about their travel plans, she outlined the complexities in a dispatch to Libby: "Paul tries to travel with me because we can share a cabin and can see me through mobs at the boat in New York and I just hang on to him," she told Libby. "Crowds confuse me and though I can see perfectly well straight in front of me I don't see on the sides and keep loosing sight of people at which point I can get Panicky—still I have all my pills which I'd clutch and somehow I'm sure I'd get through. At any rate I'd preffer it [to] the claustrofobic nightmare of a plane. God knows that would be simpler (that is if you could meet me at the airport) but I suppose the best would be to see you after you came back from Europe if you weren't staying too long. . . ."

Before Paul and Jane sailed on the *Independence* in March, they called several times on Alfred Chester. Alfred reported that he and Dris had worked a spell against their upstairs neighbor, a Swiss spinster who had complained to the landlord about their "nocturnal scandals" and petitioned to have them evicted. While Chester believed that she hated "having a common Arab in the house," Paul suggested that she was simply "hot for Dris," in Alfred's words. (By his account, Jane tried to comfort Chester by saying that his adversary had heard that he was a celebrity and had begun to speak well of him.)

Aside from that news, there was talk of the crimes that had sent shivers through the expatriate community. Chester recounted the tales in a letter to Edward Field: "Such terrible things have been happening," he wrote.

> . . . Some women were raped by three Arabs in the Foret Diplomatique, French women I think, and one was a virgin. So they captured three guys, who knows if they are the rapists, and tortured them and knocked their teeth out and hung them by their heels outside the gendarmarie and admitted the public at 50 francs apiece. Then the sultan ordered them to be hung by their wrists until dead, no water, just a crumb of bread per day. Last I heard one was dead. Probably the others now. . . . Also a little boy was raped by

the barman at the Merkala [café] . . . and I heard the boy too was dying. [Another] boy was murdered in the medina and his djellaba was sewn up like a sack. Another detail: from Paul, about a murder that took place two months ago. The boy's asshole was sewn up and he was left at the door of his parents' house. It all sounds terrible, but you have to remember that any little thing immediately gets great notoriety here.

Still binging on the mind-altering confections that were popular in the medina (including mescaline imported from England and the *kif*-infused "white cookies of Marrakech"), Alfred was deliciously high when the Bowleses dropped in on the eve of their departure. Sitting with a sliver of bitter opium dissolving under his lower lip, he imagined that he could see the two more clearly than ever. In a letter to Field, he said that the fragile Jane and the distant Paul had seemed "a ridiculous and pathetic pair," and added, "Ira tells me Paul is afraid to show me his new book because he thinks I'm a famous critic and would do him harm if I hated it. . . ."

After the Bowleses sailed for America, Chester turned his attention to *The Exquisite Corpse,* which he had decided to revise. As he labored over its surreal scenes, he was overtaken by a kind of giddiness; at the end of March, he sent a dispatch to Norman Glass in London, reporting that "publishers all over the place have their tongues hanging out for [the novel]." To Field, he confided: "It's very strange, everyone loves me these days. Dris told me a friend of his heard that I am the father of the American community here. Even the kids and the beatniks love me, though I guess they always did, and I'm just as fresh and bossy as ever." A few weeks later— with the amphetamines and the adrenaline still coursing through his system—he caromed into a queasy depression. With the festival of Aïd el-Kebir approaching, it was impossible to escape the cries of sheep and goats being dragged through the streets, or to forget that knives were being sharpened for the sacrifice.

When Alfred went to celebrate the feast with Dris's family in Asilah, he watched the ritual slaughter of a magnificent ram, and the scene had all the intensity of his first trip on acid. "It was the most horrible thing I ever saw," he told Field.

... It was a great lovely ram, tied up in the kitchen, sort of smelling the floor and people's feet, and really quite happy. . . . The mother poured a tablespoon of flour and a glass of water into the ram's mouth. Dris told me it was to make peace with him, so that when he goes to heaven he will have no complaints against the family. Anyhow, it ate, poor thing, lying on the floor with its eyes bulging. . . . [Then] the father cut its throat in one strike, I guess right through the windpipe and the gullet and jugular. The blood shot across the room like from a hose and kept coming. The ram jumped around. . . . I don't know whether I actually rose in my chair; in any case no one even noticed me, which is good because they never would have understood my reaction. . . . It probably only lasted a minute or so, but it seemed forever, that jumping and the blood shooting out and a horrible noise like snorting that I think came from the windpipe and lungs. . . .

Added Alfred: "I really wanted to scream. And my mind was saying the whole time, 'This is the truth. This is the truth.' "

At the end of May—after three more weeks of frantic revisions—Chester mailed *The Exquisite Corpse* to Field, who was to forward it to Alfred's agent. In the note that accompanied the manuscript, he said: "I'll probably be sick after I mail it, ashamed, etc. But it is MY book. Good, bad or indifferent, it is mine, which is the nicest part of all." Instead of feeling wretched after he sent it off, however, he was overtaken by a kind of manic joy; to Norman Glass, he confided: "I'm thrilled to pieces about [the novel]. I spent all last night and this morning being high and thinking about it, and laughing. . . . I think it is so sweet of God or the Devil or whoever to have given me this book to write. I think it may make my fortune."

As summer began, Alfred prepared for a trip with Dris to London, where *Behold Goliath* was to be published by André Deutsch—and where he hoped to be greeted with wild acclaim. While he was still spinning out fantasies about becoming the darling of the British press, he received a visit from Edward Field and Neil Derrick, who told him that they were delighted with *The Exquis-*

ite Corpse. During a cocktail party for them at his flat, Alfred tried out his London persona: Wearing a gold turban, an embroidered waistcoat and dark sunglasses, he looked "stunning," as he reported it to Glass. "[It was] a roaring success," he said. "I made an orange punch with black market rum . . . very potent. Ira had some Congo hash which everyone smoked. So they all got very drigh (drunk plus high) except me. . . . I am going to be very outrageous in London. Prepare yourself."

By Field's account, Alfred seemed merely exuberant during their brief stay in Morocco. If anything was unsettling, it was the drug-steeped scene in the medina: At a gathering at John and Natasha Doughertys' house, everyone was hopelessly *kif*ed, and the hostess herself "kept breaking out in peals of crazy laughter," as he remembered it. Years later, he said, "I think everybody [in the medina] was trying to see how crazy they could be, or how many drugs they could take and still come back. It was like playing Russian roulette—and Paul Bowles was the inspiration for that."

With the tourist season beginning, the Tangier police made another swift raid on the native quarter. At the Fat Black Pussy Cat (the club where the Marrakech Express crowd collected), it was said that twelve Americans had been hauled from their lairs and left to languish in the Casbah jail. The American consul reportedly had lodged a protest, but it seemed that the authorities had renewed their campaign to discourage indigent visitors. Determined to make Tangier attractive to free-spending middle-class travelers, they did what they could to give the city an aura of respectability. Despite the harassment, the medina crowd saw no reason to look for a new haven. Sent to Spain on the ferry, deportees were still coming right back to Tangier—and to the *kif* dealers who collaborated with the police.

Like many Tangerinos, Paul and Jane Bowles talked at times about where to resettle if the authorities ever turned out the entire expatriate community. Before sailing back to Africa in June, Paul made a solitary scouting trip to Santa Fe, where his friend John Goodwin lived. In a letter to his parents he reported, "Jane and I had wanted to come out here . . . to look around at the place as a possible settling-spot once we have to leave Morocco (which will come sooner or later, everyone is sure)." Deciding that the outpost was "the least objectionable city in the United States," he looked at a few houses—all of which seemed vastly expensive—and then put the notion aside. As uncertain as it could be, life in Tangier had a kind of anxious momentum; again and again, it gave him the opportunity to observe that he was living in the midst of chaos.

At that moment, however, the most disturbing development in Paul's life had nothing to do with Morocco. After weeks of deliberation, editors at Random House had turned down *Up Above the World;* as he reported it to his mother, they had said that they couldn't comprehend his understated novel. In many ways, the rejection was ironic: While *A Hundred Camels in the Courtyard* had transformed him into a guru, Bowles had fallen out of sync with the literary establishment; in a setting where Tom Wolfe and Norman Mailer were now the stars, his new work seemed anachronistic.

Rather than obsessing about whether the novel would find a publisher, Paul went straight to work when he and Jane returned to Tangier. Although *A Life Full of Holes* had been seized by the authorities, as Larbi had feared, he continued to record and translate Mohammed Mrabet's stories. Mrabet was inventing a lengthy tale about a calculating Moroccan struggling between loyalty to his wealthy patron and his love for a young girl, and the two were spending long hours together as the saga unfolded.

At the same time, Bowles began editing a collection of Jane's stories that had been proposed by Peter Owen. Jane, of course, said that she had neglected to keep anything that she had produced since 1944, and that there was hardly enough material for a book. "She said, 'I'm not a writer. I don't want to be published. It's all a big mistake,'" Paul remembered. "But I knew the material, and I thought it should be published whether she wanted to or not." After unearthing his own copies of her work, Paul had begun to retype the lot and to transform her 1951 essay "East Side: North Africa" into a short story.

For Jane, the prospect of having another book published was only slightly more traumatic than events on the domestic scene. As Paul began spending more time with Mrabet, the young Moroccan began to look more and more like a rival. In a perpetual state of need, she focused her anxiety on her involvements with the neurotic "Lady Anna," whom she had seen in New York, and with Martha Ruspoli, who remained tantalizingly aloof. After she and Paul had been in Tangier for several months, she reported to Libby Holman, "I am really in a black state and trying to keep it from Paul as much as possible—which means that I don't discuss myself and my life and my work too much. . . . I miss you and I miss being near you and the friends I have left very badly." Added Jane, "I should really be in East Hampton. I don't know what I'm doing here."

As always, she welcomed the noise of "the David life" and of the sideshows at the Itesa. Since Bowles had become a polestar for the post-Beats, it seemed that every day brought a new drama; aside from wanting to simply sit at his feet, visitors often felt compelled to create scenes in Paul's *sala.* At one point, he was dismayed to see Natasha Dougherty at his door wearing an assortment of thrift-store cast-offs and carrying a large pouch filled with *kif* and bread-crumbs. By Paul's account, she was a startling apparition: "She said she'd been attacked in the street and needed a new passport, et cetera, and needed to borrow thirty thousand francs, which was about sixty dollars. Well, ten days later she came back with the same story and asked for thirty thousand more francs. I thought, 'This is where I came in. . . .' "

As it happened, Alfred Chester was also at Paul's, and he spoke up while Bowles was searching for a reply. "He told her, 'Get out of here—you stink,' " said Paul. "I hadn't noticed anything, but he apparently had. . . . She went into French and began quoting Rimbaud. I said, 'What are you *doing* in Tangier?' She said, 'I am looking for amphetamines, which are cheaper in Marrakech than anywhere in the world.' "

Somehow, Paul managed to rid himself of Natasha, but she materialized soon afterwards at Jane's flat. When Aicha told the Bowleses that a crazy woman was at the door, "Jane grabbed my arm and told me, 'Don't go,' " he remembered. "She went to the door and said, *'Qu'est-ce que vous voulez?'* Natasha went through the same story, and Jane, who had a bowl of cold rice that she had been eating with her fingers, as she liked to do, upended the bowl on her head. Natasha simply picked the rice out of her hair and bent down to pick up the mess from the floor and started eating it. Jane slammed the door, but Natasha had the last word."

*   *   *

That summer, Alfred's friend Susan Sontag was among those who wrote Paul to announce that she was coming to Tangier. Chester himself received a letter from her after he returned from London; as he reported it to Norman Glass, Sontag had told him that she had been thinking about him a great deal, and that she would be in Morocco for a week or so. Said Alfred, "Of course I've written back saying I'd love seeing her. She wants her Roger Straus[1] to see [*The Exquisite Corpse*]. . . . That whore."

Alfred's feelings about Sontag, it seemed, had little to do with her actual behavior. Like many of those who admired his writing, she had supported him even when he seemed spectacularly irrational, and she had taken his part in public battles. In 1964, while Alfred was denouncing her in his dispatches to Harriet Sohmers and Edward Field, she was facing off against the critic Saul Maloff, who had taken apart *Behold Goliath* in *The New York Times Book Review*. (In a letter to the editor, Sontag had argued that Alfred's stories were "ingeniously fashioned and intelligent" and suggested that Maloff's reaction had been distorted by homophobia.) Her loyalty had not impressed Alfred, who could find ominous meanings in the most innocuous acts. To Edward Field, he reported that Susan had sent him "a very strange twisted letter that makes you wonder why she wants to come here." Wrote Alfred, "Is she afraid I will become famous and powerful and be her enemy? I will try to fathom her black sinister depths."

By Alfred's account, he discussed Sontag with Bowles, who brought out the two notes that she had sent him. "We compared [our letters] and roared with laughter as they go together so interestingly," he told Field. "A woman, Paul kept saying, she's a woman. Naturally. I think she is trying to make us compete for her. . . . In her first letter to Paul she says she is coming with Carlos somebody. In her second letter to me, she says she is coming alone. And the whole situation threading between me and Paul is a riot. In the end she will wind up not having a room as no one is getting her one. . . ."

With London and *The Exquisite Corpse* behind him, Chester himself was in a precarious state. Not only had he lost the connection to his fictional characters, but the novel had yet to find a publisher:

André Deutsch had made a low bid, and editors at the *Paris Review* "didn't understand it and said it was offensive," as Alfred reported it. Still dosing himself with tranquilizers and codeine and *majoun,* he continued to feed his paranoia. On August 18, he wrote a letter to Field that sounded alternately rational and skewed; saying that he wanted to talk Deutsch into upping the stakes, he wrote:

> Paul says I have been promoted from one kind of schlemiel to another. He says publishers always consider you a schlemiel, but there are different levels or categories. . . . Oh, I read his book. Simon and Schuster gave him a $70,000 [*sic*] advance. . . . It's a mystery story, a sort of parody of *The Sheltering Sky.* The best part is the beginning which is like Jane's book and describes him and Jane. (. . . I finally saw her yesterday. He dragged her over and we had a row about my doorbell. I was high and was getting furious, then suddenly my eyes met Paul's and I began to laugh and couldn't stop. I adore him this week, which usually means that he will do something horrible. He lures me into dropping all my defenses, then does something monstrous.) I'm dying to know what he's cooking up for me and Susan.

In spite of his truce with Paul and Jane, Alfred had continued to believe on some level that they were satanic figures who were plotting to destroy him. When the "sinister" Sontag arrived in mid-August and contacted the Bowleses, he decided that she had joined their conspiracy. Already convinced that Paul wanted to steal Dris, Chester seized upon the notion that Susan, too, would become fascinated with his lover, and that she would take him with her when she left Morocco.

During the two weeks that Sontag was in Tangier, Chester's connection to reality somehow was broken. In the past, he had been able to travel between sanity and dementia; now, he was locked into the prison of his own madness. Overtaken by the idea that his brain had been destroyed by X-rays when he was seven, he decided that he was being poisoned with LSD. He imagined that Sontag was taping his conversations and that the "intelligence section" at the American consulate had him under surveillance. In a fit of terror, he burned his own diaries and letters and destroyed a group of water-colors that Dris had done. Even for those who had seen Chester at his worst, the change was shocking. "Susan asked me, 'Is Alfred always like this?'" said Ira Cohen, who invited her to hear Jilala musicians at the Bat Palace. "I think he asked her to marry him, and was coming on a bit hysterical. I said, 'No, no, he just finished his book—he's just somehow worked up and unusual in these few weeks.'"

After his visitor left in September, Alfred's letters betrayed a startling change: His sense of irony had vanished, and his terror was palpable. To Field, he said, "Susan's visit was catastrophic. I didn't entertain her at all because I was nuts, out of myself or induced, I don't know. Are you really Edward? And how can I know? . . . I feel as though I've had a lobotomy by long distance, that my dreams are visible, that my thoughts can be read, that I've been fed *yage.*" In a letter to Glass, he reported that he was thinking of fleeing: "There's no point in staying in Tangier among the poisoners," he said. "I see no one except Paul and I wonder if too much slimy water hasn't flowed under the bridge for us to really be friends. Besides, you never know where he'll strike next."

Instead of avoiding the desperate Chester, Bowles continued to call on him. At some point, he offered to take Alfred on a scorpion hunt, and they hiked into the country, where he taught him to use palmetto leaves to lure the creatures from their lairs. For Alfred, the interlude seemed weighted with hidden meaning, and he used it as a springboard for a short story called "Safari." Modeled on Paul, its protagonist is a Merlin figure who kindles the narrator's insanity. "Here's what I have to say about him in my short story," Chester told Field:

"Sometimes I think Gerald is God and sometimes I think he's the Devil. I have the strange feeling his mind can make things out of nothing like the road we were on, the plain we'd just crossed over, the mountain above us. I know this is insane. Probably I am insane. None the less I think a madman can be logical and right. If I see too much of Gerald he spreads insidiously through my life like ink on blotting paper. I go out at night and hear a strange bird cry in the trees and I think: That's Gerald. Or a dog baying. If I'm with someone I may say, 'Do you hear that bird? It's Gerald. He can turn himself into a bird.'"

Years later, Paul Bowles claimed to remember little about Alfred's psychotic break, save for a conversation that he had had with Sontag. "She and I were talking at Guitta's, and I told her I didn't see him at all because he'd become impossible," he remembered. "She said, 'Alfred is crazy.' I said, 'Oh, well, we're all crazy.' She said, 'No, he's certifiable. He's really crazy.'" Added Paul, "He wouldn't have acted so crazy other places. People think Tangier is the sort of place where you can behave strangely."

By late fall, Alfred had grown so erratic that his landlord had petitioned the Moroccan government to deport him. Feeling intolerably isolated, he asked friends to find a place for him in New York, where he hoped to shake the panic and the horror. Dris, it seemed, had no desire to come along; saying that he wanted to go to work in a factory in Belgium, he told Alfred that they should rendezvous in Morocco in six months.

On a drizzling day in December, Chester boarded a ferry for Gibraltar. Before putting Tangier behind him, he wrote a businesslike note to Paul, saying that he could reach him at his mother's house in Brooklyn, "if you care to write." Later, from the safety of New York, he began a mad, elegiac story in which he talked about his idyll in Morocco: "Oh, ladies and gentlemen," he said, "dear reader, if you knew what they had stolen from me. A kingdom. It couldn't be harder to lose a real kingdom. Land and power and money. But to be robbed of that which is not merely your own living heart but a geography of paradise and your dream of the perfect. . . . I have lost it."

Chapter 21

On Christmas Day, 1965, Jay Haselwood died of a heart attack on his way to lunch with the venerable Jessie Green. To Haselwood's admirers, it seemed that an era had ended; apart from being a font of Tangier mythology, Jay had been a link to the days when an ex-GI could get picked up by a hard-drinking countess who would buy him a bar. Held at St. Andrew's Church, where David Herbert was a pillar, his funeral was a state occasion that attracted every aging socialite, every penurious blueblood, every old-guard expatriate in Tangier.

William Burroughs happened to be in town when Haselwood dropped dead, and he went to the service with Brion Gysin. After taking in the scene—where the gin-soaked poseurs and the spongers were out in force—Burroughs went to dinner at the Bowleses'. As Paul remembered it, he seemed to relish the absurdity of the occasion; wearing a black suit, he had dressed the part of a foppish mortician, complete with trilby and furled umbrella. Standing before the fireplace, Burroughs unbuttoned his kid gloves and droned, "Well, Paul, you missed a very enjoyable funeral."

If Burroughs could find a trace of dark humor in Haselwood's death, Jane Bowles could not. Since autumn, she had been in a steady decline; often, she confined herself to her bedroom. Dizzy, overcome by anxiety and depression, she had stepped up her drinking, although her physician had long since forbidden her to use alcohol. She slept at odd hours, waking in the middle of the night and rousing her entire household, and she alternately binged and fasted. Unable to keep track of the medication for her hypertension, she took her pills when she pleased. "She was on so many," Paul said. "Epanutin, which is for epilepsy; Serpasil, which was well known to be a powerful depressant, not only of the blood pressure but of the mind. She would take too much Serpasil mixed with Mellaril and God knows what other soporifics." In her fragile state, the loss of Jay Haselwood seemed insurmountable. "For me it was the death of an eppoc," she told Libby Holman. "The depression after[ward] was bad and . . . the confusion in my life has been fantastic." Added Jane, "I am not sick but I am not well or I am having change of life and the dissiness gets better and then worse. . . ."

More dependent than ever, Jane began to clutch at Paul, whose attention was focused on Mrabet. To placate her, Bowles had an intercom system installed between their two bedrooms. "She wasn't herself for all that time," he remembered. "She was desperate. Day and night, I'd hear the tinkle and she would say, 'Can you come down, my bed is crooked,' or I'd go down to give her her medicine. She'd take three times as much medication as she was supposed to be taking—her argument was, '[The doctors] don't know how I feel.' " By Paul's account, she was obsessed with the idea that she was doomed: "She never believed she'd get better," he said. "She wanted to discuss the state of her health constantly. I wasn't supposed to say anything—she wanted me to share her terrible experiences, not to assuage her fears."

"There was a great self-destructive streak in Jane, and it came out during that period," said her friend Charles Gallagher, who had been away from Tangier for several years. "I noticed that all of her neuroses were much worse. She kept saying, 'I'm through,' but she talked herself into a lot of that—just as she talked herself into not being able to write anymore."

With Jane on the brink, Paul received an offer from Little,

Brown to write a travel book—this one set in Bangkok. Eager to see Thailand (and, as he later admitted, to reclaim his independence), he began making plans for an extended journey. Terrified of staying in Morocco alone, Jane "begged . . . for months [for me] to take her along," as he remembered it. Paul stood his ground—arguing that she would hate the climate and saying that it would be impossible for him to work if she were with him. "I said, 'Jane, you won't be able to stand it, and every day you'll say, "When can we get out?" She said, 'I wouldn't, I'd be quiet.' She wanted to go very much."

Finally, Jane decided to make a long trip to America, where she planned to stay with her mother in Florida. After offering to accompany her, Martha Ruspoli announced that she couldn't leave until the fall, and Jane was gripped by the fear of traveling alone. In a note to Libby Holman, she gave a disjointed summary of Martha's reasons for delaying her own trip, and added, "[But] if I go into that and who she is and why I even know her, etc., I might as well ask you who is going to finish this biography after my death. . . . Libby, my spelling worries me so much that I am afraid to come home and see what is wrong with me that wasn't wrong with me before. Maybe some premature deterioration due to the original stroke. I don't know. I don't know what is physical any longer and what is mental. . . ." Adding that she was "frightfully depressed," she reported, "My book, *Two Serious Ladies,* I made no money at all or to be exact about four hundred dollars since publication including the advance. It is at the same time considered To be a literary success in certain circles which I never get into since I am not there, I am here."

As it happened, Jane had just received a letter from Farrar, Straus & Giroux proposing a volume that would include *Two Serious Ladies,* her short stories and *In the Summer House.* Titled *The Collected Works of Jane Bowles,* the book was to have an introduction by Truman Capote, who had not seen its author for years. Prodded again by Paul, she agreed to the proposition, and Capote wrote an admiring essay describing a Jane who existed only in memory. Calling her a "modern legend," he said: "I am sure she is unchanged; indeed, I am told by recent travelers from North Africa who have seen or sat with her in some dim casbah cafe that this is true, and that Jane, with her dahlia-head of cropped curly hair, her tilted nose and mischief-

shiny, just a trifle mad eyes, her very original voice (a husky so-
prano), her boyish clothes and schoolgirl's figure and slightly limp-
ing walk, is more or less the same as when I first knew her. . . ."

While Jane's collection was being readied by Farrar, Straus,
Paul's own novel was arriving in bookstores in America. In a letter
to Ira Cohen (who had returned to New York) Bowles noted gloomily that Simon & Schuster had chosen to publish *Up Above the World*
on the Ides of March, and that the reviews "undoubtedly [would]
be awful." Although his agent immediately sold the film rights, the
response from critics was indeed restrained. To many, it seemed that
the novel was an anemic echo of *The Sheltering Sky;* as *The New York
Times*'s Conrad Knickerbocker put it, "Mr. Bowles performs like a
musician who has fallen in love with one tune which he plays
magnificently, but over and over again." Noting that "existential
despair is already a well-worn dramatic convention, as artificial as
Restoration wit," *Life* reviewer Wilfred Sheed observed that Bowles
was "telling the same tale" seventeen years after the appearance of
his first novel.

As the Bowleses prepared for their separate journeys, there
was a development at the Itesa that Paul, in particular, deemed
portentous. At the end of April, their parrot Seth died suddenly, and
Mrabet (a misogynist who loathed Cherifa) took it as a sign that
someone in the household was using black magic. To Ira Cohen,
Paul reported, "Aachor is coming up, and the women apparently are
practicing their tsoukel.[1] A very bad month, according to the male
Moslems. Someone killed our grey parrot; he dropped dead while
Aicha was giving him water. According to the vet, an embolism
caused by terror. Who knows? He also said it could have been a
result of poison, but that the corpse would have to be taken to the
Institut Pasteur.[2] . . . Mrabet insists ten men died yesterday, all
victims of tsoukel."

That season, Brion Gysin was living in the flat next to Jane's,
and he shared it with John Giorno, a poet whom he had met in
New York. As Giorno remembered it, Bowles had rushed over
to Brion's just after the parrot was stricken. "Apparently, the
bird had eaten some of Jane's food and just keeled over," said
Giorno. "Paul was really alarmed." With Brion, he said, Paul had
spun a fantasy about Jane being poisoned—saying that she

looked deathly pale, as though she had been fed arsenic. All the signs, they decided, pointed to Cherifa: "Jane was still having the affair with Princess Martha Ruspoli, and they had thought earlier that Cherifa must be in a state about it," said Giorno. "She was a very simple woman, and jealousy comes to the fore very quickly in that sort of character."

The incident only underscored Paul and Brion's shared distrust for Jane's companion, who seemed more hostile by the hour. In a letter to Andreas Brown,[3] Paul reported that Brion's presence "elicited from Cherifa endless dire monologues: the women in Gysin's life are going to come with the police and drag him off to jail. This of course is what she hopes for, and I made her admit it in front of Jane, which helped a bit. As you know, Cherifa carries a switchblade always, in order to castrate any male who may say good evening to her. Never knew a woman who hated men so violently. . . . And always I'm more appalled by her than before."

Despite the bad blood, Bowles was stricken that summer by a rare bout of nostalgia about his years in Tangier. Sensing, perhaps, that Jane had turned a corner, he felt reluctant to dismantle their lives together. He decided that he would miss the Itesa, where he could hear the sounds of frogs and owls at night, and where he could record music from the nearby village of Ain Hayani. Later, he remembered: "Jane had made excellent cooks out of both Cherifa and Aicha. Although she could not work in the kitchen as she had before, we continued to have magnificent dinners. . . . I realized that I should miss our evening meals by the fireplace and the hour of stretching out on the cushions afterwards. Now that the time to leave approached, it was suddenly clear that . . . these things were of great importance to me, and that no matter what sort of life I found for myself in Bangkok, I would be very sad to have left Tangier."

Finally, it was an unexpected loss that helped Bowles to make the break. That June, Rena Bowles suffered a heart attack and fell into a coma. A few weeks after her death, Paul received word that Claude, too, had died. Suddenly, he felt less attached to the city that he had chosen as a refuge; as he explained it, "The death of my parents diminished my unwillingness to leave Tangier; very likely the shock made itself felt by leaving me in a state of indifference.

the affair between Gysin and Giorno. Uncomfortable with monogamy and haunted by his sense of failure, Brion began to cavil about
John and to say that he would never regain his sexual freedom. By
the end of August, Giorno was ready to return to New York—and
Gysin was ready for him to leave. And while their friendship would
survive, Brion would always display the same sort of cynicism
about him that he exhibited towards his other admirers. For an
aging prince with an urge to destroy himself, even friends could be
cast as jesters.

Four months after he reached Bangkok, Paul Bowles cut short his
trip to Thailand. Although he had yet to finish his research, he had
little choice; Jane herself had returned to Tangier in September, and
her condition had deteriorated once again. Although she had told
him nothing, he had received a dispatch from her physician, Dr.
Yvonne Marillier-Roux, reporting that she was suffering from in-
testinal adhesions that might require surgery. Dr. Roux also told
Paul that his wife's psychological condition was precarious, and that
she "couldn't take responsibility for her." In a letter to Edouard
Roditi, Paul reported: "Jane hasn't written to me since September,
and I have no idea what she's doing. I write her regularly, but she
is too depressed to reply. Madame Roux writes that she does not
even go into the street or talk on the telephone. It sounds bad.
Cherifa writes merely that Jane is unhappy and smokes many cigarettes. Since she hasn't smoked in years, it still sounds bad."
    Without Paul, Jane had simply given in to the malignant anx-
iety that had taken seed the previous fall. Rather than remaining
with her mother, as planned, she had hurried back to Tangier,
convinced that she would never be allowed to return if she stayed
too long abroad. Once she was back at the Itesa, she was overcome by dread and depression; terrified of being alone, she
clutched at Cherifa and Aicha the way she had clutched at Paul.
Still taking her medication without regard to her doctor's instructions, she was dizzier and more confused than ever, and she continued to drink even after suffering a severe seizure—her first in
three years. Unable to read or to write, she began to focus her
anxiety on the issue of money. She decided that her bank accounts
had run dry, and no amount of reassurance would convince her

that she wasn't about to be dragged off to the poorhouse.

Although Paul had reported that he had heard nothing from Jane, she had, in fact, dictated a letter to him that was typed by a friend who had volunteered to help her with correspondence. In it, she had said, "I should have gone with you no matter how hot or uncomfortable it might be. I could have stayed in the room. It particularly worries me that you don't have any idea of when you're coming back. . . . It terrifies me to live from month to month and so I have sent for extra money, via the bank, but even so until it comes I will be on tenterhooks, and *will* it come? . . . I naturally want to be well covered, particularly with you not here. What can I do if I suddenly have no money? You were always here to handle these things."

As frightened as she was of losing her money, Jane was infinitely more afraid of losing her mind. Since her stroke, she had been haunted by the specter of the "looney bin," as she called it, and her jokes about being committed failed to conceal her fright. For a woman whose intellectual acuity was her only weapon, being trapped inside a mind that was beyond repair was the worst fate imaginable; only the notion of being locked away from the world— and from Paul—seemed worse.

According to Charles Gallagher, Jane had a sense of morbid destiny that, by the end of 1966, was playing itself out: "When she referred to herself as 'finished,' I always thought she meant that metaphorically, as a writer; but in fact she probably meant it in another way. She seemed to know what was in store for her."

To Libby Holman (who was sending her a monthly stipend) Jane had confessed that she was frightened of being exposed as a madwoman. After Libby's nephew David Holman visited Tangier, Jane had managed to compose a dispatch in which she reported that he had found her in the throes of a "nervous breakdown." Wrote Jane, "I wanted [David Holman] to hide from You the state I was in—and it is not a state that is so noticeable except that I am very quiet. . . . I told [David Herbert] that I was very much frightened that if You heard anything about a nervous breakdown you would cut me off I was half joking but it was a feer. David Herbert said I was crazy, but there is no limit to what I fear. . . . Than David Herbert told the story to David Holman, which made everything terrible. Worse than that I told David Holman not to repeat it to you because it does sound crazy and he said he wouldn't dream of it so I'm repeating it to you and I'm sure that David Holman will tell you that I'm not crazy. Just depressed and with reason. . . . Anyway please Don't cut me ough because you think I'm crazy or for any other reason."

In Paul's absence, friends like David Herbert and the Gerofis tried valiantly to keep Jane from sinking, but she seemed beyond their reach. "Paul wrote to us, 'Tell Janie to write,' " remembered Isabelle Gerofi. "He didn't imagine what state she was in." On her fiftieth birthday, Herbert gave a small party for Jane at his house, and she was eerily unresponsive. "I had a little baby Pekingese, and I took it to give it to Janie," said Gerofi. "She didn't say a word—she was out, *ailleurs.* She was sitting in a red dress, like that [pantomiming abjection], with the little Pekingese on her lap, thinking of what I don't know."

Even a surprise visit from Libby herself failed to reach the distant Jane. When Holman arrived at the Tangier airport in February 1967, she screamed joyfully and ran to embrace Jane, who responded only with a weak smile. Deciding that Jane needed a change of scene, Libby told her that she was welcome to stay at Treetops for as long as she liked. After a few days, however, it became evident that Jane was in no state to travel; she stayed in her room for hours, and her mind was hopelessly clouded. Devastated, Libby became violently ill herself, and she and Louis Schanker made plans to leave after just a week. When Paul finally arrived, a weeping Holman came to him and said, "I can't take another hour of Jane."

Bowles himself was unprepared for what he encountered when he saw his wife. Although he had hoped that Jane "was merely in a surly mood because I had refused to take her along with me," as he put it, he found her to be in a profound depression. While she could be lucid at times, she spoke only of her illness, and the hysteria that he had seen in July had been replaced by a strange detachment. As Paul reported it to Peter Owen (whose letter to Jane apparently had gone unanswered), "The truth is that she cannot read her mail, nor does she bother to open it or save it for me to open, so it's next to useless to write her about anything. Her health is extremely bad, and she spends most of her time lying in bed looking at the ceiling." In a letter to Charles Henri Ford, he said that Jane's condition seemed to be linked to her drug-taking, rather than to any neurological problems. Wrote Paul, "Her medication begins to tell. . . . Ten years of constant sedation can't help anyone into superior health."

For six weeks, Paul watched and waited, searching for some improvement. Urged by Dr. Roux to place his wife in a sanitorium, he hoped to avoid the decision to send her away. As Mohammed Mrabet remembered it, the strain was obvious: "Jane had been ill for many years, but now she began to grow worse," he wrote. "Some people claimed she had been given tsoukil, and others thought she had drunk too much alcohol. Each one had his own idea, but no one really knew what had broken the blood-vessel in her brain in the first place. She did not go out of the house very often, and she stayed in bed a lot. As time went by, Paul began to look sick, too."

At length, Dr. Roux convinced Paul that Jane needed to go to a psychiatric hospital where she could be placed under observation—and where her medication could be controlled. That spring, he wrote to his friend Oliver Evans (with whom he had rendezvoused in Thailand) "Jane is very ill. Last week I went to Málaga to look into possible hospitals there. I found one to which I hope to take her on Friday. Only she has let her passport elapse, as well as her resident carnet and her exit-visa. (They won't let one out of the country without a visa.) The departure is thus dubious. . . . I hope that once I've settled her in Málaga and don't have to worry constantly about her as I do now, I can start on my Bangkok book." Added Paul, "Get pachouli oil in Penang. . . . I envy you Angkor and Bali so much."

Arguing that she didn't need to be hospitalized, Jane refused to leave Tangier—or her husband. "She was terrified of being subjected to shock treatment again," Bowles remembered. "She hated it—*hated* it." In her feeble state, however, she was unable to hold up her end of the battle. "She always knew that I would have my way, so it didn't really matter what she said, but she continued to object," he remembered.

By the middle of April, Bowles had taken Jane across the

Straits to the sanitorium that he had chosen. When he returned to Tangier, he wrote to Virgil Thomson, saying that the decision had been inescapable: "It was painful, but there was no possible way of allowing her to stay here in the state she was in," he said. "She could be lucid only if one managed, for a minute or two, to get her mind away from her 'illness.' Behind it all she seemed to be quite clear about her state, and could discuss it rationally now and then in moments of stress. Fundamentally the trouble was that she did not seem to care one way or the other. It was all happening to someone else about whom she didn't give a damn. I'm hoping the hospital can get her interested in something, if only in getting out."

David Herbert was among the friends who made the trip to Málaga to see Jane in the sanitorium. Hoping that she would be buoyed by the fact that *The Collected Works* was receiving high praise, he brought along the best reviews. "As reading was such an effort, Janie made me read them to her," he remembered. "She looked very sad and, for a little while, said nothing, then, hopelessly, she said: 'I know you meant this kindly, darling, but you couldn't have done anything more cruel!' I was aghast. 'You see,' Janie went on, 'it all makes me realize what I was and what I have become.' I was terribly upset. Janie, seeing this, looked up with the ghost of a smile. 'Give me the book,' she said. I handed her *The Collected Works*. With a trembling hand she picked up a pencil and added, 'of Dead Jane Bowles.' "

In Tangier, Paul found it difficult to concentrate on anything apart from Jane's plight. With the "thunderheads of [her] illness on the horizon," as he described it, focusing on the Bangkok book seemed impossible, and writing fiction was out of the question. Between trips to Málaga, he worked on the translation of Mrabet's second novel, *The Lemon*, [5] and saw friends like John Hopkins, Joe McPhillips and Louise de Meuron—one of the few Tangerinos who still entertained on a grand scale.

During Paul's absence, Brion Gysin had taken on the role of ringmaster at the Itesa, and that spring he played host when the Rolling Stones drove down from London. Introduced to the group by a friend who was an art dealer, Brion made a point of arranging for them to meet Bowles. Later, Paul remembered that he had been decidedly unimpressed when he and Mrabet encountered the young musicians in Gysin's flat: "I hated rock music," he said, "so I wasn't very excited about meeting them. I scarcely knew who they were— I'd never heard a note that they'd played. There was no one to be introduced to except Mick Jagger and I think Keith Richards—the others were lying there on the floor asleep or unaware." In a letter sent to Charles Henri Ford just after their departure, Paul observed that the visitors had been "very much rolling (in money) and very stoned. Supposedly," he said, "they're on a musical tour of Morocco; that is, they are looking for Moroccan music. But I think the jduq jmel and the raita (datura)⁶ will get them before the Gnaoua or the Djelala do. Or perhaps LSD immunizes them to such simple substances. . . ."

After Brion left with the group on their pilgrimage to Marrakech, the Itesa was oddly quiet. To Ira Cohen, Paul reported: "I'm here alone with Cherifa to get dinner and Aicha to get lunch, an idiotic system, but one which I can't very well alter, since this is a transitional period. Naturally I'd like to fire Cherifa for good, but she has it all set up with Jane to remain, surely knowing what I had in mind."

The silence was broken when the volatile Mrabet finally faced off against Cherifa. Still convinced that she was using black magic to control Jane, he told Bowles that he wanted to inspect a sickly looking philodendron at Jane's flat. At Mrabet's insistence, Paul went to retrieve the plant, but he was stopped by a hysterical Cherifa. ("She tried to gouge my eyes out," he said, "and I decided it wasn't worthwhile.") Mrabet then stormed into the flat, forced his way past Cherifa and seized the plant himself. He carried it back upstairs, where he and Paul unearthed a magic packet like the one that Jane had found in her bed years earlier. "The maid screamed and said, 'Don't touch it—it's very dangerous,'" remembered Bowles. "It was as though it had been a cobra. We got it out and opened it up and there were fingernails and all sorts of things that had been burned. It had allowed Cherifa to use the plant as her proxy. When she went home to sleep, she could have the plant do her bidding, so that was why she didn't want to be without it."

Mrabet and other Moroccans believed in Cherifa's magic, of course, and even Bowles was half-convinced that she could influence Jane with her incantations. Later, he said, "I believed [in magic] in the sense that since I was surrounded by people who were absolutely convinced of it, I had to modify my own beliefs in order to live with them. I couldn't deny it, and the more I accepted it, at least superficially, probably the closer I came to believing it myself."

When he went to Málaga again, Paul said nothing about the incident. After weeks at the sanitorium, Jane was still despondent, and her physicians were recommending electroshock therapy—an idea that sent her into hysterics. Convinced by her doctors that it was her only hope, the agonized Bowles finally gave his permission for the treatment to proceed. "My feeling is that it blots out whole departments of memory permanently, which isn't so good," Paul wrote to Virgil Thomson. "Of course, she is dead set against it. But if she can't get well without it . . . ?"

That spring, Jane composed a note to Libby Holman in which she tried to describe her stay in the hospital. "I am very sad and also Bewildered. . . ." she wrote. "I cannot right you very much because I write the words with being able to see them yet—so there isn't as much privacy as I could have if I needed no guidance. Readis is allmost out of the question but I am so much Better that I hope write you to write you so y." Ending abruptly, the letter was unsigned.

Although the shock therapy produced no radical improvement, Jane's condition had stabilized somewhat by midsummer, and she continued to plead with her husband to bring her home. Before allowing her to come back to Tangier, however, Paul wanted to banish Cherifa. "Everybody had been telling me, 'You've got to get rid of that woman.' Dr. Roux said, 'The only thing to do is push her out—get rid of her before Jane comes back,' " he remembered. "The day Jane was to return, I said, 'You have to leave—she's coming back. You can't see her.' Cherifa said, 'Oh, I see, the bride is coming back.' Very nasty. I said, 'Go, go, go'—you know. She went, and she said [menacingly], 'I'll be seeing you.' "

On July 27, Bowles went to Málaga to fetch Jane. Oddly agitated, she had dropped a great deal of weight, and she seemed to have aged several years: Underneath the short brown wig[7] that she wore, her face looked drawn and haggard. Friends who saw her in the following weeks were startled to see how wraithlike she was, but Paul was determined not to let her slip into the role of an invalid. In a letter to Peter Owen, he reported that she had even shown an interest in returning to her fragmented play. Wrote Bowles, "She seems to think of nothing but getting back to work at writing, which is an excellent sign, I must say. We bought notebooks and pens, so she would have materials. . . ."

Under the circumstances, writing proved out of the question. As soon as she was back at the Itesa, Jane was compelled to spend ten days under the scrutiny of Jane Howard and Terence Spencer, a writer and a photographer who had been sent to Tangier by *Life*. On the theory that a profile would give momentum to her *Collected Works* (and, presumably, to *The Time of Friendship*, the volume of his stories that Holt had just published), Paul had agreed to the story over Jane's objections. Now, it would be impossible for her to shut herself in her room—or to gather strength in peace.

Later, Howard would remember Jane as a frail creature who exhibited a childlike charm and slept with a stuffed koala bear. To Howard, the bond between the Bowleses was clear; as she reported it, they sounded like a pair of Noël Coward characters trading wry witticisms. When Jane went into a modest panic before one outing, Howard noted, she lurched into a disjointed monologue that was directed at Paul: "Okay, Tuesday we'll have the couscous," she said, "but should it be with chicken or lamb? How can I put my eyeliner on with this brush? What if it smears? I'm so frightened of this atomizer! *Oy!* Help! If we go in the Volkswagen, who should ride in the front seat? If Bob and Tom come to the party, should we ask Emma and Nora? But Nora can't stand John, can she? Where should we go if we decide just to have a snack?" By Howard's account, Paul said, "Snack? How would I know? I haven't had a snack since 1957." Later, there was a discussion of the sanitorium: "I was thrilled to see how *short* everyone there was," Jane confided. "I've never been anywhere else where everyone was smaller than I am." According to Howard, Paul told her, "Now Janie, remember, there are pygmy tribes to be visited."

With Howard and Spencer on their trail, the Bowleses went to a party given by Joe McPhillips and John Hopkins at their villa on the Mountain. A group of Jilala musicians had also been invited, and the entertainment proved more dramatic than expected: After dinner, the seductive music began and Mohammed Mrabet (who, as it happened, was a Jilala adept) fell into a trance that grew deeper as the music became more intense. Brandishing a long, curved knife, he crouched and swayed and leapt like a wild man. "He was really out of control, making animal noises," remembered Hopkins. "He was behaving like a maniac—getting his face closer and closer to a charcoal brazier. Finally, he was down on the ground, and it looked like he was going to immolate himself." Hopkins dashed in and tried to drag him away from the burning embers, but the ecstatic Mrabet put up a fight. "He was quite athletic—always priding himself on his muscles—and it was like wrestling King Kong," Hopkins said. "Other people got into it and there was a free for all on the ground next to the fire. I looked up and Paul was standing there like a scientist—he had that cigarette holder in his hand, and he was just inspecting the scene."

Apart from that soirée, the *Life* team followed the Bowleses to David Herbert's and to a party at Martha Ruspoli's. Although Cherifa had been banished, Jane had begun to slip away to meet her at the movies, and she appeared at Martha's as Jane's chaperone. Wearing a black *haik* and litham along with dark sunglasses, she seemed thoroughly unrepentant: "She looked like a terrorist," remembered Bowles. "She *was* a terrorist."

To Howard, Jane confided, "I feel guilt and affection for [Cherifa]. If it weren't for us she'd never have been introduced to European ways at all. She's a freak, and I'm afraid she'll get worse and worse as she realizes she isn't popular."

As soon as their visitors had left Tangier, Jane was compelled to undergo an operation for hemorrhoids. While she was still recuperating, the stitches ripped, and in spite of the agony she refused to return to the surgeon. Finally, she relented—only to be told that she needed more surgery. By the end of October, she was recovering from the second operation, and both her household and Paul's were in chaos. "She lies screaming all night, and there doesn't seem to be anything the doctors can do for her," Paul told Oliver Evans. "No injection calms the pain. This preoccupation keeps me from doing much of anything, as I'm always on the alert for poundings on the ceiling by one of the maids, summoning me; it happens any hour of the day or night. The trouble is that she sometimes tries to get out of bed by herself, and falls, and that always makes things worse. . . ."

In a letter to Libby Holman, Paul reported that Jane's illness had heightened the agitation that he had observed when he brought her home from Málaga. "As Jane recovers she gets onto a higher and higher horse, I find," he told Libby. "And the reason for that is that she has suddenly cut out *all* medication, for the first time in ten years; as a result of 'being on her own,' as it were, she is extremely energetic, and the energy releases heretofore unsuspected reserves of aggression. So she has her own way or else."

While she was still recuperating, the defiant Jane invited Cherifa to return from exile. Paul saw that there was little to be done about it: "She always said, 'I hired her and I'll fire her—you have nothing to do with it,' " he remembered. And if discovering the packet of *tseuheur* had underscored his belief that Cherifa meant to keep Jane in her sway, he never broached the topic with his wife. "She wouldn't have gotten rid of Cherifa even if she'd believed it, and she wouldn't have believed it," he said.

As much as he disliked the notion of returning his advance, Bowles decided to abandon his book on Bangkok. Lukewarm about the city itself, he was unable to establish any creative momentum. "The city doesn't deserve [the book], and I don't feel that I deserve the punishment it has been inflicting on me, the attempt to say something valid . . ." he told Edouard Roditi. "It's a question of sending back $5,000 and resigning myself to the unfavorable financial result. . . ."

That fall, there was little relief either for Paul or for Jane. Even when she gained enough strength to make morning trips to the market, her moods were unpredictable. "She was up and down by the minute," he remembered. Since writing even a letter was impossible, Paul sat by her bed and took dictation when she wanted to send a dispatch to Libby or to her mother. Still hoping "to pull her out of the dark place where she would like to stay," as he described it, Bowles continued to insist that she was, in fact, improving. To Roditi, he reported, "I'm convinced, even if she isn't, that she's definitely on the road to recovery."

*   *   *

With Jane in desperate straits, Paul took only passing notice of a drama that was unfolding elsewhere in Tangier. Somehow, Alfred Chester had made his way back to Morocco, and he had taken a villa on the Mountain, where he was closeted with his madness. His months in New York had been long and lonely: Although Simon & Schuster had published *The Exquisite Corpse,* the book had drawn hardly a glance from the literary community that he had courted for so long. Struggling with a new novella, he had gone into therapy with Laura Perls, but it had been impossible for him to regain his footing. After receiving a long-awaited inheritance, he had left for Europe, and his illness had waxed and waned as he skittered from London (where he had been treated at R. D. Laing's clinic) to Paris. Alienated from most of his friends, he had convinced himself that he was being followed by an army of little green men—men whom he believed had followed him to Morocco.

By November, Paul had seen Alfred several times. Drinking heavily to quiet the voices in his head, he was still obsessed with Bowles; during the months he had been away, he had written him a series of chilling letters that betrayed his fixation. (From New York, he had sent a dispatch addressed "Dear Great Man, Monster," saying, "You gave me the greatest gift I've ever had, by which I mean, in short, of course, what else, Morocco. . . . Could you please like my magic father promise me Morocco again?") And while most of the expatriates who had seen Alfred had been taken aback, Paul continued to regard him with sublime dispassion. In a letter to Ira Cohen, he reported merely that he had gone with him to a Chinese restaurant and that Chester was "still on his lost identity kick." Added Paul, "He says that yesterday he passed through a trauma having to do with his work. First time he's mentioned work since I started seeing him again. . . ."

John Hopkins was with Bowles one evening when he went to look in on Chester. "We had had dinner with a friend on the Mountain, and Paul said, 'Let's stop in and see what Alfred's doing,'" remembered Hopkins. "He was in one central white-washed room with rooms running off of it, and he slept with dogs that crapped and pissed on him. In one room there was a dump truck's worth of wood; in the other there was an equally vast amount of oranges. He had a great fire going and it was blazing right up to the ceiling and into the room. It was so hot that he was walking around in a G-string, and he was ranting and raving." Paul, he said, showed no reaction to Alfred's tirade. "We left after ten minutes," he remembered, "and Alfred ran out after us in that G-string, sweating like a little fat blimp of a lobster, shouting that we'd been invited to a dinner party he hadn't been invited to. He looked and acted so weird, you didn't know if he was human."

After Chester had been in Tangier for a month or so, Paul decided to introduce him to Louise de Meuron, who was a neighbor on the Mountain. The generous Louise took him under her wing, as did a handful of other expatriates with a taste for the bizarre. As Bowles reported it to Cohen, Alfred was soon seen in the company of "a nucleus of tattered friends whose presence here I'd been ignorant of. Unbelievable old French junkies and queens and English lady lushes who live with Moroccans." Added Paul, "[He] finds them in the smaller bars, where it seems he himself is always to be found, from noon on."

Although she, too, was sinking, the loyal Jane also renewed her friendship with Alfred. As Paul remembered it, the alliance between them seemed a kind of folie à deux: "Alfred had done everything to make her hate him, but she felt sorry for him because he was psychotic," he said. "[But] they were both out of their minds— that's what they had in common."

Living at the end of the world had proven disastrous for Jane Bowles. No longer the spirited, urbane creature whom Truman Capote and Cecil Beaton had found so seductive, she had been robbed of her independence, her momentum and her sense of self. By choosing to stay in exile with her husband, she had abandoned the milieu where she had a presence as a writer. From *The Sheltering Sky* onward, she had said that Paul was the artist—that her own career was "a mistake." Adrift in a setting dominated by idlers and misfits, she had ceased to bring forth her own fiction; instead, she had used her creative energy to perfect the character who was Jane Bowles. When her stroke came, it merely sent her down a path that she had already chosen; like Kit Moresby, Jane had always felt herself to be under a curse. And, like Kit, she eventually tumbled into a nightmare from which there would be no awakening.

It was at the end of December, 1967, that Jane's darkest prophecies finally were fulfilled. Somehow, the fragile thread that had been holding her together was snapped: Sliding into a manic state, she became impossible to control. Without a word to Paul, she packed her belongings and moved with Cherifa into the Atlas Hotel—an establishment notable only because it was close to the Parade. Each day, she sat in bars for hours, drinking and delivering disordered monologues; and each day, Paul tried to persuade her to come home.

Seized by a vehement urge to self-destruct, Jane began to give away everything she owned. "She met hippies in the street and said 'Come back to my hotel,' " Bowles remembered. "She gave them all her clothes, what jewelry she had, and the money out of her purse. Who were they? She didn't know. They were just hippies walking the street saying, 'Groovy.' "

Borrowing money from friends and shopkeepers and writing checks on her joint account with Paul, Jane managed to hand out hundreds of dollars to people whom she barely knew. In bars, she picked up tabs for the strangers who drank with her. Agitated, disheveled, she frightened the barflies who were alert enough to see how disturbed she was.

"She drove me mad," remembered Peter Pollock, who owned a restaurant called La Pergola. "She came to my bar every day, and she didn't know what she was saying or what she meant—she was so far gone by then. It was all very unpleasant, really, because she obviously didn't know why she was there."

In her confusion, Jane decided that she was in love with Lily Wickman, the new proprietor of the Parade. An aging French-woman with heavily painted eyes and a poodle haircut, Wickman once had worked as part of a motorcycle act called the "Wall of Death." Said Isabelle Gerofi, "Mme Wickman was an ugly woman who had a past, so she was a special person for Janie. She went to the bar every day to see her, but of course she never answered."

As Wickman remembered it, Jane created an upheaval every time she appeared at the Parade—walking back and forth and wringing her hands until Wickman threatened to banish her. Talking constantly, repeating herself, Jane would remove her wig and play with it while she flirted with the tough-talking barkeep. Years later Wickman recalled, "Jane was in fact very gay when she was here. . . . She would go into the kitchen and talk to the cooks and laugh. One day she came without clothes. Finally," she said, "the customers began to be very upset."

At that point, Wickman called Bowles to tell him that Jane was being incorrigible. But while he was appalled by her behavior, her husband could find no way to rein her in. Frenzied and disordered, she seemed beyond Paul's grasp, and her will was stronger than ever. Desperate, he asked a few of her friends to help subdue her.

"Paul said we should try to talk to her," remembered John Hopkins. "McPhillips and I went to see her [in her room] at the Atlas, and we found her dressed like she was going to a party, completely manic. I've never heard anyone so funny—the Moroccans were rolling on the floor with laughter. A few days later she was still handing out money and drinks, and every kind of toady in town was right there next to her."

When Paul himself tried to pry her out of bars, she turned on him. "She was very excited and furious when Paul refused to allow her to drink," said Isabelle Gerofi. "He came to get her one day at the Parade and she pushed him. After that, Paul was in a terrible state. And Janie knew perfectly well what would happen: She said, 'I will be a stupid girl and it will be irreversible.' "

Early in January, Hopkins and McPhillips went to the Itesa to visit Bowles, who was thoroughly traumatized. "We found him in the flat, huddling in the corner," said Hopkins. "He pointed downstairs, towards Jane's, and he said, 'She's spent all my money—she's gone crazy.' " As disturbed as he was, however, Paul said little about Jane to other friends; cloaked in his old pessimism, he watched as she acted out a script that seemed to have been written long before. "Jane was helpless, and Paul was very withdrawn," remembered Edouard Roditi. "There were very few in Tangier who were close to either of them at the time."

In fact, Jane's remaining friends had begun to fall away; even in Tangier there were limits, and no one wanted to watch as she approached the end of the line. "They deserted her because people don't like strange people, and Janie had lost her usefulness," said Gerofi. In typical Tangier fashion, members of the expatriate community began to gossip about Paul's "indifference" to his wife, and to trade stories about her exploits. By the middle of January, every-one in the expatriate community knew about her epic scenes. As Paul himself reported it to Ira Cohen, she went at one point to the American consulate and staged "a lie-in strike" in an attempt to get cash—a stunt that she repeated several times. Wrote Bowles, "[She said] when you give me the money I want, I'll get up. She finally settled for a glass of whiskey and went on her way, only to return there the following day and every day thereafter, in order to try to work the same strategy. But they got in touch with me. (I knew nothing about any of it, as she was living at the Atlas Hotel all those weeks.)"

For Bowles, such public displays were excruciating. It was one thing for Jane to play out her mad scenes in private, and quite another for her to establish herself as a woman too troubled to walk the streets. In January, he renewed his pleas for Jane to return to the Itesa, and by the middle of the month, she relented.

Even when she was back at the Itesa, however, there seemed to be no way to subdue Jane. She was infuriated when Paul told the servants to hide the liquor, and his attempts to supervise her drug-taking were no more successful than his efforts to stop her drinking. "She was taking more and more medicines any old way," he remem-bered. "I tried to get the maids to hide the bottles and only give her what she was supposed to take. Impossible—she had complete power over them. 'I don't care what Monsieur Bowles says—get that bottle!' [she'd say]. And then they'd go and get it."

Still writing checks to strangers, Jane eventually overdrew the Bowleses' joint account. The Moroccan government quickly moved in on Paul—claiming that it was his responsibility to cover her debts. To Cohen, Paul wrote, "No end to her troubles. Or mine . . . she ran up enormous bills all over town, and I am still paying them off. Have sent for three thousand dollars so far with which to do it (as she emptied the bank account) and still haven't got them all."

Alternately penitent and defiant, Jane dictated a note of apol-ogy to Paul while she was sitting at the Atlas bar. Her amanuensis was Alfred Chester. Said Jane, "Darling Paul—It will be all ex-plained—I mean, your financial dilemma—in one half hour. I mean, by me. It's true you should have a separate account. I have not spent as much money as you think. Please don't think it's your financial problem, *but mine.* We will talk it over and understand everything. All my Love Jane." Underneath, Jane scribbled two lines in her own unsteady hand: "Alfred is the secretary. Part of the love is for Alfred—"

By the middle of January, Paul was convinced that his wife was no longer able to function outside the hospital. Again and again, he tried to persuade her to return to Málaga. Still terrified of being locked away, she resisted. Isabelle and Yvonne Gerofi joined the campaign, but Jane dug in her heels. Unable to help herself, unwilling to be saved by others, she was impelled by a destructive energy that her friends found frightening.

Still, the end was approaching: On January 17, a disoriented Jane appeared with her servant Aicha at the Librairie des Colonnes. After asking the salesclerk for a few dirham, she collected two books and began to walk out of the store without paying. Aicha objected, and Jane became furious—lunging towards her and going for her throat, as though she wanted to choke her.

At last, Jane realized that there would be no turning back. Shortly after the scene at the bookstore, she told Paul that she would return to the sanitorium. On the evening before they were to depart, "She looked as though she was going to be violent," Bowles remembered. "The expression on her face, the fact that she would seize heavy instruments and hold them [as though she wanted to hurl them]—she wasn't herself."

On January 20, 1968—a clear, springlike day—Paul and Jane Bowles left Tangier together. On the ferry with them was an intern from the local psychiatric hospital. Aside from helping to monitor Jane, he was prepared to give her an injection if she became uncontrollable. When the boat docked in Algeciras, the party took a taxi for the two-and-a-half-hour trip to Málaga. As Paul remembered it, Jane seemed to be "rather out of her mind," during the journey. "She said, 'There are so many refugees on this road. They're all trying to get out of Morocco, and I think we're very lucky that we got out.' Of course," he added, "I agreed with her."

Long after Jane Bowles left Tangier for the last time, a new edition of a volume called *World Authors* was published in New York. In it was an autobiographical essay that she had been asked to write in the fall of 1967, and that she had dictated to Paul from her sickbed in Tangier. An elliptical, Jane-like account of her life as a writer and an expatriate in Europe and Mexico and Morocco, it began, "I started to 'write' when I was about fifteen and was obliged to do composition in school. I always thought it the most loathsome of all activities, and still do. At the same time, I felt even then that I had to do it." In the end, Jane said, "From the first day, Morocco seemed more dreamlike than real. I felt cut off from what I knew. In the twenty years that I have lived here I have written only two short stories, and nothing else. It's good for Paul, but not for me."

Epilogue

Jane Bowles never regained her sanity. Diagnosed as a manic-depressive psychotic, she spent almost five years in psychiatric hospitals in Spain. Her husband made the journey to visit her every few weeks, and each time he saw her, she begged him to allow her to return to Tangier. Only once did he try to care for her alone; in 1969, he brought her back to the Itesa for four months, but the experiment was a dismal failure. Disoriented, despondent, she asked friends to help her kill herself. On May 4, 1973—blind, mute, devastated by a series of strokes—she died at a Málaga sanitorium called the Clínica de Los Angeles. She was buried in an unmarked grave in the nearby San Miguel Cemetery.

As it happened, Jane's decline and death coincided with the end of an era in Tangier. In the late sixties and early seventies, the city attracted few new expatriates. Beset by all-too-modern problems including inflation and unemployment, it greedily played host to hordes of British, German, Dutch and American tourists who hiked through its derelict medina and tried to avoid the rapacious "guides" who offered everything from carpets to camel saddles. The shops on the Boulevard Pasteur grew more and more tawdry-looking, and the streets, muddier and more crowded. Hustlers eager to sell their sexual services haunted the cafés in the Ville Nouvelle, and it became impossible to leave one's hotel without being followed by a multilingual youth whispering, "Madam, madam . . ." By the early eighties, Tangier had the air of a city that had never possessed the slightest charm. Still, the end of the decade brought signs of better times: Long forgotten by the *haut monde,* Tangier came back into focus in 1989, when Malcolm Forbes gave a $2 million birthday party for himself at the Palais Mendoub, which he had bought in 1970. His eight hundred guests—Elizabeth Taylor, Henry Kissinger, Beverly Sills, Oscar de la Renta, William Buckley and Barbara Walters, among them—were followed by a flock of *paparazzi,* and the celebration itself recalled Barbara Hutton's most extravagant fêtes. In the meantime, the city had begun to attract a new group of investors—members of the Arab petrocracy who wanted a playground outside the Middle East. As the nineties began, wealthy Kuwaitis and sheiks from the Emirates were building homes on the Mountain (where property values were soaring), and a Saudi Arabian prince had just given the city an imposing new mosque.

Many of those who enlivened the expatriate scene during the sixties abandoned Tangier as it faded. Separated permanently from Raymond Doan in 1971, Barbara Hutton made her last visit to Sidi Hosni in 1975; when she died in 1979, the house went to her friends Silvia de Castellane Hennessy and her husband, Kilian. In 1973, Brion Gysin left for Paris, where he took an apartment near the Beaubourg. Stricken with cancer the following year, he died in 1986; at his memorial gathering in Tangier, mourners tossed his ashes in the sea near the Caves of Hercules. Jane's friend Charles Gallagher left for Marbella, and John Hopkins (who wed a wealthy American) moved to England, where he continued to write fiction. Tamara Dragadze also settled in England, where she published a novel called *Like Milk on the Fire,* which was set in Morocco. The mother of two, she later became an anthropologist whose area of expertise is the Soviet Union. Devastated by the death of his wife, Tamara's stepfather Narayan went to live in a monastery in the Atlas Mountains in 1965; when it was closed by the Moroccan government, he made a spiritual pilgrimage on foot through Spain, France and England before succumbing to lung cancer. Ahmed Yacoubi published *The*

Alchemist's Cookbook (which contained recipes for hashish cookies, *majoun* and other delicacies) and then immigrated to America to continue his work as a painter. In 1986, he, too, died of cancer. After her trip to Tangier in 1966, Libby Holman never saw the Bowleses again. Five years later, she died of carbon monoxide poisoning— apparently, by her own hand.

Some members of Paul and Jane's circle refused to leave the city during its long decline. Princess Martha Ruspoli kept her house on the Mountain until she died in 1984, and Countess Louise de Meuron did the same. Joseph McPhillips stayed on to become headmaster of the thriving American School, and Christopher Wanklyn, to live and work in Marrakech. Isabelle Gerofi, her husband, Robert, and Robert's sister Yvonne remained on the Boulevard de Paris, living in the same well-preserved building where Ruth Hopwood kept a flat.

By 1990, the expatriates who dominated the city in the postwar era were leading exceedingly quiet lives. Stalwarts like the ebullient David Herbert continued to entertain at their homes on the Mountain, although the gatherings were less ambitious than they once were. For the old guard, mornings were devoted to shopping at the Fez Market, and afternoons, to gardening or gossiping or sipping Grand Marnier at a quiet restaurant like the Nautilus. Nightlife in Tangier was desultory, at best; one occasionally took visitors to the "folkloric" show at the Minzah, but the Parade had been razed and the bar owned by the late Joseph Dean was a dour-looking establishment that had long since been abandoned by Those Who Mattered.

Although he pronounced Tangier to be "radioactive" when he left for England in the mid-sixties, William Burroughs returned to Morocco several times. At work on his novel *The Wild Boys* in 1967, he stayed for a month in Marrakech and a month at the Atlas Hotel, where he stoked himself with *majoun*. In 1985 (after he had settled in Lawrence, Kansas), he went back to Tangier with his assistant, James Grauerholtz. With Grauerholtz, William visited the Itesa, and he and Paul Bowles reminisced about the gruesome incident in which the madman Marnissi had hacked his way through the medina. The two also spoke of Alfred Chester: "He heard voices . . ." Bowles told Burroughs. "He used to come and complain to me because my voice seemed to predominate. . . .

[He'd say] 'Leave me alone! When you go to bed, don't think about me! I don't want to hear what you're saying.' "

In fact, Alfred Chester was destined to spend the rest of his life in the grip of madness. Living with Dris in Asilah in 1968, he was driven wild by the noise of children playing outside his window, and he often engaged them in stone-throwing battles that drew the police. (By one account, his neighbors were so upset by his behavior that they finally tied him to a tree in the belief that it would cure him.) Ejected from Morocco that May, Alfred returned alone to New York, where he tried to finish his novella, *The Foot.* Paranoid, reclusive, he alienated his remaining friends before moving on. After sojourns in London, Paris and an Israeli seaside community called Herzlia, Alfred turned up in Jerusalem in 1970. With his illness in full bloom, he had only his dogs and the poet Robert Friend for company. In August 1971, he succumbed to a lethal combination of cognac and barbiturates. Obscurity had claimed him long before, and the news of his death traveled slowly.

On December 30, 1990, Paul Bowles turned eighty. He still lived in the two-bedroom flat at the Itesa that looked much as it had when his wife died: Worn leather suitcases were stacked in the entranceway, and a dusty velvet curtain hung between the front door and the cushion-lined living room. Bookcases were filled with French, English, Spanish and Japanese editions of his own novels and of Jane's work, and a painting by Ahmed Yacoubi was hung above a low table piled with mail from abroad. On the terrace was a profusion of plants (including the ancient philodendron that had been snatched from Cherifa) that blocked the strong Moroccan sun. Lamps were kept low, and on chilly days, a smoky fire burned in the small grate. Despite his age, Bowles still had no telephone; anyone who wanted to make contact with him was compelled to send him a letter or to turn up at his door.

In some ways, age had taken its toll on Paul: His hair was white, his hearing had deteriorated and he suffered from bouts of sciatica that left him with a slight limp. Still, he had lost none of his elegance; he favored cashmere dressing gowns and English tweeds, and he smoked the occasional *kif* cigarette through a black holder. Over the years, he had fallen into a routine that seldom varied. In the mornings, Rodrigo Rey Rosa (a young Guatemalan writer who had become a protégé) often came to prepare his breakfast. After working on fiction or on translations, Bowles dealt with his correspondence. At two o'clock, visitors invariably arrived—friends, as well as journalists or film crews who had traveled thousands of miles. At 4:30, Paul's driver, Abdelouahaid Boulaich, would come to his rescue, and he would announce to his guests he was leaving to do errands. The two would make their slow rounds in Paul's vintage Mustang—first, a trip to the post office, then on to the Fez Market or the bank. At 6:00, Rodrigo or Mrabet (who lived in the country with his wife) would be in the kitchen, preparing the supper that Bowles often ate in his narrow bed. When he went out, it was usually for a quiet dinner with Tangerinos whom he had known for years—Herbert, McPhillips, Marguerite McBey, the writer Gavin Young or the painter Buffie Johnson, who had taken the apartment at the Itesa where Jane had lived.

Bowles produced no novels after Jane died, but he did continue to write. In 1972, Ecco Press published his autobiography, *Without Stopping*—a starkly noncommittal book that William Burroughs christened *Without Telling*. Five collections of his stories appeared between 1977 and 1988, and *Points in Time* (a "lyrical history" of Morocco, as he described it) was published in America in 1984. During the same period, Paul also translated works by Isabelle Eberhardt, the Swiss-born adventuress who lived in the Sahara at the turn of the century; by Moroccans including Mrabet and Mohammed Choukri; and by Rey Rosa, who wrote in Spanish. But while Bowles remained productive during his years alone, it seemed to many that his work lost its edge—that, without the wife who had been his muse, he took little pleasure in the business of writing. After Jane's death, Paul himself confessed to Virgil Thomson, "My degree of interest in everything has been diminished almost to the point of nonexistence . . . there is no compelling reason to do anything whatever." As their friend Charles Gallagher would say, "Her life wouldn't have had any meaning if she [hadn't had] him. And perhaps his writing [had no] meaning if he didn't have her to outshine."

Whenever Paul spoke of Jane, it was clear that she had been the source of his inspiration. His face changed completely when her name cropped up, and he was pleased to talk about her eccentricities, as well as her work. (Years after she died, he told a visitor about the afternoon when she had been standing by his fire, chewing on a greasy lamb shank, when a group of strangers were ushered in. ("Jane looked up from her gnawing and said, 'I have a spiritual side,' " he laughed.) To one journalist, he allowed that it was Jane who had kept him from becoming a recluse, and that he felt lost without her. "I think I lived vicariously . . . and didn't know it," he said. "When I had no one to live through or for, I was disconnected from life."

While Bowles always refused to court fame, it found him again in the early months of 1990, when the Italian director Bernardo Bertolucci arrived in Tangier with a movie company. Bertolucci had acquired the rights to *The Sheltering Sky,* and he had arranged to shoot parts of his film in Tangier. His company laid tracks at the foot of the Casbah for a scene that required a trolley car, and the crew took over the once-grand Hotel Continental, which served as a backdrop in several shots. Pirated copies of the screenplay were circulated among Tangerinos, and journalists made pilgrimages to interview Paul and John Malkovich and Debra Winger, who were Bertolucci's Port and Kit. Although Bowles said repeatedly that he expected the worst, he was pressed into duty to serve as the film's narrator, and he agreed to fly to Paris that November for its premiere.

That excursion was a rare event, for after he took Jane to Málaga, Tangier's most prominent expatriate expressed no desire to explore the world outside Morocco. In 1974, he told Virgil Thomson, "Perhaps the best thing about [Tangier] is the feeling it gives one of being in a pocket of suspended time and animation. Nothing happens for such long periods . . . that one dreads any change which might upset the status. That's the way it affects me, at least."

Of course, Paul Bowles never stopped complaining about his adopted home. At the end of 1990, he was lamenting the fact that the Ville Nouvelle had been marred by construction projects that would never be finished, and that the price of cookies at the Fez Market jumped from one week to the next. He talked about the absurdities of Moroccan bureaucracy, and he shuddered over the gloomy weather. But if some failed to see how Tangier had held him for so long, Bowles knew why he had stayed on after the dream had died: "Tangier," he said, "is like a gong that rang [forty] years ago. I still hear the resonance."

Notes

PROLOGUE

1. The predominant nationalist party.

CHAPTER 1

1. *Djellabas* were hooded robes. Once worn only by men, they were being adopted by women in place of the more traditional outer covering, which was called a *haik*.
2. A palm garden.

CHAPTER 2

1. The wealthy, Harvard-educated Perdicaris (the son of a Greek-American diplomat) ran away with a married Englishwoman named Ellen Varley and settled in Tangier in 1872. The following year, Emily Keene, Ellen's lady-in-waiting, scandalized society by accepting a marriage proposal from Hadj Abdeslam, the Grand Cherif of Wazzan. In 1904, Perdicardis and his stepson were kidnapped by the brigand Ahmed er Raisuli, and the incident prompted an international uproar. Teddy Roosevelt dispatched seven warships to Tangier, and Secretary of State John Hay sent a telegram to the American Consul in which he declared, "This Government wants Perdicaris alive or Raisuli dead." After agreeing on a ransom of $70,000 worth of Spanish silver dollars, Raisuli allowed his guests to go free.

CHAPTER 3

1. Powell is a pseudonym.

CHAPTER 5

1. The cloth that covers the lower portion of a woman's face.
2. A merchant's stall.
3. *Bisteeya* is a pie made with chicken or pigeon and sprinkled with cinnamon and sugar; a *tagine* is a traditional slow-cooked stew often made with lamb or poultry, and *mechoui* is lamb that has been roasted over a spit.
4. Tetum was the woman from the market whom Jane had dubbed "The Mountain Dyke."
5. After a few years, the three came to a parting of the ways, and their bar was briefly closed. Belline opened a flower shop and later became Barbara Hutton's housekeeper; Chase left Tangier, and Haselwood (who was still bankrolled by the Countess) refurbished and reopened the Parade.

CHAPTER 6

1. It was never clear just how the party got back to Tangier without the car keys.

CHAPTER 7

1. A low table.
2. The Arabic term for the region that includes Morocco, Algeria, Tunisia and Libya.

CHAPTER 10

1. Ampules of dolophine, which was later called methadone.

CHAPTER 11

1. Bowles took the title from a passage in the Koran: "The likeness of those who choose other patrons than Allah is as the likeness of the spider when she taketh unto herself a house and lo! the frailest of all houses is the spider's house, if they but knew."
2. Years later, Paul Bowles allowed that he had christened Lee Burroughs in honor of William. Still, he noted, "They had nothing in common; Lee was such a *square.*"
3. A "raking-in," or roundup.
4. The French minister of Moroccan and Tunisian affairs, who had just offered autonomy to Tunisia.

CHAPTER 12

1. The "ex-captain" was a smuggler and a neighbor of Dutch Tony's.
2. After the French accepted the plan for Moroccan independence, Spain negotiated a separate peace; in April, 1956, Franco agreed to abolish the Spanish protectorate and recognize the country's independent status.
3. Georges Bidault was France's foreign minister.

4. Isherwood had appropriated Paul's surname for his character Sally Bowles, who was the protagonist of the stories upon which the play *Cabaret* was based.

5. In fact, Paul kept much of his money in travelers' checks that were hidden under his bed.

6. Years later, Burroughs denied that his wall had been scarred by bullets, saying, "I had a little air pistol and I used matchboxes for target practice, but there were no holes in the wall or anything like that."

CHAPTER 13

1. Much of Kerouac's account of his sojourn is taken from the fictionalized version that appears in *Desolation Angels.* In it, a very recognizable Burroughs appears as Bull Hubbard.

2. William noted that he had come to understand the phrase's true meaning only after the fact; in his introduction to the novel, he wrote, "The title means exactly what the words say: NAKED Lunch—a frozen moment when everyone sees what is on the end of every fork."

3. Taprobane had proven a financial drain, and Paul arranged to put it on the market when he was in Ceylon. Although the island eventually was sold, a government ban against taking money out of Ceylon prevented him from collecting a single rupee.

4. Themistocles Hoetis was an editor who was interested in republishing Jane's novel in America.

CHAPTER 14

1. Berred was Jane's cat.
2. If Allah wills.

CHAPTER 15

1. Some of the selections were included on a two-volume record released by the Library of Congress in 1972; others were never made available to the public.

CHAPTER 16

1. The Mouloud is the celebration that marks the Prophet's birthday.
2. In fact, the Surrealists had experimented with an almost identical method during the twenties.

CHAPTER 17

1. A pseudonym.
2. Inspired by his sojourn in Morocco, Hopkins's first novel, *Tangier Buzzless Flies,* was published in 1974.
3. The plural of *sebsi* is *sebassa.*
4. John and Natasha Dougherty are pseudonyms.
5. In 1961 King Mohammed V had died after minor surgery, and Crown Prince Moulay Hassan had ascended to the throne as King Hassan II.
6. An American-born painter, Marguerite McBey was the widow of the Scottish artist James McBey. She lived in a house on the Mountain.

CHAPTER 19

1. When she became estranged from Doan, Hutton took Herbert back into the fold.

2. After his breakup with Barbara, Lloyd Franklin married a British heiress named Penny Ansley and moved with her into a house on the Mountain; in 1968, the two were killed in a car crash when they were driving home from a party in Marrakech.

3. Held in the Grand Atlas and the territories to the south, an *ahouache* is a formal celebration that features singers, dancers and percussionists.

4. By Glass's account, Alfred's editor at *Commentary* failed to up the fee, but a few months later the *Tribune* began to pay him more. Explained Dris, "It took a long time for my words to reach New York."

5. Although the piece was commissioned by *Show,* it was turned down; in 1965 it was published in *Evergreen Review.*

6. Despite his gallant recovery, David Herbert was shocked; years later, he said that he had felt "terribly sorry" for Chester.

7. A *tageeya* is a skullcap.

8. By that point, Brion had made his peace with the "Pan people" who had cast a spell on him in 1957.

9. Jane often used the Yiddish term *ganseh megillah,* which means a rigamarole.

CHAPTER 20

1. Roger Straus was Sontag's publisher.

CHAPTER 21

1. Aachor is a Moslem holiday that comes ten days after Moharram (New Year's Day); *tsoukel* is a kind of poisoning that is associated with the practice of black magic.

2. Later, Paul reported to Cohen, "Jane refused to take the parrot to the Institut Pasteur for fear of what they might discover."

3. Andreas Brown was a bookseller who later bought the Gotham Book Mart in Manhattan.

4. Gysin's novel was published in 1987 by the Overlook Press.

5. This, despite the fact that Mrabet's first novel, *Love with a Few Hairs,* had been seized by the authorities in Tangier.

6. Sold in magic stalls, *jdug jmel* are tiny seeds that are used to intensify the effect of *kif* preparations like *majoun.* Datura is a medicinal herb used as an hallucinogen.

7. Jane had begun wearing wigs in the early sixties.

Sources

Letters written by Paul Bowles and Jane Bowles are taken primarily from three sources: The Humanities Research Center at the University of Texas at Austin (abbreviated as HRC); the Virgil Thomson Archive at the Music Library at Yale University; and *Out in the World: Selected Letters of Jane Bowles, 1935–1970,* a collection edited by Jane's biographer. Many of the letters written by William Burroughs in Tangier are in the Rare Book and Manuscript Library at Columbia University, which also has a collection of letters written by Allen Ginsberg and Peter Orlovsky. Alfred Chester's letters have been compiled by Edward Field and Neil Derrick, and are used by permission of Jeffrey Chester, Alfred's nephew and literary executor.

PROLOGUE

xi "I relish the idea" Paul Bowles in *Without Stopping* (New York: The Ecco Press, 1985), p. 366. Hereafter abbreviated as WS.

xii "had not taken a bath" William Burroughs, *Naked Lunch* (New York: Grove Press, 1966), p. xli; "walk[ed] like a rope unwinding" Truman Capote, *The Dogs Bark: Public People and Private Places* (New York: Random House, 1973), p. 89.

xiv Dr. Leslie Croxford in conversation with author, August 26, 1987.

xvi "on top of the wave" PB to Michael Rogers in *Rolling Stone,* May 23, 1974.

CHAPTER 1

Much of the biographical material on Paul Bowles in Chapter 1 comes from his accounts in *Without Stopping.*

1. Paul Bowles in WS, p. 274.

3. "Paul and I are so incompatible" Jane Howard, "A Talk in the Casbah,"

Washington Post Book Week, March 19, 1978; "could have been invented by Kafka" PB in conversation with author, December 4, 1987; "an opium trafficker" Lawrence D. Stewart, *Paul Bowles: The Illumination of North Africa* (Carbondale: Southern Illinois University Press, 1974), p. 114.

4. PB in WS; Jay Harrison, "Composer at Home Abroad," *New York Herald Tribune,* May 17, 1953; "Even as a small child" Richard Patteson, *A World Outside: The Fiction of Paul Bowles* (Austin: University of Texas Press, 1987), p. 13; "delightful and sensible" Gertrude Stein, *The Autobiography of Alice B. Toklas* (New York: Harcourt, 1933), p. 309.

5. "The heat here is like that of a Turkish bath" PB to Daniel Burns, undated, HRC; "a madhouse" PB in WS, p. 127; "Up here on the mountain" PB to Gertrude Stein, August 22, 1931, Gertrude Stein Collection, Beinecke Rare Book and Manuscript Library, Yale University; "everything [in Fez to be] ten times stranger" PB in WS, p. 130; PB in conversation with author, January 13, 1988; "baptism of solitude" PB, *Their Heads Are Green and Their Hands Are Blue* (New York: Ecco Press, 1984), pp. 143–44.

6. PB to Charles Henri Ford, undated (1933), HRC; "There is one drawback" PB to Charles Henri Ford, March 23, 1933, HRC; "each day lived through" PB in WS, p. 164; "spin fantasies about how amusing it would be" PB in WS, p. 207; PB, *Their Heads Are Green and Their Hands Are Blue,* p. 21.

7. PB in WS, p. 275; "Just before the car came" ibid., p. 276.

8. "As for packing your passport" Jane Bowles to PB, undated (late August, 1947), in Millicent Dillon, ed., *Out in the World: Selected Letters of Jane Bowles, 1935–1970* (Santa Rosa, Calif.: Black Sparrow Press, 1985), p. 37. Hereafter cited as *Out in the World.*

CHAPTER 2

9. Much of the historical information in Chapter 2 comes from Lawdom Vaidon [David Woolman], *Tangier: A Different Way* (Metuchen, N. J.: Scarecrow Press, 1977); Harold D. Nelson, ed., *Morocco: A Country Study* (Washington, D.C.: The American University, 1985); and *International Tangier* (Tangier: The International Bank, 1949).

10. Vaidon, *Tangier: A Different Way,* Chapter 18; PB to Charles Henri Ford, December 13, 1947, HRC; PB to Charles Henri Ford, October 24, 1947, HRC.

11. Vaidon, *Tangier: A Different Way,* Chapter 18; PB in conversation with author, November 20, 1987.

12. Vaidon, *Tangier: A Different Way,* Chapter 18; *An American Guide to Tangier: The Golden Gateway* (Tangier: The Mediterranean American Press, 1952).

13. Vaidon, *Tangier: A Different Way,* Chapter 18; Kathy Jelen in conversation with author, January 12, 1988; Robert Shea in conversation with author, November 11, 1987; "dainty little tea parties" Daphne Fielding, *The Nearest Way Home* (London: Eyre & Spottiswoode, 1970), p. 67.

14. "Babs Buys Palace in Tangier Casbah," *New York Mirror,* September 20, 1946; "Barbara to Live in Casbah Home," *New York Journal-American,* September 20, 1946; Ruth Hopwood in conversation with author, December 2, 1987.

15. Ruth Hopwood in conversation with author, December 2, 1987; "I inherit six servants" *Time,* September 30, 1946; *Time,* September 1, 1947; C. David Heymann, *Poor Little Rich Girl* (New York: Pocket Books, 1983), pp. 244–51.

16. Vaidon, *Tangier: A Different Way;* "without plumbing" Heymann, *Poor Little Rich Girl,* p. 246; Comtesse Guillaume Lecointre in conversation with author, November 27, 1987.

17. Comtesse Guillaume Lecointre in conversation with author, November

27, 1987; PB, "Post Colonial Interlude in Tangier," Rare Book and Manuscript Library, Columbia University; Ian Selley in conversation with author, December 5, 1987; Vaidon, *Tangier: A Different Way.*

CHAPTER 3

19. PB in WS, p. 277.

20. "The lake in Bou Jeloud" PB to Charles Henri Ford, undated (1947), HRC; Stewart, *Paul Bowles: The Illumination of North Africa,* p. 149; "where there [is] only the sky" PB in WS, p. 275; "become whatever [Port] wanted" PB, *The Sheltering Sky* (New York: Vintage Books, 1990), p. 99; "It was as if always" ibid.

21. "You know" ibid., p. 100; PB in WS, pp. 277, 278; PB in conversation with author, January 19, 1988; PB in conversation with author, January 13, 1988.

22. PB in conversation with author, January 13, 1988; PB in WS, p. 277; PB to Charles Henri Ford, November 19, 1947, HRC.

23. "rhymes with horror" Tennessee Williams to Donald Windham in *Tennessee Williams' Letters to Donald Windham* (New York: Holt, Rinehart and Winston, 1976), January 26, 1949; "the Boom Town" PB to Charles Henri Ford, October 24, 1947; "You ask about" PB to Charles Henri Ford, November 19, 1947, HRC; PB in conversation with author, January 13, 1988.

24. "It was the cheapest kind" and "The effect came upon me" PB in WS, p. 278.

25. "without any relation" PB in conversation with author, January 13, 1988; "striking him with the weight" PB, *The Sheltering Sky,* p. 243; "opened his eyes" and "His cry went on through" ibid., p. 245; "She had more angst" PB in conversation with author, December 4, 1987.

26. "threw [her] into a state" and "Naturally all during the summer" Jane Bowles to PB, undated (December, 1947), in Dillon, ed., *Out in the World,* pp. 64, 66; PB in WS, p. 279; "cozy as a raspberry tart" Truman Capote in the introduction to *My Sister's Hand in Mine: The Collected Works of Jane Bowles* (New York: Ecco Press, 1978), p. vii; PB in WS, p. 279; "Please take care of yourself" Jane Bowles to PB, undated (December, 1947), in Dillon, ed., *Out in the World;* PB in conversation with author, December 14, 1987.

27. PB quoted on Yacoubi in Stewart, *Paul Bowles: The Illumination of North Africa,* p. 160; PB, *Their Heads Are Green and Their Hands Are Blue,* p. 156; "I'm in slow route" PB to Charles Henri Ford, December 13, 1947, HRC; PB in WS, p. 282; PB, *Their Heads Are Green and Their Hands Are Blue,* pp. 128–44.

28. Ibid.; "There are probably few accessible" PB, *Their Heads Are Green and Their Hands Are Blue,* p. 143; "a question of finding" PB to Charles Henri Ford, November 19, 1947, HRC; "the horror that lies above" PB, *The Sheltering Sky,* p. 328.

29. PB in WS, pp. 282, 283; PB, *Their Heads Are Green and Their Hands Are Blue,* p. 136; "a ridiculous, libelous" and "describ[ed] me" PB to Charles Henri Ford, January 25, 1948, HRC; "Of course I was really" PB to Charles Henri Ford, January 25, 1948, HRC; "A horror of slowness" ibid.

CHAPTER 4

30. PB in conversation with author, November 20, 1987; "All the people in the town" Jane Bowles, "Everything Is Nice," in *My Sister's Hand in Mine,* p. 314; "You tell me you are going to Fez" PB, *The Spider's House* (Santa Rosa, Calif.: Black Sparrow Press, 1987).

31. David Herbert in conversation with author, December 7, 1987; Charles Gallagher in conversation with author, January 30, 1987; Christopher Wanklyn in

1986; other material on this page is based on interviews with sources who wish to remain anonymous.

59. "He had one eye higher" David Herbert, *Second Son*, p. 66; "ushered into an immense" Diana Cooper to Alfred Duff Cooper, February 23, 1936, in Artemis Cooper, ed., *A Durable Fire: The Letters of Duff and Diana Cooper, 1913–1950* (New York: Franklin Watts, 1984).

60. "a remarkably common" and "very smart stomach-dancers" ibid; Beaton quoted in Vickers, *Cecil Beaton*, p. 222; "After three weeks" ibid., p. 223; "His father . . . a millionaire" David Herbert, *Second Son*, p. 120; Beaton quoted in Vickers, *Cecil Beaton*, p. 341.

61. Smith quoted in Vickers, *Cecil Beaton*, p. 341; Vaidon, *Tangier: A Different Way;* Ian Selley in conversation with author, December 5, 1987; Dunphy in conversation with author, August 3, 1987; Clarke, *Capote*, pp. 154, 199.

62. "a deep, murky well" *Newsweek*, January 26, 1948; "It is impossible" *The New York Times*, January 21, 1948; "Gore told Truman" Clarke, *Capote*, p. 141; PB in WS, p. 288; "wrapped around [Jack]" Tennessee Williams to Donald Windham, April 8, 1949, in *Tennessee Williams' Letters to Donald Windham;* PB in WS, p. 291.

63. Dunphy in conversation with author, August 3, 1987; "a dump, depressing beyond words" Jack Dunphy, *Dear Genius: A Memoir of My Life with Truman Capote* (New York: McGraw-Hill, 1987), p. 209; "Janie and Paul Bowles" Truman Capote to John Malcolm Brinnin, quoted in Brinnin, *Sextet: T. S. Eliot & Truman Capote & Others* (New York: Delacorte, 1981), p. 45; PB in conversation with author, January 7, 1988; Vickers, *Cecil Beaton*, p. 341; PB in WS, p. 292.

64. "Everything went wrong" David Herbert, *Second Son*, pp. 121–22; "Many of them had not spoken," ibid.

65. "built a fire" PB in WS, p. 292; "a curious place" Truman Capote to John Malcolm Brinnin, quoted in *Sextet*, p. 45; "a display ground" and "The Soko has its own celebrities" Capote, "Tangier," in *The Dogs Bark*, pp. 88–89.

66. "An exotic young man" and "a beautiful girl," ibid; "Each morning [they]" ibid., pp. 89–90; "She has not visited" ibid., p. 93; Ian Selley in conversation with author, December 5, 1987.

67. "A hundred or so of these" David Herbert, *Second Son*, p. 168; Herbert, *Second Son*, pp. 121, 169; PB in conversation with author, January 7, 1988.

68. "genius imp" Truman Capote, *Answered Prayers*, p. 76; "She seemed the eternal" and "a charming series" Capote in introduction to *My Sister's Hand in Mine*, p. v; "Everything has changed" Jane Bowles to Katharine Hamill, undated (late summer, 1949), in Dillon, ed., *Out in the World;* PB in conversation with author, January 7, 1988.

69. PB in conversation with author, January 7, 1988; "one day Truman" PB quoted in Clarke, *Capote*, p. 202; Clarke, *Capote*, p. 111; Jack Dunphy in conversation with author, August 3, 1987; "Among the planet's most pathetic" Capote, *Answered Prayers*, p. 72; Jack Dunphy, *Dear Genius*, pp. 209, 210.

70. Ibid., p. 211; "Before coming here" Truman Capote, "Tangier," in *The Dogs Bark*, p. 88; David Herbert in conversation with author, August 26, 1987; Herbert, *Second Son*, p. 123; PB in conversation with author, January 11, 1988.

71. Herbert in conversation with author, August 26, 1987; Herbert, *Second Son*, p. 123; Joseph McPhillips (on the Bowleses' relationship with each other) in conversation with author, January 26, 1988.

72. PB in conversation with author, November 20, 1987; Herbert, *Second Son*, p. 124.

73. "He still did not know" PB in WS, p. 293; "the lingering descriptions" PB in WS, p. 293; PB in conversation with author, January 11, 1988; PB in WS, p. 294; "parties were given for him" and "I know it did him" Jane Bowles to Libby

Holman, undated (November, 1949), in Dillon, ed., *Out in the World; The Times Literary Supplement* (London), September 30, 1949.

74. *Time,* December 5, 1949; Tennessee Williams in *The New York Times Book Review,* December 4, 1949; Norman Mailer, *Advertisements for Myself* (New York: G.P. Putnam's Sons, 1959), p. 468; PB, *Let It Come Down* (Santa Rosa, Calif.: Black Sparrow Press, 1985), Introduction, p. 7.

75. "started right in" PB quoted in Stewart, *Paul Bowles: The Illumination of North Africa,* p. 87.

CHAPTER 7

76. Terry Wilson in conversation with author, November 26, 1987; Felicity Mason in conversation with author, September 27, 1987; Brion Gysin and Terry Wilson, *Here to Go, Planet R-101* (San Francisco: RE/Search Publications, 1982).

77. Felicity Mason in conversation with author, September 27, 1987; William Burroughs in introduction to Brion Gysin, *The Last Museum* (New York: Grove Press, 1986); "some of the cleverest" Robert Palmer, "Memories of a Jack of All Arts, Ever on the Move," *The New York Times,* August 21, 1986.

78. Felicity Mason in conversation with author, September 27, 1987; PB in conversation with author, November 20, 1987; "slipped into the wrong colored package," Gysin quoted in Robert Palmer, foreword to Gysin, *The Process* (Woodstock, N.Y.: Overlook Press, 1987), p. xvii; Gysin and Wilson in *Here to Go;* "never been so desperate in [his] life" Jane Bowles to PB, undated (February 13, 1950), in Dillon, ed., *Out in the World;* PB in WS, p. 304.

79. "wild west of the spirit" Gysin, *The Process,* p. 144; "as a cook" PB in WS, pp. 304–5; Gysin and Wilson in *Here to Go,* pp. 26, 27.

80. Palmer in foreword to Gysin, *The Process,* p. xiv; Gysin and Wilson in *Here to Go,* pp. 27–29; "blue kif smoke" ibid., p. 30; "The Lupercalia" ibid., p. 29.

81. "Inside the village" Gysin in *Here to Go* (quoted from *Gnaoua* 1 [1964], Ira Cohen, ed.), pp. 30–31; "You know your music" William S. Burroughs and Brion Gysin, *The Third Mind* (New York: Seaver Books, 1978), p. 47; PB in WS, p. 305; ibid., p. 284; Bradshaw, *Dreams That Money Can Buy,* p. 284.

82. Bradshaw, *Dreams That Money Can Buy,* p. 284; "Libby Holman has left" PB to Charles Henri Ford, August 18, 1950, HRC; Paul Bowles, in "Dinner with Sir Nigel," in *Unwelcome Words* (Bolinas, Calif.: Tombouctou Books, 1988).

83. Ibid.; David Herbert, *Second Son,* p. 166.

84. Ruth Hopwood in conversation with author, December 2, 1987; "the smart expensive," David Herbert, *Second Son,* p. 166; *An American Guide to Tangier;* Kathy Jelen in conversation with author, January 12, 1988.

85. Kathy Jelen in conversation with author, January 12, 1988.

86. Kathy Jelen in conversation with author, January 12, 1988.

87. Kathy Jelen in conversation with author, January 12, 1988.

88. Paul Bowles in *Paul Bowles in Morocco,* a film by Gary Conklin, Mystic Fire Video; PB in conversation with author, January 4, 1988; PB in introduction to *Let It Come Down,* p. 9; "supremely conscious" PB, *Let It Come Down,* p. 101; "It's a madhouse" ibid., p. 29; "A little Moroccan boy" ibid., p. 142; "supremely anonymous" ibid., p. 117; "he was no one" ibid., p. 143.

89. "he was not real" ibid., p. 285; PB in WS, p. 305; PB in introduction to *Let It Come Down,* p. 8; "Horrific, unpleasant" *Kirkus Reviews,* November 1, 1950; "preoccupied with" *New York Herald Tribune,* December 3, 1950; "shocked, scandalized and disapproving," PB to David McDowell, August 15, 1950, Rare Book and

Manuscript Library, Columbia University; "Whether you know it or not" McDowell to PB, September 6, 1950, Rare Book and Manuscript Library, Columbia University.

90. "well organized and could cause" PB in WS, pp. 222–23; PB in WS, pp. 143–44; "I have nothing" PB to David McDowell, August 29, 1950, Rare Book and Manuscript Library, Columbia University; Vaidon, *Tangier: A Different Way*, pp. 250–51; Nelson, ed., *Morocco: A Country Study*, pp. 518–60.

91. Ibid; Vaidon, *Tangier: A Different Way*, p. 258; *Time* August 29, 1955, and September 5, 1955.

92. "Paul and Jane loved disasters" David Herbert in conversation with author, December 7, 1987.

CHAPTER 8

93. Gysin and Wilson in *Here to Go*, pp. 71–73; Felicity Mason in conversation with author, September 27, 1987; PB in conversation with author, January 28, 1987.

94. PB in conversation with author, January 28, 1987; PB in conversation with author, November 20, 1987; PB in WS, pp. 307–8.

95. "deep inside my heart" Jane Bowles to Libby Holman, undated (February 18, 1951), in Dillon, ed., *Out in the World*; Jane Bowles, letters to PB and others, January 11, 1950–February 19, 1951, in Dillon, ed., *Out in the World*; Dillon, *A Little Original Sin*; Bradshaw, *Dreams That Money Can Buy*, pp. 287–89; "sweet and trusting" and "looks not only beautiful" Jane Bowles to Libby Holman, February 18, 1951, in Dillon, ed., *Out in the World*; "many a cold evening" Truman Capote in introduction to *My Sister's Hand in Mine*, p. vii.

96. "the wife of a writer" Jane Bowles to PB, January 17, 1950, in Dillon, ed., *Out in the World*; Christopher Wanklyn in conversation with author, December 11, 1987; PB in WS, p. 310; Christopher Kininmonth, *Morocco* (London: Jonathan Cape, 1972), pp. 289–90; "With a novel" PB to Rena Bowles, July 26, 1951, HRC.

97. Stewart, *Paul Bowles: The Illumination of North Africa*, p. 122; "forced his body this way and that" PB, *Let It Come Down*, p. 269; "with each gesture" PB, *Let It Come Down*, p. 271.

98. PB in conversation with author, December 14, 1987; Edouard Roditi in conversation with author, March 28, 1988.

99. Charles Gallagher in conversation with author, January 30, 1988; Christopher Wanklyn in conversation with author, December 11, 1987; "nada es mala" Vaidon, *Tangier: A Different Way*, p. 349; Gavin Lambert in conversation with author, November 22, 1987.

100. "there [is] no longer any reason" PB, "Here to Learn," in *A Distant Episode* (New York: Ecco Press, 1988), p. 281; Noël Mostert in conversation with author, January 19, 1988; PB in conversation with author, December 14, 1987; Dillon, *A Little Original Sin*, pp. 216, 217.

101. David Herbert in conversation with author, August 26, 1987; PB in conversation with author, January 28, 1988; Hamri in conversation with author, January 18, 1988.

102. PB in WS, p. 310; "We decided that since" PB in WS, p. 311; William Burroughs in conversation with author, March 26, 1988; PB in WS, p. 311; Dillon, *A Little Original Sin*, p. 218.

103. PB in WS pp. 313–15; Vaidon, *Tangier: A Different Way*, pp. 260–62; "nightmare clarity" Robert Gorham Davis in *The New York Times Book Review*, March 2, 1952.

104. "The fruit of which" Richard Hayes in *Commonweal*, March 7, 1952; "I can imagine" L. A. G. Strong in *The Spectator*, April 25, 1952; PB in WS, p. 316; "He

has an intuitive gift" and "He can lie so well" PB, "A Man Must Not Be Very Moslem," in *Their Heads Are Green and Their Hands Are Blue,* pp. 60–61.

105. PB in WS, pp. 315–20; Bradshaw, *Dreams That Money Can Buy,* pp. 203, 211, 300, 301, 311–13, 332.

106. Ibid., PB in WS, p. 320; PB in conversation with author, December 14, 1988.

107. Ibid.; "I feel so guilty" and "you shoot yourself" Bradshaw, *Dreams That Money Can Buy,* p. 312; PB in conversation with author, December 14, 1988; Christopher Wanklyn in conversation with author, December 12, 1987; Seth Rosen and Jean Bernard Dangien in conversation with author, August 25, 1987; Bradshaw, *Dreams That Money Can Buy,* p. 313.

108. Ibid.; "Has Ahmed come back?" Tennessee Williams to PB, June 22, 1953, HRC; PB in WS, p. 321; "[Paul Bowles] has two Arabs" Tennessee Williams to Donald Windham, July 28, 1953, in *Tennessee Williams' Letters to Donald Windham.*

CHAPTER 9

110. *Time,* August 29, 1955, pp. 22–23, and September 5, 1955, pp. 18–23; *Morocco: A Country Study,* pp. 59–61.

111. Ibid.

112. Ibid.; "I was in a hurry" and "my fears seem well grounded" PB in WS, p. 322; Ian Selley in conversation with author, December 5, 1987; PB in conversation with author, November 20, 1987.

113. Noël Mostert in conversation with author, January 19, 1988; PB in conversation with author, November 20, 1987, and January 28, 1987.

114. Vaidon, *Tangier: A Different Way,* pp. 253, 263.

115. Herbert, *Second Son,* pp. 129–30; Jonathan Meades, "His Place in the Sun"; Tessa Codrington Wheeler in conversation with author, December 17, 1987; some material in this section comes from sources who wish to remain anonymous.

116. Tessa Codrington Wheeler in conversation with author, December 17, 1987; PB in conversation with author, January 11, 1988.

117. Patrick Higgins, *Madame: An Intimate Biography of Helena Rubenstein* (New York: Viking, 1971, p. 282; PB in conversation with author, January 11, 1988; Tessa Codrington Wheeler in conversation with author, December 17, 1987; Edouard Roditi in conversation with author, March 28, 1988.

118. Tessa Codrington Wheeler in conversation with author, December 17, 1987; "shattered mountains" Brion Gysin, *The Process,* p. 46; "a blue tide of darkness" ibid., p. 38; "more like yachts" ibid., p. 39; "volcanic moon-surface" ibid., p. 39; "running shadows but no shade" ibid., p. 48; "march[es] in the eye" ibid., pp. 46–47.

119. "playing about like a mind" ibid., p. 41; "all truth is a tale" ibid., p. 317; "grandiose stories" PB quoted in Mark Ellingham and Shaun McVeigh, *The Rough Guide to Morocco* (London: Routledge & Kegan Paul, 1985), p. 193; "too much in love with my husband" Felicity Mason, "The World of Brion Gysin: He Came, He Saw, He Conquered, and He Cut It Up" (unpublished).

120. Felicity Mason in conversation with author, September 27, 1987; "the most sensual city in the world" and "a dozen pairs of dark Arab eyes" Mason, "The World of Brion Gysin"; "he was a painter" ibid.

121. "felt a profound" "visited each other by punt," "Do you think they swapped wives," "turned his mysterious otherworld" and "this is my sister" ibid.; conversation with Felicity Mason, September 27, 1987.

122. Conversation with Felicity Mason, September 27, 1987; "left no room" William Burroughs in *Here to Go,* Introduction, p. x.

123. "I said, I would like to," Brion Gysin and Terry Wilson in *Here to Go,* p. 35. Robert Shea in conversation with author, November 11, 1987; Vaidon, *Tangier: A Different Way,* p. 289.

124. Terry Wilson in conversation with author, November 26, 1987; Wilson and Gysin in *Here to Go,* pp. 35, 36; "for some unforeseen, complex" Brion Gysin in William S. Burroughs and Brion Gysin, *The Third Mind* (New York: Seaver Books, 1978), p. 47.

CHAPTER 10

125. Brion Gysin and Terry Wilson in *Here to Go,* p. 161; "wheeled in . . . arms and legs flailing" Gysin in William S. Burroughs and Brion Gysin, *The Third Mind,* p. 49.

126. Victor Bockris, *With William Burroughs: A Report from the Bunker* (New York: Seaver Books, 1981), Introduction, pp. xii–xx; John Tytell, *Naked Angels* (New York: Grove Press, 1976), pp. 36–51; "I was a nobody" Burroughs in conversation with author, March 26, 1988; "I don't want that boy" Bockris, *With William Burroughs,* p. xiv.

127. "Writers were rich and famous," ibid., p. xiii; Tytell, *Naked Angels,* pp. 37–45; Barry Miles, *Ginsberg* (New York: Simon & Schuster, 1989), pp. 49–74; James Grauerholz in William Burroughs, *Interzone* (New York: Viking, 1989), pp. x–xiii.

128. "experimenting with heterosexual amity," Allen Ginsberg in William Burroughs, *Letters to Allen Ginsberg, 1953–1957* (New York: Full Court Press, 1982), p. 6; Bockris, *With William Burroughs,* pp. xvi, xvii, 44, 45; "Burroughs Heir Held After Wife's Slaying," *New York Daily Mail,* September 7, 1957; "Trial Ordered in Killing," *The New York Times,* September 11, 1951; "I thought myself to be controlled" William Burroughs in *Burroughs,* film directed by Howard Brookner, released in 1984; Allen Ginsberg in William Burroughs, *Letters to Allen Ginsberg, 1953–1957,* foreword.

129. William Burroughs in conversation with author, March 26, 1988; Burroughs, *Letters to Allen Ginsberg, 1953–1957,* pp. 11–24; PB in conversation with author, November 20, 1987; "sticking needle[s]" William Burroughs in *Naked Lunch* (New York: Grove Press, 1959), p. xli; "Meeting the local expatriates" William Burroughs to Allen Ginsberg, March 1, [1954], in William Burroughs, *Letters to Allen Ginsberg, 1953–1957,* pp. 24–25.

130. PB in WS, p. 323; Burroughs in conversation with author, March 26, 1988; "evincing no cordiality" Burroughs to Jack Kerouac, August 19, [1954], in Burroughs, *Letters to Allen Ginsberg, 1953–1957,* p. 55; "passing along a back street" PB, "Burroughs in Tangier," from *Big Table,* vol. 1, no. 2 (1959); Bowles in conversation with author, January 28, 1988; "tall, broad-shouldered, handsome" William Burroughs in *Interzone,* p. 74; "Paul Bowles is" William Burroughs to Allen Ginsberg, February 9, 1954, in Burroughs, *Letters to Allen Ginsberg, 1953–1957,* p. 24.

131. "Miggles looked up at her husband" William Burroughs to Jack Kerouac, February 12, 1956, Rare Book and Manuscript Library, Columbia University; "The only person in Interzone" William Burroughs to Jack Kerouac, December 7, 1954, Rare Book and Manuscript Library, Columbia University; "It has occurred to me" William Burroughs to Allen Ginsberg, July 15, [1954], in Burroughs, *Letters to Allen Ginsberg, 1953–1957,* p. 47; "Paul Bowles invites the dreariest" William Burroughs to Jack Kerouac, June, 1954, Rare Book and Manuscript Library, Columbia University.

132. "[sat] around smoking" William Burroughs to Allen Ginsberg, January 26, [1954], in Burroughs, *Letters to Allen Ginsberg, 1953–1957,* p. 15; "encountered a barrage" and "Dean wanted not to" William Burroughs to Allen Ginsberg, June 24, [1954], in Burroughs, *Letters to Allen Ginsberg, 1953–1957,* p. 37; "Tanger is a marrow-

bone" and "Jane Bowles" William Burroughs to Allen Ginsberg, June 24 [1954], in Burroughs, *Letters to Allen Ginsberg, 1953–1957,* p. 38; "disturbance of erotic" and "shack up with a fellow" Allen Ginsberg in Burroughs, *Letters to Allen Ginsberg, 1953–1957,* foreword, p. 6; "appeared as a terrible affront," ibid., p. 7; James Grauerholz in conversation with author, March 26, 1988; "write me a fix" William Burroughs to Jack Kerouac, April 22, 1954, Rare Book and Manuscript Library, Columbia University.

133. "snails to Camembert" William Burroughs to Allen Ginsberg, March 31, 1955, in Burroughs, *Letters to Allen Ginsberg, 1953–1957;* "[Burroughs] spends more money" PB in "Burroughs in Tangier," *Big Table,* vol. 1, no. 2 (1959); William Burroughs in conversation with author, March 26, 1988.

134. William Burroughs in conversation with author, March 26, 1988; William Burroughs to Allen Ginsberg, May 11, [1954], in Burroughs, *Letters to Allen Ginsberg, 1953–1957;* William Burroughs to Allen Ginsberg, July 3, [1954], July 8, [1954], July 15, [1954], in Burroughs, *Letters to Allen Ginsberg, 1953–1957;* "Kiki and I," "in case a mob" and "And me caught" William Burroughs to Allen Ginsberg, August 19, [1954], in Burroughs, *Letters to Allen Ginsberg, 1953–1957.*

CHAPTER 11

135. "a startling change" PB in WS, p. 323

136. "political disagreements" PB to John Lehmann, March 20, 1954, HRC; "Ahmed is on his way" PB to John Lehmann, April 27, 1954, HRC; "not about the traditional" PB, *The Spider's House* [Santa Rosa, Calif.: Black Sparrow Press, 1987], Introduction; PB in WS, p. 324.

137. "supremely deserted" PB, *The Spider's House,* p. 399.

138. "decomposing before my eyes" PB in the preface to *The Spider's House;* "Everybody was expecting" PB to Oliver Evans, August 24, 1954, HRC; Vaidon, *Tangier: A Different Way,* p. 270; *Time,* September 5, 1955, pp. 18–23.

139. Ibid., Dillon, *A Little Original Sin,* p. 235; "Scene by scene" Brooks Atkinson in *The New York Times,* December 30, 1953.

140. "There's no point" Jane Bowles quoted in *Vogue,* May 1, 1954, p. 137; "Is it writing" Jane Bowles quoted in Dillon, *A Little Original Sin,* p. 239; "kept out of the David [Herbert] life" Jane Bowles to Natasha von Hoershelman and Katharine Hamill, undated [June, 1954], in Dillon, ed., *Out in the World.*

141. "sat down and lowered" Jane Bowles to Natasha von Hoershelman and Katharine Hamill, undated [June, 1954], in Dillon, ed., *Out in the World;* Yvonne Gerofi to author, November 18, 1987.

142. "It's so hard to know" Jane Bowles to Natasha von Hoershelman and Katharine Hamill, undated [June, 1954]; PB to author, January 28, 1988; Christopher Wanklyn to author, December 11, 1987.

143. Isabelle Gerofi and Yvonne Gerofi in conversation with author, November 18, 1987; PB in conversation with author, December 14, 1987, and January 7, 1988; David Herbert in conversation with author, December 7, 1987; Christopher Wanklyn in conversation with author, December 11, 1987.

144. Ibid., Lyn Austin in conversation with author, March 9, 1988; PB in conversation with author, December 14, 1987.

145. "tries very seriously" Truman Capote, *Answered Prayers,* p. 77; PB in conversation with author, December 14, 1987; Isabelle Gerofi in conversation with author, November 23, 1987; Dillon, *A Little Original Sin,* pp. 254–56; Charles Gallagher in conversation with author, January 30, 1988.

146. "When she saw the island" PB in WS, p. 325; Dillon, *A Little Original Sin,* pp. 259–260.

147. "I think she was having" Guggenheim quoted in Dillon, *A Little Original*

Sin, p. 262; "my failure to like" Jane Bowles to PB, undated [July, 1948], in Dillon, ed., *Out in the World;* "I think you are, too" Charles Gallagher in conversation with author, January 30, 1988; "hit bottom" and "a nightmare to the end" Jane Bowles to PB, undated [April/May 1955], in Dillon, ed., *Out in the World;* "pounding with blood-pressure symptoms," "to ward off the evil eye" and "[They] think I am mad" Jane Bowles to PB, undated [April/May 1955], in Dillon, ed., *Out in the World.*

148. "I thought I alone" Ibid.; Vaidon, *Tangier: A Different Way.*

149. "Tanger is running down" William Burroughs, *Interzone* (New York: Viking, 1989), p. 54; William Burroughs to Allen Ginsberg, December 6, 1954, in Burroughs, *Letters to Allen Ginsberg, 1953–1957;* "Perhaps New Yorker" William Burroughs to Allen Ginsberg, January 12, 1955, in Burroughs, *Letters to Allen Ginsberg, 1953–1957;* "[Morton] twisted in hideous" William Burroughs, *Interzone,* p. 41; "lost all his savings" William Burroughs, *Interzone,* p. 50.

150. "perfidious Australian," "a cockney informer" and "he look[ed] like" Burroughs, *Interzone,* p. 51; "miasma of suspicion" Burroughs, *Interzone,* p. 47: "I started a conversation" Burroughs, *Interzone,* p. 48.

151. William Burroughs in conversation with author, March 26, 1988; "I am famous all over town" William Burroughs to Allen Ginsberg, April 20, [1955], in Burroughs, *Letters to Allen Ginsberg, 1953–1957;* "I have been buying the last box" William Burroughs to Allen Ginsberg, July 5, 1955, in Burroughs, *Letters to Allen Ginsberg, 1953–1957;* "Morphine Minnie" Charles Gallagher in conversation with author, January 30, 1988; PB in conversation with author, November 20, 1987.

152. Brion Gysin in Gysin and Wilson, *Here to Go,* pp. 161–62; "I cannot say I saw" Brion Gysin, *The Third Mind,* p. 49; Peter Pollock and Paul Danquah in conversation with author, January 23, 1988; "very charming" Francis Bacon to author, May 19, 1988.

153. "watching him like a cat" PB in conversation with author, November 20, 1987; "Ahmed and I" Francis Bacon to author, May 19, 1988; PB quoted by Michael Rogers in *Rolling Stone,* May 23, 1974; "a pipeful of kif" PB, *A Hundred Camels in the Courtyard* (San Francisco: City Lights Books, 1962), title page; Stewart, *Paul Bowles: The Illumination of North Africa,* pp. 111–13; PB in conversation with author, January 5, 1988.

154. Ibid.; Christopher Wanklyn in conversation with author, December 11, 1987. Dillon, *A Little Original Sin,* pp. 268–69; Oliver Smith quoted by Jane Howard in "A Talk in the Casbah," *The Washington Post Book Week,* March 19, 1967; "I don't want to see you" Dillon, *A Little Original Sin,* p. 269.

155. Ibid.; Christopher Wanklyn in conversation with author, December 11, 1987.

CHAPTER 12

157. Vaidon, *Tangier: A Different Way,* pp. 273–74; *Time,* August 29, 1955, pp. 22–23; *Time,* September 5, 1955, pp. 18–23.

158. Ibid.; "Tangier was more turbulent" PB in WS, p. 330; "Just had a riot" William Burroughs to Allen Ginsberg, August 1, 1955, in Burroughs, *Letters to Allen Ginsberg, 1953–1957;* William Burroughs in conversation with author, March 26, 1988; Vaidon, *Tangier: A Different Way,* p. 273; "He was so violent" PB in conversation with William Burroughs and James Grauerholz, January 20, 1985 (unpublished transcript).

159. William Burroughs to Allen Ginsberg, August 10, 1955, in Burroughs, *Letters to Allen Ginsberg, 1953–1957;* "evict the Chinaman" and "The ex-captain" William Burroughs to Allen Ginsberg, September 21, 1955, in Burroughs, *Letters to Allen Ginsberg, 1953–1957;* William Burroughs to Allen Ginsberg, October 7, [1955],

in Burroughs, *Letters to Allen Ginsberg, 1953–1957;* "artistically satisfying" William Burroughs to Allen Ginsberg, October 21, 1955, in Burroughs, *Letters to Allen Ginsberg, 1953–1957;* "seething with ideas" and "may make overland trip" William Burroughs to Allen Ginsberg and Jack Kerouac, October 23, 1955, in Burroughs, *Letters to Allen Ginsberg, 1953–1957.*

160. "I went in an Arab cafe" William Burroughs to Allen Ginsberg, October 23, 1955, in Burroughs, *Letters to Allen Ginsberg, 1953–1957;* "Tanger is the prognostic" William Burroughs to Allen Ginsberg and Jack Kerouac, November 2, 1955, in Burroughs, *Letters to Allen Ginsberg, 1953–1957; Time,* August 29, 1955, and September 5, 1955.

161. Vaidon, *Tangier: A Different Way,* pp. 275–76; "My personal feeling" PB to John Lehmann, November 16, 1955, HRC.

162. Vaidon, *Tangier: A Different Way,* p. 277; William Burroughs to Allen Ginsberg, February 17, 1956, in Burroughs, *Letters to Allen Ginsberg, 1953–1957;* "The natives are getting uppity" William Burroughs to Allen Ginsberg, February 26, 1956, in Burroughs, *Letters to Allen Ginsberg, 1953–1957;* "Instead of the customary assortment" PB in "Letter from Morocco," *The Nation,* December 12, 1956; Charles Rolo in *The New York Times Book Review,* November 6, 1955; Anthony West, *The New Yorker,* December 3, 1955.

163. "I thought the Mary McCarthy" PB to David McDowell, November 19, 1955, Rare Book and Manuscript Library, Columbia University; Dillon, *A Little Original Sin,* p. 270; "[go] out into the gale" PB in WS, p. 331; "I was on junk at the time" William Burroughs in Bockris, *With William Burroughs,* p. 109.

164. Burroughs, *Naked Lunch,* pp. xlii, xliii; "the end of the junk line" and "I did absolutely nothing" Burroughs, *Naked Lunch,* p. xli; William Burroughs to Allen Ginsberg, April 16, 1956, in Burroughs, *Letters to Allen Ginsberg, 1953–1957;* William Burroughs in conversation with author, March 26, 1988; William Burroughs to Allen Ginsberg, June 9, [1956], in Burroughs, *Letters to Allen Ginsberg, 1953–1957;* "I was staying" William Burroughs in Bockris, *With William Burroughs,* p. 12.

165. "They just came floating in" Gysin and Wilson, *Here to Go,* p. 120; "rich, far-out" ibid., p. 125; "He had big" ibid., p. 120; "Scary Mary," Gysin and Wilson, *Here to Go,* p. 119.

166. "Magic practices?" ibid., p. 123; "When guests came" ibid., p. 126; ibid., pp. 120–26.

167. Charles Gallagher in conversation with author, January 30, 1988; Vaidon, *Tangier: A Different Way,* pp. 276–77, 316–17; "the wife of one" "Thugs were to be seen" Fielding, *The Nearest Way Home,* pp. 65–66; Henry Gemill, "Tangier Turmoil," *The Wall Street Journal,* April 12, 1956, p. 1.

168. Ian Selley in conversation with author, December 5, 1987; "just beginning to sprout" Fielding, *The Nearest Way Home,* pp. 142–43.

169. PB in conversation with author, January 7, 1988; Christopher Wanklyn in conversation with author, December 11, 1987; Charles Gallagher in conversation with author, January 30, 1988; "They smoked *kif*" PB in WS, p. 332.

170. Burroughs, *Letters to Allen Ginsberg, 1953–1957;* "One wall of the room" PB, "Burroughs in Tangier," *Big Table,* vol. 1, no. 2 (1959); Burroughs in conversation with author, March 26, 1988.

171. "downright piquant" William Burroughs to Allen Ginsberg, September 16, 1956, in Burroughs, *Letters to William Burroughs, 1953–1957;* "How long does it take" and "I have seen him twice" William Burroughs to Allen Ginsberg, October 29, 1956, Rare Book and Manuscript Library, Columbia University; William Burroughs in conversation with author, March 26, 1988.

172. Ibid.

CHAPTER 13

173. "jealousy is one of the emotions" William Burroughs to Allen Ginsberg, October 13, 1956, in Burroughs, *Letters to Allen Ginsberg;* "Tell Jack that" William Burroughs to Allen Ginsberg, January 31, 1957, in Burroughs, *Letters to Allen Ginsberg.*

174. Tytell, *Naked Angels,* pp. 52–78; Dennis McNally, *Desolate Angel: Jack Kerouac, the Beat Generation and America* (New York: Random House, 1979), pp. 230–21; Joyce Johnson, *Minor Characters* (New York: Pocket Books, 1983), pp. 143–47; Jack Kerouac, *Desolation Angels* (New York: Perigee Books, 1980), p. 305; "the ancient rhythmic fishermen" Jack Kerouac, *Lonesome Traveler* (New York: McGraw-Hill, 1960), p. 147; "brown ragged robe priest" ibid., p. 148.

175. "whanging music" Johnson, *Minor Characters,* p. 148; "late afternoon cafe" Kerouac, *Lonesome Traveler,* p. 143; "I watched her flip off" ibid., p. 144; "made some home made pipes" Kerouac, *Lonesome Traveler,* p. 146; "I'm shitting out" McNally, *Desolate Angel,* p. 233; Kerouac, *Desolation Angels,* pp. 310–11.

176. McNally, *Desolate Angel,* p. 233; "the creaks of pederast love" Kerouac, *Desolation Angels,* p. 316; "stiff officious squares" ibid., p. 320; "Not too many" Johnson, *Minor Characters,* p. 151; "just for his big stupid soul" Kerouac, *Desolation Angels,* p. 314; "horrible sickness" and "the emergence of my" William Burroughs to Allen Ginsberg, undated (1957), Rare Book and Manuscript Library, Columbia University; "When will he get here?" Kerouac, *Desolation Angels,* p. 313.

177. "What's all this love business?" ibid., p. 314; "Wheaties by a pine breeze" and "Wolfe suddenly remembering" Kerouac, *Desolation Angels,* p. 317; Tytell, *Naked Angels,* pp. 79–105; "direct heart exchange" Allen Ginsberg in Burroughs, *Letters to Allen Ginsberg, 1953–1957,* p. 7; "metamorphosis from quiet brilliant" Barry Miles, *Ginsberg* (New York: Simon & Schuster, 1989), p. 196; "angel-headed hipsters" Ginsberg in *Howl and Other Poems* (San Francisco: City Lights Books, 1956), p. 9.

178. Miles, *Ginsberg;* "big lovely arrival" Kerouac, *Desolation Angels,* p. 318; PB in conversation with author, December 4, 1987; Allen Ginsberg in Winston Leyland, ed., *Straight Hearts' Delight: Love Poems and Selected Letters, 1947–1980* (San Francisco: Gay Sunshine Press, 1980), pp. 111–18; Miles, *Ginsberg,* pp. 181–82; "he was very moody" Ginsberg in Leyland, ed., *Straight Hearts' Delight,* p. 116.

179. Miles, *Ginsberg,* pp. 224–25; Allen Ginsberg to Peter Orlovsky, January 20, 1958, in Leyland, ed., *Straight Hearts' Delight;* "At the time" Jack Kerouac, *Desolation Angels,* p. 317; "one afternoon high on hasheesh" Jack Kerouac, *Lonesome Traveler,* p. 146; Allen Ginsberg to Lucien Carr, April 4, 1957, Rare Book and Manuscript Library, Columbia University; "It was a little sad" Jack Kerouac, *Desolation Angels,* p. 318; "clear sharp images" Allen Ginsberg to Lucien Carr, April 4, 1957, Rare Book and Manuscript Library, Columbia University.

180. "veiled women" ibid.; "crazy jukebox hangout" and "an absolutely cool bunch" Kerouac, *Desolation Angels,* p. 318; "the only danger here" Allen Ginsberg to Lucien Carr, April 4, 1957, Rare Book and Manuscript Library, Columbia University; "All of a sudden" Jack Kerouac, *Desolation Angels,* pp. 319–20.

181. "To think that I had" and "sit on the edge" Kerouac, *Desolation Angels,* p. 321; "take care of yourself" Kerouac, *Desolation Angels,* p. 322; Miles, *Ginsberg,* p. 224; Tytell, *Naked Angels,* p. 46; "Anson arrived from Venice" Allen Ginsberg to Lucien Carr, undated (Spring, 1957), Rare Book and Manuscript Library, Columbia University; Allen Ginsberg in conversation with author, April 8, 1988.

182. Allen Ginsberg in conversation with author, April 8, 1988; "Zen Buddhist-Bebop" Jane Bowles to PB, undated (mid-April, 1957), in Dillon, ed., *Out in the World.*

183. PB in conversation with author, December 4, 1988; Jane Bowles to PB,

undated (February 24, 1957), in Dillon, ed., *Out in the World;* "It is impossible to write," "a bad shock" and "failure follows me" Jane Bowles to PB, undated (February 1, 1957), in Dillon, ed., *Out in the World;* "sheer hell" Jane Bowles to Libby Holman, undated (April 10, 1957), in Dillon, ed., *Out in the World.*

184. "We had fish" and "truss-like corset" Jane Bowles to Libby Holman, undated (April 10, 1957), in Dillon, ed., *Out in the World;* "because I went into" and "Cherifa and I almost" Jane Bowles to PB, undated (mid-April, 1957), in Dillon, ed., *Out in the World.*

185. "in my innocence" PB in WS, p. 336; Christopher Wanklyn in conversation with author, December 12, 1987; PB in conversation with author, November 8, 1990; Dillon, *A Little Original Sin,* pp. 285–88.

186. Ibid.; PB in WS, pp. 338, 339; PB in conversation with author, November 8, 1990; Edouard Roditi in conversation with author, March 28, 1988; Yvonne Gerofi in conversation with author, November 23, 1988; "in the night, all around me" PB in *WS,* p. 336.

187. PB in conversation with author, December 14, 1987; Eduoard Roditi in conversation with author, March 28, 1988; PB in conversation with author, November 8, 1990; Dillon, *A Little Original Sin,* p. 289.

188. PB in conversation with author, December 4, 1987; Charles Gallagher in conversation with author, January 30, 1988; Tennessee Williams to PB, undated, HRC; PB to Peggy Glanville Hicks, July 11, 1957, quoted in Dillon, *A Little Original Sin,* p. 289.

CHAPTER 14

190. PB in conversation with author, December 4, 1987; Allen Ginsberg to Jack Kerouac, May 31, 1957, HRC.

191. "It was always Bill" PB, "Burroughs in Tangier," *Big Table,* vol. 1, no. 2 (1959); "shouting in his cowboy voice" PB, ibid.; PB in conversation with author, December 14, 1987; "short frail blond" and "He took me out" Allen Ginsberg to Lucien Carr, undated (1957), Rare Book and Manuscript Library, Columbia University; Allen Ginsberg in conversation with author, April 8, 1988.

192. Allen Ginsberg in conversation with author, April 8, 1988; "Klee like in work" Allen Ginsberg to Lucien Carr, undated (1957), Rare Book and Manuscript Library, Columbia University; Peter Pollock and Paul Danquah in conversation with author, January 23, 1988; "I was only afraid" Francis Bacon to author, May 19, 1988; "wears sneakers" Allen Ginsberg to Jack Kerouac, May 31, 1957, HRC.

193. Allen Ginsberg in conversation with author, April 8, 1988; Allen Ginsberg to Jack Kerouac, May 31, 1957, HRC; Miles, *Ginsberg,* p. 225.

194. William Burroughs to Allen Ginsberg, August, 1957, in Burroughs, *Letters to Allen Ginsberg, 1953–1957;* "lost what was left" and "the simple fact" PB to Virgil Thomson, August 3, 1957, Virgil Thomson Archive at the Music Library, Yale University; PB in conversation with author, January 22, 1988; Dillon, *A Little Original Sin,* pp. 290–91; "My dear Mrs. Bowles" PB in WS, p. 338.

195. PB in conversation with author, January 22 and 28, 1988; Dillon, *A Little Original Sin,* pp. 291, 292, "an undercurrent of violence" and "take hold of heavy objects" PB to Virgil Thomson, September 10, 1957, Virgil Thomson Archive at the Music Library, Yale University; Dillon, *A Little Original Sin,* p. 292; Christopher Sawyer-Lauçanno, *An Invisible Spectator* (London: Weidenfeld & Nicolson, 1989), p. 339; "profoundly unhappy and depressed" PB to Virgil Thompson, October 2, 1957, Virgil Thomson Archive at the Music Library, Yale University.

196. "She sees its effect" PB to Virgil Thomson, October 2, 1957, Virgil

Thomson Archive at the Music Library, Yale University; PB in WS, p. 338; PB in conversation with author, January 4, 1988; Dillon, *A Little Original Sin,* p. 295.

197. "Sonia had to call" PB in WS, p. 339; "Jane is with me" PB to John Lehmann, November 23, 1957, HRC; Edouard Roditi in conversation with author, March 28, 1988; William Burroughs in conversation with author, March 26, 1988; Sawyer-Lauçanno, *An Invisible Spectator,* p. 341.

198. William Burroughs in conversation with author, March 26, 1988; Sawyer-Lauçanno, *An Invisible Spectator,* pp. 341, 342; David Herbert in conversation with author, December 7, 1987; "I don't think" Jane Bowles to PB, undated (early May, 1958), in Dillon, ed., *Out in the World,* p. 300.

199. Vaidon, *Tangier: A Different Way,* pp. 324–25; "sick of Tangier" and "It is really disgusting" William Burroughs to Allen Ginsberg, November 26, 1957, Rare Book and Manuscript Library, Columbia University; "Brion Gysin has opened" William Burroughs to Allen Ginsberg, December 8, 1957, Rare Book and Manuscript Library, Columbia University.

200. William Burroughs in conversation with author, March 26, 1988; "Changes in my psyche" William Burroughs to Allen Ginsberg, November 10, 1957, Rare Book and Manuscript Library, Columbia University; "must have some cunt" William Burroughs to Allen Ginsberg, November 26, 1957, Rare Book and Manuscript Library, Columbia University; "I confessed all my doubts" Allen Ginsberg to Peter Orlovsky, January 20, 1958, in Leyland, ed., *Straight Hearts' Delight.*

201. Brion Gysin and Terry Wilson, *Here to Go,* pp. 39–40; Hamri in conversation with author, January 18, 1988; "They poisoned my food twice" Brion Gysin and Terry Wilson, *Here to Go,* p. 34; "A treasure trove" Brion Gysin in Burroughs and Gysin, *The Third Mind,* p. 48.

202. Terry Wilson in conversation with author, November 26, 1987; "a gray-green" and "I really don't know" Burroughs and Gysin, *The Third Mind,* pp. 49–50.

CHAPTER 15

203. Vaidon, *Tangier: A Different Way,* pp. 317, 320–23.

204. Ibid.

205. "The Tangier of the dubious" PB, "Post-Colonial Interlude in Tangier," undated, n.p., Rare Book and Manuscript Library, Columbia University, Charles Gallagher in conversation with author, January 30, 1988; "The Tangier situation" Christopher Wanklyn to Jane Bowles, March 21 [1958], HRC.

206. "Their foreign journalists" Francis Bacon to PB, April 5, 1958, HRC; "Tanger is finished" William Burroughs to Allen Ginsberg, August 25, 1958, Rare Book and Manuscript Library, Columbia University; "As to the adviseability" [sic] William Burroughs to PB, October 19, 1958, HRC.

207. Ahmed Yacoubi to PB, September 9, 1958, HRC; Vaidon, *Tangier: A Different Way,* p. 325; PB to Virgil Thomson, December 27, 1958, Virgil Thomson Archive at the Music Library, Yale University.

208. "she began to" ibid., PB in WS, p. 344; Christopher Wanklyn in conversation with author, December 12, 1987; "It was summer" PB in WS, p. 345.

209. Ibid., "These men" PB in WS, p. 346; Christopher Wanklyn in conversation with author, December 12, 1987; "In Tamanar" PB in WS, p. 346.

210. "During dessert" PB, *Their Heads Are Green and Their Hands are Blue,* p. 120; Information Bulletin, Library of Congress, October 17, 1960, Christopher Wanklyn in conversation with author, December 11, 1987.

211. William Burroughs in conversation with author, March 26, 1988; "Telegram from Interpol" William Burroughs to Allen Ginsberg, September 11, 1959, Rare Book and Manuscript Library, Columbia University.

212. Tytell, *Naked Angels;* Allen Ginsberg in conversation with author, April 8, 1988; William Burroughs in conversation with author, March 26, 1988.

213. Ibid.; "Look down LOOK DOWN" William Burroughs, *Naked Lunch,* p. xlviii; Ian Selley in conversation with author, December 5, 1987; Charles Gallagher in conversation with author, January 30, 1988; *Time,* November 2, 1959; "the rowdy, rollicking" Robert Ruark in *The New York World Tribune,* December 18, 1959.

214. Ibid., "Most people have left" PB to Charles Henri Ford, January 1, 1960, HRC; "You want to know" PB to Lilla van Saher, April 3, 1960, HRC.

215. Charles Gallagher in conversation with author, January 30, 1988; "I don't think it would" Jane Bowles to Libby Holman, undated (1960), in Dillon, ed., *Out in the World;* David Herbert in conversation with author, December 7, 1987.

216. Ruth Fainlight in conversation with author, November 28, 1987.

217. Isabelle Gerofi in conversation with author, January 22, 1988; Ruth Fainlight in conversation with author, November 28, 1987; PB in conversation with author, January 7, 1988.

218. Tamara Dragadze in conversation with author, December 16, 1987; PB in conversation with author, January 4, 1988; Christopher Wanklyn in conversation with author, December 11, 1987.

219–222. Tamara Dragadze in conversation with author, December 16, 1987.

CHAPTER 16

223. Vaidon, *Tangier: A Different Way;* "the whole town is crammed" PB to Rena Bowles, September 4, 1960, HRC; PB, "The Ball at Sidi Hosni," *Big Table,* vol. 5 (1960).

224. Heymann, *Poor Little Rich Girl,* pp. 245–46; PB, "The Ball at Sidi Hosni"; "Jane was busy for a week" September 4, 1960, HRC; Ruth Hopwood in conversation with author, December 2, 1987.

225. Ibid.; Christopher Wanklyn in conversation with author, December 11, 1987; "The floodlighting of their" PB, "The Ball at Sidi Hosni," *Big Table,* vol. 5 (1960); "She liked everything around her" PB in WS, p. 347.

226. Heymann, *Poor Little Rich Girl,* p. 326; Ruth Hopwood in conversation with author, December 2, 1987.

227. Ruth Hopwood in conversation with author, December 2, 1987. David Herbert in conversation with author, August, 1987.

228. Ruth Hopwood in conversation with author, December 2, 1987; Heymann, *Poor Little Rich Girl.*

229. Ibid.; David Herbert in conversation with author, December 7, 1987.

230. Suzy, "Bab's Casbah Party Stuns 'Em," *The New York Mirror,* September 2, 1960; David Herbert in conversation with author, December 7, 1987; Tessa Codrington Wheeler in conversation with author, December 18, 1987.

231. William Burroughs in conversation with author, March 26, 1988; "The Beatniks have invaded" PB to Rena Bowles, June 12, 1961, HRC; *Life,* November 30, 1959; *Time,* November 30, 1962.

232. PB in conversation with author, December 4, 1987; Terry Wilson in conversation with author, November 26, 1987; Felicity Mason in conversation with author, September 27, 1987; Brion Gysin in Burroughs and Gysin, *The Third Mind,* pp. 42–46; "a project for disastrous success" Burroughs and Gysin, *The Third Mind,* p. 45.

233. "writing is fifty years behind" Burroughs, *The Third Mind,* p. 51;

"rub[bing] out the word" Brion Gysin in Burroughs and Gysin, *The Third Mind,* p. 46; Burroughs in conversation with author, March 26, 1988; "cold metal excrement" William Burroughs, *The Soft Machine* (London: Paladin/Grafton, 1968), p. 69. Terry Wilson in conversation with author, November 26, 1987.

234. Ibid.; Felicity Mason in conversation with author, September 27, 1987; Ira Cohen in conversation with author, November 16, 1988; "whispered to me" Allen Ginsberg to Jack Kerouac, May 11, 1962, Rare Book and Manuscript Library, Columbia University; Allen Ginsberg in conversation with author, April 8, 1988; "sitting at home" and "rather indifferent" Allen Ginberg to Jack Kerouac, May 11, 1962, Rare Book and Manuscript Library, Columbia University.

235. "Bill had declared," "little English boys," "angelic looking" and "old amity," ibid; Allen Ginsberg in conversation with author, April 8, 1988.

236. PB in conversation with author, December 4, 1987, and November 20, 1987.

237. "when he played" PB in WS, p. 349; Sawyer-Lauçanno, *An Invisible Spectator,* p. 356; "huge casual pageant" PB to Allen Ginsberg, June 21, 1961, Rare Book and Manuscript Library, Columbia University; Miles, *Ginsberg,* p. 290.

238. Allen Ginsberg in conversation with author, April 8, 1988; Tamara Dragadze in conversation with author, November 25, 1987.

239. "rapped it in newspaper," Peter Orlovsky to Janine Pommey, July 8, 1961, Rare Book and Manuscript Library, Columbia University; "Me and Bill B." Peter Orlovsky to Janine Pommey, July 8, 1961, Rare Book and Manuscript Library, Columbia University; "as I am 35 and half my life" Miles, *Ginsberg,* p. 291; ibid., pp. 276–82.

240. Ibid., pp. 276–82; Timothy Leary, *Flashbacks: An Autobiography* (Los Angeles: J. P. Tarcher, 1983), pp. 95–96; "Knew more about drugs," "Allen Ansen and Gregory" and "We were all" Leary, *Flashbacks,* pp. 95–96.

241. "I'm not feeling" ibid.; Allen Ginsberg in conversation with author, April 8, 1988; Miles, *Ginsberg,* pp. 291, 292; "The review of" Allen Ginsberg to Barney Rossett, August 4, 1961, Rare Book and Manuscript Library, Columbia University; PB in WS, p. 349, "I think Bill & Leary" Allen Ginsberg to Peter Orlovsky, August 2, 1961, in *Straight Hearts' Delight.*

242. PB in WS, p. 349; Allen Ginsberg to Peter Orlovsky, August 3, 1961, in Leyland, ed., *Straight Hearts' Delight;* "It really shook" Allen Ginsberg to Jack Kerouac, May 11, 1962, Rare Book and Manuscript Library, Columbia University.

243. Nancy Randolph, "Chic-Chat," *The New York Daily News,* August 16, 1961; Nancy Randolph, "Survivor Recounts Babs' Bash," *The New York Daily News,* August 19, 1961; "a hundred ill-assorted" Cecil Beaton, *The Restless Years* (London: Weidenfeld and Nicolson, 1976), pp. 134–35.

244. Cholly Knickerbocker, "Helpful Babs Embarrasses a Polo Club," *The New York Journal-American,* June 1, 1962; Cholly Knickerbocker, " 'Babs' Hutton Admits She's Happy at Last," *The New York Journal-American,* November 89, 1961; David Herbert in conversation with author, December 7, 1987.

245. David Herbert in conversation with author, December 7, 1987; *Life,* February 2, 1962.

CHAPTER 17

246. "He was always loose" PB to Rena Bowles, October 18, 1961, HRC; "She is covered" PB to Rena Bowles, December 23, 1961, HRC.

247. PB in conversation with author, January 7, 1988; "Seemed to be enjoying" and "Charles Addams household" Harold Norse, *Memoirs of a Bastard Angel* (New York: Morrow, 1989), p. 387; "Jane would sulk" ibid., p. 386.

CHAPTER 19

277. William Burroughs to Allen Ginsberg, November 20, 1963, Rare Book and Manuscript Library, Columbia University; "a horse's ass" William Burroughs to Allen Ginsberg, October 26, 1961, Rare Book and Manuscript Library, Columbia University; Burroughs and Gysin, *The Third Mind*, pp. 107–8.

278. William Burroughs III, *Kentucky Ham* (New York: E. P. Dutton, 1973), pp. 42–43; William Burroughs in conversation with author, March 26, 1988; Ira Cohen in conversation with author, November 16, 1988; Alfred Chester in *Commentary*, January, 1963; Terry Wilson in conversation with author, November 26, 1987.

279. William Burroughs in conversation with author, March 26, 1988; "accosted by an aging" and "half the old" William Burroughs III, *Kentucky Ham*, p. 38; "looking at me like a loving" ibid., p. 39.

280. Ibid.; William Burroughs in conversation with author, March 26, 1988; Joseph McPhillips in conversation with author, January 28, 1988; Vaidon, *Tangier: A Different Way*.

281. Ibid; Edouard Roditi in conversation with author, March 28, 1988; David Herbert in conversation with author, December 7, 1987; Heymann, *Poor Little Rich Girl*, p. 339; Herbert, *Engaging Eccentrics*, pp. 30–31; Ruth Hopwood in conversation with author, December 2, 1987.

282. David Herbert in conversation with author, December 7, 1987; Herbert, *Engaging Eccentrics*, pp. 30–31; Suzy, "The Troubadour" *The New York Mirror*, September 16, 1963.

283. Heymann, *Poor Little Rich Girl*, pp. 342–43; PB in WS, p. 354.

284. "[it] sounded too Moroccan" ibid., pp. 354, 355; Joseph McPhillips in conversation with author, January 28, 1988; "[Jane] says everyone" Alfred Chester to Edward Field, November 27, 1963; Alfred Chester to Harriet Sohmers, October 10, 1963; "It would be a perfect place" Alfred Chester to Harriet Sohmers, November 22, 1963; "Occasionally I see" Alfred Chester to Edward Field, November 27, 1963.

285. Edward Field and Neil Derrick in conversation with author, March 5, 1988; "I've been starving lately" Alfred Chester to Edward Field, December 20, 1963; Alfred Chester to Edward Field, October 2, 1963.

286. "I waited two hours" ibid.; Sawyer-Lauçanno, *An Invisible Spectator*, p. 364; "Jane says Moroccans" Alfred Chester to Edward Field; December 20, 1963; "Dris emerged" Glass, "The Decline and Fall of Alfred Chester," in *Head of a Sad Angel*, p. 338; "Sometimes I get panicky" Alfred Chester to Edward Field, November 27, 1963.

287. "stripped to the waist" Glass, "The Decline and Fall of Alfred Chester" in Chester, *Head of a Sad Angel*, p. 345; "It is eight P.M." Alfred Chester to Edward Field, January 29, 1964.

288. "The winds fly in from all directions" from "Glory Hole," in Chester, *Head of a Sad Angel*, p. 220.

289. "A local millionaire" Alfred Chester to Edward Field, February 19, 1964; "I'm scared" Alfred Chester to Edward Field, February 25, 1964; Ira Cohen in conversation with author, November 16, 1988.

290. Ira Cohen in conversation with author, November 16, 1988; Alfred Chester to Norman Glass, February 28, 1964; Alfred Chester to Edward Field, February 28, 1964; Alfred Chester to Edward Field, February 29, 1964; "The people here" Alfred Chester to Edward Field, March 10, 1964; "Naturally I want" Alfred Chester to Norman Glass, March 1, 1964; "Afraid, don't fail me" Alfred Chester to Edward Field, March 31, 1964.

291. Edward Field in conversation with author, September 5, 1990; "Forget

other wire" Alfred Chester to Edward Field, March 4, 1964; Edward Field in conversation with author, September 5, 1990; PB in conversation with author, December 4, 1987; "against the rules" Alfred Chester to Norman Glass, March 17, 1964; John Hopkins in conversation with author, November 28, 1987; "We are pretending" Alfred Chester to Edward Field, March 10, 1964; "the dinner was stupendous" Alfred Chester to Edward Field, May 6, 1964.

292. PB in conversation with author, December 4, 1987; PB in WS, p. 355; Alfred Chester to Norman Glass, May 22, 1964.

293. "a purely pleasurable" PB in WS, p. 355; Joseph McPhillips in conversation with author, January 28, 1988.

294. John Hopkins in conversation with author, November 28, 1987; Joseph McPhillips in conversation with author, January 28, 1988; Tamara Dragadze in conversation with author, December 17, 1987.

295. William Burroughs in conversation with author, March 26, 1988; Felicity Mason in conversation with author, September 27, 1987; "promises a new kick" PB to Rena Bowles, December 12, 1964, HRC; John Hopkins in conversation with author, November 28, 1987; "the sinister servant" Gysin, *The Process*, p. 169; Terry Wilson in conversation with author, November 26, 1987; "death rattle fandango" Jane Bowles to Libby Holman, undated (October 4, 1963), in Dillon, ed., *Out in the World*.

296. Jane Bowles to Audrey Wood, undated (March, 1964), in Dillon, ed., *Out in the World*. PB in conversation with author, December 14, 1987; "the first publication" PB to Peter Owen, January 26, 1964, HRC; "I do get worse" Jane Bowles to Libby Holman, undated (June 30, 1964), in Dillon, ed., *Out in the World*.

297. "I could go on forever" Jane Bowles to Ruth Fainlight, undated (September, 1964), in Dillon, ed., *Out in the World;* Dr. Palma Ruspoli in conversation with author, January 19, 1991; Kathy Jelen in conversation with author, January 12, 1988; Buffie Johnson in conversation with author, August 17, 1987; Isabelle Gerofi in conversation with author, January 27, 1987; Dillon, *A Little Original Sin,* pp. 353–54.

298. Isabelle and Yvonne Gerofi in conversation with author, January 27, 1987; Buffie Johnson in conversation with author, January 17, 1990; David Herbert in conversation with author, December 7, 1987.

299. Some material on this page is based on conversations with a Tangerino who wishes to remain anonymous. PB in conversation with author, December 14, 1987.

300. Theodore Solotaroff in *Book Week,* June 7, 1964.

301. "I loved it" Alfred Chester to Edward Field, November 25, 1964; Alfred Chester to Edward Field, December 17, 1964; "I walk more or less" Alfred Chester to Edward Field, December 21, 1964.

302. "Paul and Jane have come over" Alfred Chester to Edward Field, December 21, 1964.

CHAPTER 20

303. Terry Wilson in conversation with author, December 17, 1987; Edouard Roditi in conversation with author, March 28, 1988; PB in conversation with author, December 4, 1987; Sawyer-Lauçanno, *An Invisible Spectator,* p. 378.

304. Mohammed Mrabet, *Look and Move On* (Santa Rosa, Calif.: Black Sparrow Press, 1976); PB in conversation with author, January 28, 1988; "English disgrace" and "I guess it hasn't" Jane Bowles to Libby Holman, undated (late January/early February 1964), in Dillon, ed., *Out in the World*.

305. PB in WS, p. 355–56; "Paul tries to travel" Jane Bowles to Libby Hol-

man, undated (February, 1965), in Dillon, ed., *Out in the World;* "nocturnal scandals," "hot for Dris" and "such terrible things have been" Alfred Chester to Edward Field, March 2, 1965.

306. "a ridiculous and pathetic pair" Alfred Chester to Edward Field, April 2, 1965; "publishers all over the place" Alfred Chester to Norman Glass, March 30, 1965; "It's very strange" Alfred Chester to Edward Field, April 2, 1965; "It was the most horrible thing" Alfred Chester to Edward Field, April 14, 1965.

307. "I'll probably be sick" Alfred Chester to Edward Field, May 4, 1965; "I'm thrilled to pieces" Alfred Chester to Norman Glass, May 22, 1965; Edward Field and Neil Derrick in conversation with author, March 5, 1988.

308. "It was a roaring success" Alfred Chester to Norman Glass, June 3, 1965; Alfred Chester to Edward Field, June 3, 1965; Edward Field and Neil Derrick in conversation with author, March 5, 1988; "Jane and I had wanted" PB to Rena Bowles, May 5, 1965, HRC; PB in WS, p. 356.

309. Ibid.; PB to Rena Bowles, July 29, 1965, HRC; Sawyer-Lauçanno, *An Invisible Spectator,* p. 378; Dillon, *A Little Original Sin,* p. 367; PB in conversation with author, December 14, 1987; Edouard Roditi in conversation with author, March 28, 1988.

310. "I am really" Jane Bowles to Libby Holman, undated (May 14, 1965), in Dillon, ed., *Out in the World;* PB in conversation with author, January 4, 1988.

311. PB in conversation with author, January 4, 1988; "Of course I've written" Alfred Chester to Norman Glass, August 2, 1965; "ingeniously fashioned" *The New York Times Book Review,* May 31, 1964; "a very strange twisted" Alfred Chester to Edward Field, August 5, 1965; "We compared" Alfred Chester to Edward Field, August 18, 1965.

312. "Paul says I have been" Alfred Chester to Edward Field, August 18, 1965; Edward Field and Neil Derrick in conversation with author, March 5, 1988; Alfred Chester to Edward Field, September 17 and 27, 1965; Ira Cohen in conversation with author, November 16, 1988.

313. Ira Cohen in conversation with author, November 16, 1988; "Susan's visit was" Alfred Chester to Edward Field, September 17, 1965; "There's no point" Alfred Chester to Norman Glass, October 8, 1965; Alfred Chester, "Safari," in Chester, *Head of a Sad Angel;* "Here's what I have to say" Alfred Chester to Edward Field, September 27, 1965.

314. "She and I were talking" PB in conversation with author, December 4, 1987; Alfred Chester to Edward Field, October 10, 1965; Alfred Chester to Nadia Gould, October 28, 1965; Alfred Chester to Harriet Sohmers, November 7, 1965; "if you care to write" Alfred Chester to PB, undated (Monday, 1965); "Oh, ladies and gentlemen" Alfred Chester, "The Foot," in *Head of a Sad Angel,* p. 297.

CHAPTER 21

315. Jane Bowles to Libby Holman, April 1, 1966, in Dillon, ed., *Out in the World;* PB in conversation with author, December 4, 1987.

316. Dillon, *A Little Original Sin,* p. 369; PB in conversation with author, November 8, 1990; "For me it was the death of" Jane Bowles to Libby Holman, April 1, 1966, in Dillon, ed., *Out in the World;* PB in conversation with author, January 4, 1988; Charles Gallagher to author, January 30, 1988.

317. "But if I go into that" Jane Bowles to Libby Holman, May 10, 1966, in Dillon, ed., *Out in the World;* "begged . . . for months" PB in WS, p. 359; PB in conversation with author, November 8, 1990; "I am sure she is unchanged" Capote in Jane Bowles, *My Sister's Hand in Mine* (New York: Ecco Press, 1970), introduction.

318. "undoubtedly [would] be awful" PB to Ira Cohen, February 25, 1966,

Rare Book and Manuscript Library, Columbia University; Conrad Knickerbocker in *The New York Times,* March 12, 1966; Wilfred Sheed in *Life,* March 25, 1966; "Aachor is coming up" PB to Ira Cohen, April 29, 1966, Rare Book and Manuscript Library, Columbia University; John Giorno in conversation with author, August 1, 1987; PB in WS, p. 358.

319. "Elicited from Cherifa" PB to Andreas Brown, October 15, 1965, HRC; "Jane had made excellent" PB in WS, p. 358; "The death of my parents" Ibid., p. 359.

320. John Giorno in conversation with author, August 1, 1987; Felicity Mason in conversation with author, September 27, 1987.

321. John Giorno in conversation with author, August 1, 1987.

322. Ibid.; John Hopkins in conversation with author, November 28, 1987; Dillon, *A Little Original Sin*, pp. 383–384; PB in conversation with author, November 8, 1990; "Jane hasn't written" PB to Edouard Roditi, January 17, 1967, Department of Special Collections, University of California at Los Angeles; Isabelle Gerofi in conversation with author, November 23, 1987.

323. "I should have gone with you" Jane Bowles to PB, n.d. (September/October? 1966) in Dillon, ed., *Out in the World;* Charles Gallagher in conversation with author, January 30, 1988; Christopher Wanklyn in conversation with author, December 11, 1987; "a nervous breakdown" Jane Bowles to Libby Holman, undated (October, 1966), in Dillon, ed., *Out in the World.*

324. Ibid.; Bradshaw, *Dreams That Money Can Buy,* p. 369; "was merely in a surly mood" PB in WS, p. 363; PB in conversation with author, November 8, 1990; "The truth is" PB to Peter Owen, March 17, 1967, HRC.

325. "Her medication" PB to Charles Henri Ford, March 18, 1967, HRC; Mohammed Mrabet in *Cook and Move On*, p. 92; "Jane is very ill" PB to Oliver Evans, May 11, 1967, HRC; PB in conversation with author, November 8, 1990.

326. PB in conversation with author, November 8, 1990; "It was painful" PB to Virgil Thomson, April 27, 1967, Virgil Thomson Archive at the Music Library, Yale University; "As reading was such an effort" David Herbert, *Second Son,* p. 127; "thunderheads of [her] illness" PB to Oliver Evans, May 11, 1967, HRC.

327. PB in conversation with author, January 4, 1988; "very much rolling" PB to Charles Henri Ford, March 18, 1967, HRC; "I'm here alone" PB to Ira Cohen, April 20, 1967, Rare Book and Manuscript Library, Columbia University; PB in conversation with author, November 8, 1990.

328. PB in conversation with author, November 8, 1990; "My feeling is" PB to Virgil Thomson, May 1, 1967, Virgil Thomson Archive at the Music Library, Yale University; "I am very sad" Jane Bowles to Libby Holman, undated (1967), in Dillon, ed., *Out in the World.*

329. David Herbert in conversation with author, December 7, 1987; "She seems to think" PB to Peter Owen, June 5, 1967, HRC; Jane Howard, "A Talk in the Casbah," *The Washington Post Book Week,* March 3, 1978.

330. Ibid.; John Hopkins in conversation with author, November 28, 1987; PB in WS, pp. 363–64; PB in conversation with author, January 19, 1988; Jane Howard, "A Talk in the Casbah," *The Washington Post Book Week,* March 3, 1978; "She lies screaming" PB to Oliver Evans, November 13, 1967, HRC.

331. PB in conversation with author, November 8, 1990; "As Jane recovers" PB to Libby Holman, September 9, 1967, quoted by Dillon, *A Little Original Sin,* p. 396; "I'm convinced" and "the city doesn't deserve" PB to Edouard Roditi, August 28, 1967, Department of Special Collections, University of California at Los Angeles; "that dark place" PB to Jane Howard, April 9, 1969, Rare Book and Manuscript Library, Columbia University.

332. Edward Field and Neil Derrick in conversation with author, March 5,

1988; Diana Athill in Chester, *The Exquisite Corpse,* Introduction; "Dear Great Man" Alfred Chester to PB, March 5, 1966; "still on his lost" PB to Ira Cohen, November 21, 1967, Rare Book and Manuscript Library, Columbia University; John Hopkins in conversation with author, November 28, 1987.

333. John Hopkins in conversation with author, November 28, 1987; "a nucleus of tattered" PB to Ira Cohen, November 21, 1967, Rare Book and Manuscript Library, Columbia University; Dillon, *A Little Original Sin,* pp. 398–401; PB in conversation with author, November 8, 1990.

334. PB in conversation with author, November 8, 1990; Peter Pollock and Paul Danquah in conversation with author, January 23, 1988; Isabelle Gerofi in conversation with author, January 22, 1988; Dillon, *A Little Original Sin,* p. 398.

335. John Hopkins in conversation with author, November 28, 1987; Isabelle and Yvonne Gerofi in conversation with author, January 22, 1988; "Jane was in fact" Dillon, *A Little Original Sin,* p. 399; PB in conversation with author, November 8, 1990; Edouard Roditi in conversation with author, March 28, 1988.

336. Edouard Roditi in conversation with author, March 28, 1988; Isabelle Gerofi in conversation with author, January 22, 1988; "[She said] when you give me the money" and "no end to her troubles" PB to Ira Cohen, February 9, 1968, Rare Book and Manuscript Library, Columbia University; Dillon, *A Little Original Sin,* p. 400; PB in conversation with author, November 8, 1990; "Darling Paul" Jane Bowles to PB, undated [January 11, 1968], in Dillon, ed., *Out in the World.*

337. PB in conversation with author, November 8, 1990; Isabelle and Yvonne Gerofi in conversation with author, January 22, 1988; Dillon, *A Little Original Sin,* p. 401.

338. Jane Bowles quoted in *World Authors, 1950–1970* (New York: H. W. Wilson, 1975), p. 203.

EPILOGUE

343. "My degree of interest in everything" PB to Virgil Thomson, June 26, 1973, Virgil Thomson Archives at the Music Library, Yale University; "I think I lived vicariously" PB quoted in Dillon, *A Little Original Sin,* p. 421.

344. "Perhaps the best thing about Tangier" PB to Virgil Thomson, March 29, 1974, Virgil Thomson Archive at the Music Library, Yale University.

345. "Tangier is like a gong" John Giorno in conversation with author, August 1, 1987.

Index